The Thirty Years War

Also by Peter H. Wilson

WAR, STATE AND SOCIETY IN WÜRTEMBERG
THE HOLY ROMAN EMPIRE 1495–1806
FROM REICH TO REVOLUTION 1558–1806
EUROPE'S TRAGEDY: A HISTORY OF THE THIRTY YEARS WAR

The Thirty Years War

A Sourcebook

PETER H. WILSON

First published 2010 by
PALGRAVE MACMILLAN

Palgrave Macmillan in the UK is an imprint of Macmillan Publishers Limited,
registered in England, company number 785998, of Houndmills, Basingstoke,
Hampshire RG21 6XS.

Palgrave Macmillan in the US is a division of St Martin's Press LLC,
175 Fifth Avenue, New York, NY 10010.

Palgrave Macmillan is the global academic imprint of the above companies
and has companies and representatives throughout the world.

Palgrave® and Macmillan® are registered trademarks in the United States,
the United Kingdom, Europe and other countries

ISBN 978–0–230–24205–0 hardback
ISBN 978–0–230–24206–7 paperback

This book is printed on paper suitable for recycling and made from fully
managed and sustained forest sources. Logging, pulping and manufacturing
processes are expected to conform to the environmental regulations of the
country of origin.

A catalogue record for this book is available from the British Library.

A catalog record for this book is available from the Library of Congress.

10   9   8   7   6   5   4   3   2   1
19 18 17 16 15 14 13 12 11 10

Printed and bound in Great Britain by
CPI Antony Rowe, Chippenham and Eastbourne

For Jeremy Black

Contents

List of maps, figures and illustrations

MAPS

FIGURE

ILLUSTRATIONS

Chronology

[Numbers in square brackets refer to the documents]

1517	Conventional start date for the Reformation signalled by Martin Luther's public protest against the Catholic church.
1555	Peace of Augsburg grants legal rights to Lutherans in the Empire [Docs 1–2].
1556–8	Abdication of Emperor Charles V splits the Habsburg monarchy into Spanish and Austrian branches.
1560	Conversion of the Lutheran elector Palatine to Calvinism. Followed by other conversions (mainly from Lutheranism), including that of the Brandenburg elector (1613), the landgrave of Hessen-Kassel and various minor counts.
1562	Start of the French Wars of Religion (to 1598), a three-way fight between a weak Catholic monarchy, Calvinist nobles and townsmen (Huguenots), and their hardline Catholic opponents (led by Lorraine). Spanish intervention from 1590 simplifies this into a struggle between the monarchy (now backed by the Huguenots) and the League (backed by Spain). Association with Spain discredits the League, which fragments. Edict of Nantes grants freedom of worship and military autonomy to the Huguenots (1598), effectively ending the war.
1563–70	First Northern War signals the start of the struggle between Denmark and Sweden for dominance of the Baltic. Denmark asserted its pre-eminence in the Treaty of Stettin (1570).
1566	Dutch revolt against Spanish Habsburg rule (until 1648). English support for the Dutch leads to war with Spain 1585–1604 (Spanish Armada 1588).
1568–78	Concessions to the Austrian and Bohemian Protestants by the Habsburg archdukes.
1576	Accession of Emperor Rudolf II (until 1612).
1580s	Emergence of a confessionalised generation: people who had grown up since the Reformation only knowing religious schism. Worsening economic and climatic conditions (especially c.1590–1640). Resumption of witchcraft accusations and trials, peaking around 1610–30. The German princes revise and expand their territorial militias [Doc. 113].
1583	The elector of Cologne converts to Calvinism and is deposed by both pope and emperor in favour (eventually) of a Catholic

	Bavarian candidate. Small-scale Spanish intervention and limited fighting 1583–7.
1592	Brief Bishops' War over who should rule the bishopric of Strasbourg. Ended by compromise negotiations.
1593–1606	Long Turkish War between Rudolf II (with financial support from the Empire) against the Ottoman Empire. Rudolf forced to make a compromise truce with the sultan in 1606 (renewed periodically until 1662). Habsburg monarchy virtually bankrupt.
1600	Controversies stirred by the Palatinate impair the operation of the imperial supreme court (*Reichskammergericht*).
1605	Donauwörth incident (sectarian riots). Rudolf II authorises Bavaria to restore order, which annexes the city as recompense for its action (1607) [**Doc. 3**].
1608–12	Succession dispute between Emperor Rudolf and his brother, Archduke Matthias, in the Austrian Habsburg lands as the increasingly unstable Rudolf refuses to marry. Concessions made to the Protestant nobles and burghers in the provincial Estates, including Rudolf's 'Letter of Majesty' to the Bohemian and Silesian Protestants (1609). Counter Reformation continues in Styria [**Doc. 8**].
1608	Protestant Union formed by the elector Palatine who orchestrates a walk out of his supporters at the Reichstag (imperial diet) meeting in Regensburg. Saxony and many Lutheran territories refuse to join the Union [**Doc. 4**].
1609	Catholic League formed by the duke of Bavaria and many ecclesiastical territories [**Doc. 5**].
1609–21	Twelve Year Truce between Spain and the Dutch.
1609–10	First Jülich-Cleves succession dispute between Brandenburg and Pfalz-Neuburg (second in 1614). Limited Dutch, French and Spanish intervention.
1611–13	Second Northern War between Denmark and Sweden signals the latter's growing power.
1612	Accession of Emperor Matthias (till 1619). Partial relaxation of tension (e.g. League dissolved 1617).
1613	Reichstag meeting at Regensburg. The Palatinate and most Union members refuse to sign the concluding Recess which is passed by the Catholics with the support of Saxony and many Lutheran imperial Estates. Tension eases, but anxiety and suspicion persist [**Docs 6–7**].
1617	Bohemian diet accepts Ferdinand II as their king with only two dissenting votes. The Oñate Treaty settles the disputed Austrian Habsburg succession [**Docs 9–10**].
1618	Defenestration of Prague (23 May) starts Bohemian Revolt. Fighting begins in June between Habsburg and Bohemian forces, but both sides continue negotiations until March 1619 [**Docs 11–13**].

1619	Bohemians depose Ferdinand II as their king and form a Confederation (22–26 August) [**Doc. 14**]. Accession of Emperor Ferdinand II (28 August). Frederick V of the Palatinate accepts Bohemian crown (September), but finds little support [**Docs 15–19, 30**]. Transylvania intervenes in support of Bohemia [**Doc. 20**]. Bavaria backs Ferdinand II in return for being allowed to re-establish the League (Treaty of Munich, 8 October) and (soon) also the promise of Palatine lands and title. Saxony backs Ferdinand (but withdraws into neutrality in 1622 once the Bohemian Revolt is suppressed) [**Docs 21–4, 131**]. The papacy and Spain provide additional assistance [**Docs 129–30**].
1620	Imperial victory at White Mountain (8 November). Frederick V a fugitive. Expropriation of opponents within Habsburg lands begins early in 1621 [**Docs 25–9**].
1621–2	Resumption of Spanish–Dutch war (April) [**Docs 31–6**]. Thirty Years War shifts to the Rhineland where the Palatinate is defeated by 1624 [**Docs 37–8, 121, 140**]. Extension to the Empire of the Habsburg policy of expropriation. First of three Huguenot revolts in France (till 1629). Start of Swedish–Polish War (till 1629). Currency speculation and the impact of the war fuel the hyperinflation known as the *Kipper und Wipper* [**Doc. 145**].
1623	Palatine lands and title transferred to Bavaria [**Docs 39–40**].
1625	Danish intervention restarts the war and moves it to northern Germany. Limited English and French financial and material support for Denmark (Hague Alliance) [**Docs 41–4, 46**]. Wallenstein appointed to raise a new imperial army [**Docs 47–50**].
1626	Danish offensive in northern Germany ends in defeat at Lutter (August). Bavarian and imperial forces crush the Upper Austrian Peasants' Rising against Bavarian occupation (since 1620, held in lieu of compensation for Bavaria's expenses in helping the emperor against Bohemia) [**Doc. 28**].
1627	Mainland Denmark overrun by imperial and League troops. Extension of expropriation policy to northern Germany where land belonging to princes and lords who had backed Denmark is taken and given to imperial officers and supporters (Wallenstein given the duchy of Mecklenburg in 1628 [**Docs 51–2**]. Bavaria returns Upper Austria to the Habsburgs and receives confirmation of its possession of the Lower Palatinate and the Palatine electoral title). Attempts to build an imperial navy on the Baltic (at Wismar in Mecklenburg) financed by Spain (the Baltic Design) [**Docs 53–4**].
1628	Stralsund repels Wallenstein's siege [**Doc. 55**]. Mantuan succession dispute. France eventually backs an anti-Spanish candidate as new duke of Mantua. Imperial intervention to enforce

Ferdinand II's jurisdiction over imperial (northern) Italy. Imperial forces besiege Mantua (captured in 1630) and repel Venetian intervention, while Spanish troops try to block French intervention by (unsuccessfully) besieging Casale. The Mantuan dispute is eventually settled by compromise in 1631 [**Docs 56–9**].

1629   Denmark agrees the Peace of Lübeck, recovering its mainland provinces in return for allowing the emperor a free hand in northern Germany [**Doc. 45**]. Ferdinand II issues Edict of Restitution (in March) demanding return of former Catholic church land taken by Protestants since 1555. Imperial and League troops spread across northern and much of southern Germany to enforce the Edict and the ongoing policy of expropriations [**Docs 61–4**]. The French broker the Truce of Altmark between Sweden and Poland (September) ending hostilities since 1621.

1630   Swedish invasion of Pomerania (in June) interrupts Ferdinand's attempts to settle matters in the Empire and Italy at the Electoral Congress of Regensburg [**Docs 66–73**]. Concerned at the disproportionate growth of the imperial army (now four times larger than that of the League), Maximilian of Bavaria forces Ferdinand to dismiss Wallenstein and replace him with Tilly (who remained commander of the League) [**Doc. 60**].

1631   France agrees financial support for Sweden (Treaty of Bärwalde, January), intending to use Sweden to keep the emperor busy and unable to help Spain in its struggle with the Dutch [**Doc. 77**]. France would have preferred an alliance with Bavaria to block both the emperor and German Protestants. Bavaria agrees to cooperate with France, but also refuses to abandon the emperor (because Ferdinand had given the Palatine lands and title to Maximilian). France directs Sweden not to attack Bavaria or the League territories [**Doc. 78**]. Saxony tries to organise a neutral group of Protestant princes opposed to both imperial power and Swedish invasion (Leipzig Convention, February–April) [**Doc. 65**]. Few princes join the Swedes who are unable to break out of north-east Germany [**Doc. 73**]. With Tilly commanding both the imperial and League armies, it proves impossible to prevent clashes between League and Swedish forces. Tilly besieges Magdeburg, which had refused to admit a garrison. Sack of Magdeburg (May) after the city refuses to surrender, because its Swedish commander claimed it would be relieved in time. Fire spreads accidentally, killing most of the population [**Docs 79–90**]. Swedes meanwhile bully Brandenburg into joining them (April–June) [**Docs 74–5**]. The Swedes then advance into Saxony which declares for Sweden. Saxony intends its alliance merely to pressure Ferdinand into being more reasonable and abandoning the Edict [**Doc. 76**].

Swedish–Saxon victory at Breitenfeld (September) [**Doc. 117**]. Rapid escalation of the war as Swedes overrun much of central and western Germany. Start of the worst period of destruction (to about 1640) [**Docs 122–6, 146–53**].

1632   Having already conquered many League territories (Würzburg, Bamberg, Mainz, etc.) since October 1631, Sweden no longer recognises Maximilian as neutral and invades Bavaria in April [**Docs 91, 114, 135, 146**]. Maximilian accepts Wallenstein's recall as imperial commander [**Doc. 97**]. Sweden begins reorganisation of its conquered territories [**Doc. 92**]. This is interrupted by the death of its king, Gustavus Adolphus, at the battle of Lützen (November) [**Doc. 93**]. Government passes to Chancellor Axel Oxenstierna, on behalf of six-year-old Queen Christina. The Catholic territories in the Rhineland believe the emperor and League can no longer protect them and open negotiations for French protection.

1633   Sweden organises its German allies into the Heilbronn League (April) in attempt to secure funding for its army [**Docs 94–5**]. Saxony and Brandenburg refuse to join, but remain allied to Sweden. Sweden's German generals (led by Bernhard of Weimar) force Oxenstierna to step up the policy of 'donations', distributing captured territory to them. France invades the duchy of Lorraine (part of the Empire, but its duke was also a French vassal) in June, bringing its troops into the Rhineland and in a position to offer 'protection' to German territories. Only the elector of Trier and a few minor Alsatian territories accept. The growing French presence threatens the Spanish Road, or route from the Alps down the Rhine to the Spanish Netherlands. Spain sends an army over the Alps from north Italy to clear the Rhineland (September), but the forces are decimated by plague that is now spreading across the Empire. Wallenstein opens secret negotiations to detach Saxony and other territories from their Swedish alliance [**Doc. 98**].

1634   Fears that Wallenstein is planning to defect prompts Ferdinand to sanction his assassination (February) [**Docs 99–102**]. The command is reassigned (initially to Archduke Ferdinand, the future Ferdinand III). Spain sends a second army over the Alps which assists in the imperial victory at Nördlingen (September), but then continues its march northwards to the Netherlands. The Swedish position collapses in southern Germany. Part of the Swedish army (containing the few native troops) retreats north to the Baltic coast. The other, mainly German, part under Bernhard of Weimar retreats to the Rhine.

1635   France and Spain are already heading towards war which becomes official in April when France declares war on the excuse that Spanish troops have arrested the elector of Trier who was under French protection. France signs an offensive alliance with the Dutch and begins operations against Spanish possessions in the Netherlands, Italy and Iberia. France does not declare war against the emperor [Docs 109–10]. Some imperial troops assist the Spanish in the Rhineland and defend the southern frontier of the Spanish Netherlands, but the emperor and the Dutch remain at peace. The collapse of Sweden's position in southern Germany enables Saxony to change sides in the Peace of Prague (May) [Doc. 103]. Bavaria also signs, dissolving the League in return for renewed guarantees for its possession of the Palatine lands and title. The Saxon and Bavarian armies become autonomous corps within a single imperial army. Brandenburg and most of Sweden's other German allies follow Saxony and accept the peace which offers concessions over the Edict of Restitution. Some are excluded from the emperor's amnesty (which was part of the peace) because their territory had already been distributed to imperial supporters: the Palatinate, the Bohemian and Austrian rebels from 1618, Württemberg and a few minor counts. Hessen-Kassel is also excluded, but remains neutral along with the Guelph dukes (ruling Brunswick and Lüneburg in northern Germany) during negotiations to include them in the peace [Doc. 105]. Sweden's remaining German officers in its army in north Germany mutiny until Oxenstierna promises to include their pay arrears as a Swedish war aim (Powder Barrel Convention, August) [Doc. 104]. France brokers a twenty-year extension to the Truce of Altmark (1629) between Poland and Sweden (Truce of Stuhmsdorf, September). With this and the army secure, Sweden rejects the emperor's peace terms relayed through Saxony and the war resumes in the Empire [Docs 106–7]. Bernhard of Weimar and Sweden's south German army pass into French pay. France intends to use them for a surrogate war in Germany to keep the emperor from assisting Spain, without having to declare open war against him.

1636   The Saxon army, backed by an imperial contingent, fails to drive the Swedes from north Germany [Docs 111–12]. Another imperial contingent assists the Spanish advancing into France from the Netherlands. The offensive leads to an unexpected French collapse (the 'Year of Corbie'), but fails to make permanent gains. The papacy attempts to mediate by sponsoring a peace conference in Cologne, but its refusal to negotiate with Sweden prevents this from getting off the ground [Doc. 148]. Ferdinand II meets the electors at Regensburg and secures the succession of his son Archduke Ferdinand.

1637   Accession of Emperor Ferdinand III (till 1657). Ferdinand tries to consolidate the Peace of Prague by widening the amnesty.

Sweden and increasingly France encourage Hessen-Kassel and the Guelph dukes not to abandon their pro-Swedish neutrality. Weimar's inability to break across the Rhine from Alsace obliges France to send reinforcements from its own army, drawing it deeper into the war in the Empire [Doc. 115].

1638 Renewed Saxon-imperial failure against the Swedes in northeast Germany. The French finally secure a foothold east of the Rhine by capturing Breisach (December), but are unable to break further east across the Black Forest [Doc. 149].

1639 France absorbs the Weimar army on Bernhard's death as the French 'Army of Germany'. A Swedish offensive hits Saxony and Bohemia, encouraging Hessen-Kassel and the Guelphs to rejoin Sweden. The emperor recalls most of the units that had served with the Spanish since 1635. Effective end of Spanish imperial–military cooperation [Doc. 129].

1640 France moves its German army to north Germany to support Sweden's German allies. Revolts in Catalonia and Portugal seriously undermine Spain's war effort against France and the Dutch. Spanish subsidies to the emperor dry up. Ferdinand III makes a further effort to save the Peace of Prague and rally all German territories behind him by summoning the Reichstag in Regensburg (1640–1). They renew support, but there is growing disillusionment with the cost of the war and the failure to defeat Sweden and France [Docs 128–9].

1641 Franco-Swedish alliance consolidated as both agree not to make a separate peace in the Empire (Treaty of Hamburg, 30 June) [Doc. 108]. Ferdinand III signs the Hamburg Peace Preliminaries (25 December), agreeing to convene a general peace congress in the Westphalian towns of Münster and Osnabrück to be chaired by Denmark [Doc. 157]. Sweden does not join France's war against Spain. Brandenburg's truce (24 July) with Sweden signals drift of German princes into neutrality. The imperial army defeats the Guelph dukes who remain neutral for the rest of the war (Peace of Goslar, January 1642). Hessen-Kassel is Sweden's only remaining important German ally, which survives by overrunning much of Westphalia (north-west Germany). The elector of Cologne organises a Westphalian army with the assistance of local (largely but not exclusively) Catholic minor territories. This army resists Hessen-Kassel, while the main imperial army supports the Saxons against the Swedes. Defence of the Rhine is devolved to Bavaria.

1642 The main imperial army is defeated at the Second Battle of Breitenfeld (November), weakening its operations against the Swedes who capture Olmütz as a base in the Habsburg lands [Docs 118–19, 125–6, 133]. Franco-Swedish military cooperation breaks down as France's Army of Germany retreats south-west back to its original area of operations in the Rhineland [Docs 134, 136].

1643   Congress of Westphalia opens in the towns of Münster and Osnabrück. This merges with earlier Danish mediation. Denmark had grown alarmed by the prospect of a permanent Swedish presence in northern Germany. Sweden fears that Denmark will mediate the peace in the emperor's favour and moves its main army rapidly out of Germany to attack Denmark [Doc. 162]. France's Army of Germany is defeated by the Bavarians and driven back to the Rhine (Battle of Tuttlingen, November).

1644   The Swedes overrun mainland Denmark, but are unable to gain full command of the sea needed to attack the Danish islands. The emperor is unable to profit from Sweden's temporary distraction. The army sent to assist Denmark collapses in disorder as its supply arrangements break down. Meanwhile, a renewed French offensive finally secures a strong foothold east of the Rhine (Battle of Freiburg, capture of Philippsburg and Mainz). Brandenburg renews its truce with Sweden to last till a peace settlement is formulated i.e. 1648 [Doc. 158].

1645   France, England and the Dutch broker the Peace of Brömsebro between Denmark and Sweden (August). Denmark abandons attempts to mediate and surrenders some of its territory in southern Sweden. The main imperial army is defeated at Jankau (March) by the Swedes, while the French (after an initial reverse at Herbsthausen) defeat the Bavarians at Allerheim. Saxony makes a truce with Sweden (extended in March 1646 to last till a peace settlement). These setbacks force Ferdinand III to send secret instructions to his envoy, Maximilian von Trauttmannsdorff, to start serious negotiations at the Westphalian congress [Docs 159–61].

1646   Franco-Swedish military cooperation becomes more effective. Sweden concentrates on defeating the main imperial army which is now defending Bohemia and Austria. France uses its Army of Germany to pressure Bavaria in the hope it will also make a truce. Hessen-Kassel meanwhile keeps the Cologne–Westphalian army busy. Negotiations intensify at the Westphalian congress [Docs 163–5]. Operations are linked to these negotiations as a way of pressuring opponents to give ground in the talks.

1647   Spain agrees a truce with the Dutch (January) and defeats a revolt in Naples. Bavaria accepts the Truce of Ulm (March) with France and Sweden, but rejoins the war in September following renewed imperial guarantees for its retention of the Palatine lands and title [Doc. 166]. Sweden is unable to use this opportunity, because France switches its Army of Germany for an (unsuccessful) attack on Spanish-held Luxembourg. Temporary Bavarian neutrality gives Ferdinand III an excuse to break dynastic solidarity with Spain and open serious negotiations with France, as well as Sweden.

1648   Spanish–Dutch talks conclude with the first Peace of Münster (15 May): Spain accepts Dutch independence. Franco-Spanish talks collapse as another French victory (Battle of Lens) prompts France to demand too much. Spain continues fighting, because of the aristocratic revolt against the French government (the Fronde, lasting till 1653). Franco-Spanish war continues till the Peace of the Pyrenees in 1659. The combined imperial-Bavarian army is defeated by the combined Franco-Swedish army at Zusmarshausen (March), but survives. A Swedish assault on Prague is resisted. The war in the Empire is concluded through the dual treaties of Münster (IPM with France) and Osnabrück (IPO with Sweden and Hessen-Kassel) (both 24 October) [**Docs 167–8**].

1649   Ratification of the Peace of Westphalia (18 February). Execution Congress opens in the imperial city of Nuremberg to implement the peace within the Empire (May). Demobilisation and withdrawal of all garrisons arranged by two Recesses (September 1649 and March 1650) [**Docs 169–71, 173–4**].

1650   Troop demobilisation and withdrawal largely complete. Widespread official peace celebrations and start of formal commemoration of the peace [**Docs 172, 175–6**].

1651   'Düsseldorf Cow War' as Brandenburg tries to settle the Jülich-Berg inheritance dispute by force against Pfalz-Neuburg. Both parties obliged to accept a settlement brokered by the emperor.

1652   Spain evacuates Frankenthal, while Hessen-Kassel evacuates its last garrison in Westphalia (Lippstadt).

1653   Sweden finally accepts Brandenburg possession of eastern Pomerania (as agreed at Westphalia) in return for formal enfeoffment of its new German possessions by the emperor (May).

1653–4   Reichstag meets in Regensburg and passes wide-ranging legislation, including annulment of many wartime debts, but postpones most of the outstanding constitutional issues left open in the Peace of Westphalia. The concluding Recess includes both the IPM and IPO, confirming that both treaties are integral parts of the imperial constitution.

1654   Sweden evacuates its last garrison (Vechta, in Westphalia).

1659   Peace of the Pyrenees concludes Franco-Spanish war.

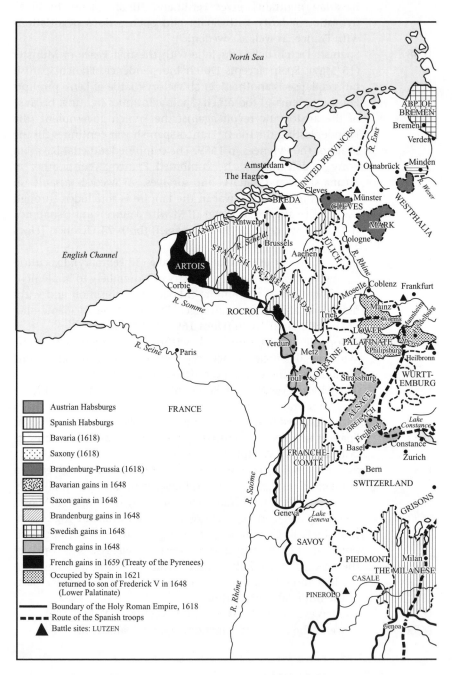

Map 1   The Holy Roman Empire during the Thirty Years War

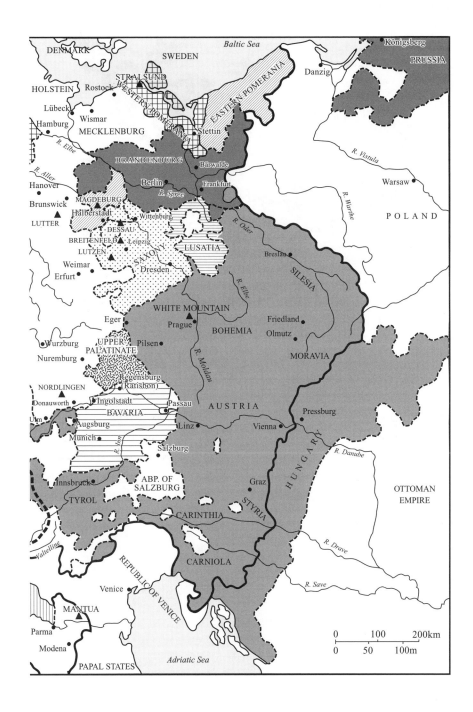

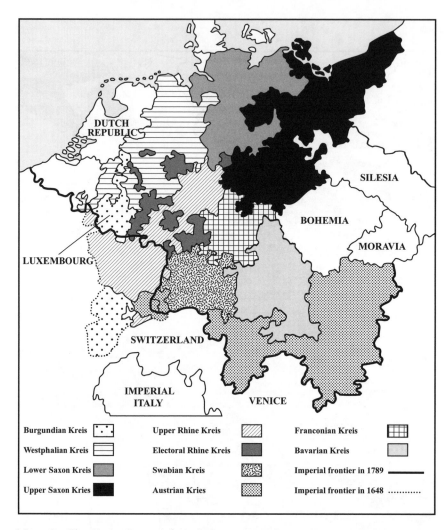

Map 2 The *Kreise* (imperial circles)

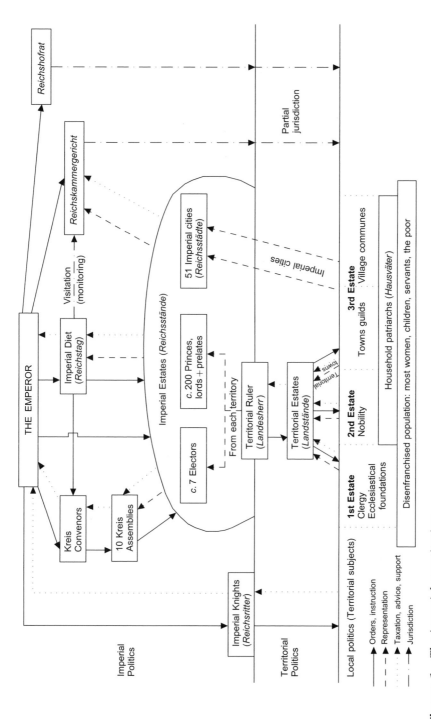

Figure 1 The imperial constitution

Acknowledgements

The author and publishers wish to thank the following for permission to reproduce copyright material:

Aschendorff Verlag GmbH & Co. KG for pp. 440–52 and pp. 453–55, translated from Fritz Dickmann *et al.* (eds), *Acta Pacis Westphalicae*, series I *Instruktionen* vol. I *Frankreich – Schweden – Kaiser* (1962); Aschendorff Verlag GmbH & Co. KG for pp. 357–60 from Elke Jarnut and Rita Bohlen (eds), *Acta Pacis Westphalicae*, series I *Korrespondenzen* section B vol. 3 part 1 *Die französische Korrespondenzen 1645–6* (1999); Cambridge University Press for p. 132, from J. V. Polisensky, *War and Society in Europe 1618–1648*, translated by Robert Evans (1978); Columbia University Press for pp. 223–26, from *The Secret Diplomacy of the Hapsburgs, 1598–1625*, by Charles Howard Carter, copyright © 1964 Columbia University Press, reprinted with permission of the publisher; Geschichts- und Altertumsverein Ellwangen eV for pp. 110–11 and p. 112, translated from Karl Schumm, 'Die Hohenlohe Herrschaft über Ellwangen 1633/34' in *Ellwanger Jahrbuch* (1956/57) vol. 17; Historical Union for Upper Palatine and Regensburg for pp. 185–86, translated from J. Staber (ed.), 'Die Eroberung der Oberpfalz im Jahre 1621 nach dem Tagebuch des Johann Christoph von Preysing' in *Verhandlungen des historischen Vereins für Oberpfalz und Regensburg* (1964), vol. 104; Kommission Für Bayerische Landesgeschichte Bei Der Bayerischen Akademie der Wissenschaften for pp. 254–55, translated from Memorandum of Count Heinrich Schlick, president of the Habsburg Court War Council, edited by Eugen von Frauenholz as 'Zur Geschichte des Dreißigjährigen Krieges' in *Zeitschrift für Bayerische Landesgeschichte* (1941/42) vol. 13; Oldenbourg Wissenschaftsverlag GmbH for pp. 242–7, translated from Georg Franz *et al.* (eds), *Die Politik Maximilians I. von Bayern und seiner Verbündeten 1618–1651* (*Briefe und Akten zur Geschichte des Dreißigjährigen Kriegs*, new series vol. I, © 1966 by Oldenbourg Wissenschaftsverlag, München; Oldenbourg Wissenschaftsverlag GmbH for pp. 653–59, translated from Bernd Roeck, 'Die Feier des Friedens', in Heinz Duchhardt (ed.), *Der Westfälische Friede*, © 1998 by Oldenbourg Wissenschaftsverlag, München; Oldenbourg Wissenschaftsverlag GmbH for p. 7, translated from Hans Sturmberger, *Aufstand in Böhmen. Der Beginn des Dreißigjährigen Krieges*, © 1959 by Oldenbourg Wissenschaftsverlag, München; The Orion Publishing Group Ltd for p. 311, from D. P. O'Connell, *Richelieu*, Weidenfeld & Nicolson, London (1968); Oxford University Press for p. 30, from Hans Medick, 'Historical Event and Contemporary Experience: the Capture and Destruction of Magdeburg in 1631' in *History Workshop Journal*

(2001), Autumn, 52, pp. 23–48, by permission of Oxford University Press; Peter Lang GmbH for p. 197, translated from Franz Maier, *Die bayerische Unterpfalz im Dreißigjährigen Krieg: Besetzung, Verwaltung und Rekatholisierung der rechtsrheinischen Pfalz durch Bayern 1621 bis 1649* (1990); Professor Dr Jan Peters for extracts from Peter Hangendorf's diary, translated from J. Peters (ed.), *Ein Söldnerleben aus dem Dreißigjährigen Krieg*, Akademie Verlag GmbH (1993); Philipp Reclam J. Verlag GmbH for pp. 133–4, pp. 366–7, pp. 371–4, translated from Bernd Roeck (ed.), *Deutsche Geschichte in Quellen und Darstellung* vol. IV *Gegenreformation und Dreißigjährige Krieg 1555–1648* (1996); The Random House Group Ltd for p. 54, from *Letters of Elizabeth, Queen of Bohemia*, compiled by L. M. Baker, published by Bodley Head, reprinted by permission of The Random House Group Ltd (1953); University of North Carolina Press for pp. 83–4, *Religion and Politics in the Age of the Counterreformation: Emperor Ferdinand II, William Lamormaini, S. J., and the Formation of the Imperial Policy* by Robert S. J. Bireley, copyright © 1981 by the University of North Carolina Press, used by permission of the publisher, www.uncpress.unc.edu; University Press of America for pp. 77–9, from Theodore K. Rabb (ed.), *The Thirty Years War; problems of motive, extent, and effect*, pub. D. C. Heath 1964, 2nd edition published University Press of America (1981); WBG Wissenverbindet for p. 160, translated from Hanns Hubert Hofmann (ed.), *Quellen zum Verfassungsorganismus des Heiligen Römischen Reiches Deutscher Nation 1495–1806,* Wissenschaftliche Buchgesellschaft (1976); Yale University Press for pp. 217–18, from Steven Ozment (ed.), *Three Behaim Boys: growing up in early modern Germany* (1990); akg-images for the image in Doc. 153: Thirty Years War 1618–1648. – 'Rapacious Attack'. – Woodcut after an etching by Hans Ulrich Franck, 1643, photo: akg-images; The Bridgeman Art Library for the image in Doc. 154: The Raising of an Army, plate 2 from 'The Miseries and Misfortunes of War', engraved by Israel Henriet (c. 1590–1661) 1633 (engraving) (b/w photo) by Callot, Jacques (1592–1635) (after) / Grosjean Collection, Paris, France / The Bridgeman Art Library. The Bridgeman Art Library for the image in Doc. 155: The Hanging, plate 11 from 'The Miseries and Misfortunes of War', engraved by Israel Henriet (c. 1590–1661) 1633 (engraving) (b/w photo) by Callot, Jacques (1592–1635) (after) / Grosjean Collection, Paris, France / The Bridgeman Art Library; akg-images for the image in Doc. 156: Callot, Jacques; French engraver; c. 1592/93–1635. – 'Beggar', c. 1622/23. – Etching, 13.7 x 8.6 cm, from the series 'Les Geux' (The Beggars), private Collection, Photo: akg-images / François Guénet.

Every effort has been made to trace all the copyright holders, but if any have been inadvertently overlooked the publishers would be pleased to make the necessary arrangement at the first opportunity.

Introduction

The Thirty Years War was the greatest man-made calamity to befall Europe before the twentieth century, claiming proportionately far more lives than either of the world wars. It has been variously presented as the culmination of an age of 'religious wars' beginning with the Protestant Reformation in 1517, as an international struggle against Austrian and Spanish Habsburg predominance, and, more narrowly, as a German national disaster. These interpretations are supplemented by further national perspectives, each relating events through the experience of one of the many other countries which became involved.

The main focus of the fighting was the Holy Roman Empire, a political organisation first established in 800 that claimed direct descent from ancient Rome and considered itself superior to all other European states. The Empire encompassed modern Germany, Austria, the Czech Republic, Belgium, Luxembourg, parts of eastern France, western Poland and southern Denmark. It was ruled by an emperor chosen by the seven leading princes called electors.[1] The emperor was considered sovereign, held the initiative in most imperial institutions and represented the Empire in dealings with rulers elsewhere. The electors had consistently chosen a member of the Habsburg dynasty as emperor since 1438, because this family had the largest possessions and a direct interest in defending the Empire against the Muslim Ottoman Turks, who conquered the Balkans after the mid-fifteenth century. The emperor was expected to share important decisions with the imperial Estates (*Reichsstände*), or territories comprising the Empire. Some of these were under his direct rule as hereditary possessions, since the Habsburgs held Austria, Bohemia[2] and parts of the Upper Rhine, as well as Hungary, which lay outside the Empire to the east. The rest of the Empire was ruled by the electors, princes and imperial cities, which collectively constituted the imperial Estates. They could be

---

[1] The three prince archbishops of Mainz, Cologne and Trier were the senior electors, followed by the hereditary secular rulers of Bohemia, the Palatinate, Saxony and Brandenburg. The elector of Mainz was also head of the Catholic church in the Empire and remained Catholic, like his fellow archbishops in Cologne and Trier. The elector of Saxony was the first important patron of the Lutheran Reformation. Lutheranism spread to the Palatinate and Brandenburg, but their electors adopted 'reformed' Protestantism, called Calvinism, in 1560 and 1613 respectively. The Bohemian crown was held by the Habsburg dynasty from 1526, which remained Catholic.

[2] Bohemia was an autonomous kingdom within the Empire, covering the modern Czech Republic, Silesia – which is now in Poland – and Lusatia – now in Germany.

summoned to meet the emperor in the imperial diet (Reichstag) to discuss important matters like war, peace and taxation, but were otherwise expected to manage their own internal affairs according to the growing body of written imperial law. This law underpinned the entire imperial constitution, but was far from comprehensive. The imperial Estates could also meet, either on their own initiative or when summoned by the emperor, in assemblies held for each of the ten regions known as (*Reichs*) *Kreise* ((imperial) circles), which had been established at the beginning of the sixteenth century.[3]

Rapid changes in Europe's political, religious and economic affairs posed numerous challenges to which the emperor and imperial Estates responded as they saw fit, according to precedent, custom and their understanding of religion and morality. This gave rise to considerable disagreement, not least because disputes over what constituted the correct version of Christianity became enmeshed with arguments about the imperial constitution (see Figure 1). Further difficulties arose, within the Habsburg lands and many imperial Estates, between rulers and their own subjects who were often represented as provincial or territorial Estates (*Landstände*) in assemblies roughly analogous to the imperial diet. These problems did not lead inevitably to violence, but a combination of adverse circumstances rendered them more intractable around 1600 and contributed to the Bohemian Revolt which started the Thirty Years War in 1618. The subsequent course of events is outlined in the Chronology and explored further in the introductions to each document section.

The book is intended to allow readers to understand the war through the words of those experiencing it and to explore what drove them to fight ferociously for three decades. It is designed to be used in a variety of ways. Its basic layout derives from my own special interest in the Thirty Years War, but it is constructed so as to allow tutors to make their own use of the material. The

---

3 Of the ten *Kreise*, the Electoral Rhenish Kreis on the middle Rhine encompassed the three ecclesiastical electorates, the Palatinate and a few minor territories. The lands immediately to the south and east formed the Upper Rhenish Kreis whose principal territory was the *Landgraviate* of Hessen-Kassel. Bavaria, Salzburg and their immediate minor neighbours formed the Bavarian Kreis. The south-western territories were grouped into the Swabian Kreis, while those to the north of Bavaria formed the Franconian Kreis (chiefly Bamberg, Würzburg, Ansbach, Bayreuth and Nuremberg). The north-western territories constituted the Lower Rhenish (also called Westphalian) Kreis, those of northern Germany formed the Lower Saxon Kreis, and those of the north-east composed the Upper Saxon Kreis which included the electorates of Brandenburg and Saxony. The Spanish Habsburg lands west of the Rhine in the Netherlands formed their own Burgundian Kreis, while Austria's possessions in Alsace, on the Upper Rhine and along the Danube around Vienna constituted a separate Austrian Kreis. Neither the Austrian nor the Burgundian Kreise held assemblies, since they were entirely dependent on the two branches of the Habsburg dynasty, but their formal existence offered both monarchies an additional means to legitimate policy within the Empire. Bohemia was excluded from this regional subdivision entirely.

supporting material (this Introduction and the commentaries to each section of documents) are deliberately brief, so as not to answer pre-emptively questions that tutors may set students. The remarks are restricted to raising questions and setting the context of the individual documents. All the documents are referenced and (where necessary) annotated to identify named individuals and explain potentially obscure terms. They are also keyed into the chronology at the start of the book, which offers a short summary of the causes, course and consequences of the war. The Guide to Further Reading at the end offers suggestions for those seeking more information on specific points.

The material follows my own interpretation of the war as a struggle about the religious and political order in the Empire. The war was related to other conflicts in Europe, but nonetheless remained distinct. This dictates the selection of material that includes Spain's struggle with the Dutch, as well as Swedish, French, Danish, British and Polish policies, but only as far as these related to the war in the Empire.

The organisation into 19 sections is based on my own teaching experience, but tutors can combine, skip or split sections as required, and the longer sections have subdivisions to assist in this. The material is arranged broadly thematically, but in roughly chronological order, to combine the advantages of both approaches. Sections 1–3 include material relating to the causes. Section 4 covers not only the Bohemian Revolt, but allows exploration of its consequences within the Habsburg monarchy. The resumption of the Dutch War (1621) is covered by Section 5, that also includes material explaining why Spain was unable to assist Austria more forcefully. The main military and political events of the 1620s are covered in Sections 6–8. Swedish intervention restarted the conflict in 1630. Section 9 includes material on the controversy surrounding Sweden's motives and methods once in Germany. The material on the destruction of Magdeburg (1631) is particularly rich. The significance of this event and the issues it raises warrant a separate Section (10). It also provides a convenient change of focus halfway through the book, shifting from the arena of religious controversy, high politics and military events, to a more immediate, personal perspective of those caught in the conflict. The main events of the early 1630s are covered by Sections 11–13: the controversy surrounding Wallenstein, Sweden's defeat and the emperor's attempt to settle the war in the Peace of Prague. Section 14 includes material on why that peace failed and why the war continued. Questions of military organisation and practice, the war economy and the wider impact have been separated into sections 15 and 16. Some of the material in the other Sections (especially 4 and 10) also deal with these issues, and users of the book are alerted to this and to connections between other topics by the cross-referencing of the documents, as well as through the Index. However, it makes sense to devote more space to these issues, given the interest in the wider impact of the conflict. Placing them at this point in the book allows those working through the material sequentially to approach these questions with a firm grounding in the wider political background. Sections 17–19 conclude the war with peace making, implementation and commemoration.

In selecting the documents I decided to include the most important material on the key events and issues across the entire scope of the war, as well as representative samples of different types of sources and kinds of authors. This necessitates the inclusion of a few texts already available elsewhere, though the bulk of the documents appear in English for the first time and include some directly from the archives. Four of the statistical tables derive from later calculations, but otherwise all the material is contemporary. The translations aim to convey the meaning of the text without compromising too much of the original style. Official titles were not standardised in the seventeenth century and the translation follows the original rather than imposing anachronistic uniformity. The Empire's designation is a good example. Few documents used the full 'Holy Roman Empire of the German Nation', which was in fact never the exclusive official title. Protestant texts tended to drop 'Holy' and most generally omitted 'of the German Nation'.

Dates are given in the Gregorian New Style used by Catholic Europe, unless the original uses both this and the Julian Old Style retained by Protestants and which was ten days behind. Currency is presented as in the original. The Empire had two principal coins, though their precious metal content, and hence value, varied depending on where and when they had been minted. The south, west and Habsburg lands used the florin (fl.), which was divided into 60 *Kreuzer* (xr.), each worth four pfennigs (pennies). The subdivisions of the taler (tlr.) used in the north and east varied from 24 to 36 smaller coins of different names depending on the territory. One taler was generally reckoned to be equivalent to 90 *Kreuzer*.

Some of the documents are edited to reduce length, especially where the passages can be omitted as redundant or can easily be summarised. However, the general principle favours presenting material at length to give readers a fuller picture and allow the same text to be 'interrogated' for different questions. The selection includes contrasting material on the same issue or event, as well as different kinds of source material, such as a variety of textual and visual sources on military discipline and experience. It also includes diverging viewpoints, such as the inclusion of both Catholic and Protestant, civilian and military, accounts of the sack of Magdeburg. A number of cryptic documents have been chosen deliberately to prompt discussion of interpretation and meaning in such sources.

The length of the documents varies. Political texts are generally longer than those on other issues, but have been balanced by the inclusion of some substantial extracts from diaries and memoirs. The 19 sections are also of different length. The first three are a little shorter. This is deliberate, since tutors using the book in sequence may need to concentrate on fewer documents at the beginning of a course, covering more material as students gain familiarity with the subject in later sections.

I would like to thank the cohorts of students who have taken my special subject at the universities of Sunderland and Hull and who have posed many of the questions prompting the selection of material here. Michael Schaich took particular care in reading the entire text and offering numerous valuable suggestions. I am indebted to Janine Marret and my wife Eliane for assistance in translating Documents 25, 93 and 169, as well as Thomas Biskup for help with Document 121 and Charles Prior for help with Document 25. Unless otherwise stated, I am responsible for all other translations and for any mistakes they may contain. Kate Haines, Jenni Burnell and the team at Palgrave have been a delight to work with. Finally, it is my pleasure to dedicate this book to Jeremy Black, a true friend and colleague.

1

Political and religious tension in the Empire after 1555

It was long customary for historians to blame the outbreak of the Thirty Years War on the failure of the Peace of Augsburg to resolve tensions in the Empire arising from the disputes over the Protestant Reformation **[Doc. 1]**. This treaty was deliberately ambiguous in its language to allow both Catholics and Lutherans to sign it whilst still disagreeing fundamentally over what constituted supposedly absolute and singular religious truth. The ambiguity was not immediately a problem and the treaty proved surprisingly durable, helping to sustain the longest period of peace in modern German history prior to the tranquillity that has lasted since 1945.

Nonetheless, three issues emerged as serious, long-term problems. The most significant was the fate of the ecclesiastical principalities and other lands of the Catholic imperial church (*Reichskirche*). These were full imperial Estates, represented in imperial institutions where their numbers gave the Catholics an inbuilt majority. They were ruled by relations of the Catholic princely and noble families, who had embarked on church careers and were elected by the senior clergy in each territory. Many of these clergy converted to Lutheranism, leading to the election in some principalities of sons from Protestant princely families eager to advance their political influence and confessional interests. These elections and the conversion of some incumbent ecclesiastical princes, like the elector of Cologne in 1583, threatened the influence of Catholic families and their majority in imperial institutions.

The second issue was the fate of the church property still in Catholic hands but lying within territories now ruled by Lutheran princes. The last issue was the presence of dissenting minorities in both Catholic and Lutheran territories. Most princes wanted to expel minorities in their own territory, but demanded toleration for their co-religionists living in someone else's lands.

Emperor Ferdinand I (1503–64, r.1558) addressed these problems in a separate declaration **[Doc. 2]**, but many Catholics denied this was a binding part of the Peace. Meanwhile, Lutherans rejected Article 18 of the Peace, claiming they had never agreed this during the negotiations. This article became known as the 'ecclesiastical reservation' and was intended to reserve the church principalities for Catholicism.

Further difficulties emerged with the spread of Calvinism after 1560. Though called a Religious Peace, the 1555 treaty did not define doctrine. Lutherans were referred to as the adherents of the Confession of Augsburg, a religious statement first issued in 1530 but revised subsequently. However, the treaty did not specify which version enjoyed the protection of imperial law. Calvinists claimed inclusion as a set of believers who were simply continuing Luther's original mission. Catholics and most Lutherans rejected this; the latter often hating Calvinists more than the Catholics did, because most conversions to Calvinism came at their expense.

The 1555 treaty has entered history as the Religious Peace, but it was referred to in the later sixteenth and seventeenth century as the 'Religious and Profane Peace' because it also addressed other issues like public order. Disputes over doctrine were supposed to be settled by theologians, while those over legal jurisdictions and other matters would be adjudicated by the two imperial supreme courts. Unfortunately, the theologians could not agree, while many people found it hard in practice to distinguish between religion and law, since Christian morality was a benchmark for both. The Imperial Cameral Court (*Reichskammergericht*) was entrusted with adjudicating disputes arising from the 1555 treaty. It was an independent supreme court composed of Catholic and Lutheran judges selected by the imperial Estates. The court handled most cases with relatively few problems before the 1580s when the issues became increasingly politicised by the Calvinist elector Palatine and the Catholic duke of Bavaria. Both princes identified their own dynastic goals with wider confessional concerns.

The growing number of disputes prompted Emperor Rudolf II (1552–1612, r.1576) to intervene. Less circumspect than his two predecessors, Rudolf assigned cases to the Empire's other supreme court, the Imperial Aulic Council (*Reichshofrat*), on the grounds that public order also fell within its remit. Protestants and some Catholics regarded the court with growing suspicion, because it was based in Vienna and staffed entirely by the emperor's appointees. Most disputes still passed relatively smoothly, but Rudolf's personal, heavy-handed intervention in some high-profile cases seriously damaged his reputation. The most notorious was his intervention through the *Reichshofrat* in the imperial city of Donauwörth after sectarian riots in 1605 **[Doc. 3]**. This city lay in the Swabian Kreis, one of the ten administrative regions in the Empire (see p. 1 and Map 2). It was customary to assign enforcement of court verdicts to the leading princes of each Kreis. In this case, Rudolf appointed the duke of Bavaria as imperial commissioner, even though his lands were in the Bavarian, not Swabian, Kreis. He then allowed the duke to annex Donauwörth in lieu of the costs he had incurred. It is easy to see why militant Protestants felt the emperor was deliberately promoting Catholic 'tyranny' in the Empire.

1. The Religious Peace of Augsburg, 1555

15 In order to bring the highly necessary peace to the Holy Empire of the Germanic Nation between the Roman Imperial Majesty and the Electors, Princes and Estates, let neither His Imperial Majesty nor the Electors, Princes, etc., do any violence or harm to any Estate of the Empire on account of the Augsburg Confession, but let them enjoy their religious belief, liturgy and

ceremonies as well as their estates and other rights and privileges in peace; and complete religious peace shall be obtained only by Christian means of amity, or under threat of the punishment of the Imperial ban.

16 Likewise the Estates espousing the Augsburg Confession shall let all the Estates and Princes who cling to the old religion live in absolute peace and in the enjoyment of all their estates, rights and privileges.

17 However, all such as do not belong to the two above-named religions shall not be included in the present peace, but be totally excluded from it.

18 And since it has proved to be a matter of great dispute as to what was to happen with the bishoprics, priories and other ecclesiastical benefices of such Catholic priests who would in course of time abandon the old religion, we have in virtue of the powers of Roman Emperors ordained as follows: where an archbishop, bishop or prelate or any other priest of our old religion shall abandon the same, his archbishopric, bishopric, prelacy and other benefices together with all their income and revenues which he has so far possessed, shall be abandoned by him without any further objection or delay. The chapter and such as are entitled to it by common law or the custom of the place shall elect a person espousing the old religion who may enter on the possession and enjoyment of all the rights and incomes of the place without any further hindrance and without prejudging any ultimate amicable transaction of religion.

19 Some of the abbeys, monasteries and other ecclesiastical estates having been confiscated and turned into churches, schools and charitable institutions, it is herewith ordained that such estates which their original owners had not possessed at the time of the Treaty of Passau [1552] shall be comprised in the present treaty of peace[1].

20 The ecclesiastical jurisdiction over the Augsburg Confession, dogma, appointment of ministers, church ordinances and ministries hitherto practised (but apart from all the rights of the Electors, Princes, Estates, colleges and monasteries to taxes in money or tithes) shall from now cease and the Augsburg Confession shall be left to the free and untrammelled enjoyment of their religion, ceremonies, appointment of ministers, as is stated in a subsequent separate article, until the final transaction of religion will take place.

---

[1] The Peace of Passau concluded the so-called Princes' Revolt which overturned the temporary ascendancy of Emperor Charles V in the Empire following his victory over the Saxon elector and his Lutheran allies in the Schmalkaldic War (1546–7). The Peace recognised the possession of all former Catholic church property which had passed into Lutheran hands by 1552. Negotiations to consolidate these arrangements continued at the Reichstag which met in Augsburg, with Charles's brother and successor designate, Archduke Ferdinand (1503–64), representing the emperor. These talks produced the Peace of Augsburg in 1555.

21 While the Estates of the old religion are entitled to their rents, interest, dues and tithes, those who pay them are to remain under the same secular jurisdiction of the Estate under which they stood at the start of this religious dispute. Likewise, these rents, interest, dues, tithes and properties are to sustain the necessary work of the church and schools, as well as poor relief and hospitals as before, regardless of religion.

22 If any disputes or misunderstandings arise over the use of such rents, interest, dues, etc., each party is to select one or two impartial arbiters to decide within six months. No one is to prevent such rents, interest, dues, etc. from being used to support their previous purpose until such a decision has been reached.

23 No Estate shall try to persuade the subjects of other Estates to abandon their religion nor protect them against their own magistrates. Such as had from olden times the rights of patronage are not included in the present article.

24 In case our subjects whether belonging to the old religion or the Augsburg Confession should intend leaving their homes with their wives and children in order to settle in another place, they shall be hindered neither in the sale of their estates after due payment of the local taxes nor injured in their honour.

Source: Karl Zeumer (ed.), *Quellensammlung zur Geschichte der Deutschen Reichsverfassung in Mittelalter und Neuzeit* (Tübingen, 1913), pp. 341–70.

---

2. The Declaratio Ferdinandea, 24 September 1555

We, Ferdinand, by the Grace of God King of the Romans[1], permanent enlarger of the Empire, king of Germany, Hungary, Bohemia, Dalmatia, Croatia and Slavonia, etc., ... hereby announce publicly through this letter that the adherents of the Augsburg Confession humbly submitted a petition at this imperial diet during the discussions to agree the religious peace that many knights, towns and communes in the territories of the archbishops, bishops and other ecclesiastics have long adhered to the Augsburg Confession and still do, and it was of concern that they are being pressured by their rulers ... running the risk of violence between rulers and subjects. In order to prevent this and to preserve the most necessary peace in the Holy Roman Empire of the Germanic Nation, they humbly petitioned that the ecclesiastics be instructed to leave their subjects unhindered to observe the Augsburg Confession until these disputed points of religion can finally be resolved

---

[1] The title King of the Romans was given to the person elected as successor designate whilst a reigning emperor was still alive. Archduke Ferdinand had been elected King of the Romans in 1531 and was accepted as emperor once his elder brother Charles abdicated (1556) and died (1558).

through amicable agreement. The adherents of the old religion, however, objected to this, so that neither party could agree this point.

Therefore, by the power of the plenipotentiary powers granted us by our dear brother and lord, His Roman Imperial Majesty [i.e. Charles V], we hereby rule and declare that the ecclesiastics' knights, towns and communes, that have adhered to the Augsburg Confession for a long time and for years, and have used that religion's church customs, ordinances and rites publicly and continue to do so until the present date, shall be left their religious beliefs, church customs and rites, to be disturbed by no one by force, until a Christian, final settlement of religion.

Source: Karl Brandi (ed.), *Der Augsburger Religionsfriede vom 25. September 1555. Kritische Ausgabe des Textes mit den Entwürfen und der königlichen Deklaration* (Göttingen, 1927), pp. 52–4.

_____

3. The Donauwörth Incident, 1607: Emperor Rudolf II's imperial ban, 3 August 1607

We, Rudolf the Second, by the grace of God Elected Roman Emperor ... offer grace and all the best to all and everyone ... who receives our ban letter and is summoned by it. High, and honourable, also high-born dear friends, nephews, cousins, brothers-in-law, electors and princes, also high-born nobles and subjects. Having received complaints and requests from the honourable Heinrich Bishop of Augsburg[1] ... we have placed the mayors, council and commune of the City of Donauwörth through verdict and law under the Holy Roman Imperial Ban and have authorised our respectable commissioner, the high-born Maximilian Count Palatine of the Rhine, Duke of Upper and Lower Bavaria,[2] our dear cousin and prince, to announce this publicly with due solemnity through the appointed imperial herald and exclude them from the peace, and apply the ban to their persons, property and possessions, credit and complaints. By the power of our open imperial letter, the aforementioned mayor, council and commune of the City of Donauwörth are denounced and are hereby declared open outlaws of ourselves and the Empire, and ... you are all requested by Roman Imperial Authority upon pain of punishment to regard the entire oft-mentioned mayor, council and commune of the City of Donauwörth as our and the Empire's outlaws, and not to admit, shelter or house, nor care, feed or water them on any account in our and the Empire's, nor in our hereditary, lands, nor your principalities, lands, houses or accommodation, nor provide any assistance, help, furtherance, or promotion, nor

_____

[1] Heinrich V. von Knöringen (1570–1646), bishop of Augsburg from 1598.
[2] Maximilian I (1573–1651), duke of Bavaria from 1598 and the founder of the Catholic League [**Doc. 5**].

purchase, sell or indeed have any other contact with them ... Furthermore [if you] discover and find their persons, property or possessions, whether on land or water, [you are to] attack, seize, lay low, occupy and arrest and act as is due to such outlaws, for as long and as far as they resist their due punishment and can be brought back to obedience to us and be released from the ban according to the law. Whoever disobeys or opposes this our Imperial order, or intends to do so, will forthwith likewise fall under our and the Empire's ban ... Given at our royal palace in Prague, the third day of the month of August in the year sixteen hundred and seven.

Rudolf

Source: Bernd Roeck (ed.), *Deutsche Geschichte in Quellen und Darstellung, Vol. IV: Gegenreformation und Dreißjähriger Krieg 1555–1648* (Stuttgart, 1996), pp. 133–4.

2

Confessional polarisation? Protestant Union and Catholic League

The elector Palatine fanned the controversy from the Donauwörth incident [**Doc. 3**] to rally support for his programme of reorganising the Empire along confessional lines. Though a senior prince, he felt marginalised as an adherent of a minority confession (Calvinism) within a political minority (Protestant imperial Estates) in the Empire. He wanted the imperial Estates to meet in two confessional groups, rather than in the customary three 'colleges' of electors, princes and imperial cities in the imperial diet, since Catholics held the majority in all three. However, religious groupings had been controversial in the Empire since the earlier Schmalkaldic League of Lutheran princes and towns, formed in 1531, which had been defeated by Emperor Charles V in a short, but decisive, war in 1546–7. Lutheran Saxony consistently opposed such sectarian alliances thereafter, preferring to cooperate with the emperor and moderate Catholics to safeguard the rights gained in 1555. Relatively few Protestant imperial Estates thus joined the elector Palatine in the Protestant Union founded in 1608 [**Doc. 4**].

Nonetheless, the move sufficiently alarmed the Catholic ecclesiastical princes that they accepted the duke of Bavaria's invitation to form a rival alliance which became known as the Catholic League [**Doc. 5**]. Neither organisation was particularly robust. Emperor Matthias (1557–1619, r.1612) opposed both, recognising their contribution to tension in the Empire. Bavaria was eventually obliged to dissolve the League in 1617, while the Union was in a state of collapse, as many members dissented from the increasingly conspiratorial and reckless Palatine policy. Nonetheless, anxiety persisted [**Docs 6–7**].

CONFESSIONAL PARTIES

4. The Protestant Union, 1608

Auhausen, 4 May 1608 [OS]
In the name of the Holy and Indivisible Trinity. Amen. We, the undersigned electors and Estates of the Holy Roman Empire,[1] on behalf of ourselves, our

---

[1]   The signatories were Christian of Anhalt-Bernberg on behalf of the Elector Palatine; Count Palatine Philipp Ludwig Duke of Pfalz-Neuburg; Margrave Christian von Brandenburg-Bayreuth (Kulmbach); Duke Johann Friedrich von Württemberg; Margrave

heirs and descendants, declare to all. Our beloved ancestors through particular care agreed, established and set up a general public peace and unity in the Holy Roman Empire of the German Nation, our beloved fatherland, so that everyone had equal rights, all violence ended and if anyone was transgressed, then the Estates of the Holy Roman Empire immediately offered their assistance through the Kreis and Execution structure as was their duty. However, part of the Holy Imperial Recess and the associated Executive Ordinance[2] have become the subject of a damaging misunderstanding, as well as being broken and illegally opposed by many with hostile and violent actions, so that one is no longer sure of certain aid. For many years the obedient Estates have protested that, despite keenly observing the imperial constitution, they have been denied such help. Instead, they have been shoved from one imperial diet, Kreis Assembly and Deputation Meeting[3] to another, while the problems grew more dangerous all the time. It is clear that if these matters are allowed to continue and not stemmed with God's help, that various parties, both outside and within the Holy Empire, will use them to cause one problem after another in the beloved fatherland and overrun the obedient imperial Estates and fight them and do so much as to overturn the entire ancient, venerable imperial constitution and grind into the dust that which has so long been built and improved and so achieve nothing less than the final destruction of all good order, regulation and prosperity, and the end of all peace-loving beings in the Holy Empire, as already the cries of the neighbourhood reveal all sorts of secret and public military preparations that have even, according to the public press reports, already started, so that, in order to pre-empt and ward off the damage and destruction, it will not simply be sufficient to maintain the beneficial good order of the Holy Roman Empire of the German Nation, but it will be highly necessary that every Estate, especially those that live in peace, together with their subjects, will have to establish a friendly understanding and composition so that they are ready with the necessary and permitted defence against those who oppose common law, Imperial Recesses and ordinances, and the noted and oft-confirmed public peace. Therefore, in view of the urgent necessity, we, the undersigned electors and Estates of the Holy Empire, to avoid such a terrible state of affairs, as well as from other good and valid reasons

---

Joachim Ernst von Brandenburg-Ansbach; Margrave Georg Friedrich von Baden. Elector Johann Sigismund of Brandenburg joined later (29 January 1610), followed by Landgrave Moritz of Hessen-Kassel, Gottfried Count von Öttingen, and the imperial cities of Nuremberg, Strasbourg and Ulm.

2   This is a reference to the Peace of Augsburg which had been issued as the Recess, or concluding document, of the 1555 imperial diet. The associated Executive Ordinance contained the regulations governing the enforcement of verdicts issued by the Reichskammergericht, the supreme court charged by the imperial diet with upholding peace within the Empire.

3   Imperial Deputations were special committees composed of representatives of selected imperial Estates to discuss particular problems. They often met when the imperial diet was not in session.

mentioned above, but not at all against His Roman Imperial Majesty, our most gracious lord to whom we owe all humble obedience, nor against those Estates of the Empire that obey its ordinances, to whom we show all good neighbourliness, nor against any person to their disadvantage or oppression, let alone against the Holy Imperial constitution, but on the contrary to strengthen it and to better uphold peace and unity in the Empire, and the former understanding that existed, as dedicated and obedient Estates of the Empire of the German Nation, our beloved fatherland, in order to advance the common well-being, our land and people and also those Estates who will in future join us to further peace, order and protection in the name of God the Almighty, have one and all reached the present amicable and confidential agreement which we acknowledge by virtue of this letter, as follows:

1 That each member shall keep good faith with the others and their heirs, land and people, and that no one shall enter any alliance against the others; also that no one shall damage, feud, fight or in any way harm another Estate or its jurisdiction, territory or subjects, nor break the laws of the imperial constitution, nor give aid in any manner if such a break should occur.

2 That we and all our heirs who are in this Union shall maintain a confidential correspondence effectively to inform each other of all dangerous and offensive affairs which may threaten each other's heirs, land and people, and to this purpose each will keep in good contact with the other.

3 Whenever important matters arise that concern the common good, or us, our lands and people during the duration of this Union, we and our heirs will help each other with faithful advice in order to uphold each and every one as far as possible unharmed in his Estate and territory. If there are disputes amongst ourselves or our heirs during the Union, the nearest Unionists are to seek an amicable compromise to the problem, as is customary in the Empire for matters of common rights and the like. No violence is to be permitted within the Union. In particular, if a member acts against the Union, or is otherwise in breach of it, they are to be dealt with by the other members …

4 It is our wish that in matters concerning the liberties and authority of the German Electors and Estates, as also of the Evangelical Estates' grievances as presented at the last imperial diet concerning infringements of the said electors and Estates and the Holy Imperial constitution, these shall all be presented and pressed at subsequent imperial diets and Imperial Circle assemblies, and not merely left to secret correspondence with each other. We also agree to try to influence other Evangelical Estates[4] towards a common understanding with us.

5 We also agree that this confidential Union shall not affect our disagreement on several points of religion, but that notwithstanding these, we have agreed

---

4   That is, Saxony.

to support each other. No member is to allow an attack on any other in books or through the pulpit, nor give cause for any breach of the peace, whilst at the same time leaving untouched the theologian's right of disputation to affirm the Word of God.

6 If one or other of us or our subjects are attacked by enemy force, it will be as if we have all been attacked, and the remaining members of the Union shall immediately come to his aid with the entire quota of the Union, as necessity may demand, and as set out in the detailed separate agreement …

7 If one or other of the united Estates is overrun, attacked or otherwise injured contrary to the public peace, without their giving any cause, and it does not expect aid from the Union, nor is able to defend himself, but has to make an agreement with the enemy to avoid further damage, such an agreement will not prevent the Union from acting. On the contrary the director, together with the committee, or each member on their own, can, according to this Union, offer aid as soon as they hear of the need without being asked, and act as if the matter was not settled until the injured party receives what has been taken from him or similar reparations …

[Art. 8 stipulated that the Elector Palatine was to be director in peacetime[5], but that he was not to interfere in the internal management of each member territory. In wartime, each member was director in his own lands.]

9 So that no irregularities occur, each elector and reigning prince is to have a vote, as are all counts and lords to have a vote for each Kreis, and likewise the honourable cities are to have a vote.

[Art. 10 stated that each member had rights of transit and billeting across another's territory in case of action through the Union, and that this was to be at the expense of all members.]

11 Since this aid is to be at the expense of the United Estates, no conquest is to be taken from those that make it, except movable property that will be common booty. However, towns, castles, fortresses and other fixed property, large cannon and the like, shall be retained by us until an agreement is reached or at least after the war, and then divided amongst us according to our quotas. In addition, if any in our service are captured by the enemy, or we take their people, then these are to be exchanged like for like, or otherwise ransomed.

12 If towns, castles, fortresses or other property is taken from a member in the duration of this Union and then recovered by us, these are to be restored without any deduction or reduction to the Estate to which they belong.

---

5   The members agreed later on 16 May that the Elector Palatine was to be director for three years, and the post was then to alternate between the princes every 18 months.

13 No member is to take anything from a fortress, town, castle, territory or subjects of another member during wartime without proper recompense. Any income from contributions, extortion and the like will be used to cover our common military expenses and shall be properly accounted for to members.

[Art. 14 stated that the Union was to last ten years, with the possibility of renewal within two years of the expiry, and regulated the financial repercussions of leaving within this time. Art. 15 stated penalties for not fulfilling Union obligations. Art. 16 opened the Union to further members. Art. 17 made the treaty binding on heirs and successors should any member die before the Union's expiry.]

18 Finally, should any member of the Union inherit or enlarge his territory, people, rights and jurisdictions in the Holy Roman Empire of the German Nation in the future, then these additions will be included in the Union. It is agreed that that Estate will pay an additional contribution proportional to the imperial tax schedule[6] according to the needs of the treasury of the Union.

This agreement is authenticated with our own signatures and seals, and a copy given to each member. Done at Auhausen on the fourth day of May, in the year sixteen hundred and eight.

Source: Hans Schulz (ed.), *Der Dreißigjährige Krieg*, 2 vols (Leipzig, 1917), I 2–12.

_____

5. The Catholic League, 1609

Munich, 10 July 1609

It is known that, for some time, affairs in the Holy Roman Empire of the German Nation have been growing more dangerous and of more concern, and that the beneficial imperial constitution, in particular the religious and profane peace accepted by the Estates to preserve peace, quiet and unity, have not only been the subject of dangerous misunderstanding, but have been violently attacked and often actually breached. It is much to be feared that if this state of affairs continues much longer, the violence will mount progressively in the Empire so that the peace-loving, obedient Catholic imperial Estates will be overrun and violated by the troublemakers and consequently nothing less can be expected than further oppression of the old true Catholic religion, the unique route to salvation, and its adherents, contrary to justice and imperial law.

_____

6   This is the *Reichsmatrikel* or list codified in 1521 specifying how many soldiers or their equivalent in monthly taxes (known as Roman Months) each imperial Estate was obliged to provide for common enterprises agreed either by the imperial diet or the assembly of the Kreis to which it belonged.

All this has convinced us[1] of the necessity of combining defensively to further implement and uphold the Holy imperial laws, and their beneficial and worthy religious and profane peace, and its associated executive ordinance.

1   First, we agree that our alliance is purely for the defence and maintenance of the true Catholic religion and the preservation of the common peace, quiet and welfare, as well as the rejection of danger and so, as stated above, for the implementation of the Holy Imperial Recesses, religious and profane peace and other worthy customs of the Empire.

Above all allies are to remain true to one another, not to attack, damage or feud with each other or each other's subjects and in short abstain from all violence against each other. If, contrary to hope, division or disagreement shall arise between the united Estates,[2] the League commander shall gather other members and diligently seek an amicable resolution. If such a solution is not possible, the disputed point is to be referred to a rapid legal process, compromise or negotiation with the assistance and agreement of one or more interested, benevolent parties. If neither the amicable nor summary process and negotiation proves acceptable to one or other party, then the matter will be referred according to the proper way to the appropriate place through the general written laws of the Holy imperial constitution. In the meantime all illegal actions and violence are strictly forbidden throughout this process.

If there are disagreements between the League commander and one or more member Estates, the adjutants are to act according to circumstances and at their discretion with the assistance of other member Estates to resolve these according to the methods set out above.

We agree that no one of us shall aid each other's enemy, but instead upon receipt of a full report to give advice and real aid to prosecute such an enemy just as if he were one's own enemy. And any such action is to be reported immediately to the League commander who will be requested to provide advice and aid.

2   Since we live in these dangerous and warlike times as well within as outside the Empire, the members of the League are to exchange information of any clandestine or open recruiting of soldiers, armaments or similar activities that come to their notice, in order to warn all their fellow members in good faith, and to inform the League commander by letter, or where the matter is too dangerous for that, by word of mouth. He will then know what action to take and, depending on circumstances, will call a League Assembly or arrange the

---

1   At this point the text lists the rulers whose representatives signed the treaty: Julius Echter von Mespelbrunn, Bishop of Würzburg; Duke Maximilian I of Bavaria; Jakob Fugger von Kirchberg-Weissenhorn, Bishop of Konstanz; Heinrich von Knöringen, Bishop of Augsburg; Archduke Leopold of Austria, Bishop of Strasbourg and Passau; Wolfgang von Haussen, Bishop of Regensburg; Johann Christoph von Westerstetten, Prior of Ellwangen; Heinrich von Ulm, Prince-Abbot of Kempten.

2   This means those united in the League, not the members of the Protestant Union.

necessary League assistance through consultation with his adjutants and other League members.

3 Should anyone among our federated ranks actually be attacked violently, be violated or damaged by anyone acting against the public and religious peace of the Empire, its constitutions and Imperial Recesses, as well as the worthy customs of the Empire, for whatever pretext, and should all attempts at legal resolution through the Empire and peaceful mediation be of no avail, then the aggrieved party is to inform the League commander, who will immediately write to the aggressor to desist, inviting him to leave the League member alone, or accept the mediation of the League. If this does not work, then the League commander will consult the members and proceed to the necessary League assistance. But if a League member himself attacks another, whoever that might be, contrary to the law, or acts belligerently without good cause, or cites a matter to the League that is still awaiting formal legal resolution through the Empire, then the League is not bound to support that member in his specific conflict.

4 The aggrieved party is nonetheless warned that this union is primarily intended to adhere to the religious and profane peace, and in cases where there is no particular *periculum* [danger], but which concern private interests and welfare, rather than the Catholic religion and the preservation of the general peace and quiet in the Empire, namely the *publicum bonum* [common good], they should use the proper legal process and refer their complaint to the *Reichshofrat*, or *Reichskammergericht* or elsewhere as appropriate according to the imperial ordinances and conduct their case at their own expense. If one or other member Estate has used these means and still requires League assistance, he should report this to the League commander. He will then know how to decide having consulted his adjutants how and if the member is to be assisted.

5 If an aggrieved member recruits soldiers and incurs other expenses in addition to those entailed in his quota to the League assistance, he is to report this to the League commander and members if he wants them refunded.

6 The League commander is to have the deciding vote at meetings of the adjutants or in plenary congresses of the League if the others are unable to reach a majority decision, except in matters concerning him alone.

7 If there is an urgent need and danger and not enough time to assemble the Estates and the assistance, then the League commander is empowered to consult his adjutants and, according to the level of danger, to recruit cavalry and infantry at the common expense to assist those in need. However, the commander must also summon a League assembly to discuss whether more assistance is required.

8 The aggrieved members are also permitted in such pressing and dire circumstances where the danger is so serious and *extremen periculum in mora* [there is danger through delay] to recruit soldiers themselves at the common

expense. However, he should report his intention and action to the League commander, who will then consult the other members as what to do about these expenses.

9 So that the intended defence is not brought into question, all of us will forswear violence amongst us in future. However, if one of us violently attacks another and invades with soldiers and refuses the amicable resolution set out above, but instead insists on violent threats, then the others should not delay, but should immediately assist the aggrieved member, particularly to forestall invasion and destruction of land and people.

10 Because it is unfortunately foreseeable that the present danger will not cease soon, we have decided to keep our present alliance for nine years ... [This agreement is also binding on heirs and descendants.]

[Art. 11 permitted other imperial Estates to join, but kept the level of contributions and assistance secret until they had joined. Art. 12 appointed Duke Maximilian of Bavaria as League commander; made Prince Bishop Julius Echter of Würzburg and Archduke Leopold as the adjutants of the Bavarian Kreis; and made Bishop Heinrich von Knöringen as adjutant of the Swabian Kreis. Art. 13 fixed membership contributions prior to the accession of further members on the basis of the Roman Months,[3] without specifying how many were to be paid.]

14 If the united Estates are attacked at several places simultaneously, assistance shall be provided according to the danger and need, and if the League commander and his assisting adjutants decide that it is better to direct the entire assistance to one place, then so be it. The League commander is to be left with the complete direction of all matters relating directly or indirectly to the League assistance, if this is summoned into the field against an enemy or violator of one of the members. He is to have complete power and authority to decide matters as he sees fit and to take what action is required by the time and circumstances according to his discretion and judgement, without anyone objecting or obstructing. We the united Estates have hereby freely entrusted the League commander with such *liberam dispositionem, directorium* [free judgment and direction] and authority. Only excepting that the members understand that there will be qualified military advisors proposed by the adjutants and accepted as such by the League commander.

15 If one or other member of the League is directly attacked, all the other members are by virtue of this alliance bound to provide assistance or other help, but the attacked member shall have no right to make a separate peace with his attacker. Instead he shall negotiate peace to the full satisfaction of all his fellow members in the League.

---

3   See Doc. 4 note 6.

16 Henceforth every Estate and member of the League shall undertake to keep his land and people in good military preparedness, in order to be ready to defend himself against any disadvantage or damage, and should such disadvantage and damage nevertheless occur, all the members of the League shall be committed to help and to compensate him for his losses.

17 All the costs he incurred shall be refunded. Equally, those League members who have loaned artillery or incurred other expenses in the common cause will be appropriately compensated by the others.

18 We the united princes and Estates hereby protest and announce *per expressum* [expressly] that this present union is solely for the preservation of the beneficial revered religious and profane peace and for the legally permitted defence and security of ourselves and our principalities, lands and peoples, and not the slightest infringement or prejudice to His Roman Imperial Majesty, but on the contrary intended for His Majesty's own good, as will be reported to him at the appropriate time.

19 We, the above named princes and Estates, have agreed all this by our solemn oath and princely honour as binding upon ourselves and our heirs. ... Done at Munich on the tenth day of the month of July in the year sixteen hundred and nine.

Source: Hans Schulz (ed.), *Der Dreißigjährige Krieg*, 2 vols (Leipzig, 1917), I 12–20.

ASTROLOGICAL PREDICTIONS

6. Johannes Kepler's prognosis for May 1618

Then May will not pass without difficulty in the places and the affairs, especially where the commons otherwise have great freedom, because everything is ready shattered.

Source: Johannes Kepler's prediction for May 1618 in his *Prognosticon Astrologicum* (1617), quoted in Hans Sturmberger, *Aufstand in Böhmen. Der Beginn des Dreissigjährigen Krieges* (Munich/Vienna, 1959), p. 7.

7. The comet of 1618

Around the start of our destruction, that is not only already well underway in Bohemia, but is appearing elsewhere, a dreadful comet with a long burning tail appeared in the sky causing terror throughout most of Europe ... including here in Frankfurt am Main.

With this terrible torch God Almighty signalled his place as a preacher of atonement at the high altar of heaven, so that people could see how he would punish them for their sins and had decided to bring his punishment rod over them, and thereby gave ample warning of damage and admonished them in times of grace to abstain from sin and plead for divine mercy.

Source: *Theatrum Europaeum*, 21 vols (Frankfurt, 1662–1738), vol. I, p. 100–1.

3

Crisis in the Habsburg monarchy

The Habsburgs' ability to deal with problems in the Empire was impaired by mounting difficulties in their own lands. The dynasty remained solidly Catholic, but most of their nobility and many urban burghers converted to Protestantism from the 1560s. Unlike the Reichstag where the Catholic imperial Estates retained a majority, the Protestants outnumbered the remaining Catholic nobles, burghers and clergy in the provincial Estates (assemblies) of the Habsburg lands. They used the power of the purse to bargain religious concessions from the dynasty in return for taxes (paid largely by the peasants!) to amortise the dynasty's large debts and to maintain defences against the Turks along the Hungarian frontier. This policy split the provincial Estates, where the Catholic minority, whilst not always agreeing with the dynasty, nonetheless opposed the Protestants' special privileges.

The dynasty began a coordinated counter-attack in 1579 by restricting future ennoblements and crown appointments to Catholics, thus making religion both a test for political loyalty and a criterion for social advancement and material reward. The policy stirred resentment amongst Protestant nobles, many of whom were finding it hard to live from peasant rents alone and looked to crown employment to supplement their incomes. The Habsburgs were careful to remain within what they regarded as the law, but growing confidence encouraged ever more brutal persecution. The document included here as an example of the mounting protests in fact contains two complaints [Doc. 8]. The first dates from around 1610 following a series of anti-Protestant measures by the archduke of Inner Austria (Styria), the future emperor Ferdinand II (1578–1637, r.1619) [Doc. 10]. The second complaint dates from about 1620 and reveals the already brutal impact of the war which was blamed on the foreign troops Ferdinand II had recruited.

The progress of the Habsburg Counter Reformation slowed after 1605, as the dynasty became distracted in a long, but relatively bloodless, dispute over the succession provoked by Rudolf II's refusal to marry. The Protestant factions in the Estates extracted further concessions by playing the feuding Habsburgs against each other. These privileges included the famous Letter of Majesty extorted by the Bohemians and Silesians from Rudolf in 1609.[1] The dynasty resolved its succession dispute in a treaty brokered by the Spanish ambassador who extracted concessions in return for Spain's backing for Ferdinand II [Doc. 9].

---

[1] Available in English translation in C.A. Macartney (ed.), *The Habsburg and Hohenzollern Dynasties in the Seventeenth and Eighteenth Centuries* (London, 1970), pp. 22–33.

8. The Counter Reformation in Habsburg Austria

TWO VERY LAMENTABLE RELATIONS:

THE ONE,

THE GRIEVANCES FOR RELIGION,

OF THOSE OF STIRIA, CARINTHIA, AND CRAYNE,

UNDER FERDINAND THEN DUKE OF GRATZ, NOW EMPEROUR.

THE HABSBURG DYNASTY

THE OTHER,

THE NOW PRESENT MOST HUMBLE SUP-

PLICATION, OF CERTAYNE OF

THE STATES OF LOWER AUSTRIA, UNTO THE SAID

EMPEROUR.

WHEREIN IS SHEWED THE MOST TERRIBLE, INHUMANE,,

AND BARBARIAN TYRANNIES, COMMITTED BY

THE EMPEROURS SOULDIERS, SPECIALLY THE

CASOCKES AND WALLONS, IN THE

SAID COUNTRIE.

DONE OUT OF THE DUTCH[1]

AND PRINTED

1620

The grievances for Religion of those inhabiting in the Provinces of *Stiria*, *Carinthia*, and *Cragne*;[2] not onely in their Bodies outwardly, but also in their Consciences inwardly, for the Testimonie of the true Gospell; most cruelly persecuted, by the enemies of the Truth, and their Commissaries; Under Ferdinand, now Emperour, then Duke of Grafts [Graz] etc.

To declare to the World the hourely and minutely griefe of Conscience and grievances for the Religion which wee have had, were almost impossible and also unnecessary, since it is, alas, too well knowne to this Land, to the Empire, and to a great part of the World; yet neverthelesse we will rehearse a few.

1. First, by priviledge, and good will of the illustrious Arch-Duke *Charles* of *Austria*, of famous memory, our gracious Lord and Prince, was granted to the professors of the Gospell, many special Ministers in principall Townes as in *Grate*, *Indenburgk*, *Clagenfourt*, and *Labach*.[3]

---

1 That is, Deutsch, or German.

2 The provinces of Styria, Carinthia and Krain (usually called Carniola in English) were the principal parts of Inner Austria which was governed by a separate branch of the Habsburg dynasty between 1564 and 1619.

3 Duke Charles II of Styria (1540–90) was the younger brother of Emperor Maximilian II (1527–76, r.1564), founder of the Inner Austrian Habsburg line and father of the future

2. *Item*, their Colledges and free Schooles of learning, for instructing Noblemens, and others Children, were admitted and granted them, in the foresaid Townes of Grafts, *Clagenfourt*, and *Labach*, all which priviledges are most violently taken from them.

3. *Item*, in the Countrey of *Stiria*, were many Cathedrall and other Parish Churches also violently taken from them.

4. Also many privileged Churches, pulled downe, and blowne up with Gunpowder.

5. One hundred Preachers and Ministers commanded upon paine of death to depart the province of *Stiria*.

6. A great many more Schoole-masters, and Teachers of the Youth, most pittifully banished.

7. *Item*, many Church-yards, and resting places for the dead bodyes of the faithfull, being walled and paled about, were most barbarously pulled downe, and made levell with the ground.

8. The bodies of the faithfull digged up, and given to be devoured by Dogs and Hogs; as also the Coffins taken and set by the highway side, some burnt with fire; a worke both barbarous and inhumane.

9. Also upon the burial-places of the faithfull, were erected Gibets and places for execution of malefactors. Also upon those places where Protestant Churches stood, or where the Pulpit stood, or the Font-stone, were erected alwaies most filthy spectacles most ugly to behold.

10. *Item*, many thousand of godly and religious bookes, among which were many hundred Bibles, the witnesses of Gods most holy Word, utterly burnt with fire.

11. Moreover, (a griefe above all griefes) many thousands that professed the Gospell, were most cruelly and shamefully tormented and tortured, and by the same torments compelled shamefully, to denie and renounce the truth of Christs Evangell.

12. Compelling those of the Religion to sweare upon their saluation never to renounce that damnable Popish Idolatrie, the which they were now forced to by torments.

Emperor Ferdinand II. Many Inner Austrian nobles converted to Protestantism during the 1560s and 1570s. They forced Charles to grant them personal religious freedoms in return for taxes to maintain border defences against the Turks in 1578. These freedoms allowed the nobles to build churches on their lands for their own tenants who generally also converted. Charles also extended toleration to most of the Inner Austrian towns, including Graz (the capital), Judenburg, Klagenfurt and Laibach (modern Liubljana).

13. The poore distressed people, were also compelled to their extreame cost and charges, to uphold and maintaine a strong gard of Souldiers, for those cruell Commissaries owne obedient *mancipia* and *evotoria*.

14. The constant Confessors and Professors of Christs most holy Word and Gospell, together with their Wives, and innocent Babes, were most cruelly compelled to leave their dwellings and habitations (whether it were in Cities, Townes, or Villages) at the pleasure of those barbarous Comissaries; and the longest terme of their abode was, six weekes and three dayes, sometimes but eight dayes, and sometimes they must be gonne before Sun-setting, and sometimes in the coldest time of Winter, in Frost and Snow: although it be manifest by the peace of Religion, granted in die yeere of God 1555 (as appears by the *Formalia*) that all Subiects or Tenants under Prince, or Noble-man, who were persecuted for Religion, might freely choose the time of their departure out of the Countrie.[4]

15. They were not admitted time and leisure, to make sale of their Lands and Goods, but (as may appeare by that cruell *Edict specialis*) they were constrained shamefully to sell them, to their unspeakable losse, yea, and sometimes compelled to give them; not withstanding, that it most manifestly appeares also, by the foresaid peace of Religion, that there should be no compulsion, in selling or giving of Goods or Lands, excepting only, in *amore Christianae Religionis*. And if they did sell their Goods or Lands, they were compelled to give the tenth Penny thereof, as by way of taxation; alledging that in Electorall Princes and States Lands of the Empire they did the like. But, as it appeares plainely by the aforesaid peace of Religion, it is said, those Countries shall pay the tenth Penny, who formerly did doe the same; but these our Countries have ever beene free of those taxations. We omit to remember that those Iewes who were iustly expelled not long since, were freely pardoned this taxation.

16. Notwithstanding, those Iewes were bound by bond, to pay the tenth Penny, at their departure out of the Land *per modem Compensationis*; but those poore Christian Exiles must be banished & troubled, and forced not only to quit their Countrey, Friends, alliance & acquaintance; not only debarred the fruits of their labours, but also must be bereft of that little money apointed for their maintenance, in this their wofull banishment.

17. And this was not a banishment with moderation to those devout and most faithfull Christians and our beloved Patriots, but they were exiled under paine of death never to returne. A banishment most infamous and most lamentable, that a man must bee contrained never to returne to the place of his nativitie, there, where so many yeeres he had dwelt with honor and respect; there where are the sepulchers of his dead predecessors. Although it be expresly set downe in the often spoken of peace of Religion, that it shall

---

4   See Doc. 1 article 24.

not be preiudiciall for any man, freely to visite his Countrie, and friends, from whom hee is banished for Religion.

18. Also the Noble-men, and others of those Provinces being Protestants, were not exempted this infamy, but were put by their hereditary offices of State, onely because they were of the Religion; and others were placed in their offices, being men of no qualitie or merit, and only because they were of Romish Religion. Our Protestant Noble-men, were also hindred from being Administrators, or exequutors to their friends or their children, althoug[h] they deale never so faithfully: Which shewes most plainely, that these wrongs done unto them, was not for the insufficiencie of their persons, births, or qualities, but only because they were Protestants.

19. Also the Noble-men and Gentrie of those Provinces being Protestants, were most grievously taxed and caused to pay great and grievous summes of money, over & above the tenth penny; not withstanding that they had quitted their Churches, Schooles, Preachers, and Schoole-masters: yea, even those that willingly would sometimes goe out of the Countrey for devotion, to heare a Sermon, or communicate, were constrained to pay the tenth penny, being out of his Highnesse Countries; although it be manifest *de iure*, that *nemo extra territorium suum* can punish any man.[5] All these iniuries are directly against his Highnesse (now Emperour) owne Edict, given to those of the Religion the last of April, 1599.

20. These great and grievous troubles and tyrannicall vexations, which wee have beene and are plagued withall, were not so much to be pittied, if there were any hope of our ease, or reliefe. But alas! the unmerciful answer and resolution of his Highnesse (now Emperour) given to the Protestants the eighth of December 1609 which was plainely told those of the religion, That he would never yeeld to their demandes, and that hee would continue in this his resolution even till, his grave; and that before he would yeeld for any of the least of their demands, concerning their Religion, he would rather adventure the loss of all that ever he had of God, and with a white Staffe, goe barefooted out of all his Countries.

Also his Highnesse (now Emperour) did threaten mightily the Protestant Estates, vowing that he would be revenged on them, for seeking any tolleration; alleadging that it was against his princely Authoritie.

21. To conclude, this last is the worst of all, that his Highnesse (now Emperor) will not heare his Nobility & Gentry, nor one of those of the Religion, but he oftentimes comanded them upon paine of their lives to keepe perpetuall silence: as in Anno 1598 the thirtyeth of September; the fifth of May 1599 the fifth of March 1601 and this last time, the eighth of December 1609. Also it is most manifest in that Edict, in the yeere 1599 hee

---

[5] It is clearly the law that no authority can impose any penalty for an act committed outside its jurisdiction.

absolutely forbids under the paine of death, that no man of what degree or qualitie whatsoever, should entertaine any Preacher or Minister of the Gospell; vowing also that hee will not heare any more of their grievances: Which is, *dura et acerba vox regnantis, non velle audire et scripta accipere, contra qum Vetula illa obyciebat Regi Macedonum* Philippo *audientiam recusanti: Si non vis audire, noli ergo Regnare.*[6] The abuses in Religion is no new thing, especially of the spiritual sort, but if the Spiritualite did commit any excesse, or gave any evill example, it was to be scene into by their temporally Princes and Lords, as we have a fine example in the History of *Stiria* (fol. 81,) in the yeere of God 1518. When Doctor *Luther* had gotten the upper hand, he gave in a long *Catalogue* of Complaints and abuses of the Clergie to the Emperour *Maximilian*, complayning of the abuses of their Benefices, their neglect of Gods Service, the insolencies committed in their Diocesse, the carelesnesse of their salvation, of the evill governing of Church listings, and of the too many idle persons, that were maintained to the heavie burthen of the Countrey, as sundry sorts of *Abbots, Canonicats, Prebendes, Commendats*, and many others: his Imperiall Maiestie graciously did promise a redresse, giving command to all Dukes and Lords, to see a reformation. But at this time there is greater cause of redresse of abuses, since it is to bee plainely seene, that wickednesse hath gotten the upper hand, and alas! there is no hope of helpe, or redresse.

If this Prince deales so hardly with his owne, much more cruelty is to be looked for at his hands, if he can have the upper hand of others.

The most humble Supplication of certaine of the States of lower *Austria*[7] made unto the Emperour: Wherein is shewed the most terrible, inhumane, and barbarian tyrannyes, committed by the Emperours Souldiers, by the *Casockes* and *Wallons* in the said Countrie.[8]

Most gracious Prince, the unspeakeable spoyling, destruction, miserie, trouble, calamitie, and subiection of these countries, wrought and effected by the accursed Cosackes and others your Maiesties Souldiers brought into the same, together with the robbings, murtherings, sackings, burnings, massacrings, and other barbarian cruelties used and committed therein, mooveth and provoketh us in the name and behalfe of our principall Lords & the whole Countrey, to take and have our recourse, next unto God, to your Emperiall Maiestie, with sighes and teares to renew our former complaints. In regard that the same (in the least degree) are not yet redressed, neither hath your Imperiall Maiesty, nor you[r] Generals granted any message, nor

---

6 A hard and bitter voice from a ruler, to be willing to hear and receive submissions against which that old woman objected to Philip of Macedon, when he refused her audience: 'If thou wilt not hear me, then, don't be king.'

7 The province of Lower Austria was the heart of the Habsburg monarchy and included Vienna, the capital when the emperor was not living in Prague.

8 A large proportion of the Spanish reinforcements, as well as new regiments raised for the imperial army (such as Wallenstein's cuirassiers), were Walloons recruited in the Spanish Netherlands. The emperor also received several thousand Cossacks recently discharged from Polish service.

Mandate in writing for their safe conducts; and to obtayne some reliefe therein for your poore subjects. For although your Maiesty hath heretofore oftentimes beene certified and advised, how and in what manner the Countrie in generall is spoyled and destroyed, both the Gentilmen and Commons rob'd and ransackt, some of the Pesants kild, and some of them driven from house & home into the Woods, and Mountaynes; Vines and arable Lands spoyled and laid waste, humanitie set aside; vertue, modestie, honestie, policy, law and right hindred and neglected, and an innumerable company of sinnes, and shamefull and horrible actions are daily committed, and cruelly exercised by the Souldiers. Your Maiestie having most graciously granted and promised, to take speedy order for the redressing and prevention thereof; and to that end vouchsafed your Gracious Commission to the Generall of your army, for the ceasing and stay of the same: being compelled thereunto by meere necessitie and force, your poore and humble Subjects are againe united to renew their said complaints, and to let your Maiesty know, that the said insolencies are not by any meanes ceased, nor yet lessened, but rather from day to day, and continually, are still committed, and more and more encreased and wax stronger, yea, and in such barbarian, unchristian, and inhumane manner, that we are astonished and abashed to thinke thereon, and in a manner have a detestation to name them to certifie your Majesty thereof. Therefore sith the unruly Souldiers, specially the Cosackes, stil persist in such their strange, feareful, and detestable actions, and that there is no forbearance nor distaste thereof in any sort, as also being certified, that the same is to be continued and practiced by others of your Maiesties troops. Wee, being upon more than a sure ground, for that we are certainely perswaded in our consciences, that it cannot be answered before God, together with the States, whose Officers are respectively to maintaine the Countrie, moved with no small griefe and inward vexation of mind to behold the miserable state of the country-people, & being governours and fathers of the same, (as the duty of every Governor and State-man bindeth him) most heartily and earnestly desiring and wishing to see a remedie therein. Hoping that your Imperiall Maiestie, will not in any wise be offended, nor take it in evill part, that in some sort we make the same knowne unto your Maiesty, only to the end, that your said Maiesty, as a Christian Potentate, and a most gracious Prince of the house of Austria, may the rather with all speede seeke to remedy, and take ayde for the diverting of these great, most enorme, and mischievous proceedings.

So it is, and it pleased your Imperiall Maiesty, that for as much, as the *Wallons*, and other strange Souldiers, brought into this Country, cease not continually, to make a common practise to waste, spoyle, burne, murther, and massacre the Countrie and the Commons thereof, whereby there is not any fearefull, unspeake-able, and inhumane action whatsoever, which they, and other of your Maiesties Souldiers with al cruelty, and bloud-thirstinesse, have not effected, exercised, and committed; sparing not to burne whole Villages, Hamlets, and Market-townes, and in them Storehouses for the provision of Widdowes and Orphans, (among the which we also that are Ambassadors, and have a speciall protection from your Maiety for our defence against all oppressions, are not spared) seised upon, spoyled, and burnt their Castles, houses, and their provision for their houses, being taken from them, the poore subiects that are employed about necessary defences, cannot get a bit of bread to relieve themselves withall, but are constrained to starve and die for hunger. Boys and Women being fearefully violated & ravished, are carried prisoners away, both young and old men and women, most cruelly and terribly martired, torterd, prest, their flesh pinsht, and pulled from their bodies with burning tonges, hangd up by the necks, hands, feete, and their privy-members, women, gentlewomen, and young wenches under yeeres ravished till they die, women great with child, layd so long upon the fire, untill which time as that men may see the fruit in their bodies, and so both mother and child die together, old and young, high and low states, spirituall and temporal persons, without any difference, oppressed, and many thousands of innocent people fearefully murthered. Some in their castles (and yet such as have deserved wel at your Maiesties and the house of Austrias hands, as being old & good friends to the same) not withstanding their Letters Patterns of assurance and protection, (because they professe the Lutheran Religion) pitifully murthered. Some of them with their wives and children brought forth in their shirts and smocks, and wholly bereft of all reliefe, and such as flie out into the fields, not suffred there to be free from their cruelties, but running after them, have beene most pitifully slaine, and hewed to peeces. And many men of great account have beene glad to take Pasports from their owne servants, with many other such like unspeakable and inhumane insolencies, and horrible, and cruel actions that are practiced; which although, now (as loth to make them knowne unto your Maiesty) we forbeare to write it as much as in conscience we can, and wil answere for the same before God, we wil hereafter not spare to declare.

Therefore, sith we know, that your Maiesty takes no pleasure in these feareful and horrible excesses, and intolerable abuses, & much more in respect of your Christian charitie & Princely minde, cannot but conceive a great disliking thereof; and that it is to bee feared, that your Maiesty hath not yet, or may for a long time refraine from resolving upon an answer to be made, & order to be taken touching these our obedient & humble supplications, and therefore the same will have no end nor be restrained, whereby the whole Country will bee in danger to bee laid waste, the Lords and subiects of the same brought and reduced into extreme miserie and affliction, to the great preiudice, not only of your Maiesty, but also of the whole famous and worthy house of Austria, and an unrecoverable damage unto the Empire. Wee most humbly, once againe beseech your Maiesty, in the name of our principall States, for the mercy of God, in the bleeding wounds of our Lord and Saviour *iesus Christ*, that you would be pleased, according to your naturall commendable Austrian, and Imperiall clemencie, to have compassion upon the necessitie, miserie, and pitifull estates of your faithfull States, Subjects, and inhabitants, whereby your Maiesty shall not only bee a furtherance to your owne desiring of peace, quietnesse, and prosperitie, and procure your most gracious satisfaction, but also obtayne immortall commendation of all posteritie. Which your faithfull and bounden subjects will endeavour with all dutie and obedience to deserve at your Maiesties gracious hands, wherewith we referre our selves to your most Princely pleasure and disposition.

THE TRUE NEATHER AUSTRIAN EVANGELICALL

COMMITTEES AND AMBASSADOURS

Source: Anon., *Two Very Lamentable Relations* (1620).

---

9. The Oñate Treaty, 1617

I, Don Inaco de Guevarra, Count Oñate, His Majesty's Envoy in Germany, do declare that, by this present signature and document, His imperial and also Royal Majesty in Hungary and Bohemia etc., Matthias, from his paternal and special love, care and affection for both the Catholic Faith and the entire House of Austria, has considered and decided that it would be useful and bene-ficial for their increase and welfare, if a proper succession was arranged during His Imperial and Royal Majesty's lifetime for Hungary, Bohemia and their asso-ciated provinces and lands. To this end, He has continually asked His Royal Majesty in Spain, my lord, to renounce the claims to the said kingdoms and lands, that His Catholic Majesty possesses through his mother Anna[1] who bequeathed them on 29 April in the year 1571 to the male descendants of Emperor Ferdinand, as well as his rights and claims pertaining to him, that he derives from Queen Anna through Emperor Maximilian, and to grant these to his cousin Archduke Ferdinand. Thereupon my gracious King and Master recalled the laudable footsteps and example of his ancestors who, like him, often had cause to extend and enlarge his house, and also in view of the holy religion, and the general good, and willingly agreed this time to forgo his private interest and not to mourn a gracious act. [The following section explains Oñate's powers to renounce Spanish rights in the king's name.]

In view of this, I, the above mentioned envoy and empowered representa-tive, by the power of my plenipotentiary authority, confirm and certify in the name of the king my master, and his children, the aforementioned renuncia-tion and cession of the rights derived from his mother Queen Anna. In doing so I renounce in the name of my king and his children all rights, whether those of my master the king, or the young Prince Infant, and of his sons, they possess or will have by whatever means to the aforementioned kingdoms and provinces, in favour of Archduke Ferdinand and his legitimate male heirs, without any restriction, limitation or delay, except subject to the following modification and condition, that a compensation and recompense will be provided in the form of an Austrian province, which one could and would desire, and which will be negotiated as soon as possible, thereby bearing in

---

[1]   Anna of Austria (1549–80) became the fourth wife of Philip II of Spain in 1570. She was daughter of Emperor Maximilian II, and thus sister to Emperor Matthias.

mind the protection that the House of Austria has found until now in Spain, so that appropriate satisfaction follows for all these good deeds.

Equally, Archduke Ferdinand should agree that, if his male line dies out, the aforementioned kingdoms together with their associated parts and rights, will immediately revert to Spain and its male heirs. Therefore, Ferdinand's daughters and their sons are forever excluded in favour of the king's legitimate sons and their sons. Archduke Ferdinand has agreed all this and promised to direct this treaty to Emperor Matthias and ensure that everything negotiated and agreed here will be corroborated, reinforced and confirmed by Emperor and King Matthias.

[Oñate then confirms all these terms against any possible objections and disputes. The treaty is then sworn through an 'oath on the holy religion' in the name of the king of Spain.]

Done in the palace in Prague in the Chamber of His Princely Highness on 6 June 1617 in the reign of Emperor Matthias.

[Now follows the supplement: Archduke Ferdinand's declaration:]
I am convinced that my rights to as well as my conduct towards the kingdoms of Hungary and Bohemia is manifest and well grounded. However, the almighty king of Spain is also of the view that his conduct and declarations of intent towards the same kingdoms is well founded. My position derives from this situation: not merely to avoid any cause for strife and disputes – in view of the current political situation which necessitates a swift settlement of the succession to both these kingdoms and the empire – but also to reinforce and consolidate the bonds of mutual love, beneficent goodwill and blood ties between us, I, Archduke Ferdinand of Austria, in view of the imminent renunciation of all rights of the Spanish king to the aforementioned kingdoms (as related above), will grant the said king or his successors everything that is asked of me, that I am able to grant, if I, by the grace of God, receive the dignity of the title of Roman Emperor and, in the course of exercising that title, will in particular grant the investiture of Finale and Piombino should these fall vacant.[2]

Regarding the province of Alsace, I ask His Majesty not to hold it against me that I cannot yet make this available, because so many difficulties and problems arise that prevent me from offering it. However, should the time come, for him to demand this of me, but it appear neither advantageous nor advisable, I promise to provide appropriate compensation.

The articles concerning the aforementioned renunciation and the public agreement between us make no mention of this secret pact, but instead refer to other considerations, namely the natural reasons for the correspondence of

---

[2] Finale (south-west of Genoa) and Piombino (on the Tuscan coast) were fiefs within the emperor's jurisdiction over northern (imperial) Italy. Their strategic location made them attractive to Spain as potential naval bases.

law with the public good, as well as the king's tender inclination towards me – reasons that could move him to make such a renunciation, to which the circumstance is added that of course the male line of the king takes precedence in the case (which God forbid) that none of my male descendants remain. In addition I must not divulge the aforementioned renunciation and on no account remove or diminish the security of the secret agreement, so that no clauses stand in the way and that no connection can be made between the general renunciation and the aforementioned future cession.

It will not be necessary, however, to publish this agreement at any time, but instead to enact and implement in full at the proper time what has been agreed. Of course, this will be presented under another pretext, e.g. as gratitude and in the conviction of personal sympathy and similar expressions. I have given my word, written my signature and affixed my seal to reinforce and attest this treaty.

Done in Graz on 31 January in the year of our Lord 1617.

Source: Main treaty from Franz Christoph Khevenhüller, *Annales Ferdinandei*, 12 vols (Leipzig, 1716–26), vol. 8, ss 1100–3. Secret declaration from Otto von Gliss, *Der Oñate-Vertrag* (Frankfurt, 1933), pp. 60–1.

_____

10. The character of Emperor Ferdinand II

The Papal nuncio Carlo Caraffa writing in 1628:

The emperor is now 51 years old. He is of medium build, a strong constitution, red-tinted skin, very approachable, well-disposed towards all. He normally drinks and sleeps very little. He goes to bed around 10 in the evening as is the German custom; he is already up around four in the morning or earlier ... Once he has got up, his majesty goes to the chapel to hear two masses, one for the soul of his first wife, who, though of shaky health, was tenderly loved by the emperor. If it is a feast day, the emperor then takes holy communion, for which purpose he goes to the church and hears a German sermon. This is usually given by a Jesuit and lasts an hour. After the sermon he remains at the high altar, usually for an hour and a half accompanied by specially selected music ... On those days that are not feast days, the emperor, after attending two masses (something from which he never deviates), spends the rest of the morning and often much of the afternoon in council meetings. When he is not doing this he goes hunting, of which he is much enamoured. Generally, he tends to have one day for the council and the next for hunting, from which he often only returns at dusk rather than in daylight.

Source: Friedrich von Hurter, *Friedensbestrebungen Kaiser Ferdinands II* (Vienna, 1860), pp. 212ff.

_____

4

The Bohemian Revolt and its aftermath

The Habsburgs had ruled Bohemia since 1525 and regarded it as a hereditary possession. The Bohemians saw the formal acceptance of each new king through their diet (assembly) as an election. Religious differences partly overlapped these constitutional disagreements, because most Bohemian nobles were Protestant and associated their religious freedoms with political autonomy. Emperor Matthias moved the Habsburg court back to Vienna on his accession in 1612, leaving the government of Bohemia in the hands of ten regents, including three Protestants. The regents continued the earlier policy of restricting crown appointments to Catholics and applying a narrow interpretation of Protestant religious and political privileges. This was stepped up after 1617 when Matthias arranged for Ferdinand II to succeed him as Bohemian king, whilst he remained emperor. A group of Protestant aristocratic malcontents staged the Defenestration as a calculated coup, hoping that throwing the regents out of the palace window would radicalise the more moderate majority into following their confrontational policies [**Doc. 11**]. The rebels' 'Apology' attempted to justify this and enlist foreign support to forestall a violent Habsburg backlash [**Doc. 12**]. The ailing Matthias initially tried to negotiate [**Doc. 13**], but both sides swiftly resorted to arms, and the conflict escalated once Ferdinand II became emperor in 1619.

The Bohemian rebels formally deposed him, reorganised Bohemia and its associated provinces of Moravia, Silesia, Upper and Lower Lusatia into a confederation [**Doc. 14**], and chose the elector Palatine, Frederick V (1596–1632, r.1610), as king. Frederick's decision to accept the crown automatically made him a rebel in Ferdinand's eyes and linked the war in the Habsburg lands with the political and confessional tension in the Empire [**Doc. 15**]. Frederick received little support. The Dutch were divided between those who wanted to extend their truce with Spain and a radical group around the army commander, Maurice of Nassau (1567–1625), who saw renewed war with Spain as inevitable and wanted to stir trouble in the Empire to weaken both branches of the Habsburg dynasty [**Doc. 16**]. Maurice's party seized control during 1619, executing or exiling their opponents and providing subsidies sufficient to prevent the Bohemians from being defeated, but not enough for them to win [**see Doc. 31**]. King James I disapproved of his son-in-law Frederick's rash action and refused to involve England officially in the war [**Doc. 17**]. Many Bohemian Protestants remained unconvinced by the rebel leadership's arguments [**Doc. 18**]. Lack of assistance compelled

Frederick to make an unsatisfactory alliance with Bethlen Gabor (1580–1629, r.1613), prince of Transylvania, who pursued his own objective of trying to wrest Hungary from the Habsburgs and launched a series of violent, but unsuccessful, attacks on Vienna [**Docs 18–20**].

Ferdinand lacked the means to suppress the revolt alone. He won the support of Duke Maximilian (1573–1651, r.1598) in the Treaty of Munich which allowed him to re-establish the Catholic League and laid the basis for the future transfer of the Palatine lands and titles to Bavaria. He allayed Lutheran fears by guaranteeing continued recognition of the Protestants who had been elected 'administrators' of bishoprics contrary to the Catholic interpretation of the 1555 Peace [**Doc. 22; see also Doc. 1**]. This secured Saxon support and defused Protestant charges of a religiously motivated war [**Doc. 23**]. France did not support the emperor directly, but did broker the Treaty of Ulm, which removed any threat from the already fairly toothless Protestant Union and allowed the powerful Catholic League army to invade Bohemia [**Doc. 24**]. The result was the battle of White Mountain outside Prague in which Frederick's forces were routed. His commander's explanation for the defeat gives a fairly accurate account of events and a good indication of the composition of the rival armies [**Doc. 25**]. The scale of the victory was attributed by the devout to divine intervention [**Doc. 26**].

The emperor regarded his opponents as rebels who had forfeited their rights, leaving him free to abandon his earlier restraint and accelerate the policy of making Catholicism the basis of political loyalty in Bohemia and Austria. Though he did authorise a limited number of executions, he had little interest in physically exterminating his enemies, whom he was generally prepared to pardon provided they submitted to his authority and accepted the loss of at least some of their property. Rebel properties were seized after 1621 and given or sold to those who had demonstrated their loyalty during the recent fighting. Having then expelled Protestant pastors and schoolteachers, Ferdinand began insisting that the nobility – the social and economic elite – either convert or leave [**Docs 27, 29**].

These measures stirred considerable opposition, but only in Upper Austria did this erupt into full revolt. Upper Austria had been entrusted to Bavaria in lieu of its expenses from the 1620 campaign. The Bavarians left a small garrison to ensure the local taxes were diverted to them. However, the real reason behind the continued occupation was that Duke Maximilian wanted to hold onto the province to ensure Ferdinand delivered his earlier promise to transfer the Palatine lands and electoral title to him [**see Doc. 21**]. Maximilian was also keen to promote Catholicism, but not at the dangerously rapid pace urged by Ferdinand. Resentment at heavy taxation, heavy-handed re-Catholicisation and existing local grievances spilled over into revolt in 1626. The peasants drew on images and demands voiced during earlier risings in Upper Austria in 1525 and 1595 [**Doc. 28**]. After some initial successes, the peasants were crushed by Bavarian and imperial troops.

The brevity of Frederick's reign in Bohemia led Catholics to lampoon him as the 'winter king'. Even Protestants had difficulty with his legacy [**Doc. 30**].

THE BOHEMIAN REVOLT

11. The Defenestration of Prague, 23 May 1618

Wilhelm Slavata's Account[1]

It is proper that I now describe at somewhat greater length this Defenestration and how Almighty God miraculously protected the two counts.[2] Throughout the Roman Empire, in all kingdoms and principalities of Christendom, it has been seen as wicked and punishable that [certain] persons of Bohemian origin from the two higher Estates have perpetrated such a shameful evil act the like of which was unknown in the annals of the world, namely that two regents of His Majesty [Ferdinand] and highest officers of Bohemia have been cast mercilessly out of the window into a deep valley. Although the two counts clearly responded to all the evil ascribed to them, as well as protesting suffi-ciently against the malicious action taken against them, the others in their relentless wickedness wanted to hear nothing of order, truth and justice, but rushed violently upon the two counts and seized them shamelessly.

Four members of the Lords' Estate and one knight, namely Wilhelm von Lobkowitz, Albrecht Smiricky, Ulrich Kinsky, Litwin von Rican and Paul Kaplir,[3] forcibly laid hands on Count Martinitz, pinned him down and took him to the opened window whilst shouting: 'Now we will take our just revenge on our religious enemies.' The two counts thought that they would be led out of the chancellery and placed under arrest. However, when Martinitz realised the nature of his impending death, he called out loudly: 'Since I must now die for God, His Holy Catholic faith and His Royal Majesty, I will gladly suffer everything, just allow me to see my confessor so that I can confess my sins.' Those gentlemen who were there simply replied: 'We will now send a villainous Jesuit to join you.' Whilst Count Martinitz was greatly troubled at this and began heartily to repent his sins: 'Jesus, you son of the living God, have mercy on me, Mother of God take pity on me,' the afore-mentioned persons lifted him from the ground and hurled him together with sword and dagger, but without hat, which one of them had torn out of his hand, head first out of the window into the depth of the castle moat. But he ceaselessly called out the names 'Jesus, Mary' as he fell, and he landed so softly on the ground that it was as if he were merely sitting down, so that his plea to the Virgin Mary and God's protection saved him from all harm from

---

[1] Wilhelm Slavata (1572–1652) was president of the Bohemian treasury and one of the most prominent of the regents left to govern after Emperor Matthias moved the impe-rial court back to Vienna in 1612.

[2] Slavata and Jaroslav Borsita of Martinitz (1582–1649), another leading regent.

[3] Villem Popel von Lobkowitz the elder (d.1628), Albrecht Jan Smiricky (1594–1618), Ulrich Kinsky (d.1620), Jan Litwin von Racin (Rziczan) (d.1634) and Paul Kaplir were all leading radical Bohemian noblemen. The Defenestration had been planned in Smiricky's house.

his terrible fall despite his corpulent body. Several devout and trustworthy
people processing over the great bridge to the Little Side[4] have affirmed they
saw the most holy Virgin Mary catch the gentleman in the air with her cloak
and carry him to earth. Count Martinitz did not see this himself but during
the fall he had a vision that heaven was opening and that God wished to take
him up to eternal happiness. A knight, called Ulrich Kinsky, had mocked him
whilst throwing him out with the words: 'We shall see whether his Mary will
help him,' and when he [Kinsky] saw from the window that Count Martinitz
was sitting fresh and well on the ground, he exclaimed: 'I swear to God that
his Mary did help him.'

When Count Slavata had seen how they had handled his dear friend, Count
Martinitz, it was easy for him to conclude the same would happen to him.
Raising his hands to heaven, he prayed, for the sake of God and His mercy, they
would first let him confess his sins, after which they could kill him however
they pleased. However, many shouted: 'We can't bring a villainous Jesuit in here
now, you have confessed to them enough already.' Count Thurn[5] said in
German: 'Worthy lords, there is the other one,' and they seized Count Slavata,
lifted him from the ground and, together with his cloak and sword, hurled him
head first from the same window. Still at the window he made the sign of the
Holy Cross on his breast and with a humble heart said: 'Lord have mercy upon
me, a sinner.' He grasped the window sill with his right hand, holding on for a
moment, but someone hit his fingers with the hilt of a dagger so that he was
sent hurtling downwards. His hat, complete with its beautiful band set with
golden roses and diamonds, remained in the Chancellery. They tore the golden
chain with the cross from him and kept it as they threw him out.

Count Slavata hit himself on the stone sill of the lowest window and fell
to the ground with his head on a rock. Despite this, he was able to crawl down
to the bottom of the ditch, and since the blood had run into his mouth, he
began to breath like someone who is suffocating, and lay there half-dead.
Count Martinitz was resolved to come to his aid in any way possible, and
since he feared that the people at the window would shoot at him, he
pretended to be weaker than he was and rolled himself along to Count
Slavata. Though in doing so he wounded himself on his left side with his
sword and dagger, he disentangled the head of his uncle and relative[6] from
his cloak and carefully wiped the blood flowing from the wounds in his
mouth with a little piece of cloth. He quickly took a balsam from a little silver
box which was tied up in the cloth and rubbed this on the gentleman's
temples and held it under his nose, bringing him, with God's help, back to
his senses from his faint. Meanwhile, he urged him to bear his misfortunes
patiently and prayed with him. Slavata piteously repeated his earlier prayer:
'Lord have mercy upon me, a sinner.'

---

4   The Charles Bridge across the Moldau from the main city on the east bank to the Little
     Side on the west.
5   Count Heinrich Matthias von Thurn (1567–1640), main instigator of the Defenestration.
6   Terms used here to denote affection rather than actual kinship.

Meanwhile, certain servants and, it was claimed, Count Thurn's gamekeepers and soldiers went down from the great hall onto the wall. The gentlemen looking out of the window shouted to them: 'Shoot at them and finish them off,' so several shots were fired at the unfortunate gentlemen in the ditch ...

While this shouting and shooting was going on, the secretary Philipp Fabritius,[7] who had been thrown from the window just after the two counts, got up quietly and climbed out of the ditch without his cloak or hat ... Then he quickly found a coach and left directly for Vienna, reaching it after many misfortunes and dangers, and gave His Majesty and other lords a report of what had happened in Prague.

In the ditch, Count Martinitz expected a fatal shot at any moment, and desiring the palm branch of martyrdom, hoped to be hit and killed soon without much pain. He ceaselessly commended his soul to God's mercy and repeated a short prayer ... He urged Count Slavata to get up if possible and leave with him, but he replied that while he would move his hands and feet, he could not lift his wounded head. Their enemies said to others they encountered: 'Now both of them are lying dead there. The dead dogs won't bite any more.' However, they were unsuccessful, for both Counts and the secretary remained alive, thanks to God's miraculous aid, and escaped their enemies' power completely. Shortly afterwards, Almighty God sent some honest people who, through loyalty and upright love and unmindful of the continual shooting, moved them to safety. [The counts were taken initially to the chancellor's palace. Slavata hid till he recovered and then followed Martinitz in escaping.]

Source: Adam Wolf, *Geschichtliche Bilder aus Österreich, Vol. I: Aus dem Zeitalter der Reformation (1526–1628)* (Vienna, 1878), pp. 324–6.

---

12. The Bohemian 'Apology', 25 May 1618

We, the representatives of the lords, knights and cities of Prague,[1] Kuttenberg and other Estates of all three Estates of this kingdom of Bohemia who receive the body and blood of our lord Jesus Christ in both kinds, who confess to the Bohemian Confession,[2] and who are now assembled at Prague castle, unanimously make it known to all, both in the name of those gathered here and

---

[7]　Philipp Fabritius (d.1631), secretary to the regents. He was later ennobled by the emperor as 'von Hohenfall' (of the High Fall).

[1]　Prague then comprised three associated, but autonomous, towns.

[2]　The *Contessio Bohemica* from 17 May 1575 was a compromise statement by the various Protestant confessions practised in Bohemia. It had been rejected by Emperor Maximilian II in his capacity as king of Bohemia. The 'Apology' uses the terms *sub utraque* and *sub una* denoting the different forms of holy communion to identify Protestants and Catholics respectively. The latter terms have been substituted for this translation.

those absent, that: for a number of years all three Estates and inhabitants of
the kingdom have faced, suffered and endured all kinds of complaints and
hardship, both in political as well as ecclesiastical matters. These were caused
and instigated by evil, turbulent clergy and laity, most notably those of the
Jesuit sect (whose aim, writings and endeavours have always been directed at
fraudulently subjugating not only His Majesty, but also all Protestant inhabitants and Estates of the entire kingdom to the Roman See, a foreign power).
Hereafter, however, in the years 1609 and 1610 a complete peace was established through the Letter of Majesty of His Majesty Emperor Rudolf of blessed
memory, as well as a compact between both Catholics and Protestants that
was confirmed at the general diet that neither party would harm the other,
but rather both Catholics and Protestants should and could according to their
compact freely and peacefully serve the Lord God everywhere, in any place,
without interference from either secular or ecclesiastical authorities. All this
and more was contained and confirmed in the said Letter of Majesty and the
general diet. His Imperial Majesty,[3] now our most gracious king and lord,
confirmed and reiterated all this, not only generally according to the customs
of the land, but specifically upon his accession.

However, the enemies of the king, land and the general peace have not
desisted from striving to negate the peace that was so desired and confirmed,
and to further their evil, extremely dangerous and pernicious intentions
towards this kingdom and our successors.

[The authors accuse at length Catholic zealots and Jesuits of deliberately
undermining the Letter of Majesty, ignoring or misrepresenting the terms,
usurping Protestant rights by promoting fellow Catholics into positions of
power, slandering Protestants and their faith, and seeking to frustrate the
proper line of succession in the kingdom. Following complaints from the
inhabitants of Braunau and Klostergrab,[4] the Protestants twice convened their
own assembly and appealed to Emperor Matthias, but were told to disperse.]

We Estates could never have foreseen that, instead of granting our humble
petition, we would be condemned without any hearing by His Imperial
Majesty at the instigation of our enemies ...

For the reasons detailed above, we proceeded against two of them, namely
Wilhelm Slavata of Chlum and Kosumberg, and Jaroslav Borsita of Martinitz,
otherwise known as Smeczensky,[5] as destroyers of justice and the general

---

3   This refers to Emperor Matthias (1557–1619) who was crowned king of Bohemia in May
    1611. The radical Bohemian Protestant leadership refused to recognise the validity of
    Ferdinand (II) of Styria's coronation as king of Bohemia on 29 June 1617 and maintained
    Matthias was still king.

4   Two towns under the jurisdiction of the archbishop of Prague. The Catholics claimed
    such church land lay outside the provisions of the Letter of Majesty and arrested protest-
    ers in Braunau and demolished a newly built Protestant church in Klostergrab.

5   Slavata and Martinitz (see Doc. 11 notes 1 and 2) were leading figures in the Regency
    appointed by Matthias when he moved the imperial court from Prague back to Vienna
    in 1612. They were also personal rivals with the Bohemian Protestant leader, Count

peace, and also because they disrespected the offices and positions they held, and instead used them evilly to weaken the authority of His Imperial Majesty, our king and lord, and to abolish the general peace of this kingdom of Bohemia. After determining from their past actions that they were indeed such as they appeared to be, we threw both of them out of the window in accordance with the old custom, along with a secretary, their sycophant, who had, among other things, caused considerable disruption in the cities of Prague. We shall proceed further against them (because they are still alive) and their properties, as well as against all those they represent and defend, those who wish to persecute us or anyone else by whatever means, and equally all who are destroyers of the Letter of Majesty and the agreement, or who perpetrate such crimes …

To this end at our assembly at Prague castle we have established a defence system for the entire kingdom for the good of His Imperial Majesty and this kingdom, our beloved fatherland, as well as to protect our women and children from all danger. And through this action we do not intend anything against His Imperial Majesty as our most gracious king and lord, nor desire inconvenience for those Catholics who are our dear friends and peaceful people (as long as they also desire to live in peace). For it is commonly recognised and known that no other secular or ecclesiastical person will be harmed by this action, or will any unrest result, but instead a good peace will be maintained in the cities of Prague and throughout the kingdom, except for the aforementioned unavoidable reasons and only then when we neither should nor can do otherwise or any less. Accordingly, we dare to hope that His Imperial Majesty, our gracious king and lord, will not otherwise interpret our actions, nor give credence to other contrary reports about us. We also do not doubt that our dear local Catholic friends will not oppose us on account of the just punishment we enacted against the destroyers of our Letter of Majesty, agreement and freedoms and the general peace, still less openly or secretly join our enemies. Instead, we are of firm hope that, considering the reasons explained above and the sufficiently described crimes of the aforementioned persons, all will see that it was not our intention, nor is it in the slightest to act against His most gracious Imperial Majesty, king and lord, those of the Roman religion or the agreements with them, and will not only excuse this, but will like us also assist in preserving the common freedoms, territorial privileges and all that serves mutual love and unity.

Therefore, we beseech His Imperial Majesty, our most gracious king and lord, that he will send another and more detailed apology, should it be

---

Thurn (Doc. 11 note 5) for favour and high office. Emperor Rudolf II had deprived Slavata of the well-paid post of castellan of Karlstein and given it to Thurn in 1611 to placate Protestant opinion. Ferdinand of Styria transferred the post to Martinitz when he became king in 1617, compensating Thurn with a less lucrative position. While the Apology concentrates on the two men, the Defenestrators had hoped to catch other leading Catholics, notably the Bohemian chancellor, Zdenko Adelbert Popel von Lobkowitz (1568–1628), who was absent from the meeting when they burst in.

necessary, to excuse us to the entire world. Done at Prague castle at our general assembly, Friday after the feast of Christ's ascension, that is 25 May 1618 new style.

Source: Johann Christian Lünig (ed.), *Das teutsche Reichs-Archiv*, 9 vols (Leipzig, 1710–20), vol. 6, part 1, pp. 133–40.

---

13. Emperor Matthias's open letter to the Bohemians, 18 June 1618

Dear subjects. You will know what happened to our regents, secretary and dear loyal subjects on Wednesday 23 May and subsequently in the Bohemian Chancellery in our palace and residence in Prague which should be a place of the highest respect and security. And all this is because it has been alleged that the Letter of Majesty and the free exercise of religion will be abolished. We want to make it clear to you through this open letter that we have no intention of rescinding the Letter of Majesty, or the agreement between the religions, still less want anyone else to do this, despite what others among the Estates of our Bohemian kingdom may have said. Moreover, we have always intended, and still intend, to preserve all the Estates' privileges, liberties, Letters of Majesty, diet recesses and treaties. Anyone who claims otherwise slanders us before God and the world. Rest assured, dear obedient, loyal and true Estates of our Bohemian kingdom, and do not give credence to such falsehoods.

We would like nothing more than to return in person to our royal throne and residence amongst our loyal and obedient subjects and inhabitants from all three Estates and clear up these misunderstandings with God's help. However, we cannot come to our Bohemian kingdom at the moment, partly through poor health, but also pressure of other important affairs. Capable and prominent individuals will be appointed to clear up this misunderstanding.

Since no enemy threatens us as Bohemian king, nor the three Estates and all inhabitants, there are no constitutional grounds to raise soldiers to defend the country, and thus no grounds for anyone, whoever they might be, to use the territorial privileges, letters of majesty, ordinances, freedoms, or laws to justify arming. Accordingly, we graciously order you to disband the soldiers you have recruited to prevent further damage, expense and ruin of the common man. Furthermore, no more troops are to be recruited and the militia is to stand down. All subjects of either faith are to stop attacking each other by word or deed, and instead to deal with one another peacefully as friends. We do not doubt that the loyal Estates will obey these orders. We will stop our recruiting, that was in response to yours, as soon as all the soldiers have been discharged in the kingdom of Bohemia and the militia stood down. We want to spare our loyal subjects the damage and expense that soldiers cause. If our gracious and paternal warnings and our just orders and instructions are ignored and the soldiers and militia are not immediately disbanded in the kingdom of Bohemia, we will be obliged to accept that order and justice are being disregarded. We will be left no choice, but to take the necessary measures to maintain our authority with the help of the Almighty by whose grace we are your rightful king and master. It will be obvious to all that war and unrest bring great inconvenience, hardship and misery to the poor people. We testify before God and the entire world that we have given no grounds for this situation and are entirely innocent. Those who heed our royal order and remain obedient and do not support the unruly (who will not receive another warning) are assured of our royal grace, protection and goodwill.

Source: Michael Caspar Londorp, *Acta Publica*, 2 vols (Frankfurt, 1668), vol. II, p. 445.

_____

14. The Bohemian Confederation, 31 July 1619

Prague, 31 July 1619

In the name of the Holy and indivisible Trinity, God the father, son and Holy Spirit, the only God in eternal praise, amen.

The directors, regents and councillors of the land, our representatives empowered through patents from us, the three Estates of the kingdom of Bohemia, summoned an assembly for Tuesday 23 July at Prague Castle.

Imposing envoys for this assembly were sent with plenipotentiary powers by their graces, the worthy Estates of the margraviate of Moravia, their graces the lord princes and Estates of Upper and Lower Silesia, Upper and Lower Lusatia as incorporated lands, as well as their graces the Evangelical Estates of Lower and Upper Austria.

[The preamble stresses the legitimacy of the Confederation, based on earlier agreements between the Estates in 1609 and the Letter of Majesty. All actions were directed to upholding these privileges in the face of 'evil people' bent on undermining them and bringing violence and ruin to the land. For these reasons, the Estates had agreed the following terms:]

1 Since the Almighty has also given his grace and blessing as this Confederation is solely in defence of religion, the territories have agreed that each and everyone of their co-religionists should follow a Christian life according to the Evangelical teaching and faith, avoid and prevent sin, vice, public trouble, hypocrisy, in whatever form, and follow strictly the admonishments from the pulpit and the authorities.

2 Following this from the beginning the king shall also be included in this Confederation, provided he pays gracious attention to the privileges, Letters of Majesty, concessions and terms of this Confederation, adjusts his rule accordingly and offers equal protection to all territories in matters of religion and justice, regardless of religion.

3 The king should not take advice from Jesuits, foreign envoys or councillors in any matter concerning these territories, nor appoint such foreigners to prominent offices or councils, or for other tasks, or any civic office.

4 And the Jesuits are now and henceforth never to be introduced under any pretext or [in the guise of other religious] orders into these united territories. And where they or their disciples remain or creep back in, they are to be abolished entirely. Their revenue and property and that of other orders concealing them and their disciples is to be confiscated and used to fund territorial defence ...

5 Further, no other [religious] orders are to be introduced to these united territories, other than those already present.

6 Equally, those foundations, churches, monasteries and the like that are currently left waste and abandoned are to be given to the eternal possession and free disposition of the Evangelical Estates for the use of Evangelical [church] services and schools.

7 Above all, the king must confirm without any exception or restriction, both the Letters of Majesty and the religious concessions, as well as the union between the Evangelical Estates of Bohemia and those of Silesia in 1609 that was confirmed by His Imperial Majesty, and the confederation of 1614 between the territories permitted by Emperor Matthias of blessed memory.

8 All churches in these united territories currently in Evangelical hands are to remain so in perpetuity.

9 Those united and confederated lands, namely Moravia, Upper and Lower Lusatia, which do not have a special Letter of Majesty concerning the free exercise of religion but which join this agreement, may enjoy the free exercise of religion in all the clauses, points and articles of the Bohemian and Silesian Letters of Majesty.

10 The free exercise of Evangelical religion of the Bohemian and Augsburg Confessions is extended to every man and woman in all united territories and towns regardless as to whether they belong to the king or queen, permitting the construction of churches, schools and cemeteries, and the appointment of Evangelical pastors and school teachers. Everyone shall be allowed to follow the old ceremonies of their Christian conscience in their own church. However, to ensure better unity and to prevent all kinds of difficulties and bitterness, there are to be no insults or personal attacks from the pulpit upon pain of removal from office.

11 Similarly, no foundations or benefices, be they bishoprics, abbeys, commanderies, priories, prelatures, or the like in these united territories are to be conferred on foreigners, but only upon natives of the lands of the Bohemian crown, and no further foundations or benefices are to be established, either by the king or anyone else.

12 All Roman Catholics in all the united lands are bound by law of the Estates of each territory not to undertake anything against the Letters of Majesty and agreements regarding the free exercise of religion ...

13 No Roman Catholic may hold a high or low civic office without first swearing obedience to abide by the Letters of Majesty, unions and above all this agreement as specified in the seventh and twelfth articles.

14 No Roman Catholic from the highest to the lowest status present in the united territories shall be tolerated unless they have also sworn obedience to the religious concessions and unions and above all this agreement as specified in the seventh and twelfth articles.

15 No Roman Catholic higher or lesser cleric may, as they did formerly, exercise either spiritual or above all secular jurisdiction or hold office over the Evangelicals under any pretext.

16 The following offices in Bohemia are reserved for Evangelicals: the senior castellan, the senior chancellor, both castellans of Karlstein, the senior administrator, treasurer and president of the court of appeal, both under-treasurers, the captain of Prague Castle, the senior mint administrator and both court judges.

In Moravia: the lord lieutenant, senior territorial treasurer, under-treasurer. In Silesia: the senior lord lieutenant, all lieutenants, and [the] chancellor; in the two hereditary principalities of Upper and Lower Lusatia: both bailiffs and the lord lieutenant, district lieutenants and territorial judge.

17 To ensure that qualified candidates are appointed to the above senior and territorial posts, the Estates shall have the right of selecting certain individuals in their territories, while confirmation of appointment rests with the king. As far as what happens in Bohemia and Moravia, each Estate shall name four individuals for each post in its power, without hindrance from other Estates, and the king shall choose and confirm [from these four] the candidate to be appointed. These matters concerning Bohemia and Moravia shall not infringe the concessions and privileges of the princes and Estates of Silesia, or the Estates of Upper Lusatia.

18 Those councillors' posts that until now have been occupied exclusively by Roman Catholics in the towns of all united territories are henceforth to be filled half by Roman Catholics and half by Evangelicals, but the most prominent among them, either as the presiding member, or where there is not such a person, the mayor, shall always be an Evangelical, well-qualified person.

19 In the three towns of Prague and those other towns in Bohemia, Moravia, Silesia, Upper and Lower Lusatia where the Evangelicals already hold the majority of council posts, these are henceforth exclusively reserved for Evangelical persons in perpetuity.

20 All privileges, title deeds and the like that have been used to oppress Evangelicals, such as in Budweis, Pilsen, in almost all royal towns in Moravia, in Oppeln, Ratibor and other places in Silesia, [and] in Wettigerau, Bernstadt,

Osterriz, [and] Hennersdorf unter dem Königsholz in Upper Lusatia, are declared null and void, and Evangelicals living amongst Catholics in those places are to enjoy equal protection.

[Art. 21 protected Evangelicals from being dismissed from their posts or being denied trade qualifications due to their religion and granted them freedom to exercise trades.]

22 And since these territories of Bohemia, Moravia, Silesia, Upper and Lower Lusatia are not hereditary lands, but have the right of free election, and have freely joined together, no king shall dare to have the audacity to make a prejudicial judgement against them.

23 Thus, no one shall be designated successor, still less be elected or crowned, during the reign of a future king, unless the united territories consider this necessary or desire this.

24 The oath of allegiance shall henceforth apply only to the king and not to any heirs …

25 The recent treaty with the House of Spain regarding the kingdom of Bohemia and its incorporated lands to their devastation and against their will is hereby declared null and void.[1]

26 Henceforth all discussions regarding the entire Corpus [body] and especially those where a king of Bohemia is elected, are to be held together with all territories of Bohemia, Moravia, Silesia, Upper and Lower Lusatia present and voting, unless one territory is unable to attend through pressing need. If that be the case, then the absent land is not bound by, or obliged to contribute to, any decisions or elections of the king, taken by the others.

[Art. 27 specified that royal elections were to be held at a general diet in Prague Castle. Art. 28 specified that the five territories took turns to vote in a specific order with Bohemia voting last.]

29 Once a king has confirmed this Confederation and assumed government, he is to use the following defence arrangements against all enemies always with the advice of the Estates.

30 Should, contrary to hope, a king attempt anything contravening the religious concessions, unions, and this constitution, and thereby force the territories to take defensive measures, then all Estates of these united kingdoms and provinces are *ipso facto* [by that very fact] released from their duty and cannot be subsequently held to account for any insults to the royal sovereignty and majesty.

31 The king is not permitted to start a war without the agreement of the territories, nor undertake any recruitment [of soldiers], nor permit foreign troops

---

[1] A reference to the Oñate Treaty of 1617. See Doc. 9.

into these territories, or post garrisons in country or town, or demand restitution from anyone for marching, transit, mustering or disbandment.

32 Further, the king does not have the power to build a castle or fortress in any of the united territories without their consent.

33 Similarly, the king shall henceforth not be allowed to contract debts on any of the united lands without their consent, not compel the Estates and towns to stand surety.

[Arts 34–5 charged the Bohemian Chancellery with administrative oversight which was to be exercised in conformity with the Letters of Majesty and the constitution. Arts 36–43 made each territory autonomous for administrative and judicial purposes. Art. 44 stated that royal orders contrary to the rights and freedoms of the Estates were not binding.]

45 While it is only the Evangelicals in the aforementioned territories who have agreed this Confederation and defensive measure, the Roman Catholic Estates and foundations may enjoy its protection against their and our own enemies, provided they abide peacefully by the Letters of Majesty and religious concessions, as well as this union, and do not instigate evil practices against the Evangelicals.

[Arts 46–54 made the Confederation and its associated defence system binding on all members against their enemies and all threats to their privileges. Art. 52 threatened a territory trying to secede with common military action. Art. 55 made the Confederation eternally binding.]

56 Henceforth all these united territories belonging to the Bohemian crown are to behave towards each other only as true members and no territory is to assume superiority over another, except for the traditional ceremonial precedence among them.

[Art. 57 forbade one territory from suppressing the privileges of another. Art. 58 prevented any land claiming any distinctions other than those specified in the Confederation. Art. 59 provided the text of a common oath for the Defensors.[2] Arts 60–8 specified the Defensors' duties to uphold the constitution. Art. 69 allowed each territory to consult another for advice.]

70 Concerning the common defensive measures, it has been agreed between the territories of Bohemia, Moravia, Silesia, Upper and Lower Lusatia that each shall help the other without fail in all emergencies with the following assistance.

[Arts 71–9 specified quotas of varying size depending on which territory was being helped. The maximum total strength was set at 3,250 cavalry and 9,500 infantry, with Bohemia, Moravia and Silesia each obliged to send 4,000 men,

---

[2]   The executive committee appointed by the Confederated Estates to uphold their constitution and privileges.

and the two parts of Lusatia only sending 750.[3] Art. 80 said more could be summoned if necessary. Art. 81 agreed a common commanding general, but each contingent was to serve under its own lieutenant general, with precedence amongst them regulated according to seniority in Arts 82 and 85. Arts 83–4 stated that territories that were themselves attacked were not to recall their contingents, but were to wait for assistance from those not currently under attack. Art. 86 obliged each to stockpile munitions.]

87 And since no defence can be established or maintained without money, the willing contributions of the beer levy and the like are initially to be used to fund this until a tranquil peace can be obtained, because the king will need his domains in Bohemia and in his own lands to finance his court.

[Arts 88–94 specified common administration of military finances and permitted confiscation of ecclesiastical land to help fund defence if the relevant Catholic clergy opposed the Confederation.]

95 Otherwise, whatever is agreed by the Estates of this or that territory at diets, princely congresses and meetings between the territories and is proposed to the king and granted, is to remain binding and not to be contravened …

96 No diet is to last longer than fourteen days, unless the Estates agree this is necessary for the common good.

[Arts 97–8 stated that emigrants and other 'disloyal children of the fatherland' were not to hold public office and were subject to any future decision of the Estates.]

99 Finally, the next diet shall decide what to do about the hereditary alliance with his electoral grace [of the Palatinate] and other surrounding lands.

100 The terms of this Confederation shall not infringe the constitution, privileges, freedoms, rights, statutes and hallowed customs of any territory.

Affirmed by the signatures and seals of the assembled envoys of the aforementioned Estates of Bohemia and the other territories. Enacted at the general public assembly of all aforementioned territories at Prague Castle 31 July 1619.

[A separate annex of 23 articles enhanced Silesia's administrative and legal autonomy, and obliged its clergy to contribute to its taxes and defence.]

Source: Johann Christian Lünig (ed.), *Das teutsche Reichs-Archiv*, 9 vols (Leipzig, 1710–20), vol. 5, part 1, pp. 75–87.

---

[3] In practice, Lusatia bought off its obligations by paying cash instead.

PALATINE INVOLVEMENT

15. Open letter from Frederick V regarding his acceptance of the Bohemian Crown, 7 November 1619

We, Frederick by the grace of God king of Bohemia, count Palatine and elector [etc.] offer each and every Christian potentate, elector and Estate our zealous service, friendship and gracious intentions and therefore declare: That we have no doubt that everyone without and beyond the Empire is sufficiently aware of the wretched and dangerous state into which the ancient and worthy kingdom of Bohemia, that most prominent member of the Holy Roman Empire, has fallen, together with its incorporated lands and other neighbouring states, and what suffering, tribulations and hostilities have been occurring for some time with unceasing robbery, murder, arson and ruination of the territory, as well as spilling of much innocent Christian blood, violation of honourable women and virgins, hacking of suckling babes and the like inhuman, barbarous excesses, maliciousness and atrocities. Further, experience and various comprehensive reports of such evil, misery and distress that has occurred or may yet happen make the main cause so crystal clear that even those who supported it in both word and deed (and thus willingly misleading the higher powers and bringing them into the present danger and loss) must themselves be convinced of it in their consciences.

Even in these recent times, when differences of opinion have emerged in matters of belief and religion, it is clear from Holy Scripture and the teaching of the church fathers that people's consciences cannot be commanded, bound or overpowered, but that whenever such compulsion has been attempted overtly or covertly it has had evil consequences and caused marked changes in distinguished kingdoms and provinces. Furthermore and in particular, after various foreign people crept into the Empire of the German Nation and its component and neighbouring kingdoms and lands, a new teaching and opinion emerged that is fundamentally extremely dangerous to all potentates and rulers. Using the cover of apparent holiness, these people insinuated themselves not only with great lords and rulers, but also their advisors and officials and generally the richest and most distinguished everywhere, thereby promoting a marked increase in the false zeal to pressure, persecute and, wherever they failed to yield, completely recover those who had separated from the Roman Church. It followed that, though the previous worthy regents had done their utmost to preserve the common peace, despite the aforementioned disunity of religion both in the Roman Empire as well as especially in the kingdom of Bohemia, particularly by issuing concessions, arranging religious settlements and agreements, and sustaining an equilibrium between the adherents of both religions.[1] However, doubtless more due to others' instigation than their own nature and inclinations, their successors

---

[1] This is a reference to Emperor Rudolf II and the Letter of Majesty and similar concessions to the Protestants.

gave such free rein to the aforementioned malicious people and their followers that they were able to implement one innovation after the other, and not
only used public writings to cast doubt on all religious concessions, agreements and other obligations and laws, but also to actively weaken, abolish
and annul them.

We do not wish to use this time or place to go into everything that has
been begun, proposed or promoted for so many years here in the Roman
Empire, and what a regrettable situation pertains now, but rather such a
discussion will find an appropriate exposition in due course.

Instead, concerning the worthy kingdom of Bohemia and its incorporated
lands in particular, it is quite undeniable and notorious how the Roman religion declined significantly over time, while the light of the Holy Gospel
dawned and that great difficulties often arose from this, so that finally there
was no other way to preserve peace except through certain compacts, concessions and liberties, so that peaceful co-existence and human society was not
totally undermined by differences of religious opinion.

As long as things remained on these terms, both sides were content.
However, the aforementioned hotheads could not bear this peaceful prosperity any longer, but instead, as reported, preferred to push things to
extremes and risk all, rather than abandon their deep-rooted intention of
returning everything under the spiritual domination of the Pope and the
secular domination of a foreign power. It so came to pass that the religious
complaints mounted daily in the lands, especially concerning the Letter of
Majesty, as one trick and violent act followed the other with the destruction
and closure of newly built Evangelical churches, with the instigation of division amongst the Estates, with the withdrawal of the defence they had been
allowed,[2] with the un-Christian heinous persecution of the poor subjects,
with the threat of great hardship, insult and danger to life and limb, and
even death, made against those both high and low. Then, when people naturally tried to resist by whatever means they were compelled to use (as has
already been extensively reported by the Estates concerned in a public
pamphlet[3]) they were met by force of arms and open hostilities. Thus, unfortunately both the said crown of Bohemia and its incorporated and other
neighbouring lands and provinces have largely and most painfully been
ravaged by fire and sword, spoiled and ruined and literally burnt to ashes.
And though the said lands have for many years, especially recently,
contributed their utmost in goods and blood to maintain the border
defences of the Hungarian crown against the Turks, a mighty enemy, yet
matters have now come to such extremes that the said border defences are
denuded of troops, artillery and munitions, and what was intended against
the Turks is now destined for Bohemia ...

---

[2]   The Protestants had been permitted to organise a militia in 1608, but by the time of this
      letter had in fact already disbanded it (in 1610) due to lack of money.
[3]   That is, the 'Apology', see Doc. 12.

Now we hope that it is known at least throughout the Empire that we, together with some other good-hearted electors and princes and even other potentates, right from the start of this dangerous fire left nothing wanting in true-hearted warnings and appropriate intercession to find kinder ways and means to prevent further misfortune. We would have much preferred and desired, and also advised in a timely manner, that, where possible, the differences that had arisen between a lord and his Estates and subjects might be settled quickly without further complications by involving the territories concerned according to the worthy custom, as experience shows that the efforts of distant potentates and princes only takes time, does not stem the evil, but causes more delay.

[Much time was wasted discussing possible mediation and an armistice, during which hostilities continued. The situation deteriorated after the death of Emperor Matthias. The Bohemians were driven to such a state that] they established a confederation amongst themselves to stabilise and promote the defence they were entitled to make under divine and natural law, and completely altered their government with a new election. They set out the reasons and basis for this clearly in a published pamphlet [Frederick reaffirms he tried to act as a well-intentioned mediator and had no thought of personal gain].

However, as the election to the crown of Bohemia and its incorporated lands has fallen to us by the unanimous vote[4] of the Estates gathered in a general diet, we testify before God and with a clear conscience that we have always been perfectly satisfied with the electoral dignity and our hereditary principality and lands which the true God granted us, and so never sought elevation, still less tried to obtain the said Bohemian crown by force or other means. The Estates electing us have testified to this and can do so again. Furthermore, we had no reason to do so, given the deplorable situation, but would have much rather preferred the return of peace, which would have preserved the peace and security of the Empire for longer.

For we can easily see the burden, worry, effort, work and danger during the current persistent warfare and ruined lands that must arise for us, alongside many other considerations. We also do not doubt that sensible people will agree that to accept the offer of a kingdom in such a state demands a far stronger resolution than to refuse a peaceable kingdom, and for this reason many have been praised in the history books. We testify again with a clear conscience that if we had seen the means or certainty that, by repudiating the crown, we might have ended this unholy war, obtained the noble peace and thus adequately secured the entire Roman Empire, then all the goods and honour in the world would not have swayed us, but we would have not only immediately refused the offer of the Bohemian crown, but have done our utmost to this end.

---

4   Not strictly correct, since four lords and three knights voted for Johann Georg of Saxony, even though he had refused invitations to stand for election.

We have also not acted precipitously in this great work, but have first faithfully appealed to Almighty God, who takes and grants kingdoms to whoever he wishes, to put the proper intention into our heart. We also communicated the matter in confidence to our lords and friends, and finally after consideration of all the circumstances, perceived God's wondrous Providence and firm hand in this entire great work. Since we cannot, nor should, oppose God's will and calling in any way, still less as we are completely convinced that the oft-mentioned Estates of the Bohemian crown and incorporated lands had many well-founded, legitimate and sufficient reasons to change their government, and stabilise more firmly their liberty and [exercise the] ancient renowned election, which some wanted to take away from them and enfeeble by extraordinary means. Thus, the affair is in itself legal, Christian and worthy, which is also easily proven by various examples from ecclesiastical and secular history. However, we do not thereby seek unjustly to dispossess or deprive any other person of that which belongs to him, but rather to legitimise those who desire their liberty, privileges, the Letter of Majesty, the free exercise of the Evangelical religion, and other just practices; to protect and preserve them against unjust violence, and also, as far as we are able and as far as God grants us His power and blessings, to rescue and emancipate this magnificent land and its many thousands of honest people from further suffering and eventual ruin.

Since we gain no temporal joy, delight or advantage from this, but rather have before our eyes solely God's honour, the common good, its subsequent consolation, protection and conservation, and the pleas and sighs of so many pious hearts, which move us greatly, we very much hope that the true God will not abandon us in this task, but contrary to men's thoughts will grant us, from on high, the means so that, through His assistance, we can accomplish and implement that which, according to His inconceivable wisdom, has long since been decided through His divine Providence and omnipotence. And should we fail to do this, our conscience would not only be greatly burdened, but also we would have to expect God's wrath and punishment.

We have also further considered that, had we brushed aside this divine vocation, then presumably we would have been blamed, especially by the adherents of the Evangelical religion, for all the subsequent bloodshed and destruction of lands. This would have allowed the adversaries to succeed in their intended and imminent oppression of the Bohemian nation and its confederates, and this would have allowed them to turn the weapons they had in their hands against us and other Evangelical imperial Estates, so they could try to effect the same thing. For the aforementioned restless people have constantly admonished and instigated them to act like this, even using published writings, and have also stated that the little innocents should not be spared, no not even their own children, noble families or land and people. These and various similar threats have been heard constantly.

In addition, we have had to weigh and consider that were the worthy kingdom of Bohemia and its incorporated lands, which are, after all, both a distinguished member of the Empire and a bulwark against foreign nations, not immediately assisted in some way, it might well have fallen into other foreign hands, and into such a state that it would have become detached from the Holy Empire of the German Nation, or at least have been the cause of numerous difficulties, especially for neighbouring Evangelical electors and princes. On account of our electoral house and principality of the Upper Palatinate, therefore, we neither could nor should have allowed this, not only because of the obligation and loyalty that we possess and owe to the Empire, our beloved fatherland, but also because of the ancient hereditary alliance between our electoral house of the Palatinate and the Bohemian crown. For these said reasons, therefore, we had to be all the more diligent about the conservation of this kingdom, confident that no one who sufficiently and dispassionately considered everything that had actually occurred could hold it against us.

Thus, in God's name, for the advancement of His holy honour, for the consolation and protection of those who are so greatly distressed, for the maintenance of the common liberty and welfare, for other even more urgent motives and reasons, and in response to the diverse deferential and humble written appeals sent to us by the Estates of Bohemia and all their incorporated lands, their imposing delegations, and especially their ardent desire for our intervention, we finally approved the unanimous election they offered us, and so accepted and took up the crown and government of the worthy kingdom of Bohemia and its oft-mentioned incorporated lands. Then we and our dearly beloved wife, the princess of Great Britain,[5] went in person to Prague with God's assistance. A few days later, with the unanimous consent and agreement of the Estates and the great applause of the people, we, along with Her Highness, were crowned with the customary solemnities and were thus set upon the royal thrown. May the Almighty, by His mighty arm, graciously confirm us in this, and generously grant His Holy Spirit and blessing that we direct our entire reign so that the Lord of all Lords, our saviour Jesus Christ, may rule over us and our subjects, and long maintain us in both true peace and territorial prosperity.

We also attest before God and the entire world that we are firmly resolved in our reign that no one be molested or oppressed on account of religion, nor hindered in his traditional religious practice, not even those who still confess in the Roman church (when they merely abide peacefully and blamelessly by the constitution of the kingdom and the lands, and especially the Letters of Majesty concerning religion). Consequently, the aforementioned Roman Catholics in the kingdom of Bohemia and its associated lands have, in great numbers and by a solemn oath and hand pledge, accepted the commonly established defensive confederation, assented to our recent election and subsequent coronation, and pledged themselves to be obedient to us.

We are fully determined to strive with the highest seriousness and enthusiasm, and to do our utmost to see that not only is the noble peace restored and all difficulties of war set aside in our kingdom of Bohemia and its incorporated

---

5   Elizabeth Stuart (1596–1662), daughter of James I.

lands through [God's] grace, but also greater trust is sown in the Empire itself, and further danger is pre-empted and averted, if only others will also be generally similarly disposed not to hinder us in this, nor give cause for further unrest.

We also propose to cultivate and maintain the goodwill, friendship, correspondence and trust of all Christian potentates, electors and Estates and principalities of our neighbours as much as possible. We anticipate the equivalent from them, and hereby request with friendliness, graciousness and good intentions that they would spring to our aid with both word and deed against all those who, with vile intentions, would set upon us or our kingdom and lands with hostile force. We offer our services in turn to every one of them for whatever may happen that is in our power.

We have judged it to be both advisable and necessary, given the state of things and in these difficult times, to make all of this fully known through this, our public proclamation.

Source: Johann Christian Lünig (ed.), *Das teutsche Reichs-Archiv*, 9 vols (Leipzig, 1710–20), vol. 8, part 2, pp. 74–8.

_____

16. The Dutch response, 1619

Believe me that the Bohemian war will decide the fates of all of us, but especially yours, since you are the neighbours of the Czechs. For the present we shall seek out all ways of bringing you help ... though we have many difficulties to face; the Synod has indeed decreed the aid which reflects the general feelings of our Reformed Church, but ... some of our clergy are resisting with great obstinacy and we have been forced to banish them, and to punish their rebellion when they will not obey their authorities ... All this is harmful to the Bohemian cause, which we would wish to further at all times.

Abroad there is nothing new, but reports of exceptional successes in the East Indies, and we are preparing to found an East India Company. If I am not mistaken it will finally take place in the month of September.

Source: Letter from a Dutch agent to Benjamin Buwinckhausen von Walderode, envoy of the Protestant Union, summer 1619, quoted in J.V. Polisensky, *The Thirty Years War* (London, 1971), pp. 126–7.

_____

17. The British response: Queen Elisabeth appeals in vain for assistance

To Charles, Prince of Wales, 25 September 1620

My only dear brother, I am sure you have heard before this, that Spinola hath taken some towns in the Lower Palatinate, which makes me to trouble you with these lines, to beseech you earnestly to move his majesty that now he would assist us; for he may easily see how little his embassages [embassies] are regarded. Dear brother, be most earnest with him; for, to speak freely to you, his slackness to assist us doth make the Princes of the Union slack too, who do nothing with their army; the king hath ever said that he would not suffer the Palatinate to be taken; it was never in hazard but now, and I beseech you again, dear brother, to solicit as much as you can, for her that loves you more than all the world, I doubt not but you will do it, since you have hitherto solicited his majesty for us, where you do shew your affection to me, which I beseech you to continue to her that is ever, my only dear brother,

> Your most affectionate sister to serve you,
>
> Elisabeth

Prague this 15/25 of September

Source: L.M. Baker (ed.), *The Letters of Elisabeth Queen of Bohemia* (London, 1953), p. 54.

18. The Lutheran critique of the Bohemians

We issue apologies and statements of justification, but no one believes that this makes our actions right, nor do we settle our own consciences. The Turks, the king of France, the elector of Saxony, the brother-in-law of our own king: they all disapprove of our cause, even if one or the other favours the revolution. We have broken our oath and thrown respectable men, who came in the name of the king, out of the window; we did not give them time to prey, let alone defend themselves. We did not even want to listen to Emperor Matthias or King Ferdinand who still offered us peace, forgiveness, our rights and privileges as well as judicial resolution. We allied with the neighbouring lands in and outside the Empire, the Hungarians, the English, the Dutch, the Turks, the devil himself. We besieged Vienna, and opened the entire German Empire to the Turks and Tartars as far as it was in our power.

Bethlen Gabor[1] said he sought lordship, not justice. Anhalt said he sought money, just like the other colonels and captains. At least there was some honesty in that. But one needed to satisfy one's conscience, so one cited religion. In truth, confession was ten times freer under the Habsburgs than under the Calvinists. For this reason, the elector of Saxony and other Lutherans intervened with wise prudence on the side of the emperor. For what had our king done? He had smashed images, drunk the health of the

---

[1] Bethlen Gabor (1580–1629), prince of Transylvania, allied with Frederick V and invaded Habsburg Hungary in 1619. He received unofficial support from the Ottoman authorities in the Turkish part of Hungary, but failed to persuade the Sultan to break his truce (1606) with the emperor, which had been renewed in 1615. The Sultan extended the truce for 15 years in 1627 and again for 20 more in 1642. Lack of Turkish assistance frustrated all Transylvanian intervention in the war.

[Dutch] States General with Bohemian beer, and danced with Bohemian ladies.

Whether we win or lose, our fate will be heavy. Those that have helped Frederick will stand in a long queue hungry for land and money at our expense, if we win. The anger of the much maligned emperor will be upon us if we are defeated. What else can we expect! We have taken from the emperor that which belongs to him, and to God, and offered it to the Turks.

Source: A Bohemian Lutheran nobleman, quoted in Hans Jessen (ed.), *Der Dreißigjährige Krieg in Augenzeugenberichten* (Düsseldorf, 1963), pp. 85–6.

19. The invasion of Austria: Ferdinand II describes the violence, 5 December 1619

Noble dear cousin and elector!

To continue our initial well-intentioned and highly necessary correspondence about the disorder, unrest and disobedience in Bohemia and subsequently in our kingdom of Hungary, we do not want to conceal from you that Bethlen Gabor and Count Thurn, together with their infantry and cavalry, advanced again towards the capital city Vienna over the last few weeks and immediately, the day after our return from our duchy of Styria, having robbed, plundered, burned, ransomed the poor subjects without respect to their person on both sides of the Danube, similarly exercised such great mischief and un-Christian tyranny that has scarcely been heard of. A few days ago the enemy began his retreat, but not before the Hungarians had devastated, plundered and burned everything where they had been quartered, and (it is said) stripped the people to their last threads, ruined, cut them down and dragged a large number of them away as prisoners, subjected them to unheard of torture to find money and property, dragged away numerous young lads of twelve to sixteen years old, and so ill-treated pregnant women and other women, that many of them were found dead everywhere on the roads. They pulled ropes around the men's necks so tight that their eyes popped out of their heads. Indeed, this enemy has behaved so terribly everywhere, that one can almost not remember whether such tyranny was ever heard of from the Turks.

By such means and with such allies Count Thurn thinks he can save evangelical liberty.

Source: Emperor Ferdinand to Elector Johann Georg of Saxony, 5 December 1619, from Eugen von Frauenholz (ed.), *Das Heerwesen in der Zeit des Dreissigjährigen Krieges*, 2 vols (Munich, 1938–9), vol. I, pp. 105–6.

20. Bethlen Gabor's 'Blood-flag', 1620

[A printed broadsheet claiming to show the swallow-tailed battle flag of the Transylvanians as they invaded Austria. Among the devices on the flag is a ship full of Ottoman soldiers.]
Text accompanying the image:

Bethlen Gabor's Blood-flag which he had made at Neusohl of red damask and had painted with the present figures and words, and presented solemnly to the Turkish Emir as the country's ensign.

This figure shown here
Is Bethlen Gabor's blood-flag
Which he recently (understand me right)
Delivered to the Turkish Emir
The country's ensign in Hungary.
The meaning of the flag
And what the picture signifies
Time soon might tell,
But I will indicate in German
The words that appear therein
They are in the Book of Psalms,
Look them up in the sixty eighth chapter
    (Psalm 68,v2)[1]
Where David says: Let God arise,
Let his enemies be scattered:
Let them who hate him
Flee before him, etc.
Besides an inscription
Under the column goes as follows:
By God's wisdom it is made steadfast
At this time for hope and patience
May God grant success
To the dropped anchor. Accordingly,
Each for himself should imagine
What meaning of the others may be:
Such as sun, sceptre, column and crown
The sword, the palm-branch, and above all
The sailing ship together with the star
I myself would like to know the explanation,
For each for himself, as you know
Is the best interpreter of his words:
As for myself I always wish
That this flag signifies everything that is good.

---

[1]   Verse 1 in the English Authorised Version.

May God also by His grace
Prevent all who travel on this ship
From breaking in on us,
May he protect us from foreign peoples.
In this also willingly, help Christ,
Christ, the true Star out of Jacob,
    (Numbers 24, v.17).
The Sun of Righteousness
    (Malachi 4, v.2)
To whom belongs far and wide
All kingdoms, sceptre and crown.
    (Psalms 2, v.8)
As the eternal Son of God,
Who has dominion unto the ends of the earth
    (Psalms 72, v.8)
It is our duty to call upon Him
    (Psalms 50, v.15)
That he may bring our dear fatherland
To peace and prosperity again.
God help that this palm-branch
Break the sword in two at one blow.
O God, do not desert us.
    The End.

Source: Elmer A. Beller, *Propaganda in Germany During the Thirty Years War* (Princeton, NJ, 1940), p. 23.

HABSBURG TRIUMPH

21. The Treaty of Munich, 8 October 1619

On behalf of the Holy Roman Emperor, King of Hungary and Bohemia, and on behalf of the German ecclesiastical electors, His Grace Duke Maximilian of Bavaria has been requested for the common good of all of us to take over full command of the Catholic defences to which the high Catholic Estates of the Empire, His Imperial Majesty, his dynasty and the endangered lands have been constrained for their own preservation to agree. From this task His Grace, the Duke of Bavaria, has not dissented, as a sign of his friendly feelings towards His Imperial Majesty, towards His Royal Highness in Spain and towards the whole praiseworthy House of Austria, to protect the Catholic religion and all the Estates of the Empire loyal to it.

His Grace, the Duke of Bavaria, is granted free and absolute direction over the Catholic constitutional and defence system, including recruitment and movement of the troops, whom he will lead in the name of the Almighty for the common good. His Grace, the Duke of Bavaria, regardless of the difficulty of this business, danger and problems, is prepared to commit his own person, his worthy house, land and subjects, and is also prepared to give further proof of his affection and support to His Imperial Majesty, His Royal Highness in Spain and the entire praiseworthy House of Austria to defend the Catholic religion and its adherents amongst the imperial Estates, and to accept the associated heavy burdens, dangers and other consequences and to put the common good above all *privatis* [private interest] and to accept the free and absolute directorship of the Catholic defence system that is entrusted to him, along with the recruitment and leadership of the soldiers in the name of the Almighty, but on the following express condition, that this is to begin once His Grace has actually completed the collection of the necessary money, soldiers and other requirements.

I For as long as they are under threat, His Grace, the Duke of Bavaria, shall have the full support with money and troops of all the Catholic Estates as well as of His Imperial Highness, and that this aid in money and troops will be forthcoming for as long as His Grace, the Duke of Bavaria, as supreme commander, deems necessary. And furthermore, His Imperial Majesty shall not hinder His Grace, the Duke of Bavaria, in any manner whatsoever from exercising absolute and total command.

II In return, His Grace, the Duke of Bavaria, will to the best of his ability use his direction, assistance and public defence system against all the enemies of His Imperial Majesty, including any of the Estates of the Protestant Union who subsequently become his enemies. It is expressly stated that His Imperial Majesty and His House will refrain from any negotiations, suspension of hostilities or conclusion of truce or peace with the enemies without prior knowledge, consent and inclusion of His Grace, the Duke of Bavaria. His Imperial Majesty also undertakes to carry the costs of war and of war damage as outlined in greater detail below. And His Grace, the Duke of Bavaria, under-takes to support His Imperial Majesty in like manner.

III Since the lands of His Grace, the Duke of Bavaria, would remain untouched and secure from His Imperial Majesty's enemies and others if he did nothing, but as soon as he declares openly for His Majesty and the House of Austria, his own person and lands and everything that belongs to them will be exposed to the greatest danger and uncertainty since they are surrounded by the enemy, and much anxiety, effort and work will result, and in addition to these (already heavy and important considerations), they will be obliged to contribute their quota like that of other Catholic Estates of the Roman Empire. Therefore, and particularly because His Grace is likely to contribute well in excess of what is needed for the defence system, His Imperial Majesty and His entire praiseworthy House are obliged with their property and lands to refund all the … expenses incurred through the military constitution and soldiery (excluding the cost of his own territorial defence militia) provided as assistance to His Majesty, or retained in his own lands according to the circumstances to assist His Majesty … To this end, as much of the Austrian lands are to be pawned to His Grace until the debts are settled.

IV If His Grace, the Duke of Bavaria, should lose all or part of his lands through the fulfilment of this constitution [i.e. alliance], His Imperial Majesty promises to help His Grace, the Duke of Bavaria, to recover what is lost, or to compensate him for it with the equivalent from the Austrian lands if, contrary to expectation, the lost lands cannot be recovered in the eventual peace with the enemy.

V If His Grace, the Duke of Bavaria, should capture anything from the enemy during this campaign in the Austrian lands, then it, together with all associated usages, jurisdictions, rights and property, shall be pawned to him and his descendants and not released, nor the soldiers disbanded, until all his expenses have been liquidated and refunded.

[The next section covers specific arrangements to cover jurisdictions, domains, salt mines and tolls in these areas.]

VI Finally, it is highly necessary and mutually agreed that those who will command His Imperial Majesty's troops communicate diligently and confidentially everything that happens to His Grace, the Duke of Bavaria, and inform him of their intentions. Documented herein everything that has been negotiated and mutually promised by seals of His Imperial Majesty and His Ducal Grace and their own signatures. Munich, 8 October 1619.

Source: Georg Franz (ed.), *Die Politik Maximilians I. von Bayern und seiner Verbündeten 1618–1651* (*Briefe und Akten zur Geschichte des Dreißigjährigen Krieges* (Munich, 1966, new series), vol. I, pp. 242–7.

---

22. The Mühlhausen Declaration, 20 March 1620

We, by the grace of God, Johann Schweikhard[1] elector of Mainz and imperial arch-chancellor, Ferdinand[2] elector of Cologne, and the plenipotentiary of Maximilian count Palatine and duke of Upper and Lower Bavaria, hereby confirm the following in the name of the Catholic Estates as binding on our successors. We met our special friends the right honourable princes and lords Johann Georg elector of Saxony [full title] and Ludwig[3] landgrave of Hessen and count of Katzenelnbogen at the conference in Mühlhausen and discussed the numerous escalating disorders in the kingdom of Bohemia, its incorporated lands and the Holy Roman Empire, as well as the violence of Bethlen Gabor[4] and thus of the Turks. Having considered the circumstances, we believe these problems cannot be resolved through peaceful or judicial means, but

---

[1] Johann Schweikhard von Kronberg (1553–1626), elector of Mainz from 1604.
[2] Ferdinand of Bavaria (1577–1650), elector of Cologne from 1612 and younger brother of Maximilian of Bavaria.
[3] Ludwig V (1577–1626), landgrave of Hessen-Darmstadt from 1596.
[4] See Docs 18–20 for Transylvanian intervention.

instead numerous important factors compel us to extend our hands to His Roman Imperial and Royal Hungarian and Bohemian Majesty and offer all possible assistance to preserve the empire, kingdoms and lands he has acquired through just and proper means, and protect the imperial dignity and sovereignty as well as his fiefs, rights and justice, and the electoral dignity pertaining to these. A meeting of, if not all, then at least the loyal Estates of the Roman Empire was proposed to achieve this goal with fame and honour.

However, this would be very difficult owing to the suspicion that had spread amongst the Estates, especially as the elector of Saxony indicated that the Upper and Lower Saxon Kreise feared they would be forcibly deposed, deprived of their archbishoprics and bishoprics, together with their associated lands and left destitute. Having considered all this, we feel there can be no better way to dispel such fears than through a full assurance, to favour our fellow Estates and show due devotion to His Imperial Majesty. Thus, to please His Grace the elector of Saxony, whilst expressly reserving the most prized Religious Peace and its ecclesiastical reservation, we offer the following assurance binding on ourselves, our successors and all Catholic Estates: those Estates of the Upper and Lower Saxon Kreise which are secular possessors of archbishoprics and bishoprics and their associated lands but who remain loyal and provide all due assistance to His Imperial Majesty during the present Bohemian unrest, as well as in future breaches of imperial law and the constitution, that they shall not be deprived of any archbishopric, bishopric, monastery or ecclesiastical property by force or other means. Instead, they shall retain peaceful secular possession of the said archbishoprics and bishoprics and shall be assisted to defend these. No Catholics, or others acting on their instigation, shall in the future attack, infringe or ruin them or forcibly eject them. We do not wish to prevent the aforementioned possessors from seeking His Imperial Majesty's indulgence for their administration and exercise of the regalia, or letters of protection against violence. However, we do not wish our assurance or any eventual imperial indulgence or protection to grant more extensive rights regarding the Estates' representation in the Imperial Visitation, Deputation or any other general or particular meetings than they [the Protestant administrators] have hitherto enjoyed.[5] This has been affirmed as binding on us, our successors and the other Catholic Estates by the seal of we two electors and the signature of us the Bavarian envoy so as to be better observed without breach. Done at the electoral congress at Mühlhausen, 20 March Anno. 1620.

Source: Johann Christian Lünig (ed.), *Das teutsche Reichs-Archiv*, 9 vols (Leipzig, 1710–20), vol. 5, part 1, pp. 284–5.

---

5   The Catholic imperial Estates had objected since 1582 to the Protestant administrators exercising the constitutional rights associated with the ecclesiastical territories they had acquired, most notably in the Imperial Visitation and the Imperial Deputation, the two bodies successively charged with reviewing the verdicts of the Reichskammergericht in the controversial 'religious cases' arising from disputes over the interpretation of the Peace of Augsburg.

23. Saxony backs the emperor

Ferdinand II to Elector Johann Georg, 6 June 1620

Dear uncle and elector. Since I have a firm trust in you and am much obliged to you during these difficulties in the Holy Empire, I am completely assured you will do everything that a Roman emperor could expect from a loyal elector of the Holy Empire, or that a Bohemian king and Austrian archduke could expect from such a closely connected and related prince.

I have considered the trouble that my rebels and their supporters are causing me and the common good at every occasion, and wish hereby to inform Your Grace in a German, sincere, friendly and gracious manner that the execution commission, issued against those opposing me in the kingdom of Bohemia and its incorporated lands, will not infringe the privileges, Letter of Majesty or religion of those who return to their proper obedience.

This has been done simply to prevent our common enemies from resuming their Calvinist bloodthirsty [and] dangerous attacks under the pretext of the Letter of Majesty, [alleged] changes in administration, even the Religious Peace itself. I assure your grace in an imperial, German and sincere way that there will be no changes in what I have promised you or what is incorporated into the Religious Peace. The old Bohemian Hussites,[1] in conformity with the old agreements, will not be excluded from this [religious peace] either.

Source: Michael Caspar Londorp, *Acta Publica*, 2 vols (Frankfurt, 1668), vol. II, p. 633.

---

24. The Treaty of Ulm, 3 July 1620

By the grace of God, we Maximilian, count Palatine, etc., and by the same grace, we Joachim Ernst margrave of Brandenburg etc.,[1] hereby let it be known to all: That both now and for some time there has been a dangerous situation and armed uprising both in the Holy Roman Empire of the German Nation and in various neighbouring kingdoms and lands. Thus, the electors and Estates of both the Catholic and the Evangelical unions were prompted to make military preparations and ready themselves, thereby causing misunderstandings and giving offence, violation and concern among the members of both alliances and commotion in the Holy Empire. Therefore, to banish such misunderstandings, and foster better trust between both unions and in the Empire, we have agreed to a certain binding promise, commitment and

---

[1]   Agreements from 1436 and 1485 recognised the moderate Hussites, known as Utraquists, who rejected some Catholic doctrines but refused to break entirely with Rome.

[1]   Joachim Ernst of Brandenburg-Ansbach (1583–1625), acting commander of the Protestant Union forces.

assurance through the mediation of His Royal Majesty of France's right honourable envoy[2] who was present here in the imperial city of Ulm.

And first, we Maximilian etc. as general of the Catholic League, and we Joachim Ernst etc. as lieutenant general of the Evangelical Union, by virtue of the plenipotentiary powers we possess and by our word, faith and trust, and in the best legal form, promise, commit and assure that no elector, prince or Estate belonging to either union shall not in any way or manner, under whatever pretext that can be conceived, by means of either union's military preparations, offend, insult, complain about the Religious and Profane Peace, assail, molest, attack, disturb or assault one or the other's electorate, principality, land, subjects, towns, settlements, villages or ecclesiastical and secular officeholders. Instead, both Catholics with the Evangelicals, and Evangelicals with the Catholics, shall persist in righteous and unstained peace, quiet and unity, and shall leave each to his own untroubled affairs.

So that, however, this promise and good trust according to the imperial constitution between neighbouring princes and Estates shall persist always, the troops that both sides have in proximity shall be withdrawn from the places where they are now as soon as possible, without injury to each other, and no others shall be lodged in their place.

Second, it is however qualified and agreed that this or that Estate shall not refuse if an elector, prince or Estate from either union shall, due to some future necessity and according to imperial law, seek passage for its and its people's defence and safeguard and with proper guarantee. However, such a request is to be made punctually, and not unexpectedly, or with little prior notice when the troops are already on the frontier or even in another land oppressing the subjects.

And thirdly, we, Maximilian count Palatine and the other united Catholic electors, princes and Estates exclude from this present negotiation the kingdom of Bohemia, its incorporated lands as well as all the Hereditary Lands of the House of Austria, and include in this treaty only those electorates, principalities and lands that belong to the electors, princes and Estates united to both sides, including the Palatine electorate and its hereditary possessions within the Empire (because at the moment we have not experienced the aforementioned misunderstandings with these lands, but instead hope we are on good terms with them), and it [these arrangements] shall not be further extended. So this is the declaration of the Catholic electors, princes and Estates regarding the kingdom of Bohemia, its incorporated lands and all Austrian Hereditary Lands. We Joachim Ernst of Brandenburg for our part and on behalf of our allied electors, princes and Estates, likewise wish to exclude the said kingdom of Bohemia and its incorporated lands, and instead leave matters there to take their course, and equally intend this agreement to apply only to those electorates and lands within the Empire as specified above.

Fourth, since during the ongoing negotiations we frequently touched on

---

2   Charles de Valois, duc d'Angoulême (1573–1650).

the unresolved complaints in the Empire, yet because there was insufficient time and because such matters affect not merely the members of both unions, but all Catholic and Evangelical Estates by whom we were not empowered, these have been postponed until another more convenient time.

Restitution of the damages claimed by both unions on account of their soldiers, and especially what occurred at Sontheim and its neighbourhood,[3] is to be negotiated in the future in a just manner.

All of this, we Maximilian and we Joachim Ernst unswervingly, firmly and steadfastly uphold both for ourselves and for our aforementioned fellow confederate electors and Estates, and for the better assurance of this we have hereby signed with our own hands and imprinted our seals.

Source: Johann Christian Lünig (ed.), *Das teutsche Reichs-Archiv*, 9 vols (Leipzig, 1710–20), vol. 5, part 1, pp. 285–6.

---

25. The Battle of White Mountain, 8 November 1620

Letter from Christian of Anhalt to Frederick V explaining his defeat:

Sire,

As it was your majesty's order for me to relate the events of the battle of Prague, it is my duty to obey you promptly and to present briefly what I could observe and recognise.

I remember that on Thursday, 5 November, the enemy had started to break camp before Rackonitz, which we noticed at 1 or 2 in the afternoon. Your Majesty gathered the main commanders together and asked me what to do. I gave my advice, to wit that we should head towards Prague as it was our intention, and no doubt also that of the enemy. Upon this, the elder Count Thurn interrupted and said he would bet the enemy had no intention of entering Prague as it was completely impossible, and that instead we should come to the aid of the surrounding villages in order to prevent the enemy from conquering them and so forcing Prague to surrender. When evening came, however, we clearly understood what the enemy's intentions were. Then our deliberations shifted to how best to prevent the enemy from advancing. We decided that the aforementioned Count Thurn, as guardian of the crown, would march through the night towards Prague with his son's infantry regiment, and that Your Majesty would follow the next morning with the army. Both these decisions were implemented despite the road being long and arduous and not made practicable. We did so well that we arrived at

---

[3] The Palatinate had tried to rally the more lukewarm members of the Union by precipitating a crisis in June 1618 over a fortress the bishop of Speyer was constructing at Udenheim near Sontheim by the Rhine. Around 5,200 troops and peasant pioneers seized the unfinished works and demolished them. The Catholics demanded compensation. The fortress was rebuilt after 1622 as Philippsburg.

a place two leagues from Prague half a day before the enemy; it was a village called Anhost. It was Saturday, 7 November and Your Majesty arrived around midday.

I gave orders to secure billets for the army, and you decided to make a short trip to Prague. Just after you departed, the enemy started to appear and skirmish and then we heard that all the enemy armies had rejoined each other and were making their swift way straight towards Prague. They were surprised to see we had arrived before them. Upon this, I immediately sent 500 musketeers to keep a passage open, which, if the enemy had known about, would have made our arrival difficult.

So it was that at 8 p.m., I started the whole army on a night march and at 1 a.m. we arrived at the so called White Mountain in front of the city of Prague. I set up camp to rest until daybreak. The Hungarians were alarmed by the din made by some of the Cossacks who had pursued them part of the way. Some of our own infantry regiments also seemed perturbed and I wasn't used to that, so I talked to them, but it filled me with dread.

There was fog at dawn on 8 November. When it was gone, we chose the battlefield between the so-called park of the Star Palace and a slope on the other side, so that we had the advantage of the high ground: the park was on the right-hand side and the slope on the left, so that the enemy could only attack us from the front. The field having been chosen, the Count Hollach,[1] as lieutenant and general chief of staff, ordered the troops to form the order of battle according to the sketch that I enclose (as Appendix A).

The enemy had noticed (a bit late) that we had started to move; as soon as they heard they followed us and their vanguard arrived at around 9 a.m. I had called Count Thurn to ask his advice as he knew this place very well. He confirmed that it was the best place and called his son's regiment back from Prague. Meanwhile, Count Hollach had ordered the infantry regiments to guard the park at various points, to wit that of the Count of Weimar,[2] of my son[3] and the company of guards of Your Majesty. He ordered the cannon of the Duke of Bavaria to be entrenched, but the spades that I had brought to the camp at my own expense had been damaged so much at Rackonitz, that we only had 400 usable ones left. This meant we had to fetch some from

---

[1] Count Georg Friedrich of Hohenlohe-Weikersheim (1569–1645), an ambitious prince from an extended family of Franconian imperial counts, who was made senior general by the Bohemian Estates in 1618. He was jealous of both Anhalt and Thurn. His friends and relations secured him a pardon from Ferdinand II in 1623, but he joined the Swedes in 1632 and was again placed under the imperial ban in 1634. He was eventually pardoned by Ferdinand III in 1637.

[2] Johann Ernst the Younger of Sachsen-Weimar (1594–1626). His regiment held the Star Palace, though it is missing from the list in Appendix A. He joined the Danes in 1625 and died of plague during the abortive Hungarian campaign.

[3] Christian II of Anhalt-Bernberg (1599–1656). He was wounded and captured, but released in 1622, and spent the rest of the war trying to minimise the damage to his homeland. See also Doc. 81.

Prague, but they took so long that our entrenchment was hindered and remained far from perfect. The Count Thurn decided that the two cannon were to be taken to the left flank, which damaged the enemy greatly, but the said pieces were positioned too far away. The Hungarians, that is Colonel Cornis[4] and 300 men, were posted on the right flank. The remaining Hungarians stayed at the rearguard, because they wanted to be away from the cannon. They were under orders to advance through the gaps when the battle started and to strike the enemy in the flank. I ordered particularly that 1,500 Hungarians had to remain on the left flank, as marked on the plan, and I dispatched this order three times to the commander.

The Count Hollach had ordered them similarly and the Count Thurn took the above named Colonel Cornis to the very place and showed him personally how they were outside the range of the cannon and with which advantage they could do a signal service, but nobody came there. The enemy came through a village at the foot of a mountain where the path was bad but wide enough to allow the passage of formed troops on the right-hand flank. But, they would have been seen by us, which they wanted to avoid. So, they moved as I described before.

Your Majesty will find a list of the number of men on both sides to the best of my knowledge, in Appendix B. The enemy formed the order of battle at the foot of (and partially behind) the mountain, practically in the same form as us, as they mixed infantry and cavalry regiments and left very little space on their front. We could see most of the ground where our cannon were positioned on the left flank. We damaged them so much that they were obliged to pull their front back towards their left-hand flank.

When I saw them moving, I thought they were going to try something more and, finding the Count Hollach of the same opinion, I immediately informed the troops by the two adjutants of the chief of staff and other first officers. In the end I saw that the enemy's vanguard were swiftly climbing the aforementioned mountain. I was near the two cannon on the left flank, and from there I galloped at the head of Count Hollach's cavalry where my war horses were, and in no time I could see a large troop of cavalry accompanied by two infantry battalions coming straight at us. This gave me hope, as the enemy coming so fast had to have lost order and was going to find us standing firm, in good order, our chiefs in agreement and ready to fight them. Our cannon were flanking their army, we had already dislodged theirs and, although they outnumbered us, they couldn't see this because of the narrowness of the passage. Moreover, I was well aware that the Count Bucquoy,[5] who was an experienced and wise captain, would never advise to start battle under such circumstances. This made me quite sure I was able to hope for certain victory.

---

4   Also called Kornis, he commanded the Hungarian light cavalry sent by Bethlen Gabor.
5   Charles Bonaventura de Longueval, Count Bucquoy (1571–1621), an experienced soldier from the Spanish Netherlands, who was imperial field commander 1618–21.

But God, who in his divine wisdom weighs human events, demonstrated his anger at our lack of piety and at the offences of which we are all guilty. It must be God who withdrew bravery from our soldiers' hearts, because otherwise it was impossible to believe that such a sudden effeminate terror would seize so many men I had seen perform their duties so well before. As soon as the enemy arrived at about 300 or 400 paces from Count Thurn's infantry, our soldiers started to shoot without order or sense and, even against express orders, shot in the air and immediately started to flee, seemingly in the grip of fear. I then told my cousin, Count Solms, your court chamberlain (who was that day honouring me with his presence) that although this didn't begin auspiciously, I was still hoping for a positive outcome.

At the same moment, being only just armed, I saw before me my cavalry, which had been levied by Lieutenant Colonel Streiff, with some caracolling and others galloping away. So, I ran towards them and stopped them with my sword to make them return to the charge. The captains obeyed me, but most of them didn't really persevere.

Count Hollach arranged his troops so that the ones on the left flank should charge and he told them what to do. The troops of counts Solms and Bubna[6] were engaged with the enemy but with little strength or resistance, so that I could see everything of the vanguard on my left, including the three companies of the Estates of Bohemia and the one coming after. Everybody was fleeing, some with the infantry which was running the fastest. My son charged with his cavalry, fought and pushed the enemy back to where they had their cannon. There, he was wounded twice, as was his brave lieutenant colonel. My son was then taken prisoner. Count Styrum with Mansfeld's[7] troops charged on the enemy's musketeers on the side of the park and afterwards he attacked the cavalry. He did his duty with bravery and gained a good reputation. Colonel Stubenvoll[8] also led two or three good charges. I let the Austrian cavalry charge and they did well. Lieutenant Colonel Baron Hofkirchen[9] stayed put. But the latter also performed the bad caracole. It was then that I

---

[6] Heinrich Wilhelm Count Solms-Laubach-Sonnenwalde (1583–1632) was a younger son of a family of imperial counts from the Rhineland who served consistently against the emperor until his death at the battle of Bamberg. Jan Warlych of Bubna (1570–1635) was a Bohemian who had served as colonel for Rudolf II against the Turks. He was made general of cavalry by the Bohemian Estates in 1618 and later served the Danes and Swedes as an exile.

[7] Mansfeld was not present at the battle, but one of his regiments was under Count Styrum.

[8] Hans von Stubenvoll (1569–1640) was a Lower Austrian Lutheran noble who joined the Moravia Estates' forces once they allied with the Bohemians. He transferred to imperial service after the battle. He and Hohenlohe exchanged public letters blaming each other for the defeat.

[9] Georg Andreas Baron von Hofkirchen (1562–1623) was the commander of the Lower Austrian Protestant forces.

also ordered the major of the Silesians to attack as well, which he did well with the aid of his troops, but the resistance was too great. The enemy, however, was stopped and pushed back, so that some of their troops galloped away to regroup.

Two enemy infantry battalions fired a great salvo which killed the horse of my chamberlain. One of my gentlemen, Keydel, was also wounded at my side. Those two battalions decided to withdraw too. Our artillery did well and greatly damaged the enemy, which left them perplexed. The regiment of Moravia commanded by Count Schlick,[10] as well as the five infantry companies of Lieutenant Colonel Pechmann[11] showed bravery and remained until the last. As I could see no cavalry coming to our help, and as I had only 16 horsemen near me, and as the enemy was returning with many troops (both cavalry and infantry), I didn't dare to remain, but withdrew towards the main road that goes towards Prague. I went slowly, hoping that I would find some of our troops waiting, but this was in vain. When the elder duke of Weimar[12] went to stop the Hungarians, he found Colonel Cornis accompanied by very few of his Hungarians and asked him to stand firm. He answered: *Germani currunt* ['The Germans are fleeing']; the Duke then answered: *Nolo esse Germanus hac die, ero Hungarus, maneas tantum mecum* ['They are Germans in the evening, but by morning they will be the same as the Hungarians']; but Cornis although he had turned a little, did not want to understand the Latin phrase. Then, the aforesaid duke came upon an officer who was fleeing and he shouted to him that if he didn't turn back he would shoot him through the head. When he turned, the duke realised it was one of the colonels who didn't stop his flight and continued fleeing the enemy. So, I can confirm that when I withdrew, of all our Hungarians, only a hundred were left of the ten thousand, such was the diligence they showed. It was now impossible to stop the troops. I reached the New Gate where I found Your Majesty together with the routing infantry who had fled

---

10   Heinrich Schlick (1580–1650) served the Moravian Estates 1619–20, but escaped punishment. He joined the imperial army in February 1621 and converted to Catholicism, rising rapidly to field marshal (1627) and then president (1632) of the Imperial War Council, in charge of military administration, logistics, personnel policy and planning until the end of 1649.

11   Gabriel Pechmann, a Lutheran commoner. He briefly served Poland in 1621, then Bavaria (1622) where he found his faith prevented advancement. Transferring to the imperial army in 1623, he became one of Wallenstein's trusted cavalry commanders until killed in action against the Danes in 1627.

12   Wilhelm IV of Sachsen-Weimar (1598–1662) also commanded a regiment in the Estates army, but this was not present at the battle. He escaped to serve under the Margrave of Baden-Durlach and Duke Christian of Halberstadt in their respective defeats in 1622 and 1623. He was captured in the latter, but pardoned and released in 1625 and became the senior Weimar duke in 1626. He joined Sweden in May 1631. Though given the formal title of second-in-command, he felt aggrieved that he had not received better rewards and was marginalised after 1634. He withdrew into precarious neutrality after 1635.

before and had already climbed the ramparts. I could only recover six of them who agreed to defend the city walls. The fear was overwhelming and all ran through the Little Side [i.e. the western part of Prague] towards the Old and the New Town. Some of them were swimming, especially the Hungarians, some of whom were drowned.

One of our worst mistakes was that most of our cavalry would not engage properly. The proper way, which I often explained to them, was to reject the bad habit of caracolling when facing the enemy.[13] Those who had listened to my advice, although defeated, covered themselves in glory, the others in blame. I want to stress this point strongly here, so that this custom of charging without properly engaging is avoided like the plague.

Your Majesty will understand from this account the real reasons for our defeat, and will also understand that the defeat wasn't caused by the enemy's valour, but by their good fortune and the divine help they received. Surely, God wanted to punish us for our sins, mostly because of the awful treatment and bad pay bestowed on our soldiers; seeing that the Estates of Bohemia wanted their ruin and disbandment, those soldiers were reduced to extreme despair and bad behaviour, such that no chief or officer could order them to fight anymore. For me to start a proper explanation of those matters, their faults and imperfections (and why I wanted to separate from the aforesaid estates and provinces), I would need reams of paper to do them justice. Your Majesty knew about this, even if you couldn't remedy the matter in any way possible to you. However, for this generation of people, all was in vain as the unhappy outcome proved.

I will pass over the pursuit and how Your Majesty decided to withdraw to the Old Town, as all of this happened in your presence. I will add one thing though, that if the enemy had not given battle, if the affairs of our soldiers had not been so desperate, and if the Estates of Bohemia had not been so hesitant to put them right, then, as Your Majesty well knows, the city of Prague would have been looted by our own soldiers within a few days, and we would have been unable to do anything to prevent it. This would have been very damaging for us, and that is what Count Bucquoy wanted.

I have added here in Appendix C and D[14] the reasons Your Majesty invoked to justify leaving Prague and Breslau. And I want to say that I noticed a few things which confirm in my view that God has not abandoned either Your Majesty or this cause. This is because God prevented the enemy from pursuing Your Majesty and your retinue, and I am certain that God will continue his just works through Your Majesty, for which he will be eternally

---

13 The tactic of caracolling involved successive ranks of cavalrymen riding towards the enemy, discharging their pistols, and riding back to reload. Many commanders considered it less effective than a faster charge, which often intimidated an enemy into fleeing before the two sides made contact.

14 Omitted here, these appendices outline why Frederick V abandoned Prague immediately after the battle, and why he subsequently also left Breslau in Silesia and escaped to Berlin.

glorified. I only need to add that I wish you all the best and wish only to die at your feet

Sire

Küstrin, first of January of the year 1621

Appendix A Key to the Order of Battle

1. Four companies of Count Styrum (Mansfeld troops)
2. Four companies of Moravian infantry
3. Four companies of Silesian cavalry
4. Four companies of Moravian infantry
5. Eight incomplete companies of Austrian cavalry
6. Four companies of Hohenlohe's infantry regiment [Bohemians]
7. Five companies of Hohenlohe's cavalry regiment [Bohemians]
8. Four companies of Hohenlohe's infantry regiment
9. One company of royal [i.e. Frederick V's guards] and three of Bohemian cavalry
10. Bubna and Solms cavalry, nine companies
11. Six companies of Count Thurn [Bohemian infantry]
12. Five companies of Stubenvoll's Moravian cavalry
13. Two companies of Upper Austrian infantry
14. Four companies of the younger Prince Anhalt's cavalry [Bohemians and Germans]
15. Three companies of Upper Austrian infantry
16. Three companies of the younger Prince Anhalt's cavalry
17. Three companies of the Kaplir infantry regiment [Bohemians]
18. Four companies of the Borsida Moravian cavalry regiment
19. Three companies of the Kaplir infantry regiment
20. Four companies of the Künen [Kein] Moravian cavalry regiment
21. Three companies of the Kaplir infantry regiment
22. Four companies of the Thurn infantry regiment
23. Three hundred Hungarian cavalry under Cornis
24. Four companies selected from other cavalry regiments and posted as advance guard
25. A third line of Hungarian cavalry
26. Heavy guns on the right flank
27. Heavy guns on the left flank
28. The place where the 1,600 Hungarians were to stand, but they did not appear
29. A slope to the left
30. The game park and Star Palace

Note: Our cavalry and infantry numbered no more than 15,000 effectives, while around 5,000 men remained in Prague (largely against orders). Many also suffered from the sickness contracted in Austria during the summer and autumn. Others had been detached, or had straggled during the force-marching [i.e. retreat]. Of the 15,000 Hungarians, only 6,000 were present, because many left during the march or otherwise. Around 12,000 more Hungarians were supposed to arrive on the Moravian frontier two days later.

Appendix B. Copy of a list of the enemy's forces prepared on 15 October 1620 from reconnaissance and interrogating prisoners.

Infantry		Men	Companies
1.	[Infantry Regiment] Spinelli (Neapolitans)	2,500	31
2.	Don Guilhelmo Verdugo	} 3,000	42
3.	Count Bucquoy		
4.	Fugger	1,200	7
5.	Creange and Corrati	1,200	4
6.	Breuner	800	5
7.	Duke of Saxony	1,200	10
8.	Nassau	1,000	10
9.	Fürstenberg	1,000	5
10.	Tieffenbach	900	3
11.	Colonel Fuchs	600	3
12.	Collalto	1,000	5
13.	Schaumburg	1,000	5
		15,400	

Cavalry			
1.	Don Balhasar de Maradas	400	10
2.	Count Dampierre	250	5
3.	Florentines	200	5
4.	Meckau	300	5
5.	Löbell	400	5
6.	Wallenstein	800	13
7.	Gaucher	500	8
8.	La Croy	300	5
9.	Montecuccoli	300	5
10.	Isterle	300	5
11.	Poles	800	10
		4,550	

This was the strength of Count Bucquoy's army at that point.

The list for the Duke of Bavaria's army has been lost, but it was not less than:
     Infantry   8,000;   cavalry   2,000.
The ecclesiastics sent as reinforcements from Germany:
     Infantry   9,000;   cavalry   1,000.

Total infantry   32,400;   cavalry   7,550,
together with 16 or 18 heavy guns.

List of His Majesty of Bohemia's soldiers:

Cavalry

1.	My cavalry under Lt. Col. Streiff	500
2.	Count Hohenlohe	500
3.	My son	700
4.	Royal and the Dukes of Weimar's companies	250
5.	Three Bohemian companies	250
6.	Major General Bubna	300
7.	Count Solms	250
8.	Silesians	300
9.	Austrians	350
10.	Colonel Stubenvoll	700
11.	Colonel Borseda	300
12.	Colonel Kein	300
13.	Mansfelders	400
14.	Hungarians	5,000
		10,100

Infantry

1.	Hohenlohe	2,000
2.	Thurn	2,200
3.	Kaplir	2,400
4.	Moravians	2,000
5.	Anhalt	1,000
6.	Weimar	600
7.	Royal company	200
8.	Upper Austrians	600
		11,000

Since the Hungarians were useless that day and 1,800 were killed in the game park, there were no more than 500 [sic] cavalry and around 8,000 infantry, along with six large guns at the battle. If only our men had held their ground, we would have been strong enough with God's help, thanks to the advantages we had.

Source: *Relation que Son altesse Monseigneur le Prince d'Anhalt, mon Père a faict après la Bataille de Prague*, printed in Anton Gindely (ed.), *Die Berichte über die Schlacht auf dem Weissen Berge bei Prag* (Vienna, 1877), pp. 118–28.

---

26. The 'Miracle of White Mountain'

[Composite broadsheet from 1622 showing the Statue of Our Lady and a portrait of Father Dominicus of Jesus Maria, born Domingo Ruzzola (1559–1630), confessor to Duke Maximilian of Bavaria. The left-hand image reproduces the image described below. The portrait of Dominicus shows him holding this image, while below him is a picture of the imperial and League troops routing the Bohemians.]

[Left-hand text:]
Image, or Picture
of the holy Virgin Mary, that stood with her eyes poked out by godless blasphemers in the town of Strakonitz in Bohemia, and was shown to the soldiers during the battle against His Imperial majesty's enemies outside Prague in 1620 by the honourable Father Dominico of Jesus Maria, a Descalced [barefoot] Carmelite, senior prior of Castle Carmelin. And this is the picture after which the swift victory is named: Our dear Lady of Victory. Afterwards this picture was richly decorated with precious gifts from His Imperial Majesty Ferdinand II, His Highness Duke Maximilian of Bavaria and other princes, and sent to Rome where it was crowned with a golden crown by the current pope Gregory XV in the presence of the entire clergy and cardinals in the Descalced Carmelite's church of St Paul at Monte Cavallo on 1 May 1622.

[Right-hand text:]
Image or accurate likeness
of the honourable Father Dominicus of Jesus Maria born in Aragon, of the order of the Holy Virgin Maria and senior prior of the Descalced Carmelites, who was sent by Pope Paul V to the serene prince, Duke Maximilian of Bavaria, and accompanied him in Bohemia to Prague. With a cross in his hand, this cleric raised the soldiers' hopes to victory, and with the special help and support of God and the Holy Mother, brought this memorable victory on 8 November 1620.

[Published] Augsburg, by Christoph Greutter, copper engraver at the Barfusser Gate by the ditch.

Source: John Roger Paas (ed.), *The German Political Broadsheet 1600–1700*, 6 vols (Wiesbaden, 1994), vol. IV, p. 124.

STABILISING THE HABSBURG MONARCHY

27. Catholic revenge, 30 November 1620

From Prague, 30 November 1620: The generally depressed and miserable situation here could not be more wretched. Our king continues to offer promises and much consolation, as well as paying the soldiers, but the opposite happens. There was no money to pay the soldiers before; now sufficiently large sums are found, but other people get them. There is no end to the plunder and murder here. They started by plundering the houses of the Directors and those of the Reformed faith. Now it is indiscriminate, with the same robbery in the streets. One neighbour betrays the other, the soldiers started, but now the inhabitants do it disguised as soldiers, the French, Poles and Germans as well, without end, breaking in at night and extorting money. Those who have nothing, fear for their necks, and all regret not taking up arms and fighting to the last man. The Bavarian prince has returned home, taking the English ambassador with him. Bucquoy will go to Moravia. The Moravian Prince of Liechtenstein[1] and Mr Dilli [Tilly] will remain here.

Source: A Berlin newspaper from 1620, quoted in Hans Jessen (ed.), *Der Dreißigjährige Krieg in Augenzeugenberichten* (Düsseldorf, 1963), pp. 93–4.

---

28. The Upper Austrian Peasants' Rising, 1626

[A composite broadsheet showing three of the peasant leaders. The figures on the left and right both hold flags bearing inscriptions, while the peasants' demands are printed below them.]

Upper Austrian Peasant Demands:
[the text above the figures reads:]
Psalm 37 The Lord helps the just. He is their strength in need. Psalm 20 We unfurl our flags in the name of our God.

[Text on left-hand flag:]
O dear Lord deliver us from the Bavarian's yoke and tyranny and his great butchery. Since it concerns the soul and possessions, so it concerns our bodies and blood, so God give us heroes' courage.

[Text on right-hand flag:]
It must be, Anno 1626.

The entire peasantry of Upper Austria present the following 12 articles to His Imperial Majesty:

1. The word of GOD.
2. The emperor should be lord, not the Bavarian prince.
3. The governor in Linz is to be abolished.
4. A provincial captain is to live in the province.
5. Lutheran judges and mayors are to be appointed in the towns, since the Catholics are not to be trusted.
6. The prelates are to be removed from the council and replaced by peasants, as is the custom in the Tirol.

---

[1] Karl von Liechtenstein (1569–1627) had tried to steer a middle course and prevent Moravia joining the revolt. He joined the imperial army as civil commissioner and was made governor of Bohemia after White Mountain. His subsequent reputation was mired by his role in the trial and execution of the rebels in 1621, and participation in the mint consortium and dubious land deals following the confiscation of rebel property.

7. That the soldiers are to be driven out of the land with sticks, then we peasants shall protect the land.
8. The garrisons in the towns are to be abolished, and some money be paid annually instead.
9. The Jesuitical clerics are to be removed from the province apart from the prelates.
10. A general pardon for all poor and rich, high and low.
11. The agreement promised by Emperor Matthias, that every lord can keep a pastor on his property.
12. All exiles to receive their entire property back and restored to peaceful possession.

Done in the country of Upper Austria.

Source: From an illustrated printed broadsheet, reproduced in John Roger Paas (ed.), *The German Political Broadsheet 1600–1700* (Wiesbaden, 1994), vol. IV, p. 232.

29. Counter Reformation: The 'Reformation Mandate for the Austrian Lands', 31 August 1628

Since our accession nothing has concerned us more than healing the division in belief in our Austrian lands and leading all our subjects on the path to salvation. Accordingly, we have remained lenient, gentle and patient towards our non-Catholic subjects of the Lordly and Knightly Estates and refrained from starting the Reformation against them in the hope that they would grasp our good intention, reflect on their eternal salvation and follow in the footsteps of their ancestors. We have also noticed that a good number of them have abandoned their error and returned to the ancient Catholic faith. However, there are a number left in whom our tolerance and leniency have not borne fruit. Because it is our princely office and duty to care for the salvation of our subjects, and because we wish no higher reward than this road to salvation for the noble families who have acquired fame through serving our ancestors and the fatherland and who have remained loyal and firm during the last rebellion, we hereby order that all are to rejoin us in the Catholic faith and the universal Christian Church within a year. Whoever does not do so, may not remain in the land and personally own his property, but must leave the land, sell his property and, if he cannot convert it into cash within six months, must hand it to his friends and relatives to sell. After six months it will be sold by the authorities. The entailed properties[1] are not to be sold, and

---

1   The practice of entail, called *Fideikommiß* in the Habsburg lands, allowed a noble family to place its property in a trust to be passed on to future generations through primogeniture. Each entail was approved and guaranteed by the monarch, without whose permission no part of the property could be sold.

the emigrants retain the revenue. In view of their loyalty to the House of Austria, no emigration fees or tenth penny shall be levied on these properties. The emigrants can continue their court cases through their friends, but may not take their wards with them, must renounce all debts and surrender foundation and church deeds. Furthermore, the emigrants may not travel in or out without special permission.

Source: Hans Jessen (ed.), *Der Dreißigjährige Krieg in Augenzeugenberichten* (Düsseldorf, 1963), pp. 122–3.

---

30. Posthumous judgement on Frederick V and the origins of the war, 1633

[Shortly after the news of Gustavus's death at the battle of Lützen] there came too assured news from Nayence [Mainz] of the King of Bohemia's death. When this unfortunate Prince was ready to take a new possession of his Countrey, and the conditions drawne up between him, the King of Sweden, and the Governour of Frankendale,[1] hee was surprised in Nayence with a contagious disease, presently after his return from Deux-ponts [Zweibrücken], where hee had visited a Prince of his alliance. The care and sufficiency of the Phisitian was so great, that he quickly expelled the pestilent quality, and set him in all appearance free from danger, but the great calamities through which he had passed, had much estranged his Constitution from its first puritie, and quite altered his colour and complexion. When he thought to quit his tedious bed, and take possession of Frankendale, it unfortunately happened that the King of *Sweden's* death came to his eare, which wrought so on his mind, and body, that his disease was aggravated, and his death ensued on the 29 of November. His death was much deplored by those of his blood, by his servants and subjects, yet did their griefe receive an allay by his devotion and his last words full of faith and pietie.

The life of this Prince was a meere Medley, and like a Picture with many faces. His entry into the Electorate was glorious, his beginning happy, his Vertues eminent, and courted hee was by the whole Empire. His Alliance, and his friends within and without Germany, the consideration of his House, of his Dominions, and the great Bodie that depended on his direction, were the cause of his election to the Crowne of *Bohemia*, which was fatall to him, and all *Germanie*, which felt the sad accidents that attended this Comet, and was foorthwith invaded by an universall Warre in her heart, and all her quarters, which hath never since forsooke her, having engaged all the Imperiall States and Provinces, every one whereof to this day carries her markes. And though this Prince hath sought all meanes of reconciliation, hoping that way to

---

[1]   The Palatine fortress of Frankenthal just west of the Rhine had been captured by the Spanish in 1623 and was held until the end of the war.

quench this Wild-fire; yet hath hee from time to time found such fatall oppositions, and such an ingrafted malice in the incensed partie, that all the motiones, propositions and intercessions of great Kings have hetherto beene unprofitable; and this good Prince hath been conshained to live an exile from his Countrey. At length when a most pleasing prospect laid at once open to his view the frontiers of his Country, and the end of his afflictions, a suddaine death deprived him of his sight, and the fruition of so delightfull an object.

The calamitie of this Prince hath given occasion to many licentious tongues, and pens to declaime against him, and unjustly to judge of his cause by the sad event. Those that were his most inward acquaintance, avow that hee was unfortunate beyond defect, and that the most magnanimous, and Heroicke soule could beare afflictions with no greater moderation and patience, then he did. If many of his vertues have beene clouded and obscured by his infelicity, yet are there more which his darker fortune could not hinder from shining forth, and striking envie blind. His great Family, his Extraction, his Allies and Confederates, and his Princely vertues me thinkes should have contained within the bounds of Honour, and truth, certaine Mercenary, Satyricke Spirits, who have common places of prayses, and Invectines, which they draw forth to exalt, or depresse whom they please, and mainctaine their looser vaine at the cost of Princes, and play upon their persons, qualities, and estates, whom the greatnesse of their births should priviledge from such contumelies. We owe honur, and respect to Princes of whatever party soever; whether they be Friends, Enemies, or Neuters: And I thought this short Apologie due to my so much deplored Subject, whom his miseries rendered to some contemptible, though by others he was truly honoured in the midst of his disgraces, and afflications. The King of Sweden gave many brave testimonies of him, being forced oftentimes to give him a stop in the carreere of honour, lest courage should engage him too farre, exhorting him to preserve his life, the good of his Countrey, and the publike cause.

Source: Anon., *The great and famous battel of Lutzen, ... here is also inserted ... a Relation of the King of* Bohemia's *Death* (1633), pp. 24–7.

5

Spain and the Netherlands

The Thirty Years War ran parallel to the second stage of the Eighty Years War, or Dutch Revolt against Spain. This began when Philip II of Spain (1527–98, r.1558) used force to silence protests over a wide range of religious, fiscal and political grievances in the Netherlands. Military repression radicalised opposition to Spanish rule and led to a protracted struggle from the 1560s. Spanish forces recovered control of the south (modern Belgium and Luxembourg) by 1585, prompting most of the Protestants there to flee to the north, or to England and Germany. However, the rebels remained defiant in the area north of the Rhine. Leadership of the revolt passed into the hands of Calvinist nobles and urban patricians, but the majority of the inhabitants of the seven northern provinces were still Catholic or Lutheran at this point. The leaders reorganised the north as an independent republic which secured de facto recognition from Protestant countries, but also Catholic Venice.

Philip II tried to resolve the dispute by granting autonomy to the southern Netherlands in the hope of attracting the north back to a looser association with Spain. He bequeathed the south to his favourite daughter, Isabella Clara Eugenie (1566–1633) and her Austrian husband Albert (1559–1621), younger brother of emperors Rudolf and Matthias. The couple ruled as the 'Archdukes' from 1599, but the Spanish Army of Flanders defending their possessions remained under direct control from Madrid. Isabella and her husband were unwilling to continue the costly and largely unpopular war. Their offer to negotiate met a positive response from the north where a peace party was gaining ground. The result was the Twelve Years Truce agreed in April 1609 which saw mixed results for the inhabitants of both parts of the Netherlands. Some prospered from renewed trade opportunities, while others suffered unwelcome competition from producers else-where whose goods had been embargoed during the war. Three additional groups in the north resented the Truce: radical Calvinists, exiles from the south hoping to recover their homes, and investors in maritime ventures who wanted to break into Spain's closed colonial markets.

The outbreak of the Bohemian Revolt intensified international interest in nego-tiations between Spain, the Archdukes and the Dutch to renew the Truce. The victory of the pro-war hardline Calvinist party in the north in 1619 made renewal unlikely [see Doc. 16], though the Dutch leadership continued to negotiate to deceive the Archdukes. Spain and the Dutch prepared for war from 1620 and the Truce was allowed to expire in April 1621. As war became obvious, the Dutch intensified efforts to persuade other countries that they had a common cause in opposing Spain [Doc. 31].

In a development paralleling events in the Dutch Republic, Spain's government passed into the hands of those favouring war after 1618. This party was led by Gaspar de Guzmán Count of Olivares (1585–1645) who became first minister after the accession of Philip IV in April 1621. Olivares was aware of his country's mounting economic and fiscal problems, but felt he could not accept the Dutch terms for extending the Truce without compromising Spain's prestige. Like many of his colleagues in the royal Council of State, Olivares believed a loss of reputation would undermine Spain's basis as a great power by alienating allies, encouraging other parts of its empire to revolt and prompting its numerous creditors to stop providing essential loans. All the councillors considered defence of Catholicism as essential to Spanish prestige and thus could not accept the Dutch Republic's refusal to halt harassment of its large Catholic population **[Doc. 32]**.

The Spanish–Dutch war after 1621 was a largely static affair. Both sides fielded powerful armies, but had to disperse their troops to hold the numerous fortresses along the Dutch–Belgian border. It often took an entire campaign just to capture one large fortress. To break the deadlock, the Dutch used their superior navy to attack Spain's colonies. Olivares responded with an elaborate strategy to strangle the Republic by surrounding it on land and sea, thereby cutting the international trade that sustained Dutch independence. Successes like the capture of Breda in 1625 encouraged Philip IV and Olivares to think they were winning **[Doc. 33]**, but it became increasingly obvious by the early 1630s that Spain could no longer carry the huge cost of the war **[Docs 34–6]**.

DUTCH POLICY

31. Memorial presented to James I's Privy Council, 15 February 1621

Milords:

We render our most humble thanks to His Majesty for the Public Audience which His Majesty most graciously accorded us, and inasmuch as it is His Majesty's good pleasure that we make further clarification before Your Excellencies and Lordships of the contents of our Instructions, we declare that, following the greeting made to His Majesty, we are charged to treat of affairs touching the general state of Christendom, and in particular the service of His Majesty, the state of the United Provinces, and that of their good Friends, Allies, and Confederates.

Milords the Estates General of the said Provinces[1] confess and recognize that the management of their state has largely, rather for the most part, depended on the royal care and authority of His Majesty, who by his prudent and salutary counsels has deigned to kindly assist them in their most urgent need, which truly royal benefice never has and never will be forgotten, but will remain imprinted in the hearts of the said Milords and of all their posterity.

---

[1] The Dutch Republic was divided into seven self-governing provinces which sent deputies to a council called the States General for external relations and other matters of common interest. The document uses the term 'Estates' when referring to the States General.

And now: to enter into the principal subject of this Embassy, Their Lordships have charged us to remonstrate that the goal and design of the King of Spain, with his adherents, does not tend to any other end than to extend under false pretext of religion, day by day, their unbridled ambition and domination, to the prejudice and hurt of His Majesty, the State of the United Provinces, and of their Friends, Allies, and Confederates,

Attempting by this means to pull by their lead-strings all the Roman Catholic clergy and the princes who are dependent on them in order to usurp an unjust monarchy over the whole of Europe, following the footsteps and designs of their predecessors,

To obviate which our said Lords the Estates, careful above all to support their Friends and Allies against the ambitious efforts of the said King, have furnished a very remarkable aid in money amounting to 50,000 florins [£5,000] per month to the King and the Estates of Bohemia, and a similar sum to the Princes of the Union, having continued the said contributions for the space of 19 entire months to the said King and Estates and of 11 months to the said Union,

Putting in the field, in addition, in the *Pays de Clèves*, near the City of Wesel, a very powerful army, under the conduct of Milord the Prince of Orange, to prevent the aid which, without this, the Archdukes of Austria would have sent from the Netherlands to the greater burden of the said Lord Princes,[2]

For the more certain defense of whom the said Milords the Estates have sent to them at the expense of their republic 34 mounted companies and six hundred elite troops from the best of their infantry, all under the personal command of the Lord Prince Henry of Nassau,[3]

For all of which tasks [performed] and efforts, however, Milords the Estates have not been sufficient by themselves to resist the Invasions of the enemies in Germany,[4]

But already, before the arrival of the said Lord Prince Henry, a large part of

---

[2] A reference to reinforcements sent to the Dutch-held towns in the duchy of Cleves and other posts on the Lower Rhine seized in 1614 during their intervention in the dispute over which German prince should inherit the duchies of Jülich, Berg, Cleves, Mark and their associated territories. These garrisons remained throughout the war and were only removed in 1672 following an agreement with Brandenburg-Prussia which had acquired Cleves and Mark.

[3] Frederick Henry (1583–1647), younger brother and eventual successor of Maurice of Nassau as commander of the Dutch army.

[4] The 'Invasions' refer to operations of Spain's Army of Flanders based in the Spanish (southern) Netherlands under Ambroglio di Spinola (1567–1630). Spain sent one contingent from its possessions in north Italy over the Alps to help the emperor directly in Bohemia in 1619. This contingent served with the imperial army until 1623 when it was withdrawn to the Spanish Netherlands. Meanwhile, Spinola moved about half of the Army of Flanders to the middle Rhine in 1620 where it had conquered the Lower Palatinate by 1623. Spanish troops remained in occupation of that part of the Lower Palatinate west of the Rhine until 1652, but did not otherwise assist the emperor again directly in the Empire until 1633–4.

the Electoral Palatinate had been seized, as are the Cities of Aitzem and Oppenheim, assigned in Domain to Madame the Electrice Palatine, Bachrach, Coub, Pfaltz, and several other Cities and territories appertaining to the Princes of the Union, to which they had no pretensions whatever, besides which, by violence and threats to put the remainder to the torch and the sword they have extorted the payment for their soldiers, putting to ransom in this way all the Wetteravie [Wetterau] and a good part of the County of Hannau and of Hesse.

[Then the deputies, speaking not as humble suppliants but as parties to a previous agreement, brought that agreement up:] But seeing that the said Milords the Estates, by the proposition of Milord Carleton, His Majesty's Honorable Ambassador, made in their assembly the list of October of the past year, received the boon of being advised of the good resolution which it had pleased His Majesty to take for the defense of the liberty of Germany and the recovery of the Palatinate, the said proposition being confirmed by several advices of [Noël Caron] Seigneur de Schoonewalle, Ambassador in Ordinary to His Majesty,

The said Milords the Estates thank His Majesty for this most humbly, with the firmest assurance that lie, as an all-powerful and all-wise prince, will have the said resolution earnestly executed, opposing himself with simple courage to the efforts of the enemies in order to recover that which they have unjustly seized, and that by this means will be cast into confusion all those who have no other end but to subject the whole world to the whip and trample under foot all law and Justice, in order to attain such an unjust [universal] monarchy,

Following which the said Milords the Estates resolved to second the good and heroic resolution of His Majesty by the continuation of the aforesaid assistances, although in truth the charges which a war of 40 years against so powerful a king has left on their hands are so extremely great, and weigh heavily upon them still, as would be the case for anyone who, for their own defense, find themselves constrained to undertake at their expense the number of some 40,000 foot and 40 companies of cavalry, besides the ordinary charges of the navy and the excessive annual [expenses of defending their shipping] against the pirates,

Our Instructions further include [instructions] to point out with the utmost reverence how it has pleased His Majesty to recommend, advance, and conclude the treaty of the truce between the King of Spain, the Archdukes, and the Republic of the United Provinces to restore her to a firm and assured state, but under caution and promise of His Majesty as well as the Most Christian King, that all the contents of the said treaty would be punctually observed,

Notwithstanding which, the said King of Spain and Archdukes have contravened the said treaty of Truce in several points, having had arrested in their kingdoms and lands without any reason the goods, merchandise, and ships of subjects of the United Provinces, constraining the officers to accept sale of their ships and to serve them without any pay or recompense, the damages suffered by the said subjects, with their interest, amounting to the sum of 2,111,147 florins [£211,114/14s] according to the full accounting.

And although the said Milords the Estates by earnest letters to the King of Spain and the Archdukes have requested reparation of the said damages and interest they have not up till now [sought to rectify] these extortions and injuries [themselves, as would be reasonable], neither ways nor means was lacking to the said Milords the Estates; if they have always nevertheless preferred the respect due to His Majesty and found it more proper to have him particularly informed of the said contraventions, [it was] to the end that [it be] by his royal authority [that] the said torts and damages be amended, upon which we have express commission to hear the good pleasure of His Majesty.

Further, as the time of the Truce is expiring and with it the alliances and close relations between His Majesty and the said Milords the Estates, their Lordships have charged us to enter into most earnest communication on this with His Majesty to hear the overtures which it shall please His Majesty to offer us on this subject.

We beseech finally in all reverence that it please His Majesty in his grace to grant us Benefice and benign dispatch in all the above, for which the said Milords Estates will be found greatly obliged to His Majesty, in view especially of the expiration of the said Truce and the little time [five days short of two months] that remains to them to take up arms and put themselves in a posture of good and effective resistance. [Signed by the six deputies and Noël Caron.]

Source: Memorial presented to the British Privy Council on 15 February 1621 by six Dutch deputies and Noël Caron, the Dutch resident in London; translated and printed in Charles Howard Carter, *The Secret Diplomacy of the Habsburgs, 1598–1625* (Columbia, 1964), pp. 223–6.

RESUMPTION OF THE DUTCH WAR, 1621

32. Spain's reasons for war: Olivares to Philip IV, 28 November 1621

Almost all the kings and princes of Europe are jealous of your greatness. You are the main support and defence of the Catholic religion; for this reason you have renewed the war with the Dutch and with other enemies of the church who are their allies; and your principal obligation is to defend yourself and to attack them.

Source: Quoted in John Lynch, *The Hispanic World in Crisis and Change 1598–1700* (Oxford, 1992), p. 94.

---

33. Philip IV's assessment of Spain's achievements by 1626

Our prestige has been immensely improved. We have had all Europe pitted against us, but we have not been defeated, nor have our allies lost, whilst our enemies have sued me for peace. Last year, 1625, we had nearly 300,000 infantry and cavalry in our pay, and over 500,000 men of the militia under arms, whilst the fortresses of Spain are being put into a thorough state of defence. The fleet, which consisted of only seven vessels on my accession, rose at one time in 1625 to 108 ships of war at sea, without counting the vessels at Flanders, and the crews are the most skilful mariners this realm ever possessed. Thank God, our enemies have never captured one of my ships, except a solitary hulk. So it may truly be said that we have recovered our prestige at sea; and fortunately so, for, lacking our sea power, we should lose not only all the realms we possess, but religion even in Madrid itself would be ruined.

This year of 1626 we have had two royal armies in Flanders and one in the Palatinate, and yet all the power of France, England, Sweden, Venice, Savoy, Denmark, Holland, Brandenburg, Saxony, and Weimar could not save Breda from our victorious arms. We have held our own against England, both with regard to the marriage and Cadiz; and yet, with all this universal conspiracy against us, I have not depleted my patrimony by 50,000 ducats. It would be impossible to believe this if I did not see it with my own eyes, and that my realms are all quiet and religious. I have written this paper to you to show you that I have done my part, and have put my own shoulder to the wheel without sparing sacrifice. I have spent nothing unnecessary upon myself, and I have made Spain and myself respected by my enemies.

Source: Philip IV's assessment of Spain's achievements presented to the Council of Castile in 1626; quoted in Martin Hume, *The Court of Philip IV: Spain in Decadence* (London, 1907), pp. 156–8.

SPAIN'S DIFFICULTIES

34. Spanish wealth: remittances of precious metal from the New World, 1571–1660

Period	Bullion production	Ships sailing	Spanish receipts	Crown receipts
1571–5	21.6		19.7	
1576–80	44.4		28.5	
1581–5	49.0		48.6	

[1] Amounts in millions of pesos. The number of ships sailing is the total crossing the Atlantic in both directions in that period. There was an average of 548 sailings every five years between 1600 and 1650. The total tonnage crossing in 1606–10 was 273,560, compared with 121,308 in 1646–50.

Period	Bullion production	Ships sailing	Spanish receipts	Crown receipts
1586–90	61.5	886	39.4	
1591–5	59.3		58.2	
1596–1600	51.6		57.0	10.9
1601–5	39.5		44.9	6.5
1606–10	43.1	965	52.2	
1611–15	61.6		40.6	7.2
1616–20	63.1	867	49.8	4.3
1621–5	77.9	775	44.7	
1626–30	48.9	558	41.3	
1631–5	57.9		28.3	average 4.0
1636–40	64.8		27.0	
1641–5	61.4		22.8	
1646–50	45.0	366	19.5	1.6
1651–5	62.1		12.1	
1656–60	46.9		5.6	0.6

Source: Compiled from S.J and B.H. Stein, *Silver, Trade and War: Spain and America in the Making of Early Modern Europe* (Baltimore, 2000), p. 24, and John Lynch, *The Hispanic World in Crisis and Change 1598–1700* (Oxford, 1992), pp. 48, 241, 267–8.

35. Spanish Expenditure 1621–40 (millions of ducats)

Item	Total amount	Annual average
Direct on the military	44.225	3.145
Asientos[1]	175.775	8.789
Non-military expenditure	30.552	1.528
Total	250.552	13.462 (= 21.4 million fl)

Source: Compiled from Hildegard Ernst, *Madrid und Wien 1632–1637: Politik und Finanzen in den Beziehungen zwischen Philipp IV und Ferdinand II* (Münster, 1991), pp. 262–3, covering payments through the Hacienda Real.

---

[1] Asientos were bankers' contracts. Payments under this heading included interest on loans and capital repayment.

36. Fiscal–military problems: the English ambassador's view, April 1634

This great ship [Spain] contains much water [money], but many leaks, and is always dry. It is certain that they have made loans this year for 13 millions [ducats], and are still treating for more, yet at the end of the year they will neither have money in their purse, nor army paid, nor nobody contented; which is to be attributed to the hard terms wherewith they do their business. For being masters of the mines of gold and silver, and without having but few friends, nobody will serve them but for their interests: and their own subjects are so well conceited of themselves, as they think they cannot be paid enough.

In their present levies, though they are sorry men, they give them 3 reales a day, which is 18 pence English, and yet have all they can do to keep them from running away. Subjects are fearfully hard pressed. The hard wage of business men in the Indian trade had made concealment general, which has greatly reduced the revenue of the crown. Great measures were taken to discover the unregistered treasure in the last fleet, and they found 600,000 ducats, and will yet find more. But this again will stop trade.

Source: Sir Arthur Hopton to the secretary of state, London, April 1634, quoted in Martin Hume, *The Court of Philip IV: Spain in Decadence* (London, 1907), pp. 277–8.

6

The war in western and northern Germany 1621–9

The defeat at White Mountain ended Frederick V's rule in Bohemia and left him a fugitive dependent on handouts from the parsimonious Dutch and his British in-laws. The war continued because he refused to accept the loss of his electoral title and half his Palatine lands as Ferdinand II's price for a pardon. The 'Palatine Cause' became a rallying cry for all those hostile to the Habsburgs, since war in the Empire distracted Spain from its campaign against the Dutch and prevented Austria from assisting Philip IV. Various minor German princes also rallied to Frederick V for a variety of personal, political and confessional reasons, and raised troops from their own resources and by plundering neighbouring Catholic terri-tories. Bavaria continued to back Ferdinand, because it was the chief beneficiary of the emperor's desire to punish the Palatinate. The Catholic League army under Count Jean Tserclaes de Tilly (1559–1632), reinforced by Spanish and imperial contingents, advanced against Frederick's forces defending the Lower Palatinate on the middle Rhine. Frederick's commander was Count Ernst von Mansfeld (1580–1626), a brilliant organiser but a poor general who pursued his own secret negotiations with the Habsburgs, hoping for better rewards. Frederick was unable to pay Mansfeld's army properly and it quickly acquired notoriety for its plunder-ing and extortion [see Doc. 121].

Fighting on the Rhine attracted considerable attention outside the Empire. Many commentators saw the conflict in purely sectarian terms as a struggle between the shining light of the true Protestant faith against evil Catholic tyranny. At least this is how it appeared to many in Britain who could not understand why their king James I did not support his son-in-law more forcefully. The different perspectives are exemplified in the diverging accounts of the campaign's first battle at Mingolsheim on 27 April 1622 [Docs 37–8]. Tilly caught the rearguard of Mansfeld's retreating army beyond a stream at Mingolsheim village. Though Mansfeld repulsed the initial attack, he continued his fairly disorderly retreat later that day. Like the complaint from the Austrian Estates [see Doc. 8], the Protestant pamphlet [Doc. 38] makes it clear that accusations of atrocities were present from the start of the war, and not merely in its final, allegedly more destructive, stage.

Tilly's victories at Mingolsheim, Wimpfen (1622), Höchst (1622) and Stadtlohn (1623) secured control of the Lower as well as the Upper Palatinate and enabled Duke Maximilian of Bavaria to extract his promised reward from

Ferdinand II. Despite Saxon misgivings, the emperor enfeoffed Maximilian with the Palatine lands and title in 1623, confirming this five years later [**Docs 39–40**].

The activities of Frederick V's German supporters spread the war northwards into Westphalia and Lower Saxony after 1622. Tilly's victories raised fears that Ferdinand might renounce the Mühlhausen guarantee [**see Doc. 22**] and evict the Protestant administrators from the north German bishoprics – not least because one of them, Christian of Brunswick-Wolfenbüttel (1599–1626), administrator of Halberstadt, had commanded Frederick's army which had been defeated at Stadtlohn. As the self-proclaimed protector of German Lutheranism and with a direct stake in the north German church lands where two of his sons were administrators, King Christian IV of Denmark (1577–1648, r.1588) decided to intervene in June 1625. Operations quickly stalled as the Danes opened negotiations, but their presence in the Empire was welcomed by England, France and the Dutch who all opposed the Habsburgs. These powers decided to back Christian in the Hague Alliance [**Doc. 41**], prompting him to resume his campaign. Actual assistance fell far short of what was promised [**Doc. 42**], contributing to the disastrous Danish defeat at Lutter in 1626.

Danish intervention was largely unwelcome to the north German Protestant princes who recognised that it increased, rather than lessened, the likelihood of Ferdinand disregarding the Mühlhausen guarantee. Their attempt at armed neutrality merely fuelled the emperor's suspicions that they were actively assisting the Danes [**Doc. 43**]. Despite the scale of the imperial victory which spread in 1627 as mainland Denmark was conquered, the imperial commander Wallenstein [**see Docs 47–52**] urged lenient terms [**Doc. 44**] that were eventually granted in the Peace of Lübeck [**Doc. 45**].

Ferdinand regarded Christian of Halberstadt and the other Germans who had backed Frederick V and Denmark as rebels to be punished like those in Bohemia, through the confiscation of their property and its redistribution to loyal Habsburg supporters. This process had already begun in 1627, fuelling Protestant fears that the emperor really intended to destroy their entire faith [**Doc. 46**].

WAR REPORTING: TWO CONTRASTING VIEWS OF THE BATTLE OF MINGOLSHEIM, 1622

37. Memoirs of a Catholic participant: Augustin Fritsch[1]

Because it was now winter we were moved into quarters, with my colonel's regiment at Ladenburg, two [German] miles below Heidelberg. The following spring, Anno 1622, we took the field early and chased the Mansfelders back

---

[1] Augustin Fritsch (1599–1662), a Bavarian from a relatively humble background, joined the Bavarian army as a musketeer in 1618 and served throughout the war, participating in 12 battles and the capture of 75 towns. He reached the rank of colonel and was ennobled. After the war, he served as district official and commandant of Parkstein in the Upper Palatinate.

from Wiesloch to Mingolsheim, a fine, long village, which the Mansfelders set on fire. We were ordered with our regiment through the burning village. As soon as we arrived on the field with the first squadron, we were attacked by several regiments of cavalry that had been hidden behind a hill, and which set about us so severely that we had to retreat through the burning village again. We could not counter-attack and had to stand there till evening because of the fire and the high water – there had been such a terrible rain shortly before, as if the clouds had burst.[2]

We then marched through the night, because our general [Tilly] had received word that the Margrave of Durlach[3] and his army was approaching our rear. We arrived in Winsen at daybreak. We rested there a few hours. The place was garrisoned by 300 men from all regiments under Major Jung from the Hasslang Regiment. We marched onwards to Wimpfen, where we rested two days in the gardens while the boat bridge was built. Then we crossed the Neckar where we stayed a few days and entrenched until the Durlacher arrived.[4]

Source: Fritsch's autobiography in Karl Lohmann (ed.), *Die Zerstörung Magdeburgs von Otto von Guericke und andere Denkwürdigkeiten aus dem Dreißigjährigen Kriege* (Berlin, 1913), pp. 239–40.

---

38. A Protestant pamphlet

Count Mansfield, Generall of the King of Bohemia's Army in the Field, having received intelligence, that the Baron de Tilly (Generall of the Bavarian Army) sought all the meanes hee could choise, to bring this remainder of the Lower Palatinate (which yet continueth in the King's hand) under the Bavarian subjection, intending, before all else, to take in Heydelburgh, the chie[fe]st Twone thereof, and (for that end) surprised some other smaller Townes, as Hilspach and Neckergemone, distant a little mile from Heydelburgh, and lying upon the Necker with more then Turkish or barbarian cruelty he did there put them all to the Sword, making no spare either of Man or Woman, old or young, that bee and the Spaniards had set to with their rest and full account, to have the whole Lower Palatinate (in a very short space) subjected under their obedience.

Hereupon Count Mansfield accompanied with Sir Horatio Vere,[1] worthily

---

2   Mingolsheim stood along a small stream that the rain had turned into a marsh.

3   Georg Friedrich of Baden-Durlach had declared for Frederick V shortly before and began operations in support of Mansfeld's army.

4   Fritsch goes on to recount the battle of Wimpfen, 6 May 1622, in which the Margrave's army was totally destroyed by Tilly.

1   Sir Horace de Vere (1565–1635) commanded the 2,250 English auxiliaries sent by James I to assist Frederick V in 1620. The English technically served as volunteers, allowing

determined, with all their powers to withstand their intrusion; and therefore made ordination of their Armies (being in readines) to march neere, and to resist the said De Tilly.

But then considering, that Turlach, the Marquesse of Baden, being their neighbour, not having as yet shewne himselfe, which side he favoured and inclined unto, they judged it very fit and convenient, before they presumed on the enterprise; to moove the said Marquesse (as their friend and Neighbour) to lend his helping hand, so Christianlike and necessary a businesse duely considered against the precedent barbarian cruelty.

When the noble Marquesse, with a valiant and heroyick spirit, shewed himselfe willing so to doe: upon a Military Councell, first holden, it was concluded that the said Marques should quarter himselfe on the frontiers on the Palatinate, along by the Bayliwicke of Bretten and so farre as to Winxsen, a small Emperiall Towne upon the Necker, to the intent, that if the Enemy came to make his retreat there both his owne Country and that of Wertenberg, might by him bee freed and defended against the said Bavarian Army, which mustered itselfe together from Kreyckaw [the Kraichgau], towards the aforesaid Town of Wisloch, a place of good and great advantage, for him that could winne first possession thereof, by reason of the narrow passages, and a small River running by it.

While they were seriously imployed about this busines, Count Mansfield the Generall was prepared to march forward, intending to passe over the Rhine, and set upon the said Bavarians: On a sudden, the king of Bohemia himselfe in person (in very apt time, & before noone) came that day to Germmersheim; having formerly past through France, Loraine, and the Garrisons of Leopoldus and the Spaniards, in unknowne and disguised apparell. There he found an Ambassador, that had bin sent from the Infanta, whose onely message was, to intreat and perswade the said Count Mansfield, to leave & forsake the King of Bohemia; whereto he returned a rough answer, and so sent him away, resolving to proceed on in the former intended enterprise.

Count *Mansfield* having taken good order, for defence of the places belonging to the Palatinate, along by the river or Rhine: his forces & military preparations, which were on this side of the Rhine, he caused to March directly towards the Enemy, who lay encamped in the way to Kreyckaw, upon a mount and in the vineyards hard by the Towne of Wisloch, wherewith (at the first) he shot at the King of Boehemia's forces, which was on Thursday in the Evening, but did them no hurt. In the meane while, the King's Dragons skirmished with the Enemy, and tooke some of them Prisoners: but they could not get to the Enemies quarter, in regard of the narrow passages, wherefore because it was night, they were constrained to retire into Mengelsheim, a Village distant halfe a mile from thence, where now they lodge.

The next day being the 17 day of Aprill (the day of Battaile) the Army being

James to avoid formal involvement in the war and to pursue negotiations with Spain and Austria for a peaceful solution to the conflict.

ranged in good order for Fight, the Vanguard marched (led by the Duke of Weymar, Linistar, Obertrant, and the Earle of Ortenberg)[2] before Noone towards the enemy, as hoping to set upon him. But the Enemy having advantage of the Countryes scituation (which was no meane helpe to him) set furiously on them with all his Regiments, and in such sort, as, although they carried themselves valiantly; yet after they had long withstood the Enemies great power, & done them much harme, they were forced to retire with losse of about 45 men, Captaine Berlenger being one amongst them. And because the way was so straight and narrow, and the Horse paced close together in the retreat, the Switzers Regiment was somewhat hard prest on with losse of about 21 men. Therefore all the men that were lost on the Kings side, in the first fight and retreat.

The enemy being puft up with pride, upon this small advantage and successe, followed them, and changed the place of his Campe, overtaking (in the retrait) a wagon with two sicke *Switzers* in it, that could not soone enough shift for themselves. And to make apparence of his rage and crueltie, himselfe set fire to the wagon, that they might endure the more mercilesse death. Now he perswaded himself upon this poore retrait, that he had already obtained the victory; which made him crie out in a braverie: *Go on, go on, march onward, for they are ours, they are all ours.* And although the weather was exceeding foule, yet notwithstanding he used such diligence, that he got the means to place his Ordenance on a hillock beyond *Meugelsheim,* and in such a convenient place, as he shot from thence into the Kings army, but yet did them no hurt, because (from thenece) they could not well see it.

After noone, Count *Mansfield* the Generall, appointed the army to march from *Meugelsheim* aforsaid, and to take a convenient place behind the said village, in order of battell, where likewise the Ordenance was planted on a place of good advantage, to hurt the enemie. He perceiving that the Kings forces were gone from the said village, became verily perswaded that they were fled and gone, as possessed with no meane error and feare. And this perswasion was the more confidently embraced, because Count *Mansfield* had set the sayd village on fire; which was done by him to no other end, but, by meanes of the smoke, to muffle the ememyes sight, for the better clouding of his army, that the forme and condition thereof might not be discerned, untill he had settled it in a convenient place for the battell.

No sooner was the Generall gone from the village, but the enemy came & tooke it, although he was to make his way through a narrow passage, and likewise over a small bridge, upon which, not about five or six horsemen could ride in ranke; yet he made such haste, that he brought foure peeces of ordenance beneath the said village, & planted them on a small hillocke. There also he caused his Regiments to passe over the said bridge, to pursue the King of

---

[2] Duke Friedrich of Weimar (1596–1622), Lieutenant Colonel Klaus von Linstow, Colonel Johann Michael Obentraut and Colonel Heinrich Count of Ortenberg all commanded cavalry regiments in Mansfeld's army.

Bohemiaes armie; which hee thought was partly put to flight, because from thence he could not discerne it. So that all the chiefe Commanders placed themselves in the forefront of the battel, to expresse their forwardnesse and to win bootie.

When the King of *Bohemiaes* Armie was ordered in due formee for battell, the King himselfe and the Generall *Mansfield* rode round about it, exhorting them to valiant & manly behaviour, and to win againe with a sprightfull recoverie, the honor lost at *Wittenberg* [White Mountain] by *Prague*. Count *Mansfield* like a brave Generall, marching in the front of the Armie, once more moved his souldiers to carie themselves boldly and couragiously, for now they had time best fitting for it, when in the King's owne sight and presence they might make rare expression of their valour, as often before (in divers good opportunities) they had worthily done. And now the King himselfe was royally resolved to fight in person with them; not doubting but (by Gods help) he should have the victory. So he caused the Vanguard to march on, being led directly upon the enemie; & one of his ordenance having twise discharged conveniently on the enemie, the said Vanguard made a valiant assault; yet seeming as if they retired againe, the enemie pursued; but were so suddenly and fiercely assailed by the rest of Count *Mansfields* forces, as they were enforced to a disordered retyring, hoping thereby to save themselves: but by reason of the little bridge, and so strict narrownesse of the passage, within a quarter of an houres space, or thereabout, the enemy found himselfe so confounded and overthrowne, that he lost above 2000 men in the field, as the prisoners (among which were divers principall Officers, as the Sergeant Major, the Provost Generall, *Harsels* Colonell of *Wersbergh* [Würzburg], Lieutenant of the troupes of horse, and many other officers) themselves confesse.

The enemy lost eight Cornets, and among them two great Standards or Banners, one of white Damaske, wherein were these words *In Domino spenantesin eo non confunsantur*. The other Standard was of red Damaske, having on the one side a blacke Eagle, and on the other side the Armes of *Bavaria*, with the *Golden Fleece* round about it, and under it was written, *Adiutorium Domini sit inimicis terror*. In a third great Cornet, much spoyled, there stood *Fortune*, but it was so torne and tottered, that the Moto could not be read.

There were also six Ensignes of footmen found, but so much spoyled with raine and mire, that they could not be knowne. Besides, they found a great number of horses, good store of gold, silver, and other stuffe. Afterwards, there arose up some few souldiers from among the dead bodies, and one among the rest was *De Tillies* Chamberlain, sore wounded, who being demanded, where his Maister was, answered, If he be not among y dead bodies, he is sore wounded; for he had bin by him in the Vanguard having there received some wounds. In the body of the battel, there were many Commanders slain, & 4 peeces of ordnance take from them. It is written out of the army, that *Henrick Maximilian*, Baron of *Papenheim*, an Apostat, was also slain.[3]

---

[3] Gottfried Heinrich Count Pappenheim (1594–1632) had been raised as a Protestant, but converted to Catholicism after 1614 and vowed in 1620 to suffer a wound for every year

The victory being thus won, the Kings army stood in order of battell till nine of the clock at night, in which time the King himselfe visited the Regiments with a chearfull countenance, thanking them for their valiant cariage in that notable accident. After that, he retired and marched with the Vanguard to *Langebrucehn*, a burnt village, from whence (after he had refreshed himselfe about two houres, and written certaine letters, which he sent by Post to his friends, to let them understand his victory) he went to *Brussell* [Bruchsal]. And Generall *Mansfield* with the Rereguard, two houres and an half after, followed him, and arived there about breake of day.

The prisoners freeely acknowledge, that according to mans judgement, and the situation of their camp, it was reputed impossible for them to lose the battell: but they ascribe it to the permission of God, that would have it to be so.

Source: Anon., *A true relation of all such battailes as have been fought in the Palatinate, since the King's arrival there, untill this present the 24 of May* (London, 1622), pp. 1–10.

THE CONTROVERSY OVER THE PALATINE LANDS AND TITLE

39. Saxon concerns, 1621

Notes from correspondence:

1. That Archduke Karl's[1] forthcoming visit to the elector of Saxony may assist the negotiations over the transfer of the electoral title.

2. The English ambassador[2] attending the emperor is pressing strongly for the arms taken up against the Elector Palatine to be laid down. Are the weapons now to be laid down at this point? His Grace[3] has armed and is prepared to invade the Upper Palatinate and it is to be hoped the enemy will be damaged thereby.

3. Electoral Saxon concerns as to why the emperor cannot sequestrate the Palatinate himself, still less grant it to another without the consent of the other electors: (1) religion, (2) the authority which he possesses in the Empire, (3) the balance to be preserved between the three Catholic and three non-Catholic electors, (4) the [potential] increase in the emperor's power and the

---

he had lived as a heretic. He commanded a Bavarian cavalry regiment at Mingolsheim, but in fact escaped death only to be killed at Lützen (see **Doc. 93**).

[1]   Karl Joseph (1590–1624), bishop of Brixen and Breslau, younger brother of Emperor Ferdinand II.

[2]   John Digby, first earl of Bristol (1580–1653).

[3]   Duke Maximilian, who was with the army at this point.

reduction of that of the electors, (5) the entire way in which the electors should deal with the emperor in such matters.

Source: Diary entry for 14 September 1621 by Johann Christoph von Preysing (1576–1632), an official accompanying the Bavarian army and who was made Governor of the Upper Palatinate after its conquest; in J. Staber (ed.), 'Die Eroberung der Oberpfalz im Jahre 1621 nach dem Tagebuch des Johann Christoph von Preysing', *Verhandlungen des historischen Vereins für Oberpfalz und Regensburg*, 104 (1964), pp. 185–6.

40. Deed of enfeoffment from Emperor Ferdinand II, 25 February 1623

We Ferdinand the Second by the grace of God Elected Roman Emperor, permanent enlarger of the Empire etc., announce publicly by this letter and inform all how we are inclined from innate goodwill and imperial mildness to share our imperial grace to each and every one of our and the Holy Roman Empire's subjects and loyal followers. This is especially the case for those who are the closest supports of our self and the Holy Empire helping to carry its burdens and cares through loyal service, and who thereby display particular diligence on behalf of others. On the twenty-ninth of January in the year 1621, we publicly declared and placed Frederick Count Palatine of the Rhine, the then Elector, under our and the Holy Imperial Ban for having, in the years immediately preceding, been the principal instigator and ringleader of the most disgraceful and dangerous rebellion, the like of which has never been seen nor experienced in the Empire of the German Nation ... and thereby according to the law deprived him of his electorate of the Palatinate, together with the office of Arch Seneschal[1] and the associated electoral title, as well as his other principalities and lordships, regalia, fiefs, dignities, rights and jurisdictions that he held from us and the Holy Empire.

Since His Highness high-born Duke Maximilian of Bavaria etc. made himself worthy to us and the Holy Empire by displaying due loyalty and constant obedience to us as the embattled and insulted overlord, emperor and lord throughout the entire duration of the above mentioned rebellion, and willingly, bravely and successfully provided his person, property and blood, as well as his land and people, and, together with other loyal, obedient electors and Estates, assisted us in recovering our hereditary kingdom and lands, and persistently pursued the above-mentioned declared outlaw and his rebellious followers in accordance with our imperial order and defeated his assembled army with the help of God's grace and support, and thereafter spared no energy, effort, work, care or expense to preserve our due imperial authority,

---

[1] Each of the electoral titles was associated with a particular 'arch' or hereditary office in the imperial court. A seneschal was a bailiff or agent who looked after a lord's estate, so the Elector Palatine was formally the emperor's chief representative in the Empire.

suppress the oft-mentioned outlaw and rebels ... and in view of other excellent reasons, we have decided to enfeoff the aforementioned Duke of Bavaria with the Palatine electoral title, office of Arch Seneschal, as well as the vicariate,[2] seat, voice and vote all left vacant through the proscription of the above-mentioned Count Palatine Frederick. And to do so in a manner that the said enfeoffment through us and the Holy Empire does not prejudice the rights of the children of the proscribed Count Palatine Frederick, nor his brother Count Palatine Ludwig Philipp, nor our cousin and brother-in-law Count Palatine Wolfgang Wilhelm and other heirs ...[3]

[The rest instructs all to respect this enfeoffment on pain of a fine of 1,000 marks of gold, and then lists the other electors and princes present in Regensburg when the act was carried out.]

By the authority of this letter signed in our own hand and sealed with the attached golden bull. Done in our and the Holy Imperial City of Regensburg, 25 February 1623.

Source: Karl Zeumer (ed.), *Quellensammlung zur Geschichte der deutschen Reichsverfassung in Mittelalter und Neuzeit* (Tübingen, 1913), pp. 394–5.

DANISH INTERVENTION

41. The Treaty of the Hague, 29 November 1625

[The preamble refers to the dangers to the imperial constitution posed by the spread of war – dangers that also threaten other states. Therefore, the signatories felt obliged:] to intervene at the right time to prevent the all too violent and unbearable progress of these bad intentions and oppressions, to restore and conserve the aforementioned freedom, the rights and constitutions of the Empire against the foreseeable ruin and to oppose all those who currently or in the future cause such trouble.

[Then follows a list of the alliance partners and their representatives: George Villiers, Duke of Buckingham for Great Britain; Denmark, and the Dutch Republic. These representatives had met frequently in The Hague and had agreed on the following articles:]

I. First, there shall be a firm, durable and permanent alliance between their Highnesses the Kings of Great Britain and Denmark, and their Lordships of the States General of the United Netherlands.

II. To remedy the above mentioned evil, His Highness the King of Denmark shall maintain an army of 28 to 30,000 foot soldiers and 7 to 8,000 horses in

---

[2] That is, the rights of imperial vicar associated with the Palatine electoral title.
[3] All relations of Frederick who had a common male ancestor.

the field, provided his confederates support him in sufficient and appropriate manner.

III. His Majesty the King of Great Britain shall assist the king with 300,000fl per month, payable precisely every month in Hamburg, the month being reckoned 32 days.

IV. His Majesty of Great Britain, in accordance with his alliance with their aforementioned Lordships of the States General, will in addition put an appropriate fleet to sea, to join that which is already there, and thereby divert the operations of the enemy and hinder them.

V. Their aforementioned Lordships of the States General shall assist His Majesty of Denmark with 50,000fl a month, the month being reckoned as above. In addition, they shall launch a goodly cavalcade or cavalry raid to divert the enemy from the said [Danish] army, if their circumstances permit it and if the enemy forces approach and advance against the army of the King of Denmark. Furthermore, they shall raise and contribute their part of the above-mentioned fleet of the King of Great Britain in the coming summer, and put as many infantry and cavalry into the field as possible, to form a good field camp and to prevent their enemies sending reinforcements against the above-mentioned army of the King of Denmark.

VI. None of the confederates shall leave this alliance, until through God's grace, the above-mentioned [peace and order] is restored in Germany.

[Art. VII stated that the allies could only receive written correspondence with the enemy and were to agree answers with their partners. Art. VIII obliged each ally to assist the others with all available means if they were attacked on account of this alliance. Art. IX reaffirmed that the agreed terms were binding, including on the King of Denmark.]

X. And since His Highness the Most Christian Majesty of France has seen fit to send two of his ministers to the King of Denmark to seek his help in providing the means against the harmful machinations and oppressions in the Empire. Many offers of help were made to this request, so that the burdens can be borne. Therefore, the said Most Christian King shall be asked at the earliest opportunity to join this alliance, or to contribute voluntarily good subsides to support the army of the King of Denmark, in accordance with his royal offer and in agreement with the other confederates, who have joined together in the common good.

XI. And His Highness the King of Sweden has also made various offers and declarations of his favourable inclination towards this alliance. Therefore, His Majesty shall also be invited to join the alliance and, in accordance with the said offer, to help it.

XII. The serene Venetian Republic and the Duke of Savoy shall be invited to join and take part.

XIII. The electors of Germany and the other princes, Estates and cities that are interested, shall also be invited to join.

XIV. This alliance shall be notified to the Prince of Transylvania, to ascertain whether His Highness finds it appropriate to join and to contribute to the common good.

XV. This alliance shall not alter the agreement made between His Majesty of Great Britain and their Lordships of the States General, which shall remain unchanged in its present form.[1]

[Art. XVI stated that ratification was to be exchanged by 20 March 1626 at the latest.]

Source: Laurs   Laursen   (ed.),   *Danmark–Norges   Traktater   1523–1750* (Copenhagen, 1916), vol. III, pp. 638–42.

-----

42. Satire on the ineffectiveness of the Hague Alliance

The assistance His Majesty will receive against the emperor.

1. The fugitive elector Palatine sends 20 cwt of green cheese from Holland, where he is and has been working to obtain it.
2. England sends 1,000 tobacco pipes and 4 pairs of comedians.
3. Savoy sends 100 hecklers and 20 mousetraps.
4. Norway sends 30 loads of fish.
5. Switzerland sends 1,000 nubile milk maids.
6. Holland sends 50 sacks of pepper it captured in the West Indies.
7. Venice sends 100 loads of soap and 400 wineglasses.
8. From Lapland are coming 15 magicians who can make a good wind and fog, to confuse their enemies when they need to escape.
9. Finland sends 200 reindeer, so they can make a quick getaway.
10. Greenland sends 100 seals so they have something to smear on their boots when they have eaten all the bacon.
11. The Muscovites send 1,000 white fox pelts.
12. From France 10 Huguenots from La Rochelle to teach them how to be disloyal and to rebel against the authorities.
13. Bethlen sends two dozen letters he has exchanged with the Turks and the elector Palatine's former Confederation, about how to betray Germany.
14. Lübeck sends the gun it took from King Christian[1] when it held him prisoner.

-----

[1] The preliminary treaty of 17 September 1625 between Britain and the Dutch Republic to back Denmark.

[1] Christian II was captured in 1532.

15. Hamburg sends the king a copy of the imperial privileges confirming that it is an imperial city and no longer subject to him.[2]
16. Brunswick sends 1,000 cannon balls that were fired at it without effect during the siege.[3]
17. Bremen sends 6 flags they took from the Brunswicker when they chased his troops into the Weser.[4]
18. Ditmarschen sends 24 flags it took from the Danes at Meldorf when it defeated the Holstein nobility.[5]
19. The Hanseatic cities send 9 tons of credit to make Rosenobels.[6]
20. The Danes send 400 white deer and an imperial capitulation that he should reside in Denmark.
21. Sweden sends copies of old treaties the king broke when he took Stockholm that state Denmark and Norway belong to Sweden.
22. The Turks send a protest that he should not rebel against the proper authorities, and if he does not obey the emperor, they will force him to submit.
23. And if all this help is not enough, the emperor sends two guides, Prince Wallenstein and Count Tilly, who can show him the way back to Denmark.

Source: Dietrich Schäfer, 'Die Schlacht bei Lutter am Barenberge', *Neue Heidelberger Jahrbücher*, 10 (1900), pp. 36–7.

---

43. The failure of neutrality: Lower Saxon Kreis Mandate, 4 March 1626

The worthiest, serenest, worthy, serene and well-born princes and Estates etc. of the worthy Lower Saxon Kreis announce their greeting, grace and all good wishes to all and their vassals, inhabitants, subjects and members, not matter of what estate, and are in no doubt that it will be well-known both within the Holy Roman Empire and beyond that their highnesses the princes and Estates have been compelled by the most pressing circumstances to establish a defence force in accordance with the authority and guidelines of the Holy Imperial Executive Ordinance and Recesses, and that they have not only

---

[2] Emperor Matthias confirmed Hamburg's status on 26 June 1618 after Christian IV claimed the city belonged to him.

[3] Christian had backed his relations, the Guelph dukes, who twice tried to force Brunswick to renounce its autonomy (1605–6, 1615).

[4] This refers either to measures against Duke Christian of Brunswick (1599–1626), known as the Mad Halberstädter who joined the Danes in 1625, or the city's victory over Erich of Brunswick at the battle of Drakenburg in 1547.

[5] A Danish army including vassals from Holstein was routed by the Ditmarschen peasants in 1500.

[6] A reference to the high tolls levied by Denmark on ships passing the Sound that had to be paid in coins called Rosenobles.

agreed this, but have immediately informed His Roman Imperial Majesty, our most gracious lord, as well as others, to avoid all mistrust and suspicious thoughts and hostile impressions, and have done this properly in writing from an upright open German heart to say that such a force is purely defensive and not to harm His Roman Imperial Majesty, the Holy Empire or its electors, princes and Estates, but entirely and singularly for the protection and defence of this worthy Lower Saxon Kreis and to be used as a highly necessary assistance for the hard-won liberty in religious and profane matters, together with the traditional exercise of the Augsburg Confession as the highest jewel that princes and Estates in this world could have (but against which so many have complained in recent years), as well as to ward off all threatening developments and hostilities. This is also a path that other princes and Estates have followed since the start of the imperial reign of His Roman Imperial Majesty and those of this Kreis do with due devotion, love, loyalty and obedience and will insist to their graves and for all eternity that such an upright German declaration of the Kreis will neither harm nor offend anyone in the slightest.

In July of last year 1625 the Bavarian and League Lieutenant General Johann Tserclaes Count von Tilly, followed by Albrecht Wenzel Eusebius Duke of Friedland, with their large armies invaded the said Kreis, first in the worthy principality of Brunswick, then in the archbishopric of Magdeburg and the bishopric of Halberstadt, and violently attacked fortresses, cities, towns, villages and noble houses, occupied and plundered them, not sparing the churches and houses of God, tyrannically stole not only all the property and means of sustenance of many thousands of innocent subjects and their wives and children, but also in many cases their honour, bodies, lives and health, and burnt a great number of beautiful houses, villages, monasteries, farms and mills and other buildings to the ground and in short behaved so gruesomely in the Kreis that one would not have expected the same from the hereditary and arch enemy of all Christianity. And all this occurred with no more reason than blatant pretexts that were used to disguise the long-held intention to exterminate from the reformed archbishoprics and bishoprics of this Kreis the Augsburg Confession, that is the sole means of salvation, the godly, precious, true Christian religion. Such procedures not only grossly violate the proper and traditional liberty in religious and profane matters, but also completely contravene the Holy Imperial fundamental laws and constitution and stamp on all legal order together with German liberty ... [The following passage reaffirms the belief that the Bavarians and Catholics intend harm.]

Therefore, the princes and Estates of this worthy Lower Saxon Kreis to save their Christian consciences through this public notice and letter hereby remind and warn on their lives, honour and property all officers, horsemen and soldiers of the Evangelical or Augsburg Confession, regardless of their estate, who are serving in both opposing armies and who are bound by vassalage or other duties to a prince and Estate of this Kreis, to leave both opposing armies as open enemies of the Kreis within a month of the present date and go home. If they fail to do so and continue to serve against the worthy Kreis they are expressly warned that the natives amongst them will be punished without restraint on their bodies, honour and properties with the loss of all rights and jurisdictions, while the foreigners will be treated as unchristian persecutors of their fellow believers and will be granted no quarter.

[The final passage reminds all princes and Estates of the Kreis that it is their Christian duty to observe the agreed defence measures and repeats the claim of the opening passage that this is in accordance with imperial law and not directed against the emperor.]

[Dated Brunswick, 4 March 1626.]

Source: Josef Kollmann (ed.), *Doumenta Bohemica Bellum Tricennale Illustrantia* (Prague, 1974), vol. IV, pp. 100–2.

---

44. Wallenstein urges peace, 24 June 1626

I hereby obediently enclose to Your Imperial Majesty what has been communicated with General Count Tilly. You will graciously see from this what position the enemy is in. My humble opinion in this would be that it would currently be best and bring more advantage and higher reputation if Your Imperial Majesty ... negotiated peace with them, because the enemy will get more help from various quarters and his forces will greatly increase, so that he will perhaps not accept later what he could more easily be persuaded to agree to now, and this evil might not be stopped later.

Source: Wallenstein to Emperor Ferdinand II, 24 June 1626, Josef Kollmann (ed.), *Doumenta Bohemica Bellum Tricennale Illustrantia* (Prague, 1974), vol. IV, p. 124.

---

45. The Peace of Lübeck, 22 May 1629

It is known that a peace conference was arranged in the city of Lübeck to settle the differences and confusion between the all serene and omnipotent prince and lord, Ferdinand II, Roman emperor, and the serene, powerful prince and lord, Christian IV of Denmark, Norway [etc.].

[Then follow the names of the representatives, including Wallenstein and Tilly for the emperor and Bavaria, as well as envoys from Denmark.]

After much negotiation, these have agreed, discussed, negotiated and concluded a sincere, durable, secure and permanent peace in the following points and articles:

First, His Roman Imperial Majesty and His Royal Majesty of Denmark, Norway, etc. desire to maintain a mutual just and uncoloured friendship at sea and on land from now henceforth, [so that] a durable, sincere peace, permanent unanimity and unshakeable good trust will be established and preserved. To this end, His Royal Majesty will treat His Imperial Majesty as befits a prince and Estate of the Holy Roman Empire that he is in his capacity as Duke of Holstein, and will not claim the archbishoprics and bishoprics on behalf of his dear sons on whatever pretext, nor hinder His Roman Imperial Majesty in the exercise of his imperial government. In return, His Roman Imperial Majesty will not interfere in His Royal Majesty's kingdoms and sovereign lands, nor hinder their royal government. And in the unlikely event of a misunderstanding or dispute between His Roman Imperial Majesty and His Royal Majesty or their successors, heirs and descendants, this shall be settled amicably through mutually agreed arbiters, without either party using violence against the other.

Second, since every effort has been made to achieve a firm, amicable relationship between His Roman Imperial Majesty and His Danish and Norwegian Majesty that will endure for posterity, both parties agree to sweep away anything that might hinder this or leave bitterness and so no one in the Empire may claim anything from Denmark and Norway, and vice versa, [and that the emperor should] evacuate His Royal Majesty's provinces, principalities and lands of Wendsüssel, Jutland, Schleswig, Holstein, Stormarn and Ditmarschen … and restore them without charge to His Royal Majesty in every way he possessed them before, on the condition that His Roman Imperial Majesty's and the Holy Roman Empire's authority and feudal jurisdiction over the Duchy of Holstein, Stormarn and Ditmarschen remains. Imperial troops occupying these provinces and principalities are to withdraw immediately in good order and discipline without making further demands. The process of confiscation and other punishments underway in the duchy of Holstein and its associated areas is to stop completely and everything is to be left there according to the religious and profane peace and no one is to object to this.

Thirdly, prisoners are to be mutually exchanged without delay or further burden.

And fourthly, this agreement and peace applies on the part of His Roman Imperial Majesty to the crowns of Spain and Poland, Her Highness the Infanta in Brussels, together with the entire praiseworthy House of Austria, as well as Electoral Bavaria and all assisting obedient electors, princes and Estates of the Holy Roman Empire and their subjects and inhabitants, as well as on the part of His Royal Majesty of Denmark [and] Norway to the crowns of France, Great Britain and Sweden, as well as the States of the United Netherlands.

Fifthly it has been noted that His Royal Danish, Norwegian, etc. Majesty appealed urgently during these entire negotiations that the princes and Estates of the Empire should not be treated unconstitutionally. However, His Roman Imperial Majesty always responded that he never intends to do this. Accordingly, His Royal Majesty has agreed to drop the matter. However, the islands of Fehmarn and Nordstrand, together with possessions on Förder and Sylt, are to be restored to the princely House of Holstein-Gottorp without infringing the rights of the King of Denmark over these, and all [imperial] troops are to leave these areas in good order without making further demands.

These points are to be incorporated verbatim in the imperial and royal ratification that is to be binding on the successors of both signatories.
Done at Lübeck 22/12 May in the year 1629.

Source: Ernst Wilmanns, *Der Lübecker Friede 1629* (Bonn, 1904), pp. 80–3.

---

46. A religious war?

[A broadsheet printed in Augsburg in 1626 showing a standard likeness of Luther dressed in sober cleric garb.]

Actual likeness of the highly illustrious learned man of God and the heart Martin Luther, doctor of the Holy Scripture, and sometime preacher and professor at Wittenberg [1626].

[Translation of text beneath the image:]

I say freely I was born in 1483 on Saint Martin's day in Eisleben. My father was a miner. Thanks to God's grace I was preserved 63 years, and discovered schooling and church law, and the pure teaching, and continued this until God took my soul in his hand in 1546.

Source: John Roger Paas (ed.), *The German Political Broadsheet 1600–1700*, 8 vols (Wiesbaden, 1996), vol. IV, p. 209.

7

The Catholic ascendancy

Danish intervention in 1625 restarted the war which had effectively ended with the defeat, two years before, of the last of Frederick V's armies at Stadtlohn. Spain had withdrawn its contingent which had served with the imperial army since 1619, because it needed the soldiers for its own war against the Dutch. Always short of money [see Docs 127–30], the emperor could not afford a large army, most of which had to be deployed to protect Hungary against periodic Transylvanian attacks and the threat of war with the Ottoman empire. The resumption of war in north Germany exposed Ferdinand II's dependency on Bavaria and the Catholic League, since Tilly's troops were the only ones available to oppose the Danes. Bavaria also found the war costly [see Doc. 131] and Maximilian urged Ferdinand to increase his army – a request the Bavarian elector would later regret. Ferdinand responded by appointing Albrecht Wenzel Eusebius von Waldstein (1583–1634), better known as Wallenstein, to raise and command a new army in the Empire. Though a relatively junior general, Wallenstein had amassed a huge fortune through his role in confiscating property from the defeated Bohemian rebels. He was already a controversial figure, known for his haughty demeanour, seemingly boundless ambition and, as details leaked out, his theologically suspect interest in astrology [Docs 47–50].

Wallenstein pursued and destroyed Mansfeld, who had joined Denmark with a new army partly paid for by the signatories of the Hague Alliance. He then joined Tilly in driving Christian IV's main army off the mainland, forcing it to shelter on the Danish islands in 1627. These victories increased the clamour for reward amongst imperial generals to whom the emperor owed large sums spent raising and maintaining the new army. Ferdinand settled some of these debts at the expense of those princes and nobles who had supported Danish intervention [Doc. 51]. The practice was controversial, since the victims' Protestant faith made it appear confessionally motivated, while they were condemned without trial on the grounds that their service in the Danish forces already exposed them as 'notorious rebels'. Though a beneficiary of the earlier confiscations at the Palatinate's expense, Maximilian of Bavaria also grew concerned that the redistribution of property in the Empire was endangering the traditional liberties of the German princes, because land was passing into the hands of the emperor's own nobility. These fears mounted when Ferdinand deprived the two dukes of Mecklenburg, one of the Empire's oldest families, of their duchy and gave it to Wallenstein in lieu of his expenses [Doc. 52].

The retreat of the Danish army to the islands left Wallenstein powerless to deliver a final blow to Christian IV, because there was no imperial navy. Key figures in the imperial government turned to Spain, Europe's leading naval power, for assistance. Spain had long urged Ferdinand to repay the earlier help against the Bohemians by assisting against the Dutch. Olivares now offered money and expertise to develop an imperial navy, but expected this to be used to destroy the lucrative trade the Dutch conducted in the Baltic. Sigismund III (1566–1632), king of Poland from 1587, also offered help, hoping the two Habsburg powers would back his long-standing desire to recover Sweden, which he had also ruled before being expelled by his Protestant uncle in 1600 [**Docs 53–4**].

These conflicting motives frustrated the 'Baltic Design' which was dealt a fatal blow by Wallenstein's failure to persuade the Pomeranian town of Stralsund to let him use its harbour as a naval base. Convinced they would lose their property and Protestant religion if the imperial soldiers were let in, the poorer and more militantly inclined Stralsunders forced their town council to defy Wallenstein's army. Denmark sent limited assistance and was soon supplanted by Sweden which saw Stralsund's resistance as a convenient way to block Sigismund's invasion plans [**Doc. 55**].

While the Baltic Design threatened to extend the war further north, a new front opened in Italy. The north Italian states were loosely part of the Empire, though they played only a limited role in imperial politics. Spain controlled the duchy of Milan, which was a valuable base on the eastern flank of France, a Catholic country nonetheless hostile to Spanish interests. Possession of Milan allowed Spain to send troops over the Alps into the Empire if necessary (as in 1619), or further north along the so-called 'Spanish Road' parallel to the Rhine to reinforce the Army of Flanders against the Dutch. Spain's governor in Milan was concerned at French influence in the Swiss Confederation and Rhetian Republic (also known as the Grisons) since these mixed Catholic–Protestant states controlled the Alpine passes. Alarm grew when representatives of a French aristocrat, Charles de Nevers (1580–1637), seized control in Mantua after the death of its last duke in December 1627. Mantua and its dependency Monferrato lay either side of Milan along the strategic river Po. The governor quickly allied with the duchy of Savoy, which had long coveted Monferrato, and invaded to forestall Nevers taking over as Duke of Mantua. Though his action was retrospectively sanctioned in Madrid, it compromised Ferdinand II who, as emperor, was entitled to decide who should inherit Mantua. Nevers was regarded as a troublemaker by Amand-Jean du Plessis Cardinal Richelieu (1585–1642) who had led the French government since 1624. Nonetheless, Richelieu felt obliged to support him or lose influence in Italy.

Escalation of the conflict forced Ferdinand to divert part of the imperial army from north Germany into Mantua [**Doc. 56**]. Overconfident following the victory over Denmark, Ferdinand directed further detachments to help Spain defend the Netherlands and to assist Poland in its war with Sweden, which had begun in 1621. Wallenstein opposed this, believing the emperor was taking on too many commitments which were stirring fresh resentment of Habsburg successes, notably in Sweden [**Doc. 57**]. The electors also opposed widening the war and wanted Ferdinand to extend the recent treaty of Lübeck [**see Doc. 45**] into a general peace. Ferdinand needed their cooperation, because he wanted them to elect his son, Archduke Ferdinand, as his successor in the Empire. He also had little desire to become embroiled in Spain's Dutch war or in a new conflict with France [**Doc. 58**]. War with the Habsburgs was unpopular in France where key figures like Louis XIII's brother and mother hated Richelieu's influence. Richelieu sent two envoys to the congress of electors whom Ferdinand had convened in the imperial city of Regensburg in 1630. The envoys accepted Ferdinand's relatively generous settlement of the Mantuan dispute in a draft treaty signed at the congress [**Doc. 59**]. However, Richelieu outmanoeuvred his domestic opponents in the so-called Day of the Dupes (11 November 1630), allowing him to repudiate the treaty which would have obliged France not to assist any Habsburg enemies in the future. Though imperial troops captured Mantua in June 1630, the Spanish were unable to take the fortress of Casale which guarded Monferrato. Renewed French military intervention forced both Spain and Austria to recognise Nevers as Duke of Mantua in the Treaty of Cherasco in 1631.

Wallenstein's opposition to the emperor's Mantuan policy provided ammunition for his enemies in Bavaria and the imperial court who wanted him dismissed [**Doc. 60**]. Ferdinand reluctantly agreed, naming Tilly as commander of the imperial army, which nonetheless remained separate from that of the League. This concession failed to persuade the electors to surrender their trump card and vote for Archduke Ferdinand as king of the Romans or successor designate in the Empire. The question of the imperial succession remained open until a second electoral congress, which convened under very different circumstances in Regensburg in 1636–7 after the imperial victory of Nördlingen (1634) and the favourable Peace of Prague (1635) [**see Doc. 103**].

WALLENSTEIN

47. Character: Kepler's horoscope, 1608

I can truly say of this lord, that his mind is agile, active and far from tranquil ... That he yearns for many things that he does not reveal outwardly. He will certainly be merciless, without brotherly or marital affection, respecting nobody, dedicated completely to himself and his own ambition ... He will endeavour to attain many dignities and vast power – and thus he will attract many great and secret enemies, most of whom he will defeat ... Mercury stands directly in *oppositio Jovis*, and it appears that he will have a special charm for many people and that he might become the head of a company of conspirators.

Source: Johannes Kepler's horoscope for Wallenstein, 1608, quoted in J.V. Polisensky, *War and Society in Europe 1618–1648* (Cambridge, 1978), p. 132.

48. Proposal to organise an army, 1625

Because the provinces had suffered greatly already, and in addition were not to be trusted, the domains' revenues exhausted and everywhere indebted,

Wallenstein finally proposed a way to enable His Imperial Majesty to raise a powerful army and maintain it for many years. However, he insisted on having 50,000 horse and foot [soldiers] for this. And when the imperial ministers regarded this as a desperate proposal, and replied: if we do not have means to recruit and maintain 20,000, how can we raise and pay 50,000? He replied: with 20,000 he could not place the lands where he operated under contributions,[1] but he could do it with 50,000. Thereupon it was agreed with him that he should initially raise 20,000 with the rest to follow.

Source: Franz Christoph Khevenhüller, *Annales Ferdinandei*, 12 vols (Leipzig, 1716–26), vol. 10, s. 802.

49. Initial appointment, 7 April 1625

His Imperial and Royal Hungarian and Bohemian Majesty, our most gracious lord, herewith graciously appoints his Imperial Majesty's War Councillor, Chamberlain, Major General and Colonel-Commandant of Prague, the high-born Albrecht Wenzel Eusebius Prince of Friedland and ruler of the House of Wallenstein as *Capo* [head] of all his troops currently in the Holy Roman Empire and the Netherlands, as well as those that may be sent there.

His princely grace should prepare himself and await a further gracious order to go wherever his Imperial Majesty's requirements and service should send him.

Issued under imperial instructions by the War Council 7 April 1625.

Source: Hermann Hallwich, 'Wallensteins erste Berufung zum Generalat', *Zeitschrift für Allgemeine Geschichte, Kultur, Literatur und Kunstgeschichte*, 1 (1884), pp. 119–20.

50. Ambitions: Aytona[1] to Philip IV, 12 February 1628

The emperor has taken Mecklenburg from the last descendants of the old princely house that had joined the king of Denmark and given it to the Duke of Friedland. Although the Duke of Friedland maintains that peace is within his grasp, I suspect that this gift will push it further away. The Duke is very powerful. One must be thankful that he is satisfied with these possessions,

---

[1] 'Contributions' is a general term used for a variety of ways of extracting money and other resources from areas threatened or occupied by an army. See the Introduction to Chapter 15 and **Docs 121–6**.

[1] Francisco de Moncada, Count de Osuna and Marquis of Aytona (1586–1653) was Spanish ambassador at the imperial court 1624–9.

that are admittedly extensive and significant. The emperor, through his generosity and by ignoring all warnings, has made the Duke so powerful that doubts must arise; he is now the only commander, leaving the emperor with little more than his title. He constantly presents himself as the most loyal servant of the imperial family, and indeed is such, but only as long as they do not disturb his current absolute power. At the slightest objection to his plans there will be no safety from him, because his nature is so terrible and moody that he often does not know how to control himself.

Source: Anton Gindely, *Waldstein während seines ersten Generalats im Lichte gleichzeitgen Quellen 1625–1630*, 2 vols (Prague and Leipzig, 1886), vol. I, pp. 368–9.

51. Payment: Ferdinand II orders confiscation of 'rebel' property, 16 February 1628

Personal letter from Emperor Ferdinand:

Ferdinand etc.

We have graciously resolved and decided, that all those confiscations and punishments incurred by the participants of the recent unrest and rebellion in the Holy Roman Empire who have had their fixed and movable property seized by our deputised commissioners, that these are to be used exclusively to pay the army entrusted to you and not to be used for any other purpose.

In order that this can be put into effect, it is our gracious wish that you assist our commissioners with the confiscations so that these can be seized, valued and converted into cash. However, those debts and liabilities of the various properties are to be assessed and those that are found to be justified are to be repaid first, before the rest is used to pay our soldiers in future. Discretion and moderation are to be used to ensure that no one, either from the delinquents or the creditors, feel that they have been dealt with too harshly or have cause for complaint. You know well what to do to secure our grace and we remain yours with imperial and royal grace and also all good wishes.

Given at Prague 16 February 1628

Source: Karl Oberleitner, 'Beiträge zur Geschichte des Dreissigjägen Krieges mit besondere Berücksichtigung des Österreichischen Finanz- und Kriegswesens', *Archiv für österreichische Geschichte* 19 (1858), p. 34.

52. Transfer of Mecklenburg to Wallenstein, 1628 (1629)

We Albrecht, by the grace of God Duke of Friedland and Sagan, Roman Imperial Majesty's Colonel General Field Captain, as well as etc., hereby give notice to all that His Imperial Majesty our most gracious lord has granted me through the deed of purchase dated 26 January of last year 1628 as a right, good and permanent sale the Duchy of Mecklenburg, Principality of Wend, County of Schwerin, and the Lordship of Rostock and Stargard, together with all and every associated jurisdiction, regalia, rents, revenues and dues. The superior princely dignity, jurisdiction and regalia do not come as on account or valuation, but have been granted freely by His Imperial Majesty already following our loyal service. In particular, only the revenues and income of the aforementioned duchy, principality, country, lordship and lands have been bought by us for four per cent, and are to be paid, and that from this payment (that is based upon a mutually agreed estimate of the revenues) all the duchy's debts that are accepted as binding by His Imperial Majesty according to the law are to be deducted and the necessary sum left in our hands to satisfy the proper creditors and interested parties. In addition, those debts and demands that His Majesty owes us, that are found to be justified after proper accounts, as well as the gracious Imperial gift of 700,000 Rhenish florins are to be deducted from the main payment, and the surplus, together with the individual rebel properties to be found in the oft-mentioned principalities and lands, as well as the mobile and fixed property (that his Imperial Majesty has graciously resolved to confiscate at the time of this sale), are exclusively to be used to content the Imperial Army to some extent until a final settlement and agreement can be made with the army in future, but only in return for sufficient accreditation.

Therefore, we would like nothing more than that a proper estimate is made of the revenues and dues accruing from the above-mentioned lands.

Because our military duties entail continual travelling and absence, we have entrusted this to the Imperial Commissioners instructed for this purpose.

We hereby commend and promise by the power of this accreditation that the above-mentioned estimate will be undertaken and settlement of the terms of the deed of purchase will be agreed with His Imperial Majesty's Treasury in the future.

Certified by our signature and seal. Done at Güstrow 16 June 1629.

Source: Karl Oberleitner, 'Beiträge zur Geschichte des Dreissigjährigen Krieges mit besondere Berücksichtigung des Österreichischen Finanz- und Kriegswesens', *Archiv für österreichische Geschichte* 19 (1858), pp. 35–6.

THE BALTIC DESIGN

53. Polish involvement: Wallenstein to King Sigismund III, 28 October 1627

We have received Your Royal Majesty's letter dated the twenty-fourth of September safely delivered by Mr Gabriel de Roy[1] and from this have seen and acknowledged how Your Majesty desires to further the good of Christianity. We therefore report to Your Majesty that we are already busy collecting a large fleet to pursue those who disturb Christianity. We hope that Our Lord will, as till today, support the just cause, now that Your Majesty is willing to join your ships to ours and bring them to a safe port. Therefore, we report that we have captured the town of Wismar, that is the foremost harbour in the Baltic Sea, so that Your Majesty can now send them there in better security. We will issue the order there that they [the ships] should be let in and treated well, in which matters the above-mentioned de Roy will report more to Your Majesty.

Source: Wallenstein to King Sigismund III of Poland, 28 October 1627, in Josef Kollmann (ed.), *Doumenta Bohemica Bellum Tricennale Illustrantia* (Prague, 1974), vol. IV, p. 222.

---

54. Sigismund to Wallenstein, 10 November 1627

Since we have received word that Your Grace, thanks to divine grace and support, has achieved a remarkable victory over His Majesty the Emperor's enemy, the King of Denmark, in the principality of Holstein. This is not only pleasant and agreeable to us, but also most welcome. We did not want to neglect congratulating Your Grace on such a happy success and to thank the Almighty and to prey that He will graciously permit Your Grace to prosper in such a work that is most necessary to our Catholic religion and to the due extirpation of all the most damaging enemies. We also do not want to omit telling Your Grace that certain reports have arrived that Denmark is currently seeking a peace treaty with His Majesty the Emperor and eagerly wants this. However, this is not pleasant to us, since such peace negotiations will not only do more harm than good to His Majesty the Emperor and the King of Spain, but also to ourselves. Because, with God's help, victory is in His Majesty's and Your Grace's hands and, because the [enemy] population is greatly afraid, by continuing the campaign one can easily obtain the Sound and other places, and so conquer the entire kingdom of Denmark with such a powerful fleet. Furthermore, this will help the King of Spain be more powerful than his enemies, and so much more easily and quickly provide help and assistance to

---

[1]   Gabriel de Roy (*c*.1570–*c*.1646), from Artois, was a leading expert in maritime and colonial affairs and one of Spain's chief negotiators in the Baltic Design.

the King of Spain, from whom we have already had some consolation that we might recover our kingdom of Sweden. Because matters can be judged by Your Grace's customary discretion, we entrust them to Your Grace with due affection and ask your advice how assistance against Sweden could be sought from His Majesty the Emperor in the manner of the consolation that we have received from the King of Spain, so that once this has been received, Sweden can also be attacked from this side.

Source: King Sigismund III of Poland to Wallenstein, 10 November 1627, in Josef Kollmann (ed.), *Doumenta Bohemica Bellum Tricennale Illustrantia* (Prague, 1974), vol. IV, pp. 226–7.

55. The Siege of Stralsund: Wallenstein to Duke Bogislav of Pomerania, 17 June 1628

His Roman Imperial Majesty's Field Marshal Hans Georg von Arnim has reported to us how the inhabitants of Stralsund persist in their obstinacy. Accordingly, we have no choice but to attack them in order to extinguish the fire before it does great harm to the Holy Roman Empire and Your Grace's land, and since we have arrived here[1] already and have rested 2 days, we want to set out for Stralsund at once. We hereby report to Your Grace that the regiments that have marched from the Empire across the Elbe, as well as those that were in Upper and Lower Lusatia, have been ordered to proceed to Stralsund immediately. In order to preserve better discipline and to prevent the complete ruin of the country, we amicably request that Your Grace makes arrangements to provide the troops with the necessary sustenance. And since our artillery is currently in Holstein far from Stralsund, and it would take a long time to arrive during which the country would be burdened with the war, we accordingly request equally amicably that Your Grace provide whatever cannon, ammunition and entrenching tools the said Field Marshal Hans Georg von Arnim requests. We hope to bring the inhabitants of Stralsund to due obedience in a short time and to save Your Grace's lands from ruin. You will be doing His Imperial Majesty and the Holy Roman Empire a loyal and affectionate service and we will also be obliged on this occasion.

Source: Wallenstein to Duke Bogislav of Pomerania, 17 June 1628, in Josef Kollmann (ed.), *Doumenta Bohemica Bellum Tricennale Illustrantia* (Prague, 1974), vol. IV, p. 261.

---

[1] Frankfurt an der Oder.

THE MANTUAN QUESTION, 1628–30

56. Ferdinand II decides to intervene: Ferdinand to Wallenstein, 8 December 1628

We inform Your Grace of the decision made by the ordinary royal Spanish ambassador at our court, the Marquis de Aytona, regarding his efforts to remove the French troops from Italy. Although we would not have wanted to use force for this purpose if the Duke of Nevers had not insulted our imperial sovereignty and rejected our recent peace offer, to which both Spain and Savoy had willingly agreed, and if he had refrained from invading the imperial fiefs of Mantua and Monferrato and dismembering the Holy Roman Empire (of which we expect full information within a few days and will report it to Your Grace). In these circumstances, we had no choice on account of our imperial office, house and state but to oppose this start and to meet the threatened violence with force and to protect ours and the Empire's rights as best as possible. Therefore, we have warned our dear brother, His Highness the high-born Leopold, Archduke of Austria, to take steps to improve security for this place and to report to us the status of this emergency. Meanwhile, Your Grace will send us your advice as soon as possible, whether it would be appropriate to send the remaining 60 companies of horse and foot that are in the upper Kreise,[1] or at least most of them, into Italy as the situation requires, and to replace these with troops from elsewhere, that Your Grace does not need so badly in the lower Kreise. We are in no doubt that you will reflect maturely on the reason for such a necessary move and suggest the best means to us, and if necessary arrange with Count Collalto[2] the necessary ordinance (but not issue it without our order).

Source: Emperor Ferdinand II to Wallenstein 8 December 1628, in Josef Kollmann (ed.), *Doumenta Bohemica Bellum Tricennale Illustrantia* (Prague, 1974), vol. IV, pp. 278–9.

---

57. Wallenstein's concern at the strength of the imperial army, 10 October 1629

I only humbly received Your Imperial Majesty's gracious letter of the seventeenth of August on the ninth of October and have read that you would graciously prefer, at the request of Her Serenity the Infanta,[1] and in view of the daily mounting danger in the Duchy of Brabant and the violence of the Dutch States, to send another seven thousand men as reinforcements. I now

---

[1] That is, in south Germany, actually mainly in Swabia.
[2] Rambaldo Count Collalto (1579–1630), president of the Austrian Court War Council 1624–30.

[1] Isabella Clara Eugenie, Governess of the Spanish Netherlands.

humbly report to Your Imperial Majesty that after all the troops I had to send to the Netherlands and Italy, there are no more than one company of cavalry and three or four of foot left in the Empire and among those returning from Denmark, as well as this side of the Elbe. Meanwhile, the few troops that I still have on the other side of the Elbe are in posts where they must remain to keep an eye on things, because Sweden's hostile intentions are becoming clearer by the day. And because these posts are spread across one hundred [German] miles along the coast, not to mention to positions [around Stralsund], as well as posts inland and at points that have to be held, in case the Swede[2] comes, there are no troops I could lead into the field, and I had to borrow eight Pappenheim companies from Count Tilly[3] in order to strengthen the positions around Stralsund. The men that Your Imperial Majesty sent to Prussia as aid[4] have been so affected by hunger and grief that there are no more than five thousand left. From this you will see that it is not possible to send the seven thousand or even a company in these circumstances. Since there are everywhere states and others ill-intentioned whose machinations may well cause a general uprising in the Empire and force Your Imperial Majesty to continue the war, no men can be spared in the coming spring, let alone sending reinforcements to the Netherlands, but on the contrary more should be recruited so that yourself, and your kingdoms and lands, as well as the Empire, are not endangered. I also hope that the Dutch army will be depleted through the siege of Herzogenbosch and, because winter is just before the door, will not be able to do anything more. Therefore, because Your Imperial Majesty cannot spare any men or send them to the Netherlands, Your Majesty should advise the Infanta in good time that she should use the winter to collect sufficient troops in order to resist the enemy better in the spring. I humbly enclose the letters sent to me by the said Count Tilly ...

Source: Wallenstein to Emperor Ferdinand II, 10 October 1629, in Josef Kollmann (ed.), *Doumenta Bohemica Bellum Tricennale Illustrantia* (Prague, 1974), vol. IV, pp. 325–6.

58. Ferdinand prefers a peaceful solution in Italy: Ferdinand to Count Collalto, 12 December 1629

You have certainly already received my specific orders and those points concerning how things should be handled, that we sent in encoded duplicate by a separate courier a few days ago. In the meantime, the [letter] from Bruneau[1] to me is enclosed and I have no doubt that you will give it due

---

2   That is, Gustavus Adolphus.
3   The Pappenheim Regiment was a unit in the League army.
4   For Sigismund III of Poland against the Swedes.

1   Jacques Bruneau, Spanish councillor and resident at the imperial court.

consideration and reflect reasonably on the current situation in Italy, as well as that in Germany, and how one might deal with the growing power of the States in the Netherlands[2] and the obstinate intrigues of hostile parties with foreign potentates. I will prefer all the more, as I have often indicated, that the Italian differences were settled by amicable compromise, but thereby my imperial authority must on all accounts be preserved and receive due recognition and be assured of its implementation at this time. You will direct all negotiations in accordance with this our intention and direct the council so that the way is open to the amicable compromise I so eagerly await.

Source: Emperor Ferdinand II to Count Collalto, 12 December 1629, in Josef Kollmann (ed.), *Doumenta Bohemica Bellum Tricennale Illustrantia* (Prague, 1974), vol. IV, p. 345.

THE REGENSBURG ELECTORAL CONGRESS, 1630

59. Ferdinand negotiates peace: Ferdinand to Collalto, 7 September 1630

I have read your letter of 25 August and Chiesa's[1] account and other sources; meanwhile my courier will have reached you, and perhaps the suspension of arms has been agreed and decided. Meanwhile, the French envoy here[2] has presented his plenipotentiary powers to negotiate peace, in which, as you will see from the enclosed copy, are numerous matters of concern, not the least of which is that these powers are relatively old, are not signed by the royal hand, do not refer to German affairs in a single word and the like. Notwithstanding these defects, the electors believe that we should continue the peace negotiations here so as not to lose the chance of the desired goal. Therefore, I have decided in the name of God, to let the initial negotiations continue, all the more because, according to the French envoy, no one will be sent to Italy with sufficient plenipotentiary powers from the king of France. [You will be informed] so that you will know how far things have progressed here and what points have been agreed and how you are to proceed so that nothing is negotiated to the contrary in Italy. It remains that this peace with France is to be negotiated and concluded not merely for the Italian disputes, but for the entire Holy Roman Empire and its associated Estates and members, as well as our hereditary kingdoms and lands. The electors here press strongly for this, and the common good would not be served well if peace were made in Italy and then the French arms were employed against us in Germany. The French envoy has given good cause that the same

---

[2] That is, the Dutch.

[1] Colonel Johann Baptist Chiesa, imperial negotiator.
[2] At the Electoral Congress at Regensburg.

peace and unanimity will be very agreeable and pleasant to his king, and so the articles will be so arranged and phrased, so that it seems that the French ambassador is content.

[The emperor goes on to summarise the draft Treaty of Regensburg that was later repudiated by Richelieu.]

Source: Emperor Ferdinand II to Count Collalto, 7 September 1630, in Josef Kollmann (ed.), *Doumenta Bohemica Bellum Tricennale Illustrantia* (Prague, 1974), vol. IV, pp. 408–10.

60. The decision to dismiss Wallenstein: Memorandum of imperial advisors, 17 August 1630

Confidential decision of the Privy Council in regard to the replacement of the current general with His Electoral Highness [of Bavaria] and what points should be considered 17 August 1630.

The discussion addresses two main issues. First, the proposal from the electors[1] as to how the current general could be dismissed most expediently. Second, whether the vacant post should be given to His Electoral Highness of Bavaria and what points need to be considered in regard to this.

Concerning the first point, the most Honourable Privy Council agrees with the Catholic [ecclesiastical] electors' suggestion that the general should not object to his dismissal because, firstly, as a paid employee, he is free to renounce his position as it suits him, and equally His Imperial Majesty is free to discharge him. Secondly, he has himself sought discharge virtually every year and so His Majesty would be justified in granting this, or, if this could not be arranged expediently through a third party, to send him immediately against the King of Sweden. Opinion diverged on this point. Some felt the situation was too dangerous to change commander at this moment. Others believe the danger is not yet so serious that, after the current general's abdication, a new commander could not be appointed to direct affairs with greater consistency ...

Concerning the other main point, the councillors advanced many arguments both for and against the elector's suggestion to appoint himself as replacement general, and to entrust him with the arms that constitute the emperor's power. However, Your Majesty's privy councillors unanimously agreed the elector's proposal could not be rejected without serious difficulties with His Electoral Highness in Bavaria, as well as the other Catholic Estates that could lead to a complete break with them. It is, therefore, to be considered how Your Majesty wishes to proceed with regard to the succession in the

---

[1]   The three ecclesiastical electors (Mainz, Cologne, Trier).

Empire,[2] as well as the supreme command and direction of the war. On these points your obedient privy councillors advise Your Imperial Majesty to indicate your gracious decision to the Catholic ecclesiastic electors, citing the well-known superior and admirable qualities of His Electoral Highness of Bavaria who has shown constant loyalty and devotion, so that this suggestion is not unwelcome. Furthermore, it should be said such an appointment will increase Your Majesty's power and authority, as well as promote the good and piety of the Holy Empire. Finally, it should be stated that, in order to best achieve this, some issues remain to be discussed, and to resolve these Your Majesty requests that the Catholic electors despatch some of their privy councillors for close consultation with those of Your Majesty.

There are primarily two such issues. First, that imperial war-making powers are part of Your Majesty's sovereign and imperial office according to the imperial constitution. The general [Wallenstein] should be informed that Your Majesty has decided for the good of the Empire to appoint another commander. No threat is intended to his person, reputation or other slight, but the general will find it hard to accept the decision and relinquish the army and this will pose a serious danger.

Therefore, it is suggested that, firstly, Your Majesty, should ask the Catholic electors to provide the means whereby this change [of command] can be effected without compromising the honour and reputation of the general ... In addition, it is decided that trusted persons (namely Your Majesty's privy and war councillors von Werdenberg and von Questenberg[3]) be issued with credentials and instructions immediately and sent to tell the general that the entire electoral college is constantly demanding his dismissal, that there are numerous complaints about the conduct of the war, and [to ask] how the soldiers can be maintained with few complaints in the future.

He will see that Your Majesty does not consider it advisable to alienate the electors at this critical juncture, and that Your Majesty has always shown constant grace and is concerned to ensure this change does not impair the general's security, honour or reputation. He should see that he has the means himself to preserve his reputation and security, without offence to the electors or disadvantage to Your Majesty, by resigning voluntarily, rather than exercising command with narrowly restricted powers ...

Source: Hermann Hallwich (ed.), *Briefe und Akten zur Geschichte Wallensteins (1630–1634)*, 4 vols (Vienna, 1912), vol. I, pp. 47–50.

---

[2]   Ferdinand II was seeking the electors' agreement to elect his son Ferdinand (III) as king of the Romans, or successor designate. The electors refused to relinquish this leverage and Ferdinand was not elected king of the Romans until the second electoral congress in Regensburg (1636–7), just two months before his father's death.

[3]   Court Chancellor Johann Baptist baron von Verda, Count of Werdenberg, and Gerhard Baron von Questenberg (1580–1646), vice president of the Court War Council.

8

The Edict of Restitution, 1629

A major factor behind the electors' opposition at their congress in Regensburg in 1630 was their alarm at Ferdinand's unilateral attempt to settle all the disputed points of the 1555 Religious Peace by issuing the Edict of Restitution in March 1629. Restitution meant the return of all Catholic church property and rights acquired by Protestants since 1552, the normative year imposed in the 1555 Religious Peace [**see Doc. 1**]. While this involved questions of constitutional and property law, it was also clearly a religious issue, not least through the linkage of demands for restitution with attempts to reimpose Catholicism on people who had embraced Protestantism since 1555, or who had lived on land belonging to princes declared rebels by the emperor since 1618. Re-Catholicisation gained pace after White Mountain in the Habsburg lands where it targeted the Protestant nobility [**see Doc. 29**]. It was extended to other parts of the Empire in the wake of Tilly's victories, but made relatively little progress amongst ordinary subjects who were reluctant to abandon Protestantism [**Doc. 61**].

Frustrated with slow progress, the Catholic ecclesiastical princes petitioned Ferdinand to abandon the established practice of reviewing each case separately through the imperial courts and called on him to spell out what constituted the 'clear letter' of the 1555 Peace. The emperor consulted Bavaria and the other Catholic electors who were broadly supportive of the idea. However, his Edict went much further than they expected and was issued in the form of a unilateral definitive verdict, rather than new guidelines for the imperial courts [**Doc. 62**]. The ensuing controversy frustrated hopes of converting the treaty of Lübeck into a general peace and ruined Ferdinand's immediate chances of persuading the electors to choose his son as successor. Worse, it left the Empire fatally divided when Sweden chose to invade in June 1630 [**see Doc. 66**]. Regardless of confession, all electors felt the emperor had exceeded his powers in issuing the Edict. Catholic militants felt it did not go far enough. Though the pope welcomed it [**Doc. 63**], he refrained from giving it full approval since this would entail recognition of the 1555 Peace and hence Lutheranism which Ferdinand still accepted as part of the imperial constitution. Maximilian of Bavaria initially supported Restitution, but later recognised it had been a critical mistake [**see Doc. 112**].

Moderate Catholics and all Protestants were appalled and petitioned the emperor to return to the previous practice of judging each case on its merits [**Doc. 64**]. To lend weight to these arguments, Saxony, Brandenburg and other Protestant imperial Estates convened in Leipzig [**Doc. 65**]. Few wanted to join the Swedes, who at this point were still contained by the imperial army at their landing site in

Pomerania. However, the Leipzig Convention's decision to raise troops increased Ferdinand's suspicions and stiffened his resolve not to compromise on the Edict.

61. Re-Catholicisation prior to the Edict: report on Bavarian policy in the Lower Palatinate, 1628

Report of Bernhard Baumann S.J. in Heidelberg to Elector Maximilian of Bavaria in Munich, 1628 on the re-Catholicisation of the Lower Palatinate right of the Rhine:

400 in the town [of Heidelberg] and 1,200 outside it have been freed from heresy; on feast days we get around 700 communicants in the Church of the Holy Spirit. We alone look after parish duties, visit the sick and converts daily, conduct catechism inside the town and outside, [and] deliver two sermons on Sundays. These crowds are gathered with great difficulty; since only six months ago the richer burghers were so obstinate, that two or three hundred declared they would emigrate if they were forced to convert. They were examined individually ten days before Whitsun to see who belonged to our faith; then entire districts (they had arranged this in advance) declared they would keep the faith of their ancestors, because we could not steal this like other possessions. Since the orders arrived from Munich[1] they have used unbelievable deceptions to try and circumvent these. Furthermore, they want to complain to the emperor, but the secular government,[2] to its undying credit among all well-wishers, knew how to stop this.

Source: Quoted in Franz Maier, *Die bayerische Unterpfalz im Dreißigjährigen Krieg. Besetzung, Verwaltung und Rekatholisierung der rechtsrheinischen Pfalz durch Bayern 1621 bis 1649* (Frankfurt, 1990), p. 197.

---

62. The Edict, 6 March 1629

We, Ferdinand the Second, by the grace of God, elected Roman Emperor, etc., offer our friendship, grace and all goodwill to all and every elector, prince [etc.] and all other of our and the Empire's subjects and faithful followers regardless of dignity, estate or being. It is without question all too well known that our beloved fatherland the German Nation has long suffered from damaging disagreement and destruction.

[There follows a discussion of the political and legal background from a Catholic perspective.] So it follows incontrovertibly that those immediate bishoprics and monasteries that were confiscated not before, but only after and since the Religious Peace are excluded and that the followers of the

---

[1]   These were issued on 24 February 1628 to intensify the process of re-Catholicisation.

[2]   Meaning the occupying Bavarian administration.

Augsburg Confession have no right to reform these or confiscate them. On the contrary, this is not allowed and because it has happened the injured party are free to exercise their rights and justice.

And do not be misled by the Article [15] of the Religious Peace that allows the followers of the Augsburg Confession their belief, ceremonies and church ordinances, that they have established or may establish in their principalities, lands and lordships: this does not given them the power also to reform monasteries within these lands. Although such monasteries are obliged to show due respect in worldly matters, they have nothing to do with these lands and lordships in terms of their foundation and spiritual matters, but belong as before to God and the Church. Because of this they are free and exempt from secular territory and government.

[The next section extends exemption to members of the spiritual orders and their subjects.]

Furthermore it is known throughout the Empire that certain Protestant Estates have broken the express words of the Religious Peace, not least in retaining their bishoprics, prelacies and prebends and renouncing the Catholic faith, but also those who were not entrusted with such have striven for such bishoprics and prelacies under this pretext and excuse, claiming this paragraph that appears so clear to them was never part of the Religious Peace, because they never agreed to it, but instead have often protested against it. However, we regard this paragraph, that is commonly called the ecclesiastical reservation, as an actual constitution and we have diligently studied the imperial archives to see how it became part of the Religious Peace (although we regard the letter of the Religious Peace to be sufficient). We have found that as far as the Protestant contradiction and non-acceptance is concerned that the oft mentioned Religious Peace is nevertheless different in content and that it was made with the advice and goodwill of all electors and Estates of both religious parties, and so concluded and sworn and promised with firm words from all Estates, that they would observe it in each and all of its points, clauses and articles, and not deviate or oppose it in the slightest. We swore in our electoral and coronation capitulation, as did our forebears in theirs, on this Religious Peace and the same content and terms without exception or condition, to which our Holy Roman electors bound us without condition or difference, because there is nothing in this Religious Peace to which we should not be bound.

[Further arguments follow to justify the legality of the ecclesiastical reservation. The edict then discusses the religious freedoms of subjects and reaffirms the principle of *cuius regio, eius religio*, especially for Catholic territories. There had been disagreement over this point in 1555, and the Catholics had denied their subjects the right to convert on the grounds this would lead to insurrection. The Edict then disputes Protestant claims to freedom of conscience, including for the towns and imperial knights, as well as claims derived from the *Declaratio*.[1]]

---

[1] The Declaratio Ferdinandea of 1555. See **Doc. 2.**

From the preceding discussion and according to the content of the
Religious Peace and other Holy Imperial Recesses [of the imperial diet], negotiations and acts, we identify and declare three key points: First, the
Protestant Estates have no grounds for complaint or to dispute that the generals of the [holy] orders, abbots, prelates and other clergy who are not immediately subordinate to the Empire, start the necessary proceedings through us
or our Cameral Court concerning their confiscated diocese and properties,
hospitals and other spiritual foundations, or that they receive these or even
proceed to verdict and execution. On the contrary, it is right and proper that
the Catholic Estates protest and accept such mediate clergy, who, contrary to
the clear terms of the Religious Peace, have been deprived of their monasteries and spiritual properties that they possessed at the time of the Treaty of
Passau or acquired since, or their rents and dues that have been withheld as
if the Religious Peace did not exist, and [who have been] deprived of all rights
and vindication, while their properties have been occupied by the authorities
against the intentions and view of the godly founders, as well as contrary to
the clear letter of the Religious Peace.

Equally, for the second point, we see that the followers of the Augsburg
Confession have no grounds for complaint, that their co-religionists, when
they strive after diocese, bishoprics and immediate imperial prelacies and
want to be accepted as bishops and prelates, find that their participation and
voting rights in the imperial diet are disallowed by the Catholic Estates, nor
are they enfeoffed with the [associated] regalia and fiefs. On the contrary, the
Catholics protest against such complaints that contravene the indisputable
terms of the ecclesiastical reservation, and against those clergy, bishops and
prelates who renounce the Catholic Religion, yet retain their bishoprics and
prelacies and all the rights and privileges that they enjoyed when they were
Catholic, including that such bishoprics and prelacies are regarded as Imperial
Estates. Those that are neither Catholics nor qualified for the clerical estate,
but nonetheless have forced and still force their way into such bishoprics and
prelacies, and thereby intend the end of the entire Catholic clerical Estate and
religion, are also included in this.

Our third point concerns the irrelevance of the complaints of some
Protestant Estates who want to prevent the entire Catholic Estates from holding their subjects to their religion and stopping them from leaving on payment
of emigration fees, or from allowing them to attend other preaching and services in foreign places. On the contrary, as the above discussion makes abundantly clear, the Catholics have legitimate grievances that such use of the right
of Reformation is solely intended to suborn and entice their subjects from
obedience to their authority. Moreover, this Catholic grievance is all the more
just, because the followers of the Augsburg Confession refuse Catholics the
same rights they demand themselves, and want to reform their subjects and
eliminate those who disagree, but refuse to allow the Catholics to do the same.

Now that the foremost and most important grievances concerning the
general peace have been discussed, and the extent to which they are valid or
not has been more than adequately discovered, as reported above from the

clear words of the Religious Peace, the Imperial Constitution and public documents, we hereby order our [Reichs-]Kammergericht ... to judge according to this declaration, without further objection, when similar cases arise that are covered by our resolution. The *Spolia* [robberies] and *Turbationes* [confusions], such as the occupation of diocese and prelacies contrary to the content of the Religious Peace, are quite notorious in many places and cannot be disputed, while the law, as mentioned above, from the words of the Religious Peace and other Imperial Recesses, is equally indisputable. Accordingly, henceforth nothing is more necessary than actual execution of the verdict and assistance to the injured party.

So we are determined for the realisation both of the religious and profane peace to despatch our imperial commissioners into the Empire; to reclaim all the archbishoprics, bishoprics, prelacies, monasteries, ecclesiastical property, hospitals and endowments which the Catholics had possessed at the time of the Treaty of Passau and of which they have been illegally deprived; and to put into all these Catholic foundations and endowments duly qualified persons so that each may get his proper due without unnecessary delay. We herewith declare that the Religious Peace refers only to the Augsburg Confession as it was submitted to our ancestor Charles V on 25 June 1530; and that all other doctrines and sects, whatever names they might have, not included in the Peace, are forbidden and cannot be tolerated. We therefore command to all and everybody under punishment from the Religious and the Public Peace that they shall at once cease opposing our ordinance and carry it out in their lands and territories and also assist our commissioners. Such as hold the archbishoprics and bishoprics, prelacies, monasteries, hospitals, benefices and other ecclesiastical property, shall forthwith vacate them and return and deliver them to our imperial commissioners with all their appurtenances. Should they not carry out this behest they will not only expose themselves on grounds of notorious disobedience to the Imperial ban under the Religious and Public Peace and to the immediate loss of all their privileges and rights without further sentence or condemnation, but to the inevitable real execution of that order and be distrained by force.

[The Edict is to be published by the Kreis convenors in the Kreise.]

We mean this seriously. Given in our city of Vienna, the sixth of March in the year sixteen hundred and twenty nine, the tenth year of our reign in the Empire, the eleventh in Hungary and the twelfth in Bohemia.

Source: Hans Schulz (ed.), *Der Dreißigjährige Krieg*, 2 vols (Leipzig, 1917), vol. I, pp. 60–78.

---

63. The Papal response: Urban VIII to Ferdinand II, 5 May 1629

Our soul has been filled with a marvellous joy by the recent Edict of Your Majesty which orders the sectaries to return to the priestly estate the ecclesiastical lands they have long held and in which are contained other provisions (which we bless) that remove obstacles that have up to now held back the Catholic restoration. When we reported these developments in secret consistory [of the cardinals] the apostolic senate rejoiced and praised your well-deserving piety, desirous that the reward of your noble action will be [more] victorious. Thus heresy will have learned that the gates of hell do not prevail against the church which legions of angles and the arms of powerful Austria so happily defend. How closely you have thereby bound the soul of the pontiff to yourself … our nuncio will declare to Your Majesty in more magnificent fashion.

Source: Pope Urban VIII to Emperor Ferdinand II, 5 May 1629, quoted in R. Bireley S.J., *Religion and Politics in the Age of the Counterreformation* (Chapel Hill, 1981), pp. 83–4.

64. The Protestant response: complaint from the Swabian Kreis to the Reichshofrat, January 1630

We have become anxious that we and other loyal Estates are in dire poverty and are facing immediate ruin, and again voice our concern at the destruction and devastation of the entire Roman Empire to Your Imperial Majesty and humbly beseech your protection, aid and rescue, and meanwhile regard it as advisable to approach you as well, as the foremost loyal council appointed to advise the Empire. It is our diligent view and request, that you will not only take to heart sympathetically the regrettable condition of ourselves and other loyal Estates of the Empire, but also, from duty to the Empire, as well as for the good of His Imperial Majesty and his dynasty, and for the preservation of the entire Roman Empire, to remind and assist with true advice, without letting up until not only the insatiable burden of war is recognised without delay, [and that] the loyal Estates together with their subjects are being driven into the ground, despite their patience, through no fault of their own, together with all the misery and evil that entails. Moreover, thanks to the Imperial Edict, we and other Evangelical princes and Estates are threatened with judicial punishments the like of which has neither been heard nor used before in the Empire, [and] are being de facto deprived of our property that we have held for many years through legal entitlement and inherited from several generations of ancestors. Instead, the directions of the Imperial constitution should be followed to the current situation in the Empire and that such religious and church matters should be dealt with according to the usual custom, as equality and justice should apply to them, as well as the Treaty of Passau and the Religious Peace, and everything done differently, and care taken, and matters handled according to the constitutional ways and means so that no one has cause for complaint, but on the contrary the authorised separation and difficulty of the Empire and Estates can thereby be removed.

Source: Complaint from the Swabian Kreis to the Reichshofrat, *c.*January 1630; in Hanns Hubert Hofmann (ed.), *Quellen zum Verfassungsorganismus des*

Heiligen Römischen Reiches deutscher Nation 1495–1806 (Darmstadt, 1976), p. 160.

65. The Leipzig convention, March 1631

We attest before God and the world, that we are entirely innocent of all the evil, if this gruesome oppression is not remedied quickly, and we seek and wish with peace-loving hearts and souls nothing more than to isolate and resolve all defects thoroughly through amicable compromise, establish true trust as *firmissimum pacis et mutuae concordiae vinculum*,[1] observe that the *Fundamenta*[2] and imperial laws do not oppress German Freedom, leave the electors and Estates with their authority, honours, dignity, privileges, immunities and laws and justice, [and do not] coerce or oppress anyone who lives according to law and justice, end the gruesome disorder, oppression and violence, restore a general, lasting, secure peace, and finally put a stop to the lament, misery, desolation and destruction, and the terrible bloodshed ... Their electoral graces ... [of Saxony and Brandenburg] have themselves decided from their peaceful hearts that if the amicable compromise is not made the authority and dignity of the Holy Roman Empire will be endangered still further and, God mercifully forbid, will be driven into the ground to the eternal shame and rebuke of the electors and Estates. The foreign potentates will also interfere in the affair and bring misery, ruin and destruction to each Estate regardless of religion.

Source: Letter of the assembled Protestant Imperial Estates to the ecclesiastical princes, 24 March 1631, printed in Hans Jessen (ed.), *Der Dreißigjährige Krieg in Augenzeugenberichten* (Düsseldorf, 1963), pp. 251–2.

---

[1] Firm peace and mutual concordats.
[2] Fundamentals, i.e. basic laws.

9

Swedish intervention 1630

Swedish intervention immediately divided opinion in the Empire and has proved controversial ever since. The Swedish king, Gustavus Adolphus (1594–1632, r.1611), was hailed as a divine saviour by Protestant militants and those, like the Bohemian and Austrian exiles, who had suffered from the earlier Habsburg victories. Moderates and princes like Elector Johann Georg of Saxony (1586–1656, r.1611) bitterly resented the Swedes as foreign invaders whose presence gravely threatened hopes of a peaceful resolution to the crisis triggered by the Edict of Restitution [see Doc. 62].

The Swedish landing in Pomerania in June 1630 was facilitated by France which had brokered the Truce of Altmark the previous September, ending the war with Poland. Gustavus Adolphus had attacked Poland in 1621, hoping to force Sigismund III to renounce claims to Sweden and to cede valuable river and port tolls along the Baltic coast. Though the Swedes conquered Livonia, they were unable to defeat Poland. The prospect of easier and richer pickings along Germany's Baltic coast was certainly a factor in Gustavus's decision to land there instead. Confessional solidarity with oppressed Protestants played well to some of the intended targets of Swedish propaganda, but was not a major consideration. Both internal documents and those directed at external audiences stress Gustavus's fears that the development of Emperor Ferdinand's power in northern Germany and the development of an imperial navy threatened Sweden's security [Docs 66–71]. The king was also concerned that perceived slights, such as his exclusion from the peace negotiations at Lübeck in 1629, damaged his royal reputation and international status. Swedish security was to be enhanced by championing 'German Liberty', since greater princely autonomy would weaken the Habsburgs and prevent them using the Empire's resources to harm Sweden's interests. Gustavus went to considerable lengths to present this objective as in conformity with the prevailing understanding of international law. Above all, he wanted to disarm Ferdinand's charge of unprovoked aggression [Doc. 72] and so prevent the emperor from rallying the princes against him. The emperor had sent envoys to the Polish port of Danzig (Gdansk) to seek a peaceful solution to Sweden's concerns. Gustavus deliberately frustrated this effort by manipulating the situation in Stralsund where Swedish troops had remained since Wallenstein abandoned his siege in 1628 [Doc. 67, see also Doc. 55]. The lack of any German appeals for Swedish help, other than from the coerced Stralsunders, undermined Gustavus's presentation of his invasion as impartial assistance to those in distress [Doc. 66].

Once in the Empire, it became imperative to find German allies, since Sweden was too poor and under-populated to wage a major war alone. Gustavus's search for allies was hindered by his overbearing desire to reserve absolute direction of the war for himself and subordinate his potential partners' interests firmly to his own [**Doc. 69**]. Most Protestant princes were alarmed by the Edict of Restitution and had long wanted to be free of the imperial soldiers who had been billeted at their territories' expense since 1626. However, few joined Gustavus willingly and those who did were all victims of earlier imperial victories, such as Christian Wilhelm of Brandenburg (1587–1665), the Protestant administrator of Magdeburg who had been deposed in 1625 for backing Denmark. As ruler of Gustavus's chosen landing site, Duke Bogislav XIV of Pomerania (1580–1637, r.1620) had no choice but to accept Sweden's demands which amounted to de facto conquest.

Long-term success depended on Gustavus persuading the more powerful electors of Saxony and Brandenburg to abandon their attempt to interpose themselves between himself and Ferdinand as a neutral third party at the Leipzig convention [**Doc. 74, see also Doc. 65**]. Although he was Gustavus's brother-in-law, Elector Georg Wilhelm of Brandenburg (1595–1640, r.1613) had no desire to back Sweden. He already resented Sweden's war against Poland which had threatened his Duchy of Prussia outside the Empire. Now, the Swedish landing in Pomerania trumped his carefully negotiated pact with the childless Bogislav to inherit that duchy. Relentless Swedish pressure eventually left Georg Wilhelm no choice [**Doc. 75**], enabling Gustavus to advance south towards Saxony.

His approach and Ferdinand's obstinacy over the Edict convinced Johann Georg to abandon his previous neutrality and join Sweden [**Doc. 76**]. Though hailed by many commentators as a great Protestant alliance, Saxon policy in fact remained the same. Cooperation with Sweden was intended simply to increase pressure on Ferdinand to be more reasonable and to restore the imperial constitution to what Johann Georg considered its proper state. Sweden's underlying weakness is clear from the terms of the alliance, since Gustavus was obliged to grant the obviously lukewarm Saxon elector far greater latitude than he gave any other German ally.

Swedish intervention was underwritten by France which, at that point, still contested the Mantuan succession in north Italy [**see Docs 56–9**]. Richelieu would have preferred an alliance with Bavaria to convert the League into a neutral buffer between France and Austria. However, Maximilian refused to abandon Ferdinand until he secured universal recognition of his controversial possession of the Palatine lands and electoral title. These circumstances obliged Richelieu to agree two unsatisfactory and potentially contradictory alliances. He backed Gustavus in the Treaty of Bärwalde [**Doc. 77**], promising financial support in return for an unenforceable commitment that Sweden would respect Catholicism in any lands it conquered and that it refrain from attacking Bavaria or other members of the League. To ensure Bavarian neutrality, Richelieu then promised to assist Maximilian if he was attacked, potentially committing France to fight Sweden [**Doc. 78**].

MOTIVES AND OBJECTIVES

66. The official explanation: The Swedish Manifesto, 1630

WHEN WE COME to consider the business of war, the first question to be proposed is, whether it be just or no. This is the case at present with respect to that which the King of Sweden has undertaken anew, who may very justly be called great, both for his courage and valor, and other heroic virtues, for his power, strength, and endeavors, and also for all his high and mighty designs, and actions truly worthy of a great King; having for these last years, in order to support and encourage his friends, made war successfully against the Muscovites and Polanders, and then dextrously made peace still for his glory and notable advantage; and some months ago, in a very short time, brought his army into the harbors of the Baltic Sea; having made himself master of all Pomerania, and fortified the places within his conquest, not to extend his limits, and enlarge his bounds, but to deliver his relations and friends from oppression; not by the devastation of countries and cities, but at his own charges and expense, and at the hazard of his own person, as appears by the public accounts, which have spread his fame through the whole universe. It is true, such as envy his glory, and those who are not yet informed of the justice of his arms, put various constructions upon his designs, and spread sinister reports of him, to the prejudice of his reputation. It has therefore been thought fit and proper, to declare to the world the motives and reasons of his last progress and entry into Germany. And not to dwell upon what is notorious to all the people and states of Christendom, it will be sufficient to say, that the Spaniards and the House of Austria have been always intent upon a Universal Monarchy, or at least designed the conquest of the Christian states and provinces in the West, and particularly of the principalities and free towns in Germany, where that House has made such a progress, that if this brave and generous northern prince had not bestirred himself, and opposed that torrent, she had pushed her ambition and arms to the most distant kingdoms and provinces, which have hitherto preserved and maintained their liberty, notwithstanding thousands of secret and open practices and threats made use of by the Spaniards and their partisans. This is what has given occasion to His Majesty of Sweden to put fleets to sea, and bring armies into the field, in order to preserve his friends, and render traffic and commerce free through this whole climate, as well by sea as by land; being thereto invited by several princes and states of the Empire, before they were entirely reduced to servitude and misery, wherein they now find themselves shackled by the tyranny of ambitious designers, ringleaders, counselors and generals of the said House; and by all means to prevent the total ruin both of himself and his neighbors, friends, and allies, which is truly an effect of the charity and protection which a prudent and generous prince naturally owes to his own subjects, and his nearest neighbors, who are ready to fall under the oppression of their enemies, though he was scarce able to imagine that the enemies of public liberty would have rushed with so much violence and impetuosity into the countries of their neighbors as they have done. And this belief and opinion was the cause of His Majesty's stopping short in his design of succoring those who apprehended that invasion, and turning his counsels and arms in the mean while elsewhere, that he might not lose the opportunities that offered themselves.

For after the wars of Poland in the year 1626 had obliged His Majesty to march his army into Prussia (a province subject to the said King of Poland) he then began to consider more narrowly everything he had to hope or fear from those who ravaged Germany in that manner; and judged right, that his friends had not without reason or foundation advised him of what he understood the enemy always intended against him more and more with relation to the war, as they drew nearer to the Baltic provinces.

For in the first place, in the said year, the letters sent by His said Majesty to the Prince of Transylvania were intercepted; and after they had been opened, and false glosses put upon them, to load His Majesty with the people's hatred, and render him odious everywhere, they were maliciously published; and the courier who carried them was put in prison, and treated as a criminal by open and public violence contrary to the law of nations.

In the second place, the enemies of the public quiet hindered the peace, which was then treating, from being concluded between His said Majesty and the King of Poland; although there was great appearance of its being in a fair way to be brought to a conclusion, insomuch that they practiced upon and corrupted the chief ministers of the States of Poland by presents and artifices, with an intention still to continue and keep up that war, until they had executed their designs in the Empire; by making the Polanders hope that after they had subdued the Protestant party in Germany, they would not fail to assist them to invade and take possession of the kingdom of Sweden.

For confirmation of which promise, and to acquit themselves of their obligation by real effects, which tended only to animate the Polanders, and weaken Sweden, they forbade any levies to be made in Germany for Sweden, and on the contrary allowed the enemy to levy soldiers openly, and to make use of all the provisions they could draw from thence. But perceiving that notwithstanding all their prohibitions, soldiers flocked from all the countries of Germany into the service of the King of Sweden, the following year 1627, they dispatched the duke of Holsace [Holstein] with a powerful army to make head against him in Prussia, and that under the colors and banners of the Emperor himself. Besides this, and for a greater testimony of their ill will, and in order to deprive the Swedes of all conveniences, they forbade the merchants all freedom of trade and commerce, taking away all their merchandise, and even such whereof the carriage had been paid in the towns of Germany, and confiscated the Swedish ships, on pretext of establishing a general commerce in Lübeck for the Hansa towns: which in effect was driving and excluding the Swedes from the whole commerce of the Baltic, and making a naval force at the expense of the poor merchants, subjects of the King of Sweden, in order freely to range and pirate in the said sea at their will and pleasure; which they showed with a witness the following year, having newly created a General of the Seas (a new and unheard of title in that climate) and possessed themselves of the ports and fortified places in the duchies of Mecklenburg and Pomerania.

It may be objected here, that all this was tolerable, if they had gone no further. But it was to be supposed that they would not stop there, and indeed they soon began to range the sea and fortify the port of the city of Stralsund, for a receptacle and retreat to their pirates; a thing that so nearly concerned all the neighboring states and galled them so much that the King of Sweden, who from time immemorial had a right to the protection of the Baltic Sea, neither could or ought to suffer any further progress to be made.

His Majesty then, invited by the earnest prayers of his friends and allies, and irritated by the injuries and outrages done as well to his own subjects as to his friends and allies, marched a second time into Prussia about the spring of the following year 1628 with a design to remedy all those inconveniences by good and lawful ways and means. And it happened in the meantime, that the deputies of the said city of Stralsund came to wait upon him, to complain, that notwithstanding their city had not in the least offended the Emperor, although they had neither been accused, cited, or condemned, and even after they had been declared innocent by an Imperial decree, with a promise and assurance of an entire deliverance; yet the Imperial army under the command of general Wallenstein, committed ravage and devastation, and exercised unheard of cruelties upon the burgesses of that city and the inhabitants of the flat country;[1] and proceeded so far as to fortify themselves in their territory, and without any declaration of war, surprised the Isle of Denholm, over against the port of the said city, which they were going to strengthen and fortify, to the great damage and prejudice thereof: that they had besides seized the passes of the Isle of Rügen, and those of their city, in order to make their way to the continent; that they had amused the citizens with vain hopes on purpose to surprise them: that after having drained their purses, they designed likewise to oblige them to receive a garrison, and demanded their ships, guns, and harbors; and in the meantime oppressed them with all manner of violences without either regarding their innocence or the Imperial constitution or the Emperor's decree or the treaty made in Pomerania with the Camp Marshal Arnim[2] or several other factions, nor even the vast sums of money which the said city had contributed whereby they thought to have been in safety and liberty.

This poor city then finding they could not be delivered by the decrees of

---

[1]   That is, the territory of the city of Stralsund.

[2]   Hans Georg von Arnim (1583–1641), the imperial general instructed by Wallenstein to take the city. Arnim was a Lutheran nobleman from Brandenburg who served Sweden from 1613 until he fell out with Gustavus Adolphus over pay. Having briefly served Poland, he joined the imperial army in 1626 and rose rapidly to become one of Wallenstein's most trusted subordinates. He was given command of the imperial contingent sent to assist the Poles [see **Doc. 57**], but resigned after disagreements with both them and Wallenstein. He then commanded the Saxon army 1631–5.

the Emperor, and perceiving that the duke of Pomerania, their prince, was not able to assist them, and feeling themselves abandoned by their confederates, were forced out of necessity to have recourse to a foreign aid and assistance, in order to divert the ruin that threatened them, and so accept of succor from the most serene King of Denmark, in hopes that hostility and violence might either be appeased or moderated. But fearing however lest they should be accused for being allied with a King, who was then at war with the Emperor, they judged it proper and convenient to throw themselves into the hands of the King of Sweden, who was then a friend and a neutral prince.

Wherefore His Majesty, perceiving that no moderation was to be expected from an army, which had behaved themselves with so much injustice and cruelty; and feeling that the request of that city was founded upon the justest reason and equity, and considering that it had been always allied to the Crown of Sweden, as well by a common tie of religion and commerce, as by all other manner of good correspondence, and perceiving likewise that permitting the pirates to possess themselves of that harbor for a retreat was of the highest concern and importance to his own states and all his neighbors, he could not without wounding his honor and conscience refuse those poor afflicted people the succors they demanded, which he was obliged to give them for the safety of his kingdom, neighbors, and allies.[3]

And forasmuch as His Majesty of Sweden expected thereby to have the decrees of the Emperor so much the better observed and respected, and by that means to get the Baltic Sea to remain in its former state; that is to say, free and safe to his allies, and all other nations usually driving a trade upon it; and that the city of Stralsund (which had been formerly preserved by the King of Denmark, then at war with the Emperor) should be preserved in its liberty through his mediation and intervention, as evidently appears by the pacts which he entered into on that head with the said city, when he took it under his protection; yet he could not hinder those firebrands and usurpers[4] from carrying on their pernicious and ambitious designs, nor turn them from that war, which they have ever since that time continued by sea and land, with more rage and violence than ever. For not being able to make themselves masters of that port, according to their intention, they seized that of the city of Wismar, and some others that were advantageous to them, and carried out of the port of Danzig the ships of Poland, which was at that time at enmity with the King of Sweden, to make use of them; and made so many marches, and committed so many depredations and ravages upon the neighboring seas, that His said Majesty of Sweden was at last constrained, for the preservation of commerce in his own seas, to equip, at a great expense, a navy to keep in those pirates, in order to enjoy quiet the rest of the year.

Notwithstanding all this, the most serene King of Sweden was ever inclined to peace, and contributed toward it all in his power. For understanding that a

---

[3] In August 1628.
[4] Meaning the Imperials.

treaty of peace was just upon the point of being entered into between the Emperor and the King of Denmark at Lübeck,[5] he presently sent his ambassadors thither to accommodate the difference relating to the city of Stralsund, and to pacify, in an amicable way, all the other differences which had arisen in the course of several years last past, with an express charge to use all the diligence and persuasion they were masters of to facilitate the accommodation between the Emperor and the King of Denmark; reckoning that peace could not be well made with the said King without comprehending the city of Stralsund in it; and that it was comprehended therein, upon the account of the agreements and pacts formerly made between him and that city.

But although the King of Denmark received that embassy very honorably, and the other party was invited thereto in a very decent and becoming manner by several letters from His Majesty of Sweden; yet his ambassadors were inhumanly denied audience, and no answer vouchsafed them, but were commanded upon pain of death to depart immediately not only from Lübeck but likewise out of Germany. This unworthy and dishonorable treatment was held and judged by all nations a sufficient cause of a rupture, and of requiring satisfaction by arms. And His Majesty had then been very excusable, if he had had recourse to violent remedies, since there was no valid cause or reason for his abstaining from them. However, after the deputies of the Emperor in their letters of answer dated in March had acknowledged the receipt of those of His Majesty's embassy, and by that acknowledgment seemed to make an apology for their first fault, His Majesty likewise, as being more inclined to put a good than a bad construction upon them, imagined all this might have proceeded from the wicked suggestion of some malicious and ill-advised counselors, and not from the common concert and advice of all; and did not judge that offense to be yet sufficient to oblige him to show his resentment by a just war, especially since the deputies said they had no orders to treat with any but the King of Denmark. Add to this, that if the Emperor or the duke of Friedland were spoke to on this head, a favorable answer might be expected from them. It is true, affairs were then brought to such a pass, that there was no longer any room or appearance that a treaty of accommodation would be hearkened to, because of former offenses and indignities. It came also to be considered, how, and in what manner the party offended could make the first overture to the Emperor (without wounding his honor) with whom he had not yet had any communication because of the difficulty of the passes in all the Emperor's lands, which were then stopped up, and since the negotiation of the treaty of Lübeck was drawing to a period.

However, to try once more all possible ways and in order to surmount all difficulties that might stand in the way to the blessing of peace (it being impossible to find means of making an overture to the Emperor himself), the Parliament of Sweden persuaded His Majesty to write about it to the College of Electors, not imagining that they would approve such a treatment of

---

[5] Early in 1629, leading to the peace treaty [see **Doc. 45**].

foreign Kings. Accordingly this was done the April following, that so the princes, who have a great authority in the Empire, might themselves seek and find out some proper remedy for that evil. Nay His Majesty consented, that a deputy should be sent to the general of the imperial army, on the part of the said Parliament, judging that the difficulties that had crept in among them might have been amicably composed in the armies. And for that effect Baron Steno Bielke[6] was presently dispatched, with power to treat of a truce for the city of Stralsund, if he could find minds any way disposed to peace, till an occasion should offer of sending commissioners to terminate that matter entirely. But the said Baron, being arrived at Stralsund about the beginning of spring, found affairs in a yet worse state than formerly; and the enemies resolved to pursue their pernicious designs with more violence and warmth than ever.

For Stralsund was then harassed and attacked on all sides, the gates crowded with soldiers to infest the Swedish Ocean; and as the highest piece of injustice, a very great army (without any previous defiance or denunciation of war), designed for Prussia against His Majesty of Sweden, under the conduct and command of Arnim, the Emperor's camp marshal: which hindered the aforesaid Baron from proceeding any farther, who judged that it would be somewhat necessary for his discharge to write to the duke of Friedland to acquaint him with the occasion of his embassy; and having protested against that injury and injustice of the army which was upon its march, he demanded it might be sent back and that all other acts of hostility might be forbidden according to the promise made at Lübeck by the Emperor's deputies.

Notwithstanding all this, the duke of Friedland declared that he had not as yet any inclinations toward peace, and that the promises of those deputies at Lübeck were nothing but trick and chicane. For he protested he could not recall the troops under the command of Arnim, and that His Imperial Majesty having too many soldiers, was forced to discharge himself of some of them, having already sent them to the King of Poland his friend, for that reason, to make war upon the King of Sweden (all which can be made out by authentic letters), and without giving any other answer, he made the same army advance with great diligence and harassed that of the King of Sweden in Prussia during the whole summer, whereby he had doubtless suffered the entire ruin of his states, friends and allies, if God, who is the protector of righteous causes, and the preserver of his innocence, had not taken in his own hand the defense of his cause, having made his enemies justly suffer the evils which they had unjustly prepared and designed against him.

All this being considered, it is abundantly evident how much His Majesty of Sweden, who has been so often crossed in his good designs for a peace, has

---

6   The Swedish envoy Sten Bielke, a relation of Chancellor Oxenstierna's mother. He was Sweden's main diplomatic agent in the Empire until his death early in 1638 when he was replaced by Johan Adler Salvius [see **Docs 166–7**].

been constrained at last to take up arms in good earnest against his enemies in his own defense, and for the preservation of his person, states, and allies.

It may be objected here that he ought to have temporized and waited for the answer to his letters from the College of Electors, since the King of Denmark interposed in that matter; who, by the persuasion and instigation of His said Majesty, had, ever since last winter, endeavored to compose the whole by a treaty of peace. But it must also be infallibly presupposed here, that if His said Majesty had seen the least sign or appearance of receiving a just reparation for the outrages and damages done him, and some security and liberty for his neighbors, he had never been so warm in his resentment, but rather condescended to any proposals of a peace, according to his zeal and natural inclination to the public tranquillity and quiet. But after another treaty of peace was projected in the city of Danzig in Prussia, and the commissioner of the aggressor would signify or declare nothing to the commissioner of the party offended, who offered to treat with him, and fully to apprise him of his pretensions, had showed his commission; it is easy to conclude from thence, that the Swedish commissioner was entirely disposed to seek peace and that, on the contrary, the enemy had no such intention, considering the frauds and tricks they made use of formerly, and which they likewise practiced in that same negotiation at Danzig, and which are but too manifest, since at that time they seized the passes and fortified places in Pomerania to push their conquests further and continue the war with more violence; a proof too sufficient to show how little security and certainty there was in such treaties.

As to the College of Electors, there is but too much appearance that he had gained as little there; although His said Majesty was apt to believe, that had the said Electoral College had full power from the Emperor, they would have certainly fallen upon some good measures in order to a peace; not to mention the authority which the said College has had, and ought to have in all times, which is endeavored to be diminished by little and little. For by their answer of the month of April to the letters of His said Majesty, the said lords Electors approved very well the proposition which he made them of an amicable agreement and composition, promising him herein to go along with him by a mutual goodwill; but they made no mention of the reparation demanded for the wrongs, injuries and other indignities which he complained of, which however his letters required in a special manner: from whence it is easy to judge that they left him at liberty to take care of his own affairs, as he should think proper.

And for as much as His Majesty of Sweden has suffered so many outrages and injuries without being able to receive any satisfaction for them, such as having his letters intercepted, opened, falsely deciphered, and interpreted, his subjects, officers, and soldiers imprisoned, after having been robbed of all they had and prohibited commerce, which by the right of nature is common to all the world; since the Emperor has disconcerted and hindered the peace or agreement with the King of Poland, and on the contrary assisted him with a great many troops; since he has caused whole armies to march into Prussia against His Majesty and the kingdom of Sweden, to ruin them; since he has entirely denied him the passage demanded in all friendship, and under cautions and assurances; since he has plundered his friends, allies, neighbors, and relations (in hatred to His Majesty's name) who are oppressed, persecuted, and despoiled of their duchies and lordships, banished and chased from their lands and houses, and almost reduced to beggary; since he ignominiously debarred and rejected, in a most barbarous manner, his ambassadors, who were dispatched with full power to treat of a peace; and since, *in fine*, he sent two strong armies against His Majesty without any just cause or reason and even without any pretext that may serve for a color to the wicked designs of his enemies. Seeing all this, is there any person of understanding and sense, not prepossessed with passion and private interest that can deny both by divine and human laws and by the very instinct of nature it is lawful to make use of the means which God puts in our hands to resent and avenge ourselves for so sensible an injury? Especially for Kings and sovereign princes, particularly when their honor and person, the safety of their states, and the good of their subjects are concerned; when all appearance of honor and satisfaction is denied them: it being most true and notorious to all the world that not only by menaces and secret practices but also by force and violence the enemy has seized and would likewise take possession of the ports and harbors of the Baltic Sea, to establish new admiralties there, in prejudice of the ordinary commerce and ancient liberty, and to the total ruin of the maritime towns; and after such unjust enterprises and designs are yet continued by the preparations of the enemy both by sea and land: Is there anyone, I say, that can blame the most serene King of Sweden for endeavoring by his arms to defend his subjects and friends from such an oppression?

And to sum up the whole in a few words: Are not we instructed by the laws of nature to repel force by force? And who is he that will not judge that His Majesty has been really forced against his will to undertake this just war and obliged thereto by constraint and urgent necessity, after having tried all the ways of right justice and met with all sorts of obstructions and hindrances instead of the good and wholesome remedies he proposed?

Now there remaining no other means to be employed but that of arms for his own preservation and for the defense and protection of his subjects and friends, he desires that all Christendom would judge whether he has not taken them up with regret and after being forced by extreme necessity.

If there be found any one of his enemies who should blame and reproach His Majesty for having taken upon him the defense and particular protection of the city of Stralsund, (the justice whereof is however very apparent), the blame ought to be imputed to those who gave occasion to it and who without all reason first attacked that city, its ports, and territory, and exercised the ravages and barbarities mentioned above.

If His Majesty had in any manner favored the enterprises of the Emperor's and the Empire's enemies, or if he had entered into a league and association with them, people would not be surprised if they paid him back in his own coin; but having always persisted in a resolution to live in peace and constantly continued in the amity and neutrality of both parties during the wars of Germany without having ever given any cause of suspicion or offence, he hath at present all the reason in the world to complain to all Christendom of the bad and unworthy treatment he has met with.

For which cause His said Majesty of Sweden having no designs to the prejudice of the Empire, against which he protests he has no quarrel or enmity whatsoever, has only taken up arms for the public good, for his own safety, and the preservation of his friends, whom he desires to put in the same state and liberty which they were in before this war, and by the same means to secure for the future the neighborhood and the Baltic Sea, and his own kingdom of Sweden, against all violence of pirates and robbers.

And to come to a conclusion; His Majesty has this confidence, that all honest people, who shall see this manifesto and his declaration, and read it without prejudice and consider the reasons therein briefly and truely laid down, will find cause for blaming and condemning the procedure of his enemies, as most unjust and detestable, most wicked and dangerous, examples for the Electors and other princes of the Empire, upon whom the like attempts and usurpations may be endeavored to be made afterwards. He hopes also that all Germany and even all Christendom will favor the just resolution he has taken to defend himself by arms, in order to prevent and repel the violent enterprises of those usurpers, who have so unhappily conspired his ruin and given the Emperor such pernicious counsels, as tend only to the usurpation of what is another's and of the liberty of Germany; His Majesty being willing favorably to believe that they have herein exceeded the powers, instructions, and commands of the said lord the Emperor, and eluded the good and wholesome counsels of the Electors and princes of the Empire.

Source: *A general collection of treatys* ..., 4 vols (London, 1710–32), vol. II, pp. 292–304.

---

67. Internal debates: council minutes, 4 May 1630

Whether it was advisable to restore Stralsund, in the event of the Emperor's accepting the terms proposed to him [at the Danzig conference]?

Herr Gabriel [Gustafsson Oxenstierna] thought that the question was settled by the terms of our treaty with Stralsund, since they laid it down that the King is to withdraw his garrison as soon as the Emperor restores the original state of affairs [in Mecklenburg] ...

The King: ... Our basic war aim is security; and if the Emperor will grant the terms we have proposed, that would be a sufficient guarantee; but if the King were then to continue his occupation of Stralsund it would look as though he sought to enlarge his dominions ...

[Others] denied that this would be an adequate guarantee of safety; for if our security is to be assured it must be under our own control, and not in the discretion of the enemy, for ... there can be no safety if we hand back any position which we cannot immediately retake ...

Herr Gabriel thought that we ought in the first place to demand a general restitution of the Estates [of Germany] ...

The King made the point that it would be iniquitous to deprive the Dukes of Pomerania and Mecklenburg of their hereditary rights for the sake of getting an agreement with the Emperor.

The Field-Marshal [Jakob de la Gardie]: It is quite possible for the King to occupy their lands without claiming dominion over them.

Source: Michael Roberts (ed.), *Sweden as a Great Power 1611–1697: Government: Society: Foreign Policy* (London, 1968), pp. 139–40; translated from *Svenska riksådets protokoll*, vol. II, pp. 1–4.

68. Gustavus Adolphus to Chancellor Oxenstierna, 12 May 1630

[On Oxenstierna's draft of an instruction to the Swedish delegates at the Danzig negotiations:]

The King is well satisfied with the instructions as a whole, but notices that the Chancellor has omitted to bear in mind the most important point of all, namely *assecuratio* [security]. The Chancellor is accordingly to take care that the King is not engaged to quit Stralsund, or any other place which he may be able to acquire, until all the conditions of peace are carried out by the Imperialists, their armies entirely withdrawn from the Saxon Circles, and everything (especially the coastlands) restored to a secure and peaceable condition.

Source: Michael Roberts (ed.), *Sweden as a Great Power 1611–1697: Government: Society: Foreign Policy* (London, 1968), pp. 140; translated from *Axel Oxenstiernas skrifter och brevvexling*, II, i, pp. 603–4.

69. The 'norms for future action', 1631

[As dictated by Gustavus to his secretary in May 1631:]

The ultimate or supreme goal of all actions: A new Evangelical Leader.

The penultimate objective: A new league between the Evangelical Estates and such a Leader.

This to be realized by the following means:
1. By a coordinated direction of the war;
2. The foundation of it: The right a patron has over his clients.

3. The confirmation of it:

1. Lies in the concession ... and occupation of fortified places.

2. By fixed contributions, either to the expenses of the war or of troops to be maintained at the charges of each member.

3. By free access to and transit through electorates, principalities, etc.

4. By denying requisitions to the enemy.

...

7. By strong reciprocal agreements that neither party has the right without the knowledge and consent of the other to withdraw from this alliance until the ultimate objective of the war is within the reach of all. Such a group would be difficult to organise, but might best be achieved in the following manner.

...

5. If Your Majesty does receive the absolute direction of this alliance or sufficient satisfaction, you must organise your war effort from your own resources ... words and treaties will not fill the sack.

6. Unfortunately in Germany discussions are always about day and not night, while action is about night and not day. While there is nothing fundamental to be expected from the conventions and diets ... at least much occurs that is often useful and helpful. Though such discussions can be allowed to continue, it is now urgent that Your Majesty negotiates separately with one [territory] after another, and so gradually forms a solid alliance.

7. Ideally, the elector of Brandenburg would be the first (if he can be brought to a good agreement), since this would provide a bridge to electoral Saxony ... This would be best achieved through a personal meeting with Your Majesty.

8. [To persuade Saxony to join] the army should always be ready to move into the electorate of Saxony, the elector should come to a meeting and told to join his forces with ours, but first he should be notified by letter of the terms to be reached with Brandenburg. If the war should unfortunately spread to his lands, and there would be no choice but to join Your Majesty and Brandenburg ...

10. Finally, some thought needs to be given to how Brandenburg and Saxony can be compensated (but not with Pomerania), because the war will chiefly be fought at the expense of them and their lands.

Norms for future action dictated by His Majesty the King of Sweden.

Source: B. Boëthius, 'Norma futurarum actionum', *Historisk Tidskrift*, 31 (1911), pp. 200–4.

70. Sweden's explanation of Gustavus's intentions, 1633

[Minutes of two meetings between Axel Oxenstierna and the Brandenburg government in Berlin, 30–31 January (OS), 9–10 February (NS), 1633:]

De intentione regis [Concerning the King's intentions]
They were, in general, to disrupt the *conatus* [plans] of the enemy, whose intentions with regard to the Baltic are sufficiently well known. His Majesty therefore intended to ensure the safety of his kingdom and the Baltic, and to liberate the oppressed lands [of Germany]; and thereafter to proceed according as events might develop: it was no part of his original intention to press on as far as he did. He saw and clearly understood where that would lead, but the enemy and the circumstances compelled this. His Majesty was there in person wherever the greatest danger was.

Momenta temporum were always the basis of his plans.

In specie [in particular] he intended to advance down the Danube into Bavaria and take the war into the land above the Enns [Upper Austria] and then go temporarily on the defensive there. However, since the enemy moved his entire force here, the king changed his plans and moved here [i.e. northeast Germany] leaving only his officers back there. The battle [Lützen] was then fought between them; that the king, had he lived, would certainly have won and ruined the enemy. After his death things became somewhat confused, because there was no one in command and the soldiery had been quite ruined in the recent battle.

The King would have adapted his policies in the light of the enemy's action, the circumstances of the moment, and the conduct of his friends.

Source: G. Irmer (ed.), *Die Verhandlungen Schwedens und seiner Verbündeten mit Wallenstein und dem Kaiser von 1631 bis 1634*, 3 vols (Stuttgart, 1888–91), vol. II, pp. 26–7.

71. Later reflections: Oxenstierna writing in 1636

It is now certain that had His Late Majesty not betaken himself to Germany with his army, the emperor would today have had a fleet on the seas – for he had fourteen ships even then – and it would have been in his power, with no more than 2,000 soldiers, to take Copenhagen, and capture the king of Denmark himself. And if the emperor had once got hold of Stralsund the whole coast would have fallen to him, and here in Sweden we should never have enjoyed a moment's security.

Source: Quoted in N. Ahnlund, *Gustav Adolf the Great* (Princeton, 1940), p. 252.

72. Ferdinand's response, 1630

Ferdinand II to Gustavus Adolphus, 18 August 1630

We Ferdinand II, by the grace of God Elected Roman Emperor ... express our friendship to our dear friend the serene prince Gustavus Adolphus, king of the Swedes, Goths and Wends. We wish to inform you that we have reliable reports that you have collected a large army of horse and foot throughout this year and have landed on islands belonging to the Holy Empire and are now on its soil and have seized some prominent places, castles and towns in the duchy of Pomerania and levied tolls that lie within our jurisdiction and are resolved on further acts hostile to the Empire.

We know that we and the Empire have never harmed you in the slightest throughout our difficult reign, nor caused any misunderstanding that might give grounds for such open hostilities. We are completely baffled why you have effectively begun open war (that will harm both sides) over some difficulties regarding the town of Stralsund that lies on our and the Empire's soil and concern its laws and justice. ... especially as we feel that such hostilities and unnecessary bloodshed can easily be avoided through the mediation suggested and now obligingly undertaken by the king of Denmark. Unlike you, we have indicated our desire for this and have instructed and dispatched our envoys to the talks.

Regardless of this, I would have at least expected according to international law that you would have sent some prior denunciation citing an ostensible pretext or legal cause according to your view prior to this hostile invasion. We assure you that our military preparations on the Baltic and elsewhere were never, nor are, intended to give you offence. On the contrary, we wish to remain good neighbours with the kingdom of Sweden, and would like to continue so provided you do not give further cause otherwise and stop this unnecessary war.

We hereby remind you as a friend not to interfere further in the Empire's affairs for which we give you no cause. Furthermore, your troops are to leave the places they have taken and evacuate the Holy Empire's islands and lands on the continent. Maritime travel and commerce is not to be hindered, nor any intrusion made into our and the Empire's maritime jurisdiction. If, contrary to hope, you ignore or reject our imperial declaration and mandate, and continue either with open hostilities or de facto occupation of the places seized, we will be forced to take extreme measures together with the loyal electors and Estates of the Holy Roman Empire to reoccupy them and prevent further evil, and to defend our imperial and the Holy Empire's reputation and to save its loyal Estates' lands and peoples; though we hope it will not come to this. Since this letter will reach you with your court, we affirm our friendly inclinations towards you. Done in our Holy Roman imperial city of Regensburg, 18 August 1630 ...

Source: O.S. Rydberg and Carl Hallendorf (eds), *Sveriges Tractater med främmande magter jemte andra dit hörande handlingar*, 5 vols (Stockholm, 1902–9), vol. V, part 1, pp. 827–9.

SWEDEN'S ALLIANCE POLICY

73. Treaty with Duke Bogislav of Pomerania, 9 July 1630

We Gustavus Adolphus by the grace of God king of the Swedes, Goths and Wends, grand prince of Finland [etc.] on the one part
And we by the grace of God Bogislav, duke of Pomerania [etc.]
hereby declare this agreement to be binding on our successors and our kingdoms, duchies, principalities and lands to protect the innocent Pomeranian lands from the harsh suffering of the past three years against all hostile powers and through God's grace to rescue it and place it in its former condition. To this end, both parties agree a special defence pact as follows.

First, that we the king of Sweden have assumed the direction of this defence and the military obligations resulting from it and we will have absolute control of everything necessary for war. We the duke of Pomerania grant His Majesty constant and open access to allow the places, towns, fortresses and crossing points of our Pomeranian lands and allow his entire army or detachments from it to cross, supplying them as specified in the accompanying schedule. They can garrison or leave places as they see fit for as long as this war lasts or until a suitable peace is concluded. We the duke of Pomerania retain the civil administration of all places, as well as police powers, jurisdiction, government over the prelates, knights and towns and usage of all districts, monasteries and properties.

Second, any misunderstandings or disputes between the garrisons and Estates, or between soldiers and inhabitants, are to be adjudicated by a commission composed equally of royal and ducal commissioners.

Third, we both agree that soldiers billeted or marching are to observe the law and that the royal cavalry are not to demand more than fodder, hay and straw for the horses, and the soldiers are not to demand more than necessary for firewood and lighting.

Fourth, since His Majesty has incurred considerable expense in rescuing and defending Pomerania, the duke will allow him to collect tolls on the rivers and ports for the duration of the war or until a permanent peace. His Majesty will take four fifths of each per cent, while the duke retains one fifth. The tolls are levied in the duke's name but lie at His Majesty's disposition and will be received by his collector and the duke's accountant as to be specified in a separate agreement.

Fifth, we the king of Sweden have asked the duke of Pomerania and his Estates to assist us in this costly defence by mobilising the knights and inhabitants. We the duke of Pomerania, after consulting our Estates, have agreed, but in view of the difficulties have decided not to perform such military service, but to instead pay 200,000 imperial talers each year, in three instalments, first of 100,000 and then two of 50,000 each, with the proviso that no further military service is demanded, except in the case of an invasion. For this reason, and to protect against enemy incursions, the peasants are to retain their weapons, but this imposes no obligation on the Estates.

Sixth, we the duke of Pomerania allow His Majesty's warships free access to our rivers and ports, to winter there and to billet their crews but without burden to the inhabitants, to fortify the access points as His Majesty sees fit with the assistance of our subjects and officials to help in the construction of entrenchments.

If royal soldiers are also used on the work, they will receive a daily pay bonus which is to be included in the above-mentioned billeting agreement.

We affirm this agreement with our signatures and seals. Done at Stettin, 30 August, 1630 [OS].

Source: O.S. Rydberg and Carl Hallendorf (eds), *Sveriges Tractater med främmande magter jemte andra dit hörande handlingar*, 5 vols (Stockholm, 1902–9), vol. V, part 1, pp. 395–8.

---

74. Sweden's attitude to neutrality: Gustavus to Elector Georg Wilhelm of Brandenburg, June 1631

I don't want to hear about neutrality. His Grace must be my friend or foe. When I arrive on his frontier, he must declare himself cold or hot. This is a fight between God and the devil. If His Grace is with God, he must join me, if he is for the devil, he must fight me. There is no third way.

Source: Hans Jessen (ed.), *Der Dreißigjährige Krieg in Augenzeugenberichten* (Düsseldorf, 1963), p. 242.

---

75. Brandenburg's dilemma, June 1631

Elector Georg Wilhelm to Count Adam von Schwarzenberg[1] 5 July 1631

We could not let this opportunity slip without telling you what has passed between us and HMS [His Majesty of Sweden] since your departure. HMS

---

[1] Adam von Schwarzenberg (1583–1641), a Catholic from Westphalia, entered Brandenburg service in 1610 and dominated the electoral government by 1627 as Georg Wilhelm's most trusted advisor. Hated by the more militant Calvinist officials, he was vilified in later Prussian historiography for allegedly selling out the country's 'true' interests by favouring an alliance with the emperor. The letter is dated Kölln, then a separate town, but part of Berlin from 1709.

already used every opportunity during the Leipzig Convention[2] through letters or envoys to present us with this dilemma: we should either join him or fight him. HMS did not expect much from the Leipzig Convention and waited impatiently for it to end. Since then he has redoubled his efforts. Since then the imperial troops have abandoned our towns of Frankfurt [on the Oder] and Landsberg [on the Warthe] after feeble defence, and evacuated our lands this side of the Elbe from which they have drawn many millions,[3] claiming they could not trust us. HMS then advanced with his army to the [river] Havel, to the doors of our residence, which they found defenceless since the imperialists did not arrive. We learned that HMS wanted to speak to us, so we went to meet him between here and Köpenick accompanied by our mother-in-law and wife[4] and entire court and met him shortly outside our residence. He accepted our invitation to go inside where we hoped the business would be easier in those surroundings than when we negotiated through our councillors. However, we found that HMS still insisted on the same points and ignored ours (that HMS should hand the duchy of Pomerania to us, as well as evacuate our own Brandenburg lands without demanding recompense of his military expenses. In return, we would join him and the other evangelical imperial Estates already allied to him, for the security of our lands and people). Instead, he presented harsh counter-demands: (1) that we should ratify the alliance with the duke of Pomerania[5] and (2) accept what they call the laws of war that HMS claims entitles him to recover his war costs in Pomerania by, as far as we can tell, controlling the entire coast, or at least the ports in order to dominate the sea. Furthermore, (3) our exhausted lands must pay large sums to the royal army and (4) surrender the *directorium belli*[6] in our lands by handing over whichever fortresses HMS wants, allowing his garrisons in and ordering ours out, and even dismissing whichever of our commanders and officers he chooses; in short, handing over complete military control.

The duty that binds us to His Roman Imperial Majesty and the Empire; the respect we possess amongst our fellow evangelical Estates; even what the imperial and Kreis constitution, the hereditary inheritance pacts and family agreements allow – all this counts for nothing.

HMS would only accept one middle path, namely that we guarantee the safety of his person and, if necessary, retreat [back across Brandenburg] for the then long-proposed relief march to the city of Magdeburg; that we allow

---

2   The meeting of Protestant imperial Estates sponsored by Saxony, February–April 1631 [see **Doc. 65**].

3   Around 10,000 imperial troops had been billeted in the Brandenburg countryside since late 1625; an arrangement formalised as an alliance with the emperor in 1627.

4   Respectively Luise Juliane of Orange-Nassau (1576–1644) and Elisabeth Charlotte of Pfalz-Simmern (1597–1660). Elisabeth Charlotte was a younger sister of Frederick V of the Palatinate.

5   See **Doc. 73**.

6   Direction of the war, i.e. military control.

temporary access to the fortress of Spandau, but postpone all other matters till later. We were faced with the two extremes of either fully joining [Sweden] or open hostilities. The former was unacceptable, while the latter was impossible because the imperial troops had completely abandoned us, our wife and children and the most prominent and largest parts of our lands that were now in the king of Sweden's hands. There was no expectation of relief, leaving us no choice but to accept the least of all the evils and agree the proposed compromise. The fortress of Spandau was handed over to a Swedish garrison under the terms enclosed with this letter.

We hoped that this would at last put an end to the matter, but we were mistaken. The city of Magdeburg surrendered to General Tilly and HMS marched back with his army and camped between Spandau and this residence. The difficult negotiations resumed, and our commiserations at what had happened[7] were met by a letter of rejection, a copy of which is enclosed, putting the blame on us.

The business progressed to the extent that HMS returned our fortress of Spandau, but marched with his army on the 10th of this month [OS] to our residence, surrounded it and trained his artillery upon it. There was no choice but to surrender Spandau again for the duration of the war, allow HMS access at any time through Küstrin[8] and agree a high monthly contribution to be paid from our lands this side of the Elbe. HMS was at last satisfied, and promised to end all the other burdens and billeting of his troops that our lands have suffered until now.

What all this will mean, lies in the hands of God Almighty, and we must expect much harm to follow this defection from the imperial side. We can, however, take comfort in the fact that we tried everything in our power, and the situation left us no choice but to take this course. Any impartial observer will see, first, how the imperial army abandoned us after it had sucked our lands dry, second that the king of Sweden seized our lands and had our residence in his hands and could do as he pleased, and third that we were in no position to resist (though the imperialists do not accept this) and there was no hope of relief. Anyone would have found it hard to find another way out of this dilemma.

The king of Sweden returned to Pomerania after the negotiations and retook the town of Greifswald, but came back yesterday and reoccupied the positions along the Havel. It is assumed he will advance further. We have not told anyone of this course of events which you are to keep to yourself. We remain [etc.].

Source: Johann Kretzschmar, *Gustav Adolfs Pläne und Ziele in Deutschland und die Herzöge zu Braunschweig und Lüneburg* (Hanover and Leipzig, 1904), pp. 311–15.

---

7   That is, the fall of Magdeburg.
8   A fortress controlling a vital crossing over the Oder.

76. Treaty between Sweden and Saxony, 11 September 1631

Elector Johann Georg's statement.

By the grace of God, we Johann Georg, Duke of Saxony, Jülich, Cleves and Berg, hereditary marshal and elector of the Holy Roman Empire, landgrave of Thuringia, margrave of Meissen [etc.]. Since General Count Tilly invaded our innocent lands and peoples despite all efforts and contrary to the Holy Roman Empire's highly praised constitution and especially the Religious and Profane Peace, and since the serene prince and lord, Gustavus Adolphus, king of the Swedes, Goths and Wends [etc.] at our request promised to assist us with his army, we have agreed with His Majesty by our word and Christian conscience the following:

First, as soon as His Majesty has crossed the Elbe we will join him with our army and act in concert, standing as one against our common enemies. We will leave full direction of operations to His Majesty and act as far as possible according to His Majesty's advice, not withdrawing our troops from his as long as the danger persists, nor make peace without prior consent.

Second, we wish to assist His Majesty should he need to retreat across the Elbe by allowing him to place troops in the crossing points and to defend these against his enemies to the utmost, and have instructed our commandants of these towns not to hinder this.

Third, we will supply the necessary food and forage to His Majesty's army as long as it is in our lands fighting our enemies. We affirm this through our signature and electoral seal. Torgau 1 September 1630 [OS].

King Gustavus Adolphus's statement.

We Gustavus Adolphus by the grace of God king of the Swedes, Goths and Wends [etc.] hereby declare that, after we crossed with our army from our kingdoms to the Roman Empire of the German nation in order, among other things, to provide Christian assistance to our oppressed and despoiled dynastic and religious relations, we learned from the high-born prince, our dear relation Lord Johann Georg, Duke of Saxony [etc.], that General Tilly and his army was approaching his electorate and lands, we agreed today to provide all possible assistance with our army of horse and foot. We have given our royal and Christian word to stand as one against our common enemies and to help drive them from his lands with God's assistance. We will not infringe His Grace's electoral status, jurisdictions, privileges, fortresses, crossing points or territory in any way, but will behave correctly towards him, his lands and people and will do all in our power in this Christian alliance to save his status, lands and people. We affirm this with our signature and seal. Camp at Wittenberg 1 September 1630 [OS].

Source: O.S. Rydberg and Carl Hallendorf (eds), *Sveriges Tractater med främmande magter jemte andra dit hörande handlingar*, 5 vols (Stockholm, 1902–9), vol. V, part 1, pp. 513–16.

FRANCE AND BAVARIA

77. The Treaty of Bärwalde, 23 January 1631, and the Guarantee for Bavaria, 15 January 1631

[A preamble refers to the armistice between Sweden and Poland, mediated by France, as the start of Franco-Swedish negotiations towards an alliance to the benefit of the liberty of their common friends and neighbours. The plenipotentiaries were Gustav Horn, Johan and Karl Banér for Sweden, and Hercule de Charnacé for France, who agreed the following:]

1 Between Their Most Serene Majesties the Kings of Sweden and France there shall be an alliance for the defence of the friends of each and both of them, for the safeguarding of the Baltic and Oceanic Seas, the liberty of commerce, and the restitution of the oppressed Estates of the Roman Empire; and also in order to ensure that the fortresses and defence-works which have been constructed, in the ports and on the shores of the Baltic and Oceanic Seas, and in the Grisons,[1] be demolished and reduced to the state in which they were immediately before this present German war.

2 And because up to the present day the enemy has refused to give a just reparation for the injuries he has caused, and has hitherto rejected all appeals, [the allies will] take up arms to vindicate the cause of their common friends.

3 To that end the King of Sweden will take his share of the great burden of the war by bringing an army of 30,000 infantry and 6,000 cavalry at his own expense to Germany and maintaining it there. The King of France will contribute 400,000 Imperial thaler, that is, a million *livres tournois*, every year, which will be paid and accounted for without fail to the agents of the King of Sweden appointed for that purpose, either at Paris or Amsterdam, as the King of Sweden may find the more convenient; of which one half is to be paid on 15 May and the other on 15 November, each year.

4 The raising of soldiers and sailors, the export of ships and materials of war are to be free as between the territories of the allies, but are to be refused to enemies.

5 Mutineers and deserters are to be returned to their masters for punishment.

---

[1] The Grisons was the generally accepted name for the Rhetian Republic, a state composed of three alliances of Alpine communities of which the Grey League (i.e. Grisons) was the largest. The area is now south-eastern Switzerland. The Protestant Rhetians controlled the Valtellina, a Catholic valley giving access over the Alps from Spanish Milan into Habsburg Austria. The valley and other parts of Rhetia were occupied during the Mantuan war [see **Docs 56–9**], but abandoned thereafter. France had backed the Protestant Rhetians since the early 1620s, but they switched alliance to Spain after 1637 in return for Habsburg recognition of their control of the Valtellina.

6 If God should be pleased to grant successes to the King of Sweden, he is in matters of religion to treat territories occupied by or ceded to him according to the laws and constitution of the Empire; and in places where the exercise of the Roman Catholic religion exists, it shall remain undisturbed.

7 Any other Estates or princes whoever they may be within Germany as without, who may wish to join this league, shall be admitted to it. Nonetheless, care is to be taken that those that do join, do not covertly or openly favour the other side or damage the aforementioned kings and the common cause, but on the contrary everyone should contribute to the cost of this war as far as his means allow and the cause demands; to which end a special treaty is to be concluded.

8 With the Duke of Bavaria and the Catholic League in the Roman Empire friendship, or at least neutrality, is to be preserved, provided that they on their side observe it.

9 And if, by the grace of God, an opportunity to treat for peace should present itself, the negotiations shall be conducted jointly by the allies, and neither will without the other initiate or conclude a peace.

10 This alliance shall last for five years, and so from the present day till 1 March 1636 old style. Should no secure peace be concluded within this time, the alliance can be extended at the mutual agreement of the allies.

11 It is agreed, finally, that since negotiations for this alliance began last year, that the alliance was made for six years. And since the King of Sweden has in the meanwhile incurred great expense for this war, 40,000 imperial taler, that is 300,000 *livre tournois*, will be given on the day of the signature of this present treaty in the name of the King of France for this first year, which is now almost elapsed. For this purpose bills of exchange will be contracted by us and not accounted against the [already agreed] sums of the other five years.

[Gustavus Adolphus's guarantee of neutrality for the Elector of Bavaria and the Catholic League, 15 January 1631:]

We, Gustavus Adolphus, by the Grace of God etc. Be it known to all men, that whereas the most serene and mighty Prince ... Louis XIII ... our most dear Ally, has earnestly entreated us ... to take especial care to observe friendship and neutrality, on a reciprocal basis, towards the ... Elector of Bavaria and the Catholic League, we are therefore willing, out of our regard for the aforesaid Most Christian King, to indulge him, as our brother and ally, in this matter, so that the said ... Elector of Bavaria and the Catholic League shall be safe from our enmity within their own territories, and shall enjoy an amicable neutrality, for so long as the said Elector of Bavaria and the Catholic League on their side sincerely perform their parts as friends and neutrals, and abstain from every kind of hostility, open or clandestine, against us and our friends and allies, and do not consent to any hostile decrees against us ...

Source: O.S. Rydberg and Carl Hallendorf (eds), *Sveriges Tractater med främmande magter jemte andra dit hörande handlingar*, 5 vols (Stockholm, 1902–9), vol. V, part 2, pp. 438–42.

---

78. The Treaty of Fontainebleau, 30 May 1631

His Most Christian King of France and Navarre and the Elector of Bavaria are concerned to strengthen their good friendship and mutual defence and to arrange this through a treaty with the following negotiated articles.

1 Between His Most Christian Majesty and the Elector of Bavaria there will be a sincere, good and durable friendship and a firm, mutual obligation for defence to last eight years, by which the King is obliged to defend the elector and his inherited and acquired provinces in the event of a hostile attack with 9,000 infantry and 2,000 cavalry with the appropriate military equipment at his own expense. The Elector is free to choose whether to request this aid in the given number of soldiers or their equivalent in money.

2 Equally, the Elector of Bavaria is bound to defend His Most Christian Majesty and his inherited and acquired provinces in the event of a hostile attack with 3,000 infantry and 1,000 cavalry with the appropriate military equipment. The King is free to choose whether to request this aid in the given number of soldiers or their equivalent in money.

3 His Most Christian Majesty promises not to use his forces in any way against the Elector of Bavaria and his subject provinces, nor to provide soldiers or money either directly or indirectly to those who attack the said elector and his provinces, nor to allow the recruitment in his kingdom of soldiers against the said elector and his provinces, nor to permit his friends to provide secretly weapons, cannon and gunpowder to such soldiers.

[Art. 4 restated these terms for Maximilian.]

5 His Most Christian Majesty promises to recognise the electoral dignity of the said elector and his house, to defend and protect it against all who express the wish or seek to deprive him of it or prevent the exercise of it.

6 Since circumstances require that this alliance and mutual defence pact between His Most Christian Majesty and the Elector of Bavaria must on no account be divulged to others, both sides have agreed that it will not be publicly acknowledged.

7 His Most Christian Majesty and the Elector of Bavaria have all the more confirmed and promised all these articles, because they are permitted by natural law to do so and they reflect the royal majesty and the electoral dignity,

without prejudice on the part of the said elector to his oath to his emperor and the Empire. In consideration of this reservation, the aforementioned Elector promises to carry out all that is contained in this treaty sincerely, exactly and truly. ...

Done at Fontainebleau, 30 May in the Year of Our Lord 1631 ...

Source: Dieter Albrecht, *Die auswärtige Politik Maximilians von Bayern 1618–1635* (Göttingen, 1962), pp. 378–9.

10

The destruction of Magdeburg, 1631

The destruction of Magdeburg was the worst calamity to befall any community during the war. It attracted attention throughout Europe and swiftly came to exemplify a conflict which seemed to break all bounds. Pappenheim's estimate of the death toll is probably correct [**Doc. 79**]. Only about a fifth of the city's 25,000 inhabitants survived and over 4,500 of these soon fled their devastated homes, many of which were still in ruins a century later. Even after 12 years of conflict, devastation on this scale was deeply shocking, but reactions to the disaster were mixed and far more complex than the later reception in the historical literature which generally presents it merely as an extreme example of the horrors of war.

Magdeburg's complex internal politics are a microcosm of the tangled web of issues behind the war in the Empire. The city embraced the Lutheran Reformation as early as 1524, but it was also part of the similarly named archbishopric which only passed into Protestant administration in 1545. Despite sharing a common faith, the archbishop-administrator and city were often at loggerheads over the latter's desire for greater autonomy as an imperial city. The cathedral chapter consistently chose princes from the Hohenzollern dynasty ruling Brandenburg as administrators, but this became problematic when the family converted to Calvinism in 1613. Many in the chapter and city favoured closer ties to Saxony, home of the Reformation, and the Saxon electors hoped to displace Brandenburg as Magdeburg's rulers. The citizens were uniformly Lutheran, but a Catholic minority remained in the countryside and amongst the cathedral canons, as well as the monks of the Premonstratensian monastery within the city. This presence fuelled Catholic hopes that the archbishopric, one of the Empire's oldest and most prestigious, might be recovered for their church.

This already complex situation became immeasurably worse when the current administrator, Christian Wilhelm of Brandenburg, declared for Denmark late in 1625. This played directly into Emperor Ferdinand II's hands by providing an excuse to depose him and force the canons to elect the emperor's younger son, Leopold Wilhelm (1614–62), instead. Hoping to preserve their autonomy, some canons elected another candidate, August von Sachsen-Weissenfels (1614–80), younger son of Johann Georg of Saxony. The emperor expected Wallenstein to enforce Leopold Wilhelm's election. Wallenstein had already occupied nearby Halberstadt late in 1625 as an operational base in north Germany. He was keen that Magdeburg admit an imperial garrison, because the city lay on the river Elbe which flows from Bohemia across northern Germany into the North Sea. Wallenstein's army relied on the Elbe to transport grain and other supplies from the Habsburg lands. However, Wallenstein was reluctant to impose Leopold Wilhelm, knowing once the Habsburg prince was installed as archbishop, any local revenues would go to maintain him rather than the imperial army. Wallenstein thus blockaded rather than besieged Magdeburg during 1628. The blockade was tightened in 1629, but Wallenstein had no desire to use this to enforce the Edict of Restitution which formally required the archbishopric to be restored to Catholicism. He still hoped the Hanseatic League, a major commercial and maritime organisation, would back his Baltic Design [see Docs 53–5] and had no desire to antagonise it by attacking Magdeburg which was one of its members.

It became much harder to show restraint after Christian Wilhelm, who still claimed to be administrator, slipped through the cordon of imperial troops and entered the city in July 1630. Unlike his nephew Elector Georg Wilhelm of Brandenburg, Christian Wilhelm had nothing to lose and readily allied with Sweden. Magdeburg's adherence to Sweden was hugely symbolic. The city had resisted Emperor Charles V's attempt to reimpose Catholicism on the Empire and withstood a long siege before being captured in 1551. Its defiance had been instrumental in mobilising the opposition amongst the princes who eventually secured recognition of Lutheran rights in the 1555 Religious Peace. Alliance with Magdeburg thus allowed Gustavus Adolphus to pose as defender of the imperial constitution as well as Protestant champion.

The Swedish alliance divided opinion in the city. The exact details are unclear, since we are reliant on accounts composed later by participants who sought to excuse themselves from any part in the disaster. One of the best is an anonymous account generally accepted to have been written by Otto Guericke (1602–86), a city councillor and later mayor and noted physicist [Doc. 80]. Many councillors still hoped to buy off imperial demands for a garrison with a large cash payment. The poorer citizens refused, knowing this would be largely at their expense, and suspecting that if any soldiers were admitted, they would be billeted in their homes rather than on the richer patricians. The city's outspoken Lutheran pastors condemned any compromise, but it is unclear how far they encouraged the fateful defiance. Most inhabitants probably hoped some solution would be brokered by Saxony, but Christian Wilhelm's presence thwarted that. The arrival of a Swedish officer as commandant further eroded the council's ability to reach a uniform decision.

With Wallenstein dismissed [see Doc. 60], it fell to Tilly to force the city to submit to imperial authority. Reinforcements allowed Tilly to begin a siege. His repeated offers to accept surrender were refused by the council which unwisely accepted Swedish assurances that Gustavus Adolphus was marching to their aid. In fact, the Swedish king was busy bullying his Brandenburg in-law into an alliance [see Docs 75–6]. After a final summons was rejected, 18,000 imperial and League troops stormed the city early on 20 May 1631. A fire was started, probably to provide cover for the assault or to weaken defence by encouraging the citizens to leave the walls to extinguish it [Doc. 87]. Either way, there was certainly no intention to destroy the city which Tilly wanted as a base. The fire spread, adding to the confusion once the attackers broke in. The senior officers swiftly lost control which would have been difficult to enforce, given that the soldiers felt entitled to plunder the city because it had refused its chance to surrender.

Acceptance of this military convention extended even to Protestant observers, like Christian II (1599–1656), prince of nearby Anhalt, who wrote to Tilly congratulating him on his victory [Doc. 81]. Other, more militant, Protestants were openly critical, with many playing on the city's name (literally 'Maiden's castle') to present an image of a pious Protestant virgin who preferred to immolate herself than suffer rape at the hands of the papists [Doc. 82]. Confession clearly played a part in shaping how others further afield viewed events, though as always we need to be careful when interpreting texts written by clergymen [Doc. 83]. Even Catholic accounts record the general fear of the assault, as well as the atrocities which continued over the next few days [Doc. 84]. The inhabitants' experience was mixed, with individual soldiers showing kindness amidst the general horror [Docs 85–6]. Soldiers' accounts are also candid about their role in plundering and destruction [Docs 87–8]. These eyewitness texts are some of the richest sources for civil–military encounters. Though they speak to us directly, the impression they convey is far from unambiguous. Some contemporary commentary was deliberately cryptic, possibly to avoid censorship, but perhaps also because the event itself was difficult to interpret [Docs 89–90].

VIEWPOINTS

79. A general's view: Pappenheim's report, 21 May 1631

I believe that over twenty thousand souls were lost. It is certain that no more terrible work and divine punishment has been seen since the destruction of Jerusalem. All of our soldiers became rich. God with us.

Source: Pappenheim's report 21 May 1631, quoted in W. Lahne, *Magdeburgs Zerstörung in der zeitgenössischen Publizistik* (Magdeburg, 1931), p. 67.

---

80. A councillor's view: Guericke's history

Serious difficulties and hostilities developed in 1629 between Duke Albrecht of Friedland, then imperial general, and the world-famous Hanseatic city of Magdeburg. The city was subjected to tight blockade, surrounded by 16 strong entrenchments and much bloodshed. While this was going on all sorts of arguments and misunderstandings divided the city's citizens and inhabitants. One party refused to tolerate the imperial and League armies, because of the suffering of war and the feared Counter Reformation. They wanted to be rid of this burden by driving the soldiers from the archbishopric. To this end, they wished to ally with other evangelical potentates and Estates and complete the process with combined strength. Among them were several councillors, the clergy, but mainly the common people.

The other party, which included the majority and most prominent of the council, but few pastors and citizens, opposed this. They could not advise the city, as a minor, powerless, imperial Estate, to withstand the mighty army. Instead they wished to follow the example of other neighbouring electors and towns and remain neutral. In order to preserve relations with the imperial soldiers, they were willing to allow imperial officers into the city to recruit and to purchase all kinds of provisions. They were also prepared to supply all kinds of food, saltpetre and powder, and for cannon to be cast in the city foundry. Such advice made them hated by the opposing party, and drew suspicion that they supported the papists and wanted to abandon the evangelical religion.

[Wallenstein pressured the city to admit a garrison, but agreed not to enforce the Edict of Restitution. The Hanseatic League were still mediating when] the lord administrator of the archbishopric of Magdeburg[1] arrived in disguise in the evening of 27 July 1630 [OS] without the knowledge of the councillor or citizens. [The administrator forced the council to accept the alliance he had just agreed with Sweden. The need to confront the Swedes in Pomerania and Mecklenburg prevented Pappenheim from massing sufficient troops for a full siege until he was joined by Tilly on 3 April 1631. The city was heavily bombarded and repeatedly summoned to surrender.] On the following day – it was 19 May – the council summoned the entire citizenry in their districts and asked whether they should negotiate with General Tilly. The majority in some districts favoured negotiation, some simply left it to the council to decide, while others, especially those who had promoted this business from the outset, refused all talks, expecting help from the king of Sweden at any moment. Some citizens of the Johann Ludwig district feared their district representatives would not report their views correctly and sent their own delegation that evening to the presiding mayor to say they opposed all negotiations with Tilly and preferred to fight to the last man.

The pastors of the Old Town had gone again to the city hall a few days before, led by Dr Christian Hilbert, pastor of St Ulrich. They constantly urged the councillors, as their dear parishioners, to take courage and consoled them that God Almighty would surely preserve the city in its just cause. The councillors had only to remain firm and not negotiate or agree with the Catholics as enemies of the true faith. However, numerous factors suggest that some pastors also believed they should not expose the city and its many thousand inhabitants to such dire peril; that it was preferable to make an agreement and trust God who could preserve his words and faith without the city suffering such a terrible fate. Neither the emperor nor General Tilly had ever sought a Counter Reformation, simply that the city show due respect and submit. [The author reports that he climbed a church tower on the afternoon of 19 May and saw the enemy preparing to attack the battered defences. In view of

---

[1] Christian Wilhelm (1587–1665), uncle of Elector Georg Wilhelm of Brandenburg, had been 'administrator' (i.e. ruling in place of a Catholic prince-archbishop) of Magdeburg since 1598. He was captured during the assault, converted to Catholicism and received a pension from the emperor in return for renouncing claims to the archbishopric.

this and the shortage of powder, the council agreed to negotiate and sent the author to inform Falkenberg.[2]]

That evening Falkenberg urged the council not to negotiate without his knowledge, but to meet instead at 4 a.m. to discuss the talks in common. To this end the council, the [citizens'] committee and the district representatives arrived at the appointed time at city hall, together with Falkenberg, the [Swedish] envoy Stalmann, and the administrator's councillors. The council selected the mayor, Georg Kühlewein, the syndic Conrad Gerhold and the author to meet Falkenberg, who was in a separate room with Stalmann and the administrator's councillors. The council thought the negotiations with Tilly should begin and a trumpeter was sent [to announce this] to the general. As they started to discuss this, Falkenberg interrupted with high-flown assurances of the long-promised relief by the king of Sweden. He urged them again to stick to their promises and to trust him. He declared the danger was not really as acute as they believed. Since relief was only hours away, each hour more they resisted was worth more than a ton of gold. He continued this way for almost an hour. The assembled councillors then dispatched a secretary. He reported that the two look-outs on the cathedral and St Jacob's wanted to tell the councillors they had seen the imperialists leave their camps in strength and assemble in the two suburbs of Neustadt and Sudenburg and behind the trenches by the old wall. At that moment a citizen came from the wall to report that the ground between all the hills was full of cavalry, and more troops had been seen marching into the suburbs. Falkenberg replied that he wanted the imperialists to attack, since they would be resisted and would suffer badly. Then he continued his speech, until the look-out on the St Johannis spire blew the alarm and unfurled the white war banner.

I could not sit still any longer, and went outside to see what was happening. And as I reached the Fischergasse, I saw that the Croats were already storming and plundering the fishermen's houses. They had ridden through the shallow water [in the Elbe] around the low tower [at the end of the wall]. I hurried back to city hall and told the council hurriedly there was no need to sit any longer: the enemy was already in the city. No one could believe it. Then some of Falkenberg's pages arrived and reported that the imperialists were already on the walls of the New Town. He stood up, mounted his horse and rode to fetch Lieutenant Colonel Trost's regiment. He found the imperialists already in the streets when he reached the Hohenpforte [gate] with his men, but attacked fiercely and drove them back at first. However, because they received constant reinforcements and already had cavalry in the city, Falkenberg and Trost got separated from their men and were killed.

Colonel Uslar arrived with his cavalry and what was left of the reserve, but it was already too late. The committee men and district representatives immediately ran to their posts. The councillors went here and there, but

---

2   Colonel Dietrich von Falkenberg (1580–1631), a German in Swedish service, had slipped through the imperial blockade disguised as a fisherman and assumed command of the defence.

mainly remained on the marketplace to issue orders and sent several trumpeters at once to the imperialists to seek an agreement. They were met with such an answer that none returned. Finally the enemy forced their way ever further inside and each realised they had to escape as best they could.

Source: Anonymous pamphlet, 1631, generally assumed to have been written by Otto von Guericke, later mayor of Magdeburg; printed in Karl Lohmann (ed.), *Die Zerstörung Madgeburgs von Otto von Guericke und andere Denkwürdigkeiten aus dem Dreisssigjährigen Krieg* (Berlin, 1913), pp. 21–109.

---

81. A Calvinist prince's view: Christian II of Anhalt's diary[1]

[Wednesday] 11 May [21 May (NS)]
News that yesterday morning at 8 o'clock Magdeburg was captured, plundered, set ablaze, men, women and children cut down, administrator taken prisoner, Field Marshal Falkenberg remained [i.e. dead]. This is no doubt the great, mighty fire that we saw burning yesterday. Now the imperialists have attained their intention and can bend the entire Upper and Lower Saxon Kreis to their will and make such changes on behalf of religion (if God does not intervene) as they wish. This is the great victory, and both for his imperial majesty and the Catholics, and more especially for General Tilly, to the greater glory of his reputation and name.

After the sermon the provost came to me and reported more of the circumstances in Magdeburg. News that the king of Sweden is supposed to be in Zerbst.

[The next passage is in French in the original text:] I wrote in my own hand to Tilly thanking him warmly for his intercession and with the desire for a good peace in Germany, congratulating him upon his victory at Magdeburg.

Prisoners brought here from Magdeburg report that the slaughter continued this morning and the city is completely burnt down, that no building remains but the cathedral which burnt this morning. If this great and beautiful city has been destroyed in such a short time and reduced to ashes, it is to be pitied and its downfall to be lamented.

[The following entries note reports of Tilly's plans and troop movements:]
[Entry for 24 May (NS):]
It is said that the soldiers in Magdeburg initially fell out with the burghers, but that they were entirely innocent, whereas the citizenry, who were probably twelve times as numerous, made them do too much and would not give them any more bread, even for money. It is quite likely that other injustices, secret sins and [acts of] shame occurred, because the outcome suggests that

---

[1] Christian II of Anhalt (1599–1656) was the son and successor of Christian I of Anhalt who had commanded Frederick V's army at White Mountain [see **Doc. 25**]. Christian II was captured in the battle and held prisoner until 1622. He persuaded Emperor Ferdinand II to pardon his father in 1624 and spent most of his time after, becoming ruling prince in 1630, in trying to keep all sides out of his small principality.

such a beautiful, powerful city which has flourished since the days of Emperor Otto I[2] could not have met with such an unexpected, rapid [and] terrible end without a particular reason. The sins of the land will mean many changes to the principalities etc.

One should not, to be sure, judge *ex eventu* [by the outcome] whether a matter be unjust or not, but it is sometimes permitted, especially when one has gained knowledge of something of the *Circumstantiis injustitiae* [unjust circumstances], which injustice then ravaged the land and people, as we can read in the prophets of Tyre, Sidon and Babel.[3] General Tilly offered them [the people of Magdeburg] mercy on different occasions, but to no avail.

Finally, he saw his chance last Tuesday [20 May (NS)], and had fire thrown in at various points and had fire balls fired into the city, so that the burghers would leave the wall to save their houses and see to their women and children. This actually occurred, as the burghers abandoned the wall during the assault, especially after Falkenberg had fallen after having fought nobly. Thus, the few Swedish soldiers,[4] about 1,600, were unable to resist the power of their mighty, numerous and resolute foes, whereas had they been seconded by the 1,000–1,200 armed burghers, the assault would easily have been repulsed. For this reason, the imperialists forced their way in and captured the city reducing it largely to ashes, undoubtedly contrary to General Tilly's wishes. It is said that some burghers set fire to their own houses. Large quantities of gunpowder, which they had in their houses, bacon and other flammable wares greatly assisted this.

[The dead Swedish soldiers were buried, but those of the administrator, Christian Wilhelm, and of the city were thrown into the Elbe.]

The city had been burnt down apart from 10 houses.[5]

It recalls to me the destruction of the city of Jerusalem, and no such tragedy has befallen such a city in the German empire and lands, and no such excellent city fallen so rapidly and been so suddenly and ultimately ruined since the time when Bardewyck, out of whose rubble Lüneburg was built, was taken by Henry the Lion against Bernhard I of Anhalt, elector of Saxony, and finally destroyed, which reminds me of the fall of Babylon ...[6]

Source: H. Wäschke (ed.), 'Die Belagerung und Zerstörung Magdeburgs. Tagebuchsblätter', *Geschichtsblätter für Stadt und Land Magdeburg*, 41 (1906), pp. 318–27.

---

[2] Otto I (912–73), emperor from 936, who refounded Magdeburg after the first settlement had been destroyed by the Slavs.

[3] Cities which met terrible ends in the ancient world.

[4] Falkenberg was a German in Swedish service, while the garrison were also largely German professionals hired by the city before he arrived.

[5] In fact, 200 of the city's 1,900 buildings survived.

[6] A reference to one of the many civil wars in the medieval Empire, in this case the late twelfth century, involving the controversial north German prince Henry the Lion (1129–95).

82. 'The Magdeburg Maiden'

Song or poem, probably written by a Magdeburg survivor shortly after the event:

Unfortunate fortune, what dost thou recall?
Give it me, leave that for thee,
That I may have joy eternally.

Maid and castle, mighty city
To God through Roman deed
Did sacrifice her virginity.

Just as silver and all metals pure
Must everywhere be assayed
Seven times by fire.

So the Lutheran Lucretia[1]
Righteous German Constantia
Am I in eternal gloria;

Before I recognise the Papist League
And call it master
I'd rather run into the blaze.

Refuse to dance with Charles the Fifth,
I'll stand no more from Tilly too,
And chase the bloodhound through my fire.

Ancient German bravery
Arm yourself for valiant strife,
Earn the crown of constancy.

Innocent chaste maiden I,
Tormented by the bloodhound dire,
Many a mother's child roasted in the fire.

For suffered martyrdom Cologne on the Rhine
Lauds eleven thousand virgins
I mourn thirty thousand souls!

It must pain any feeling heart,
That babes still suckling at the breast,
By cruel foe into the flames are cast.

---

[1] Lucretia, wife of Roman leader Lucius Tarquinius Collatinus, who was raped whilst her
husband was away on campaign. Having made her relations promise to take revenge,
she stabbed herself to avoid living in dishonour. The event is said to have prompted the
overthrow of the ancient Roman kingdom and the establishment of the republic (509BC).

Hamburg gunpowder, lead and fuse
Delivered unto the Pope's bloodhound
Are the ruin of me, poor maid.

My own brother indeed,
Betrayed me poor maid
Through the counsel of a false Judas.

Disloyal sisters I also accuse,
Who failed to aid me in my need,
I'll not forget on Judgement Day.

The one dear Swedish hero true
Gave me tons of gold coin too
I praise his name to all the world.

But those who him no passage gave
And severed him from all succour
Must now look to their property.

Bremen, Brunswick through the foe's cunning
Towards Nuremberg too the Bavarian blasts,
Hamburg and Saxony at the last.

The Bavarian speaks pretty words,
But with his troops he strides ahead,
Putting all Lutheran folk to the sword.

Awake, thou German honesty,
And take up arms in my strife,
Thou shalt be praised eternally!

Source: Modified from the translation in Hans Medik, 'Historical Event and Contemporary Experience: The Capture and Destruction of Magdeburg in 1631', *History Workshop Journal*, 52 (2001), pp. 32–3.

---

83. Diverging Protestant and Catholic reactions: Pastor Michaelis's diary

Nicolaus Michaelis, Calvinist pastor in Hechtsheim near Mainz, on the reaction of his parishioners on receiving the news in June:

All Protestants were terribly saddened and appalled by the wretched downfall of the city of Magdeburg, but the papists rejoiced and were glad. At Mainz there were joyful gun salvoes because of the capture of the city of Magdeburg … They marched in procession to the Church of Our Lady with drums and pipes, and gave thanks to her for such a victory, as if the blessed Virgin Mary up in heaven had such a murderous bloodthirsty heart as (them) the papists who cannot get enough of innocent human blood here on earth. It is said that some sixty thousand souls lost their lives at Magdeburg.

Source: Quoted in Hans Medik, 'Historical Event and Contemporary Experience: The Capture and Destruction of Magdeburg in 1631', *History Workshop Journal*, 52 (2001), p. 37.

84. A Catholic interpretation: Prior Bandauer's account[1]

The Holy Scriptures and secular histories tell us of the zeal and gravity with which God Almighty punishes terrible rebellion against divinely ordained authority. God's punishment is not lacking if one turns away from the ancient Christian Catholic religion and embraces a new one, abandons God and his dear saints, despises and ridicules his old belief, as unfortunately the new faith does! An example of this is the city of Magdeburg that was captured, destroyed and reduced to ashes on 20 May in the year of Our Lord 1631. Many good-hearted Christians suffered a great misfortune with this city; and it is indeed a loss that such a fine city, in which so many thousands of souls died, thus had to be destroyed and wretchedly burnt. But you, oh God, are the one who ruined Israel. The city had given great cause, because it had so stubbornly resisted its overlord, His Roman Imperial Majesty, and shown disloyalty for so many years. This was most obvious once it renounced the true faith and adopted another [in 1523] ...

Before everything was destroyed in the conflagration, the soldiers broke into the city and made enough booty. They also found untold treasures in the broken cellars and larders in the days following the storm, but lost them quickly in foolish gambling. It is regrettable that the soldiers were given such latitude, that they destroyed everything by plundering. They were more concerned with robbery and plundering than with defeating the enemy and restoring the Catholic religion ... What should we say of Christian soldiers, who steal, rob, defile, fight, drive away cattle, break open barrels and let beer and wine flow wherever they come and go, just as it happened in Magdeburg? And if it pleases the commanders, this is called military discipline today; and the army leaders, captains and officers say yes and amen, so that they can participate in the theft and robbery ...

Some preachers have claimed that some Magdeburg virgins followed Lucretia's example and preferred death or suicide to losing their honour; but such Lucretias weren't heard of in the city.[2] This, however, was heard: when

---

[1] Zacharias Bandauer (1585–1657) was the son of Lutheran peasants in the territory of the archbishopric of Magdeburg. He converted to Catholicism whilst still young, and in 1628 became prior of the Premonstratensian monastery of Jerichow on the banks of the Elbe near Magdeburg.

[2] See **Doc. 82,** note 1.

the soldiers brought the Magdeburg virgins on the back of their horses as booty into their quarters outside the city, the other soldiers shouted 'Whore! Whore!' after them in the martial tradition. There was one among them of 16 or 18 who replied: 'Oh soldiers, you can't congratulate yourselves that you have made the Magdeburg virgin your whore, she was that already, before you arrived.' And so the preachers' picture of chastity isn't true.

Many of those who sought shelter in the monastery were mortally ill from fear; many were wounded, many were so naked, that they were ashamed to go out. One could not get them out of the monastery for three weeks. One gave them some bread and beer that Father Sylvius obtained from his Excellency Tilly; because the monastery had nothing at that point that could be given as refreshment. They said that they would never in all their lives have believed that Catholics were such kind hearted people who would rush to the aid of those of another religion. In the end the provost had to use strong words and dire threats to get them out of the monastery; because one was growing concerned with the terrible stench that infection would start. In fact many of these people as well as two priests died from such an infection, while others were mortally ill.

The soldiers also said that they had found children of five or six years old in various places, who were still alive, but all wasting and starving; they brought some of them with them and kept them, but others starved to death.

One sight was truly hideous to see. Two old women had collected small orphaned children in an old chapel in the monastery's vineyard, around 23, some of nine months, others six months or a year old. They sat and lay on the earth; some played in the sand, some cried, some screamed: Mother! Mother! But there was no mother there, and the women couldn't say who the parents had been; but in some cases they knew well enough. These received bread and beer, so that they didn't starve to death, because the parents were taken prisoner or killed or burned in the fire. When the Prior of Jerichow went in the garden with Father Henricus to see the poor children, he found two women burying two small children who had died. He asked them what they were doing. They replied: 'Two children have died; we have buried them here.' 'You have made the grave too shallow, that isn't good.' They said that they had had nothing with which to dig. When he returned to the vineyard three days later, he found that the dogs had dug the children up and eaten them. Oh woe, upon woe! Lament those that shed such innocent blood! Oh how, oh how the Magdeburgers could have avoided this great disaster and terrible misfortune, if they had wanted to! [Bandhauer goes on to list events he regards as divine forewarning of the disaster.]

After three days General Tilly had the dead – they were burnt and all black so that one could not tell whether they were male or female – collected from the streets and pushed into the Elbe. It was impossible to bury them all. One could not dig deep holes since all the open spaces and squares, even the churchyards, were covered with stones and rubble, that it would have taken a long time. And such time was precious to the soldiers who were looking for their booty. That made a deep impression on someone who printed a book in Frankfurt am Main. In this he wrote that Tilly committed an inhuman even devilish act in that he had the people thrown into the water. But perhaps this fellow wasn't really there to see how things really happened ... Lies were told afterwards that the corpses had swum up the Elbe. But that was neither seen nor did it happen. They were certainly carried downstream and many were left on the banks by the wind and the waves. The birds in the sky and the ravens ate whatever had not been burnt on the bodies. It does not matter much whether a dead body is buried in the water on in the ground, or otherwise consumed by fire or wild animals. He will find it again on the Day of Judgement and must stay with it with his soul in his assigned place for all eternity.

A terrible deed took place on Saturday, the 24th of May: six godless soldiers raped a girl of 12 or 13 in the churchyard of Our Lady so that she died by their hands. When this was brought to the attention of Mr Sylvius, he decided to inform His Excellency Tilly, so that such vices could be avoided. Because none of the clerics dared do this, Mr Sylvius finally went himself to Tilly in his quarters where he found him sitting at his desk. When he saw Mr Sylvius standing before the door, he asked him in French what good news he brought. He went in and said: 'Your Excellency, I don't have anything good to say. Your baggage attendants have raped a girl of 12 in our churchyard so that she died. If Your Excellency does not counter such evil and stop it with a stringent order, the Lord God will take victory from Your Excellency and give it to the enemy, the Swedes, and that will happen shortly!'

Tilly was shocked when he heard this. He stood up, went to the window and tears came to his eyes. He asked, who and where the soldiers were. Because Mr Sylvius did not know, His Excellency immediately had the drummers publicise that such pranks were forbidden on pain of death. The culprits were already on their way and were not seen again.

Source: Bandauer's diary in Karl Lohmann (ed.), *Die Zerstörung Magdeburgs von Otto von Guericke und andere Denkwürdigkeiten aus dem Dreissigjährigen Kriege* (Berlin, 1913), pp. 100, 160, 162–4, 169–71.

THE EXPERIENCE OF PLUNDERING

85. Pastor Christophorus Thodänus's account[1]

When the enemy were already in the city and driving the poor people before them along the Breiten Weg like a herd of cattle, my wife came

---

[1] Christophorus Thodänus was a Bohemian who became a school teacher in Magdeburg in 1613 and then pastor at St Catherine's church. He included an account of his experiences in a book of three sermons he published in Hamburg in 1632, commenting on Magdeburg's fate.

running with the maid to me in the room; because this was full of muskets[2] and it would be easy to see that the enemy would be very angry about it if they saw it, she pulled me forcefully from the room just as the enemy were firing in front of the windows, and the smoke was rising to the windows, and all three of us ran into the furthest chamber behind the yard and stood next to each other not far from the door to await what would happen to us. In a flash they were in front of the door; because it was bolted they hammered hard on it. It was then opened on the landlord's order and they stormed in towards us.

This first party craved immediately that I, as the priest, should give them money. I only had a small purse with me, containing about 6 to 7 taler. I gave that to one of them, and he took it eagerly. Because there was no gold in it, which was what he really wanted, he didn't accept it, [but insisted] I should fetch him gold as well. However, he listened to my excuse, accepted it [the purse] and went away. Meanwhile, everything was smashed up in the room and chamber and taken, pocketed and carried away.

A fine young lad was among them, who showed sympathy, to whom my wife cried bitterly: 'O for the love of God won't you protect us!' But he replied: 'Dear young lady, we can't do that, we still have to pursue the enemy.' And then they ran on.

And so the first martyrdom was over. We thought it was all over and done with, because I had never been to such a fencing school before.

However, it didn't take long before another group arrived; they also craved money from us. We satisfied them with 2 taler and 2 silver spoons, which the maid had hidden in our house. They took these and went on, without doing us further harm.

Soon afterwards several more men arrived, among them one who looked like the devil himself, with two muskets and in his mouth a ball in each of the cheeks. He looked at me with a grim expression and said: 'Priest, give money!' That was always their solution. When however I excused myself that I had no more upon me, and that this wasn't my house, he was not satisfied, but rather aimed a musket at me. But when the match refused to catch fire, he blew upon it and pulled. In the meantime my wife plucked up her courage, struck his musket upwards so that the ball flew over my head into the wall. She then held him by the arms so that he could not move. And because he demanded money, but we had no more of it, he said: 'Give me silver instead.' Then it occurred to her that she still had silver hooks on her bodice, which she cut off and gave to him. He stood before her, watching, but did not lay a finger on her.

Another also demanded money from me, so I dug into my pocket and found three Bohemian pennies that I didn't know I had. I put them on the table and said, that in truth I had no more. He picked them up in his hand, took them and went away. The pain was past again. It should be noted that

---

2   Thodänus had gone to visit wounded Protestant soldiers in an inn.

none of them had bothered to search us to find whether we had anything else, which is really quite remarkable.

Source: Ernst Neubauer (ed.), *Magdeburgs Zerstörung 1631. Sammlung zeitgenössischer Berichte* (Magdeburg, 1931), pp. 56–7.

86. Friedrich Friese's memoirs[1]

On 19 May, the evening before, I went with my father along the wall from the New Town at the Lakenmacher Gate as far as the Elbe Gate. The password that night was Angel. All the posts were well guarded along the wall. No one suspected that that city would be taken the following day. Because an imperial trumpeter was in the city awaiting a reply to General Tilly,[2] and in addition a truce had been granted. Despite this, all manner of heavy firing began early in the morning around 7 o'clock. We children had scarcely got up and crawled out of the cellar, where we had been hiding because of the fire bombs and other shooting. We were almost used to it now, because the Imperials had already assaulted the city over four times and been repulsed on each occasion. However, this assault got longer and fiercer. Meanwhile, our father came running from the city hall and asked where mother was. She had left our house and was at that moment in the church of the Holy Spirit, not far from the Suden Gate. Just as she had heard the heavy firing and had left the church with other people, a maid was sent running to fetch her. Father, as he often explained later, had been at city hall when the news came that the enemy were in the city. A courier had brought this to the commander, Falkenberg, at city hall. He [Falkenberg] immediately mounted his horse and went with the armed burghers, as many of them who had joined him, to the point of the assault and offered good resistance. The other councillors and mayors, on the other hand, left city hall and went to their homes. At that point they had been discussing how to answer General Tilly. My father also left city hall. It was easy to see from the exceptional, unusual firing that it was becoming dangerous. Because of this, he wanted to make a few preparations at home before the assault was over. We children prayed meanwhile and called pleadingly to God that he would spare us mercifully. As mother now arrived, she had to put on her old black torn clothes straight away; father put on an old leather waistcoat and a pair of grey trousers, so that he would be taken for a common burgher. He had been to the imperial Generals Tilly, Pappenheim and others several times as a representative of the city and was therefore quite

---

1   This account was originally written by Friedrich Friese drawing on a (subsequently lost) manuscript by his father Daniel. Daniel came from a well-educated family in the Saxon city of Leipzig and moved to Magdeburg in 1628 to take up the post of Senior City Clerk [see **Doc. 138**]. He was often sent on important missions by the city council. The family moved to Altenburg once they escaped from Magdeburg.

2   Tilly had summoned the city to surrender.

well known and feared for a large ransom. The firing now got more and more out of control until there was a final great and terrible salvo. There were no more shots after that, from which everyone deduced that there was no more resistance and the city was taken. This was obvious from the fleeing burghers. They came running with their guns and cried Oh and Woe. Everyone shut their house doors and prepared as best they could. Among them was a peasant, who had perhaps been driven by soldiers from another alley, who climbed over our door, because we had left it still unlocked. He was very afraid. We were ten times as scared as he was, because father thought the soldiers were certainly after him. But the poor peasant hadn't seen any other hole to escape from the alley; because all the doors were locked top and bottom except ours. We let the peasant out of our garden gate, and I don't know what became of him. Not long after the imperial soldiers cried in the alleys: 'All is won! All is won!' and hammered on the doors like the devil himself. We poor people were so scared that we nearly died in our houses, prayed and called to God to have mercy. Soon they thumped on our door. Our tutor, Johann Müller, a student, looked out from above and called: 'Quarter!' But two shots were quickly directed at him. The soldiers threatened they would not leave a soul alive if they got in unless we opened up. We had to let them in; they soon attacked father and mother and craved money; they were only two musketeers. Father and mother gave them the money they had with them, as well as some clothes and utensils. They were satisfied with this, and only asked for shoes and went away again. We pleaded that they help us get away; we wanted to buy ourselves free, but they didn't listen, because they said they had to find booty first. Our tutor went with them, on the pretext of fetching us a pass; he didn't know what he was doing in the terror, and if we had waited for his pass, we would all have been burnt, because he didn't rejoin us until in the camp.

Once the two musketeers had gone, father took an axe and smashed the oven, doors and windows himself, and also ripped the straw from the beds and scattered it around the house, and threw the cambric and horrible beds of the servants into the house, as well as the pots from the kitchen and left the house wide open. It looked as if the furies had danced in it. That was of some help, because no one at first came into the house because they thought the nest already destroyed, because it looked so desolate. In addition, father put a good ham, sausage, smoked meat and what we had to eat on a table, as well as a few jugs of beer, in a corner of the house from where it could not be seen from the door. He thought that if soldiers still came into the house, they would be delayed by the sight of breakfast and give us time to hide ourselves better, and that is what happened.

Although the house had been well trashed, soldiers still came in, because they had seen mother as they ran past and so discovered us all in the lounge, attacked father and mother and demanded money. There were four of them, all musketeers with burning matches. They hit and punched father hard. Mother put up her hand, but it didn't help. We children hung like chains around the soldiers, cried and screamed that they should let father and mother live for us. And though we hung on and pulled at the soldiers, God nonetheless ensured that no soldier did the least harm, hit us or beat us. On the contrary, the furies were moved to rage a little less against the parents. We now gave these guests some of our jewellery and other precious things. They also selected the best linen goods and ran away. These rioters didn't care much for the food that stood on the table.

We didn't dare to stay in the lounge once this lot had gone, but went instead to an old, desolate stable. There was an old, dark shed where we kept coal. Father had already selected this as a refuge. We ran across the yard. There was a well used by us and our neighbour. This was securely closed at the top like a shed. A student who lodged with the neighbour climbed in great fear across the well into our yard. He carried a torch he wanted to light next to us. We were very startled again, and thought that soldiers were coming again. Finally, the good man climbed over with his torch that he had lit and said that the soldiers in the neighbour's house had wanted booty. Because everything had been hidden in the cellar and they had no light, they sent him to fetch one. We could hear them crying all the time from the neighbour's: 'Get a light! Get a light! You thunder, you whore!' and similar nasty remarks and curses. Once the student had gone, father shut the two folding doors of the well and locked them on our side, so that no one could get through so easily again. He was concerned that the neighbour, from fear, would send the soldiers across to us. They were shouting and charging about in the house like bad spirits. They cried, swore and blasphemed for booty and money without end. We heard all this as we sat in our coal shed as quiet as mice. After a while father got out to see what had happened. The soldiers soon saw him, screamed and ran towards him. Mother heard the shouting and also ran out and we children all followed. There were about seven soldiers, all with burning matches. They spoke a foreign tongue and no one understood what they said. They kept putting out their hands for money. Excuses were no good, father could say what he liked. They didn't understand, but fired at him twice in the house. God mercifully ensured that the shots didn't strike father. The bullets buried themselves in the wall. Father and mother fled into the lounge. One of them who was probably an NCO, lunged at father with a halberd. At that moment father went through the lounge door; the rogue hacked a large piece out of the ledge above the door. In this way father was mercifully preserved by God. Finally, father spoke Latin to the officer, saying that the soldiers had taken everything from him, and he had nothing to give them but clothes, linen, tin and the like. The madmen and furies were quietened a little with this, but the officer still wanted money; as soon as he got this, he would lead his men away. Now, we still had a small box in a part of the house with pearls and a few other things, [as well as] our, the children's, godparent money and the like. Mother remembered this. She led the officer upstairs, but the soldiers remained downstairs and ate the fine breakfast that lay on the table. We gave the officer these things with the earnest plea that he should let us go and help us to get out; we were eager to ransom ourselves. But he was not to be induced and turned very fierce. Finally, he let us go and took father's best cloak with lace and satin cuffs, that he wore on best occasions. The fellow took this and let us go. We went across the room and were able to get through the other chambers to another place in the yard and to our coal shed in the stables. The soldiers ran about the house, smashing and searching everything for nearly half an hour, but none of them came into the stables, because this was so full of manure and straw, that no one could get in easily.

As it was now around 9 a.m. and fairly quiet again in our house, father said that we should hide ourselves properly in the old loft. There was a dovecote there that was very dark. No one could get to us easily, because we hid just under the roof. If God had not pulled us mercifully like an iron from the fire and quite miraculously led us away, we would have all burned there together. But God, I will praise and proclaim your glory for ever.

We all went up to the old loft and hid ourselves. Our old maid, who had married a tailor who had stood guard that day at the Lakenmacher Gate, was our fortune and misfortune. This maid had run to us during the great terror and wanted to stay with us, because she thought her husband was dead, since he had been on guard duty. While we hurriedly crept up to the loft, she stayed a while in the coal shed and put her things into a basket. Now she wanted to run from the stables across the yard to join us. A soldier saw her and came in after her shouting: 'Stop! Stop!' The maid, who wasn't slow on her feet, ran crying 'Oh! Oh!' quickly up the stairs to us in the loft. The soldier heard the running and crying and soon came up as well. He found us all together and ran to father who was standing with the maid at the stairs and was saying: 'Oh Anna, you will certainly lead the soldiers to us!' The soldier then came at father with a pick axe. We children crowded round the soldier, begging and crying that he should please let father live. Christian, my fourth brother, was then a small child who could barely walk and stammer a few words. He spoke in the greatest fear to the soldier: 'Oh please let father live, I'll gladly give you the three pennies I get on Sundays.' Father used to give each child something each Sunday if he learned a phrase [from the Bible]. This, coming from an unformed and in those days simple child, touched the soldier's heart, perhaps by God's merciful providence. He immediately changed and turned to us in a friendly rather than a cruel manner. He looked at us children as we stood about him and said: 'Aye, what fine little lads you are!' because he was a Nuremberger,[3] and then said to our father: 'If you want to get out with your children leave immediately, for the Croats will be here in an hour and you and your children will scarcely survive.' Meanwhile, the soldier came to his senses and said: 'Yes, I haven't got any booty, I will try and help you escape, but first I must get booty.' He wanted to leave. We fell at his feet and pleaded that he take us with him. We would gladly give him 200 taler, if he would take us to Gommern, an electoral [Saxon] district two [German] miles from Magdeburg. But he said he had to get booty first; we should just stay put, he only wanted to search a few more houses until he found booty. He swore and

---

[3]   The soldier was speaking in Nuremberg dialect.

promised solemnly that he would return and fetch us. As he was so keen on booty, the aforementioned tailor's wife said he should go with her to her house, where there was a pannier full of clothes and money and other things belonging to her husband; she wanted to give them to him. Father also asked the maid to do this last service for us and bring the soldier back. Thus, the soldier left with her. We soon despaired that she would ever return, put ourselves in God's hands and crawled back underneath the old roof. From there we heard how things went in our house. Boxes and chests were smashed open in our house and at our neighbour's. We could see through the tiles how our neighbours, the poor people, were beaten, broken on the wheel and martyred and we all foresaw the hour of death. We remained in such fear for a good half hour.

Meanwhile the soldier and the tailor's wife had gone a very long way through three or four lanes to her house. She fetched the pannier for the soldier herself. However, on the way he had asked her who we were. The good women let out that my father was the Senior City Clerk. The soldier told her several times as they were going about that she should take him back to the house where the little lads were. When the soldier came back into the house, something we had never expected, he stood in the yard and shouted up to the loft: 'Mr Senior City Clerk, come down!' These words struck father like a knife in the gut, since he believed he had been betrayed, that the maid had been martyred and had divulged where the people were in the house and who we were. 'Oh god save us!' he said with tears, 'I've been betrayed; now we are really in for it!' But the soldier cried: 'Away! You must come quick.' Father and mother blessed each other and thought we would either die or be parted. With such anxiety and deathly fear we descended. However, as we came into the yard, the soldier was standing there with the maid and greeted us. The whole house was full of soldiers, horses and the like. Some wanted to attack father immediately, but the soldier took us and said that we were his prisoners and not to be touched. Then mother went into the lounge and saw her shawl and took it, and because the soldier said that we should take bread with us to the camp, because there was little outside [the city], she also took two loaves in a basket. There were two silver spoons still hidden in the kitchen that mother also slipped in. In addition, she gave my brother Samuel a prayer book in black velvet with very beautiful heavy silver binding that still lay by the window in the lounge. Finally, the parents had hidden a small bundle up on a beam in the old stable, containing a golden and a pearl necklace, some money, a small chain and some bracelets, though not too high up. They fetched this small bundle. Father pretended he wanted to relieve himself in the yard; mother used the same excuse to take me as the eldest son into the stable and lifted me up, so that I could climb up a bit and throw the bundle down. She then put this at the bottom of the basket and put the two loaves over it and carried it out.

And so we left the house around 10 o'clock. We children went hand in hand in pairs and quickly followed the soldier under father's sternest threats in front of the parents.

Our Anna carried our small sister Anna Magdalena on her arm in her cot behind us and, together with the tailor's wife, our former maid, made sure that we children didn't fall behind or get separated. Finally, father and mother brought up the rear. The soldier gave father his musket to carry so that he could get through better. In fact, he quite resembled a soldier, because his face was blackened by the shooting and he had roughed himself up quite nastily from smashing the oven, windows and doors, and had no collar and wore a brown leather waistcoat and grey cloth trousers and old boots. He walked next to mother like this. When we encountered crowds in the alleys he often barked out like a soldier: 'Woman, get moving!' such as one would never say to strangers. Once we had walked through a few alleys we saw various dead bodies lying atop each other, and in the great crowd often had to walk and step over the corpses. Among others we saw a peasant jump down off a gable who was scalded by hot water and smoking mightily. He lay in the street writhing and crying piteously. A maid also lay in the street who had been carrying meat in a basket; she had been shot and a dog stood nearby eating the meat.

The soldier finally went into a house and we followed him. He said he had to fetch us children something to eat and drink, because it was a very long way to the camp and we wouldn't make it otherwise. He went into the kitchen himself and fetched sausages and sides of bacon, seized a colourful Turkish carpet, rolled the bacon and sausages in it and carried it out. Meanwhile, we children ate the bread that we had brought. There were about twenty small children in the house who ran to mother also wanting bread, and mother divided almost half a loaf amongst them. The soldier also went into the cellar and fetched a pail of beer; we drank and were refreshed. Then we went on a little more.

On the way a student met mother and ripped the shawl from her body. Another wanted to grab the nanny who was carrying our little sister Anna Magdalena, but our soldier took her and he let her go again. We saw many dead bodies in the streets, including some women lying quite uncovered. They lay with their heads in a great beer barrel, which stood full of water in the alley, into which they had been pushed and drowned, but half their bodies and their legs were hanging out. It was a wretched spectacle. We all praised God heartily that he took us from fire and war. To this day I praise and thank God Almighty for his paternal protection and salvation.

While we were climbing down we saw a strange affair: a soldier had grabbed a pair of fine, large oxen and wanted to drive them out [of the city], and thought he had the strength of Milo[4] and could easily hold the oxen. He had tied a rope around his waist and drove the oxen in front of him. The animals were so startled by the flash of the guns of the advancing Croats and the rest of the turmoil, that they broke away and pulled the fellow down the

---

4   A reference to a famous athlete who lived around 500BC and once carried a cow across
     the race track at the ancient Olympic games.

wall. It was as if the fellow was flying. The oxen soon ran up the other side again, dragging the good bungler behind them, screaming his head off; I think they dragged him to his death.

And so we finally reached the camp and the hut of the soldier, who had a wife who was also from Nuremberg. She greeted us none too friendly and said to her husband: 'What the devil have you got there? You're filling the hut with children; I thought you were bringing booty!' The man quietened her with the words that he had to rescue the lads, God would grant him booty and placed his carpet with the sides of bacon in the hut. We sat down and were glad to have a bit of protection and safety. The soldier's wife was at last satisfied as well. She cooked for the officers of the regiment and had a lot to do with the food. Mother helped her prepare, cook and brew and assisted her like a maid.

This night at about eleven o'clock, the entire city of Magdeburg was ablaze. Father led us out of the hut so that we could speak of it all our lives. In the camp, which was quite some distance from the city, it was so bright that you could have read a letter by the great glow of the fire.

The next day, the 21st of May, the soldier went with his wife into the city and fetched booty. Mother meanwhile had to look after the soldier's child and see to the food, which she did willingly and happily. We tidied the hut and father remained inside so that no one would recognise him. He could see through the glass in the hut, however, how many good acquaintances, friends, burghers, including women, were led through the camp on ropes. We had God to thank that we were still free and could remain. But once acquaintances from the city saw mother sitting outside the hut by the fire, they were very annoyed and addressed her and said [in the local dialect]: 'Mrs City Clerk, what are you doing here? How are you? Can you get around? I had to ransom myself.' These noble people resented our good fortune and could easily have got us into great trouble with their careless talk.

Then a soldier came to the hut who wanted to speak to our soldier. Father was resting a little in the soldier's bed that was at the very back, while mother sat in the hut and cried. We children sat around her and would have liked a drink. The soldier told of the booty he had made and showed a finger full of rings with fine, beautiful stones; he looked at them and was pleased with himself. Meanwhile, we children demanded a drink; mother didn't have enough on her to pay for a jug of beer. The soldier gave her nearly one and a half taler, so that she could fetch a jug of beer for us children. And so through God's miraculous intervention, our enemies had to save us. We saw that God does not forsake those who place their hopes and their firm trust in him; praise, glory and honour to God!

The soldier and his wife returned towards evening and brought fine jewellery, gold and expensive linen goods. The soldier said that God had granted these to him, because he'd rescued the little lads. He reproached his wife for accusing him yesterday of filling the hut with children. He was now well pleased at his great good fortune and thanked God; soldiers don't normally do this. He was a God-fearing person and very compassionate. God forever reward him for the good deed he did us: we will praise his good deed on the Day of Judgement.

The soldier had to do guard duty on the third day and so couldn't take us to Gommern as he had promised. However, he arranged for us to go with other Magdeburg people in a lieutenant's coach to Wolmirstedt, two [German] miles from Magdeburg.

That evening, the 22nd of May, the soldier returned from the watch. It was now raining quite heavily and he was wearing a long mourning cloak around himself. His wife quickly asked him: 'Oy, husband, what are you doing? What are you wearing?' He replied: 'Oy, wife, I've got a fine cloth cloak.' She: 'Oy, are you a fool! Couldn't you take a dress?' and chided him that he was drunk. He quietened her and produced a large, tin jug, gave it to her and said that he had brought fine Spanish wine with him. His wife was now somewhat mollified and disappeared into the hut to the bed with the jug, perhaps with the intention of having a good nightcap, once dinner was over. Meanwhile, her husband lay on the bed and fell asleep. Once the wife wanted to go to bed as well, she took a large draught. However, she was deeply deceived. Her husband in his drunken state had perhaps opened the wrong barrel and brought Kofent[5] in place of Spanish wine. She spat the Kofent out like a cat, swore and poured the entire contents of the jug over her husband and poked him in the ribs. She swore terribly and claimed he was being stupid deliberately. But when he woke up, he apologised. Finally, they were reconciled, but now both had to sleep in a wet nest. This tomfoolery made us laugh in the midst of our distress and fear, because the woman had looked really funny when she spat out the Kofent.

Early on 23 May, before daybreak, the soldier led us to the aforementioned lieutenant's wagon that would take us to Wolmirstedt, and asked neither for money nor ransom from us, didn't want anything and said that God had granted him enough. Finally, the wife accepted the two silver spoons that mother had hidden in the kitchen. And so we set out very early in the morning in a wagon with over 15 people sitting like geese and hens all mixed up. We arrived around 10 o'clock in Wolmirstadt. This journey cost father the pearl hat band that we had brought with us from Magdeburg.

Source: The account of Daniel Friese, actually written by his son Friedrich, and printed in Karl Lohmann (ed.), *Die Zerstörung Magdeburgs von Otto von Guericke und andere Denkwürdigkeiten aus dem Dreissigjährigen Kriege* (Berlin, 1913), pp. 197–213.

---

[5]   Kofent was a weak beer that was a by-product of the brewing process.

87. Captain Ackermann's autobiography[1]

I was detached with 200 men in the first storm during the capture of Magdeburg; as soon as the main battery in the New Town had fired the signal, we dashed to the wall and pulled out the stakes that were buried there and rushed to the inner wall that was well defended with gabions and 400 men under the Swedish marshal Falkenberg. There was such thundering and crashing of muskets, mortars and cannon [*Kartaunen*] that no one could either hear or see, and because reinforcements followed us closely, the wall was soon black with men and scaling ladders. We finally broke over the inner wall, after around 100 of the enemy had fallen, and drove the rest in flight to the Stücktor[2] towards Lakenmacher Street. Our people put at least 400 scaling ladders over the wall in this fight. We followed the fugitives through the above mentioned gate into the city; around 100 dead including Falkenberg were left on the wall.

Before the storm that began between 8 and 9 a.m.,[3] the general had distributed good Rhenish wine to all officers and men to give them courage.

We called up the pikemen because we encountered stiff resistance from horse and foot in Lakenmacher Street; but they [the pikemen] thought that the city was already won and, wanting to plunder, had broken their pikes in two to be able to search the houses and so came up holding only sticks. We were accordingly beaten back a second and third time to the wall and scaling ladders.

Meanwhile, the Adjutant General had been sent in and ordered that a few houses be set on fire, thinking that this would force the burghers to drop their weapons to put the fire out. It was now a fine, bright, still day and two houses by the Hohenpforte were duly set alight, but against our will; they burned well over an hour as bright as a light. No burghers wanted to abandon their weapons to put them out, but instead fought on desperately in all parts of the city together with the cavalry, so that we lost our strength.

Marshal Pappenheim meanwhile had a ramp hacked diagonally into the wall with hatchets and pikes so that he could break into the city with four companies of arquebusiers and a few Croats. The fighting in the alleys, that were in part occupied by detachments, had so exhausted our nine storm columns, that were each 3,000 men strong, that we could scarcely pant. The

---

[1] Georg Ackermann (1603–80) came from a family of Protestant peasants and served Christian of Halberstadt 1621–2, then Mansfeld 1622–7, then briefly the Danes, before being captured by Pappenheim at the end of 1627. As he had not been paid, he joined Pappenheim's infantry regiment in which his cousin was already captain. He was promoted captain himself in 1630 and led his company in the attack on Magdeburg. He remained in imperial service until 1636 when he retired as a farmer near Halberstadt, probably on the proceeds of the booty he had accumulated. He later suffered from plundering soldiers, including being injured by a party of imperialists in 1644.

[2] One of the city gates.

[3] More like 7a.m.

enemy now began to waver as our cavalry marched into Lakenmacher Street with kettledrums playing and trumpets blaring. We drove the [enemy] cavalry as far as Cathedral Square and the citizenry out of the Bridge Gate: the Administrator and all the other people were captured. A great wind blew up then, fires sprung up in all parts of the city, so that there was neither rescue nor help. But General Tilly was concerned for the beautiful cathedral and detached 500 infantry to fight the fire and was there himself; he saved not only the cathedral but also the beautiful monastery and all the houses on Cathedral Square.

I was, thank God, unscathed so far and, because I could see that everyone was plundering, I took a corporal and three or four soldiers from my company and took a vaulted stone house next to the Roland on the Old Market. I entered the spice store first; a sack of nutmeg had been thrown down there, from which I put one in my mouth and recovered my strength. The arrival of all sorts of people was creating a great crush. One of them had an axe: I took this from his hand and used it to break down the inner door of the house. Someone was ready with a musket as the door swung open and fired at me, only scratching my arm because I turned, but shooting down another who stood right next to me. [The shooter] ran with his gun up the spiral staircase and shut an iron door behind him.

I had had enough of breaking down doors and so searched around the lower floor with my people. We found a shop assistant there who begged us for mercy; I promised this to him if he could show us something. He said yes, he knew of good booty, [and] led us into a room and helped drag away a bed. There was a cellar from which we drew up an iron chest. There was now such a crush of different nations in the room that I had the chest taken out and carried to a bathroom behind the yard. As we were crossing the yard, the aforementioned [the man who had fired on him], who was said to have been an ensign in the wars, fired on me next to the chest from the chamber, so that I could hardly get my people across the yard. We could not get the chest open by any means, but had to hack open a large hole that was very irregular and rough; then we delved in through the hole as if on a lucky dip. Amongst other things I got some fine silver and gold cutlery, and also a beautiful gold chain with an expensive jewel. But we could not take everything out, because the hole was jagged, and also we could not carry everything, so we left the rest for others.

I took command of my company again and was immediately ordered to stand guard at the post where we had come in. As I had occupied all the posts, I walked among the dead (of whom there were 72 all told in my company including officers) and looked towards the city with sighs. Because I saw the entire city in embers and ashes, except for the cathedral, monastery and New Market. It had only taken three or three and a half hours, from which I perceived God's particular omnipotence and wrath.

Source: Ackermann's autobiography in Ernst Neubauer (ed.), *Magdeburgs Zerstörung 1631. Sammlung zeitgenössischer Berichte* (Magdeburg, 1931), pp. 15–17.

88. Soldier Peter Hagendorf's diary[1]

On 20 May we pressed home and stormed and so took [the city]. I rushed in without any injury, but once in the city at the New Town Gate, I was twice shot through the body, that was my booty. This happened at 9a.m. on the morning of 20 May in the year 1631.

Afterwards I was taken into the camp and bandaged, because I'd been shot once through the front of the stomach, and also through both shoulders, so that the ball was stuck in the shirt. The surgeon bound my hands to my back so he could cut in with the chisel. I was thus carried to my hut, half-dead. Still it troubled my heart that the city burned so terribly, because it is a beautiful place and because it is my homeland.

When I was bandaged up my wife went into the city, even though it was on fire everywhere, as she wanted to fetch a pillow for me to lie on and cloth for dressings. I was thus left with the sick child lying by me too. Then the cry came to the camp that the houses were all collapsing on top of each other, trapping many soldiers and women who were wanting to do a bit of looting. I was more worried about my wife, because of the sick child, than about my wounds. But God protected her. She returned after an hour and a half with a woman from the city. She had brought her out with her. She was a sailor's wife and helped her carry the bed linen. She also brought me a large four-measure jug of wine and in addition had found two silver belts and clothes, that I [later] sold for 12 taler in Halberstadt. That evening my comrades arrived and each one gave me something, a taler or half taler.

Source: J. Peters (ed.), *Ein Söldnerleben aus dem Dreißigjährigen Krieg* (Berlin, 1993), p. 47.

<hr>

CONTEMPORARY COMMENTARY

Two lampoons from 1631:

89. 'A Short, but Sharp ABC'

[The picture above the text shows a cage that has just been opened containing a mouse (labelled A) in the centre, flanked by a cat (labelled B) ready to

---

[1] Peter Hagendorf is the most probable author of an anonymous soldier's diary covering 1625–49. The author was clearly from the Magdeburg area and enlisted in the Venetian army during the brief conflict in northern Italy in 1625. He joined Pappenheim's infantry regiment in the League army as a lance corporal in 1627, and served against the Danes in northern Germany, before participating in the siege of Magdeburg. He was captured and forced to join the Swedish army in 1633, but deserted back to his old regiment after the battle of Nördlingen in 1634. His regiment was disbanded in September 1649, after which the text breaks off.

pounce on the mouse from the right and a fox (labelled C) chained to a rock on the left.]

A
Advise now, who can help
The sincere bacon entice me in
If I stay here, I'll surely die

B
Risk it and run away, you'll still die

C
It's better to risk it and run. It has happened before
That a mouse has jumped at the eye of a cat
I would like to help, but the chain binds me tight.

90. 'A Brief, but Thought-provoking Conversation between a Fox and a Cat'

[The picture above the text has the image of Magdeburg on fire in the distance. The same animals shown in Doc. 89 are in the foreground. The cage has been overturned and the tail of the mouse is hanging from the mouth of the cat who has rolled over onto his back with his paws in the air. The fox remains chained on the right, this time to a tree.]

The tied Fox says:
Advise now who can help, what is here, everyone can see
A cat that's so ill he's forgotten the mouse
He's fighting death, because he's eaten a sharp mouse.

The Cat says:
O misery, great need, my powers are fading
I've killed many mice and destroyed their holes
But I've never been so weakened before
Oh what can this be, it serves me right
Because what I have just done to others
(some were innocent, others much grieved for)
Is now being done to me, and I'm being cut up
An animal from midnight has treated me roughly
The mice and rats have all made friends
And the sly fox is whispering advice to them.

The Fox says
Your cruel and great trick has been discovered
The animal from midnight will not spare his strength
You can't resist his power

There's nothing that can help
The best part is that I can chew a mouse
Because we don't want to carry this terrible load any more.

Source: John Roger Paas (ed.), *The German Political Broadsheet 1600–1700*, 6 vols (Wiesbaden, 1994), vol. V, pp. 95, 248.

11

Sweden's search for security and reward, 1631–5

Magdeburg's destruction was a potential public relations disaster for Sweden, since it exposed Gustavus Adolphus's inability to protect his German allies. This explains some of the virulent polemics during 1631, which deflected attention from Swedish inactivity by emphasising how the incident demonstrated Catholic tyranny. Having persuaded Saxony to join him **[see Doc. 76]**, Gustavus finally confronted Tilly at Breitenfeld near Leipzig in September 1631 **[see Doc. 117]**. The battle was the king's greatest victory. The imperial army collapsed, enabling Gustavus to advance deep into the Catholic ecclesiastical lands in central Germany. Having taken Würzburg **[Doc. 91]**, he overran much of the Rhineland and parts of north and south-west Germany.

The king excused his conquests to France by pointing to the presence of League troops in Tilly's army at Breitenfeld. However, his successes frustrated Richelieu's efforts to control Sweden whilst still negotiating for a firmer Bavarian alliance **[see Docs 77–8]**. The scale of the conquests transformed Gustavus's position in the Empire, giving him more resources, but also raising demands for rewards from the numerous minor Protestant princes and nobles who had recruited German regiments for him since his arrival. Like Ferdinand II, he had insufficient regular revenue to repay them and so resorted to a similar policy of distributing captured property in lieu of payment. Known euphemistically as 'donations', these gifts came with strings attached to consolidate Swedish political influence in the Empire **[Doc. 92]**.

Gustavus invaded Bavaria, but was unable to force Maximilian to abandon his alliance with Ferdinand II **[see Docs 114, 135]**. On the contrary, Maximilian now dropped his earlier objection to Wallenstein, who was reinstated as imperial commander early in 1632 **[see Doc. 97]**. Wallenstein invaded Saxony, hoping to detach it from its Swedish alliance. Gustavus attacked him at Lützen on 16 November, only to be killed and his army repulsed **[Doc. 93]**. Unaware of the king's death, but acutely conscious of his own army's losses, Wallenstein withdrew in the night, allowing the Swedes to claim a great victory.

Gustavus's death was a disaster, not least because he had not yet marshalled the Protestant imperial Estates into a solid alliance under Swedish leadership **[Doc. 94; see also Doc. 69]**. Gustavus left only a daughter, the six-year-old Christina, to succeed him. Government passed to the chancellor Axel Oxenstierna (1583–1654), an outstanding statesman, who nonetheless lacked the king's personal charisma and authority amongst the German princes. He scaled down Gustavus's plans and negotiated a more modest alliance with the southern and western Protestant imperial Estates at Heilbronn in 1633 **[Docs 95–6]**.

91. The annexation of Würzburg, 26 October 1631

Gustavus Adolphus's open letter to the district officials and government employees of the bishopric of Würzburg:

Würzburg, 26 October 1631
We Gustavus Adolphus, by the grace of God, king of the Swedes, Goths and Wends [etc.] express our greetings and good wishes to the senior and junior officials, stewards, bailiffs [etc.] of the bishopric of Würzburg and duchy of Franconia. As you will already be well aware [the letter continues with Sweden's justification for its intervention in the Empire].

We entered the field ... not only because of the damaging intrigue and very strong alliance against us, but also because of the continued hostilities following the great victory [at Breitenfeld] graciously granted us by Almighty God, and we encountered so much resistance that we duly exploited our victory and pursued to thereby better bring the disturbers of the peace to justice and achieve an endurable, proper condition with the restoration of the entirely collapsed religious and profane peace, and so advanced into the Franconian Kreis, notifying both bishoprics of Bamberg and Würzburg of this in good time and, despite the fact that the first mentioned has shown us the worst hostility of all League members, we offered ways and means for them to show goodwill and friendship towards us. However, instead of the hoped-for agreement, Würzburg answered us with nothing more than fire and cannonades, giving us sufficient grounds to advance further into the bishopric and ... to storm and capture the fortress above this city of Würzburg.

This gave us all the opportunity, justification and power to do immediately *ex jure talionis* [by the law of recompense] the same that was often done by our enemies to other loyal imperial Estates and many millions of our poor fellow believers, even when they had given not the slightest grounds for it. Since our royal disposition is not at all directed towards such *enormitäten* [enormities] or revenge, but on the contrary as explained above, our sole intention is to re-establish a secure, good and permanent peace in the entire Empire, we have deemed to make use of the larger part of this diocese, for the moment without it swearing duty to a lord, while leaving the rest to pay homage to the aforementioned bishop (who had enough chance to greet us with friendship) so that he is not left in poverty. This is our gracious wish. We also regard it as an unavoidable necessity to take the land and its poor subjects into our royal grace and to put everything into a proper and secure order until all-wise God, according to His good will, directs otherwise through the desired peace. To this end, we have established a certain territorial government and appointed capable persons to it.

All senior and district officials, stewards, bailiffs, village and town mayors, councillors and communes that were mentioned at the head of this decree are hereby ordered to appear in person before us immediately following the publication of this, our patent ... and to swear loyalty and to discharge all duties and responsibilities to us, and to await dutifully our next instructions and then to carry them out obediently.

Now that we have told you your duty, we will take those who are obedient into our royal protection and shelter, and graciously maintain their freedom of conscience and the public exercise of the same, as well as other political rights and jurisdictions, customs and privileges, and to open to them the justice of our already established territorial government. Those that oppose this gracious royal offer will be dealt with as the situation demands, and are warned that such disobedience will be punished severely. Affirmed by our signature and seal, Würzburg 26 October 1631.

Source: O.S. Rydberg and Carl Hallendorf (eds), *Sveriges Tractater med främmande magter jemte andra dit hörande handlingar*, 5 vols (Stockholm, 1902–9), vol. V, part 1, pp. 561–6.

---

92. Swedish 'donations': the gift of Ellwangen Priory to Count Hohenlohe, May 1633

(i)
[From] His Royal Majesty's and Imperial Swedish Councillor, Chancellor and Plenipotentiary Legate in Germany and with the armies of Axel Oxenstierna ... The Serene, Mighty Prince and Lord Gustavus Adolphus, King of the Swedes, Goths and Wends, Grand Prince of Finland, Duke of Estonia and Karelia, Lord over Ingermannland, our former most gracious king and lord, of glorious memory, had granted from his particular royal gentleness and grace the Priory of Ellwangen that lies in the Swabian Kreis and has been acquired by the Swedish Crown through the *Jura belli* [laws of war], together with its diocese and capital with all its spiritual and secular associated colleges, communes, districts and subjects, fiefs, towns, villages, castles, houses, farms, buildings, woods, fields, meadows, pasturages, sheep farms, hunting grounds, fish ponds, lakes, rents, dues, tithes, mobile and fixed properties, and all other usages and revenues, whatever and wherever they might be within Ellwangen territory or under other jurisdiction, whatever that might be, together with all spiritual and secular regalia, higher territorial, criminal, middle and lesser jurisdiction, courts, rights, freedoms, legal and lordly rights, and everything associated with them, whatever name they might have (except the Ellwangen property in Nördlingen, or whatever may have been granted by donation to another party), to the nobly born Lord Craft Count of Hohenlohe and Gleichen,[1] Lord of Langenburg and Kranichfeld, Knight, General Governor of

---

[1] Kraft VII Count of Hohenlohe-Neuenstein (1582–1641) was the younger brother of Georg Friedrich Count of Hohenlohe-Weikershim (1569–1645) who had served as field

the Franconian Kreis for his Royal Majesty, as well as his heirs and their heirs, in view of the useful and loyal service that the Count had performed for the Swedish Crown, and will continue to perform along with his heirs, and have bound themselves to this.

In addition not excepted all those things that the previous owners possessed, enjoyed or were obtained by his aforementioned majesty through his victorious arms, that were graciously granted and promised at his field camp before Nuremberg in September of last year sixteen hundred and thirty-two.

Prior and before this could be put into effect, however, his royal blood was spilt and he departed this earthly life in victory, through God's unfathomable will, for his honour, the true and only religion offering salvation, and German liberty, and for undying fame. Therefore, to put into proper effect all that was conferred and granted by his royal majesty and the Swedish Crown regarding the aforementioned Priory of Ellwangen to the aforementioned Lord Count, his heirs and descendants, so that they can take actual possession of their rights and immunities for themselves and their heirs, that by the power of this [document] the aforementioned Lord Count, his heirs and descendants accept the aforementioned Priory with all the above-mentioned terms, rights and jurisdictions, except the Ellwangen property in Nördlingen and what has been granted from this donation to others, as a particular gift from his royal majesty and the Swedish Crown (that hereby expressly reserves the *Jus superioritatis* [superior jurisdiction] for all time) in grateful thanks and recognise it as a fief that they henceforth hold and enjoy in hereditary possession and will always be true, loyal, and present to his royal majesty and the Swedish Crown, and will do everything that a true vassal and follower should and will do, in particular [he will] fortify Ellwangen Castle at his own expense as far as the ground makes practicable, and occupy it with the necessary garrison and hold and defend the said place for his royal majesty and the Swedish Crown to the utmost against all, [and] pay the contributions from the said Priory correctly, as specified in the separate declaration with many terms from the aforementioned Lord Count. In return, his royal majesty and the Swedish Crown will, through this donation, immunity and gift, maintain, protect and shelter the oft-mentioned Count, his heirs and descendants against all. All subjects of the Swedish Crown, in particular members of its armies, senior, high and junior

---

marshal in the Bohemian army 1618–20. Both were pardoned by Emperor Ferdinand II, but joined Sweden at the end of 1631 hoping to trade their influence amongst the Franconian counts for territorial rewards at the expense of their Catholic neighbours. Kraft was named Swedish governor of Franconia, while his brother received that post in Swabia in 1633. Kraft abandoned Sweden, accepted the Peace of Prague in 1635 [see **Doc. 103**] and recovered his own lands at Neuenstein. Ferdinand II considered Georg Friedrich too complicit in Swedish policy and refused to pardon him a second time. He was eventually pardoned by Ferdinand III in 1637. Both counts are typical of the minor princes who were the strongest supporters of Frederick V, Denmark and Sweden during the war.

officers, as well as common soldiers on horse and foot, are hereby commanded not to oppose the oft-mentioned Lord Count together with his heirs and descendants, from entering, occupying and enjoying the above-mentioned Priory, as well as its rights and jurisdictions, all and every appurtenance, but are on the contrary to be of the utmost assistance. His Excellency has signed and sealed this document by the power of his office and authority. Done at Heilbronn, the first day of May in sixteen hundred and thirty-three.

Axel Oxenstierna

(ii)

Since Lord Count Kraft von Hohenlohe has been conferred and given the entire Ellwangen castle, town and territory, His Excellency hereby orders Colonel Sperreuther,[2] upon immediate receipt of this, to remove his soldiers from the aforementioned castle, town and territory, and march to join other troops without harming the subjects or demanding payment. 2 May 1633
Axel Oxenstierna

Source: Karl Schumm, 'Die Hohenlohe Herrschaft über Ellwangen 1633/34', *Ellwanger Jahrbuch*, 17 (1956/57), pp. 110–11, 112.

---

93. The Battle of Lützen, 16 November 1632: Colonel Dalbier's account

The king arrived in Naumburg on Thursday the 1st of November [OS] and heard that Wallenstein and Pappenheim had met and been given lodgings at Weissenfels. He then ordered a retreat as fast as possible into the above named Naumburg.

Whilst this was happening, the whole infantry settled in the open fields. After three days, when everything was in order, the king lodged his infantry in the town, to wit: three brigades in the town, three in the monastery and two in the suburbs. The cavalry was put up in the neighbouring villages. At that time, the king received a letter brought to him by a peasant, written by Colloredo to his officer Guisforth.[1] In it he mentioned that Pappenheim had gone with four regiments of infantry and three of cavalry to take the castle of Halle.[2]

---

[2] Klaus Dietrich Sperreuther (1600–53) was an officer from Mecklenburg who served Frederick V, then Denmark and Sweden. His regiment had captured Ellwangen. He followed the dukes of Mecklenburg, who were pardoned in the Peace of Prague, in abandoning Sweden and joined the imperial army late in 1635. He was captured three years later, but released in a prisoner exchange, and served Bavaria (1640–7) and Venice (1647–50) as a general.

[1] Major General Count Rudolfo di Colloredo (1585–1657) commander of the imperial infantry.

[2] Gottfried Heinrich Count Pappenheim (1594–1632). The actual composition of Pappenheim's corps was more probably three cavalry regiments, 650 Croats and five infantry regiments, or about 6,000 altogether.

Upon reading this, the king held counsel with Duke Bernhard and Mr Knyphausen,[3] and then it was decided to go and join the Elector of Saxony. The order was given that instant (that is Sunday the 4th of the month at 9 p.m.) to the commanders to leave the baggage and equipment behind.

On the Monday morning at daybreak the king departed and made his way towards Pegau. He intended to go from there to Grimma and the Elector of Saxony was going to leave Torgau to reach Eilenburg. As the army marched on at about 10 a.m. that day, it was brought to the attention of the king (by some local peasants and gentlemen of the enemy) that the above named Wallenstein was lodging at Lützen and its neighbouring villages without being aware of our march; and as the king was assured that there were but two leagues to march there, he decided to go and see them, and proceeded to do so.

They then encountered a narrowed pathway, which forced them to walk in a single file. This meant that night fell before the king could seize any enemy quarters apart from some troops of cavalry who had ridden early and whom we fought, killing about 40 or 50 men and capturing a standard.[4] As it was dark, the king decided to settle there, in the open fields, remaining in order of battle. Having marched all day, they were only a quarter of a league from Lützen, headquarters of Wallenstein. But the nights are long, which gave the enemy time to regroup and to send in haste for Pappenheim. He arrived with his cavalry during the next day. At daybreak the king had the reveille sounded and started on the march immediately.

Although the day had dawned, a thick mist rose up which slowed the king's progress a little. He hoped the sun would clear the mist, which eventually it did. When the sky finally became clear, the king ordered an advance. At about 9 a.m. we caught sight of the enemy in order of battle and waiting for us. They had hidden their troops well, behind a large ditch, and had planted their cannons. The king wasted no time. As he could not make use of his cannons, he started marching on his enemy, at the head of his Swedish cavalry. He charged on the enemy himself. By his side were volunteer cavaliers, amongst them the Duke Franz Albrecht of Sachsen-Lauenburg and two gentlemen.[5] According to the reports later made by the Duke of Lauenburg of the events, the king sustained a wound on his arm, was

---

[3] Duke Bernhard von Sachsen-Weimar (1609–39) commanded the Swedish left at Lützen and assumed joint command of the army after the king's death. Baron Dodo von Innhausen und Knyphausen (1583–1642) commanded the Swedish centre during the battle and was promoted field marshal in January 1633.

[4] This is a reference to the skirmish at Rippach earlier during the day that delayed the Swedish approach.

[5] Franz Albrecht von Sachsen-Lauenburg (1598–1642). The ruler of a minor north German duchy, he had served in the imperial army 1620–32 and was accompanying the Swedes as a volunteer. His actual conduct in the king's entourage was rather less noble than portrayed here and he returned to the imperialist camp, serving as a general in 1641–2.

covered in blood and shouted to the Duke of Lauenburg: 'Please my cousin, give me assistance, I am badly wounded and I need to retire from here.' Upon hearing this, the duke of Lauenburg went to give the king assistance. As he got hold of the royal horse's bridle to turn him around, an enemy came up behind the king and fired his pistol through the king's back. The king fell off his horse. A gentleman named Luchart who was following the Duke of Lauenburg killed the man who shot the king.[6] Meanwhile our side was retreating and the king stayed where he fell. A little after 3 p.m., our side regained the lost ground and reached the place where the king had fallen. He was found amongst the dead bodies, all his clothes stolen apart from the shirt on his back. As there was no coach available, he was taken away on an ammunition cart.

During the rest of the battle, a thick mist came back around 10.30 a.m. and there was a contrary wind. This meant you could not see anything beyond ten paces, especially when the muskets fired their salvoes. Nevertheless, we carried on fiercely, and around 2 p.m. our side was able to see the enemy batteries (composed of four demi cannon and two quarter cannon) which we hastily spiked. Upon seeing that no enemy soldiers were attempting to retrieve them, Monsieur de Knyphausen ordered the nails taken off and fired large calibre balls and ordered continuous fire on the enemy.[7]

Around 3 p.m., nobody remained on the enemy left wing and the right wing was fought for by Duke Bernhard who came with very few men as he thought we had lost the battle. Monsieur de Knyphausen was still holding two infantry brigades, [including] that of Duke Wilhelm,[8] and the cavalry regiment of Colonel Ohm, under the banner of which all on our side, who had come back in disorder, regrouped. So that when Duke Bernhard arrived, he found it all in good order. As we were reassembling, a little time passed without any musketry being fired. Also the heavens cleared so that we could see what was left of the enemy, namely two blocks of infantry and a few standards [i.e. companies] of cavalry that were standing behind a ditch near three windmills. The enemy realised then that our army was still firm and ready to fire; so they fired too when Duke Bernhard arrived. This lasted until nightfall at about 7p.m., when the moon disappeared and we ceased fire. The enemy then retreated towards Leipzig with whatever it had left, but abandoned 20 cannon and about 20 ammunition carts. Our side remained on the battlefield, staying wherever we had been during the day.

On the Wednesday morning, Duke Bernhard ordered that each cavalry regiment give so many horses to tow the cannons away. This was done apart from one demi cannon with a broken limber, which was dragged to the

---

[6] It is usually stated that the master of the king's horse, von der Schulenburg, killed the assailant.

[7] This is the battery on the imperial left and not the larger one by the windmills.

[8] Wilhelm von Sachsen-Weimar (1598–1662), elder brother of Bernhard, who was in the process of retiring from Swedish service at the time of the battle.

castle of Lützen. This castle was the only one [building] left in a good state, and 200 musketeers were assigned there to guard the cannon whilst a new limber was sent for in order to transport it. On that same day, the whole of our army and cannons marched towards Weissenfels in order to issue food to the soldiers, rest and look after the wounded as well as form a new brigade. In order to do so, the army remained there on the Wednesday, Thursday and Friday. On the Thursday morning, those belonging to the Chancellery showed a treaty to the general officers and to Knyphausen and Bulach.[9] That treaty had been signed by the king and by some princes who witnessed it. It was to be implemented in the name of the queen and the infant prince, under the direction of the Chancellor who named Duke Wilhelm as Generalissimo of the army. All this gave me the desire to see the dead body of the king.

Source: Colonel Johann Dalbier's eyewitness account of the battle of Lützen, written in French, held in the National Archive, London, SP81/39, part 2, fols 250–3.

---

94. Negotiations for a Protestant alliance: Gustavus's instructions for his envoy to Saxony, 11 June 1632

[Gustavus Adolphus notes the negotiations with Wallenstein that have been conducted through the Saxon Field Marshal Arnim. He directs his representative to stress Sweden's peaceful intentions, but to urge the Saxons not to do anything hasty and in the meantime to continue the war until there are sufficient guarantees from the emperor, Spain and the League. The best way to prosecute the war and secure a just peace is to form a broad Protestant alliance within the Empire.]

The principal question to be considered, is how that most necessary and indispensable *corpus* [union], which must be the basis and guarantee of peace, can be founded upon a sound footing and organised under a directory. His Majesty, for his part, considers that it would not be difficult to devise the means for creating a *corpus solide* [firm union], and is prepared to come forward with suggestions. It might be better, however, that the Elector himself should first make known his views as to whether he intends to consider His Majesty's personal participation, and to declare whether he intends that such a *corpus* should be governed and guided by His Majesty, as one of those most closely involved, and be under his absolute direction, or whether he intends to satisfy His Majesty's claims and permit him to retire; or again whether he proposes to bind himself more closely to His Majesty and the Swedish crown,

---

9 Claus Conrad Zorn von Bulach, commander of the second line of the Swedish right during the battle.

or whether the idea is to put up a leader among themselves, and entrust the direction of the *corpus* to him.

Source: Gustav Adolf's instructions for Pfalzgraf August as his envoy to Elector Johann Georg of Saxony, dated Donauwörth, 1 June [OS] 1632, from Georg Irmer (ed.), *Die Verhandlungen Schwedens und seiner Verbündeten mit Wallenstein und dem Kaiser von 1631 bis 1634*, 3 vols (Stuttgart, 1888–91), vol. I, p. 207.

95. Gustavus Adolphus's memorandum for Oxenstierna's negotiation with the imperial Estates at the meeting to be held at Ulm, 24(?) October 1632

1. Since the state of affairs in general, and especially the prosecution of the war against our formidable enemy, demands a close cohesion between those who are concerned for the common cause in Germany, as well as armies for defence and for carrying on the war into the enemy's country, together with financial resources sufficient to maintain them and to preserve military discipline, H[is] M[ajesty] has resolved to call together the Estates of the four Kreise to Ulm,[1] and has charged his Chancellor Axel Oxenstierna to represent to them on H.M.'s behalf the present condition of affairs ... and thus by gentle means to try to induce them deliberately to join together in defence of their welfare, and of the common cause, and to find means to translate their resolve into action.

2. In matters of form the Chancellor is to accommodate himself as well as he can to their customs and susceptibilities; but in matters of substance he is to make every effort to secure these three points: (1) to do all he can to induce them to break away from the Emperor, to acknowledge him no longer, and either directly ... or indirectly to renounce him, and instead to bind themselves more closely to H.M., and to come under his direction and protection; (2) to join together to prosecute the war against the Emperor and his adherents ...; (3) last and most important, that they devise means whereby the armies which H.M. has planned and ordered may be supported and discipline preserved.

3. The Chancellor may permit a free discussion, and may hear what they propose; but sooner or later, as may be most appropriate, he is to suggest to them the example of the United Netherlands[2] [and also to suggest raising money by an excise on wine, beer, bread and meat].

...

7. If the Estates cooperate heartily, or at any rate tolerably, the Chancellor shall also ... suggest that the Reichskammergericht in Speyer be entirely reconstituted ... But if he finds the Estates shy of this idea, he is not to raise

---

[1]   The Swabian, Franconian, Upper and Lower Rhenish Kreise.

[2]   That is, the Dutch Republic.

the question, but to leave it to H.M. to bring forward at the appropriate moment; though he is to take every opportunity to have the Imperial President of the court,[3] or other suspect persons, removed from the Reichskammergericht, and to make preparations for future changes.

Source: Michael Roberts (ed.), *Sweden as a Great Power 1611–1697. Government: Society: Foreign Policy* (London, 1968), pp. 145–6; from *Axel Oxenstiernas skrifter och brevvexling*, vol. II, s. i, pp. 866–8.

96. The League of Heilbronn, 13 April 1633

Confederation of Heilbronn between the Electoral Rhenish, Swabian, Franconian and Upper Rhenish Kreise on one part and the Swedish Royal Chancellor on the other, 1633.

[The preamble sets out the standard Swedish justification for intervention, stressing that King Gustavus Adolphus had been forced to take up arms because the emperor had attacked him in Prussia without provocation, insulted his envoys and showed clear] intention to create a mighty navy and to use it to conquer neighbouring kingdoms and republics and to seize and control their commerce, [the abuses suffered by the Protestants are known to the entire world and they have been deprived of their property through the Edict of Restitution and their subjects forbidden to hear the true word of God. The rest stresses the good intentions of the late king to bring about an alliance of the four south German Kreise. The subsequent negotiations had led to the following:]

First and foremost, the princes and Estates who are present, and the envoys and delegates of those electors and Estates who are absent as well as those as members of the Empire, by the power of its constitution do, for themselves, their heirs and successors, freely and collectively confederate closer with the royal dignity and majesty and most praiseworthy crown of Sweden under the guidance of its plenipotentiary legate and his excellency the royal chancellor [Oxenstierna]. They agree that all the confederates shall be faithful, and give mutual assistance, and protect each other from harm. They will also venture their persons, their lives and their fortunes in the cause, until such time as German liberty, and a respect for the principles and constitution of the Holy Roman Empire, are once again firmly established, the restoration of the Evangelical Estates is secured, and a just and certain religious and profane peace (which all confederates can enjoy) is obtained and concluded, and also until the royal dignity and majesty and crown of Sweden has been assured of

---

3   That is, the presiding judge who was appointed by the emperor to oversee the Reichskammergericht.

an appropriate satisfaction. [All the treaties made between Gustavus Adolphus and individual territories that joined the League were to remain in force.]

Second: the Estates and envoys present, having come to the conclusion that the military organisation cannot function without a competent supreme Director; and remembering that his late Majesty, the saviour of German liberty, filled that position in his lifetime including his last campaign in the north German Kreise, [they] have determined to show their respect to his late Majesty and to his successor, and also to give a testimony of their high esteem of the Chancellor's excellent qualities, by asking and entreating him to take upon himself the office of Director, for the good of the common cause in its hour of need, and for German liberty. [Oxenstierna agreed to assume the role.]

Third: Since however the burden upon His Excellency the Director would be very heavy for him to bear unaided, it has been found good to provide him with a *Consilium Formatum* [Standing Council] of well-qualified persons, furnished with detailed instructions, with whose approval his Excellency the Director is to deliberate and decide in all matters of importance; provided, however, that in military matters the final decision shall always remain with his Excellency the Director himself. Each Kreis shall appoint a Kreis councillor, subject to the Director's and Standing Council's authority, to oversee affairs in the Kreis.

In the fourth place, it is agreed that no confederate shall seek peace separately with the enemy, unless it is done with the prior knowledge and agreement of the Director and the entire confederation. All such matters shall be brought before the Standing Council and notified to the Kreis Estates to be discussed and agreed with their consent.

Fifth, if any confederate, against expectation, does not assist their fellow members or tries to pursue such dangerous policies as becoming neutral (which is henceforth forbidden amongst the evangelicals), then he will not receive aid from the confederation when he is threatened or attacked by the enemy.

Sixth, it is agreed that for the duration of the present war, and until a secure peace is obtained conformable to our desires, the confederates of the four Kreise will maintain the necessary armies, and provide them with pay, provisions, ammunition and artillery. These armies will swear loyalty to the confederation and the Swedish crown. Necessary garrisons will be provided.

Seventh, in order that the war may be prosecuted more effectively, strict discipline shall be enforced and all excesses are to be prevented for as long as the conflict lasts. All have unanimously agreed that the troops shall want for nothing and will be provided with all necessaries, including the artillery train … [A separate appendix detailed these arrangements.]

Eighth, his Excellency the Director has declared that he will take care, with the Council, that the military are duly reformed, that the burdensome staffs of the regiments are cut down, that military discipline is restored, that commerce, together with the income and nourishment of the common man, shall be firmly restored, that each Estate's jurisdiction shall be preserved, as well in criminal cases as in civil, so that they may punish all outrages except those committed in the course of military operations; that the excesses of the soldiery, as far as the times will allow, shall be suppressed; that good order shall be kept in billeting and transit, and the confederates, if at all possible, be spared; and that the allotment of quarters shall be left to the magistrates in each locality. And in return all the Estates undertake to take such measures in their territories as may ensure that the soldiery have adequate pay.

In the ninth place, the Estates and envoys here present, considering how not only his late Majesty in his day, but the crown of Sweden afterwards, have been so ready to offer them assistance, and indeed to continue it, have engaged to his Excellency the Director that in return they will help the aforesaid crown to keep possession of those enemy lands within the Empire which it already occupies, until the war is over, and a proper satisfaction is afforded; as also to take care that reasonable indemnity may be provided for the injuries sustained by others of the confederation.

Finally: as the confederation now concluded in the name of God has been a measure forced upon them by the great insolence of the enemy, and is designed as a legitimate measure of self-defence, and by no means as an offensive measure against any peace-loving state, so also it is a measure of moderation, implying no violation of the fundamental principles of the Holy Roman Empire, nor any infringement of the constitution or the Empire or the Kreise, or of any sovereignties, dignities, pre-eminence or rights within them; nor does it intend any prejudice to those Electors and Estates who are loyal to the Empire, nor to any foreign potentate or republic. And the Confederates cherish the confident hope that other Evangelical Electors and Estates of the Empire, and also foreign potentates and republics, will not be displeased at this work of salvation that promotes God's honour, conserves the Holy Roman Empire and the Estates and their eternal welfare, but on the contrary that they will take occasion to adhere to and enter so Christian and just a league and assist it ...

Done at Heilbronn, on the thirteenth day of the month of April, in the year after Christ's birth sixteen hundred and thirty-three.

Source: O.S. Rydberg and Carl Hallendorf (eds), *Sveriges Tractater med främmande magter jemte andra dit hörande handlingar*, 5 vols (Stockholm, 1902–9), vol. V, part 2, pp. 18–29.

12

Wallenstein's second generalship, 1632–4

The terms of Wallenstein's reappointment as imperial commander were negotiated at Göllersdorf outside Vienna in April 1632 [**Doc. 97**]. The original no longer exists; almost certainly destroyed deliberately to remove anything that might have incriminated the emperor. Having recovered some ground during 1632, Wallenstein concentrated his efforts the following year to persuade Saxony to change sides. This objective was pursued through a combination of military pressure and secret negotiations [**Doc. 99**]. Though Wallenstein kept the emperor apprised of general developments, he remained reticent on the details. The earlier criticism of his boundless ambition swiftly resurfaced, not least because he remained suspiciously inactive in Silesia for most of 1633, while Swedish armies overran much of south-west Germany and threatened Bavaria again [**Doc. 98**]. The emperor and his advisors hesitated to remove him, fearing they had lost control of the army [**Doc. 100**].

In fact, many officers resented Wallenstein and feared his inactivity was undermining morale. A group of conspirators emerged around Octavio Piccolomini (1599–1656), a distinguished Italian aristocrat who had been commander of Wallenstein's bodyguard, but resented his lack of promotion. Piccolomini fanned fears that Wallenstein was planning to defect to Sweden. Wallenstein's refusal to go to Vienna left him unaware as to how serious the situation had become. Nonetheless, he was sufficiently alarmed to ask the officers with him at his headquarters in Pilsen in Bohemia to swear personal allegiance [**Doc. 101**]. Coming after his earlier rejection of a direct order to march to save Bavaria [**see Doc. 100**], this Pilsner Reverse appeared to corroborate Piccolomini's charges that he planned to turn the army against the emperor. Ferdinand's advisors argued that Wallenstein's actions placed him in a position similar to Frederick V after 1618; as a 'notorious rebel', he could be punished without a trial. Piccolomini and his fellow conspirators had already found a group of Irish and Scottish officers in the imperial army prepared to do the distasteful deed. Wallenstein realised the danger as units began leaving Pilsen without his orders. He fled west to Eger, hoping to join the Swedes. Fears of the army's disloyalty proved unfounded as more regiments declared for Ferdinand. The assassins had accompanied Wallenstein during his escape and finally showed their hand, murdering his four closest companions and then forcing their way into his bedroom and killing him as well. (There are good contemporary accounts in English of the assassination in A.E.J. Hollaender,

'Some English Documents on the End of Wallenstein', *Bulletin of the John Rylands Library Manchester*, 40 (1957–8), pp. 358–90.)

Amidst the high drama, it is often forgotten that Wallenstein was married twice. Neither wife bore him a son who survived into adulthood, and it is unlikely that he really aspired to some of the far-flung ambitions he was accused of. Without an heir and with his health failing, he had already bequeathed much of his wealth to his cousin Max Waldstein (1600–55). His widow, Isabella Katharina von Harrach (1601–55), came from the ranks of the senior Habsburg aristocracy and expected to be looked after. Her appeal is representative of those of the countless widows and orphans who were left more or less destitute through their husbands' and fathers' deaths in military service **[Doc. 102]**.

97. The Göllersdorf Agreement, 14 April 1632

Content of the conditions for the appointment to the generalship agreed between the Duke of Friedland and His Roman Imperial Majesty's privy war councillors, and especially the Duke of Krumau and Eggenberg.[1]

1 That the Duke of Friedland be not only His Roman Imperial Majesty's but also the whole worthy Austrian house's and the crown of Spain's generalissimo.

2 That the generalship be conferred upon him in *absolutissima forma*.

3 That His Royal Majesty Ferdinand III should not appear in person with the army and still less exercise personal command over it; instead, when the kingdom of Bohemia is reoccupied and conquered again, the king should reside in Prague and Don Balthasar di Marradas[2] shall supply 12,000 men to protect Bohemia, who will remain there until a universal peace has stabilised the Holy Roman Empire. For he, the Duke of Friedland, finds that the Bohemians must have a real ruler with the personal presence of their king in their own country. In this way the Emperor and his general will be protected all the more from rebellion.

4 He should have as security an imperial pledge on the Austrian hereditary territory as recompense for his regular expenses.

5 As recompense for his extraordinary expenses, he should be allowed to exercise the highest jurisdiction in the Empire over the territories that he occupies.

---

1 Johann Ulrich von Eggenberg (1568–1634), Duke of Krumau, was one of Ferdinand II's most trusted advisors and counted as one of the few courtiers favourably inclined to Wallenstein.

2 Count Baltasar de Marradas y Vique (1560–1638) was appointed commander of the Spanish contingent with the imperial army in the Bohemian campaign in 1619 and remained in imperial service thereafter. Though he continued to be promoted, he lost influence during Wallenstein's first generalship and was relegated to commanding the troops stationed to defend Bohemia.

6 The right to confiscate lands in the Empire shall be his *in absolutissima forma*, in such a way that neither the Reichshofrat nor the treasury nor the Reichskammergericht at Speyer shall pretend to have any power in the matter, be it in cases of general or particular import.

7 As in confiscation of lands so also in granting of pardons, he, the Duke of Friedland, shall be allowed to act as he pleases. If anyone should obtain a safe conduct and pardon from the imperial court, such shall have no validity unless it is especially endorsed by the Duke of Friedland, and it shall apply in good faith and by word of mouth and not in full substance. Full pardons can only be sought and received from the Duke of Friedland, because the Roman Emperor would be too forgiving and would pardon all those who sought it and this would remove the means to remunerate the colonels and officers and to content the soldiers.

8 As it is inevitable that some time or other negotiations for peace will be started in the Empire, so let it be that the Duke of Friedland's private interests among other things concerning the duchy of Mecklenburg shall also be included in any agreements.

9 He shall receive all expenses and means to continue the war.

10 His army is free to move through or retreat into any of their Majesties' Hereditary Lands.

Source: This is the most likely version of the original text that was almost certainly deliberately destroyed after Wallenstein's murder; in Karl Maria Freiherr von Aretin, *Wallenstein. Beiträge zur nähren Kenntniß seines Charakters, seiner Pläne, seines Verhältnisses zu Bayern* (Regensburg, 1856), pp. 60–1.

---

98. Criticism of Wallenstein: Oñate to Philip IV of Spain, 2 November 1633

Vienna, 2 November 1633

Most gracious lord! The Duke of Friedland is stirring so much dust in Germany, that I feel obliged to report on his absolute power and the manner in which he uses it to bring Your Majesty up to date on the current situation.

The court here was gripped by such fear after the defeat in the battle near Leipzig[1] due to the feeble means of defence that, as the Prince of Eggenberg assures me, most ministers thought the emperor should flee to Graz and, if necessary, to Italy. Eggenberg, however, advised recruiting a new army to try luck one more time. The general opinion was that the Duke of Friedland was

---

[1]   Breitenfeld, 1631.

the only man for the task. I have not yet had time to discover the treaty[2] that he made with the emperor at that time, but the results indicate that, in addition to the personal promises he received that were undoubtedly extraordinarily extensive, he was also granted supreme command of the army with absolute power and complete independence, as well as the right to make war or peace, determine the number and size of the army, fill all vacant command positions with his appointees, do as he pleased with rebels' properties in the Empire and the Hereditary Lands and grant them to whom he chose. In addition, the emperor granted him the right to recruit in all his kingdoms and provinces, levy contributions, billet soldiers and do everything he felt necessary, in whatever manner he considered best. There has never been an equivalent treaty throughout history, and the Duke of Friedland has used it both absolutely and ruthlessly: he seldom writes to the emperor and when he does he only provides a superficial report on his intentions.

Source: Anton Gindely, 'Waldsteins Vertrag mit dem Kaiser bei der Übernahme des zweiten Generalats', *Abhandlungen der königlich-böhmischen Gesellschaft der Wissenschaften*, 7th series, vol. 3 (1890), pp. 19–20.

---

99. Wallenstein's secret diplomacy: minutes of the Brandenburg Privy Council, 7 February 1634

The Brandenburg Privy Council's Verdict on Wallenstein's Offer:

He [Wallenstein] agrees that Saxony is tired of war, because it has not achieved any of its objectives. Its lands are in danger, which it had brought on itself, because it remained set on its course and did not heed the advice of Your Electoral Grace[1] and wanted to communicate with others. The Saxons surely knew, when Tilly returned with his regiments, that he was stuck in it as much as the others, that the lieutenant general in Leipzig has said as much.

It is worth discussing whether the proposals merit both electors accepting them.

When one considers where they come from, it is from the enemy. It must be considered whether their heart is in it and whether these men are well-intentioned. Because one enemy seeks to harm the other; if he can do this through negotiations, it is not as hard as through force of arms.

He[2] has done this twice before with both electors. He has already wanted to leave his master, to whom he is duty bound, and join his army to ours and so turn against his master. Since Friedland[2] holds his own name and honour in

---

2   That is, **Doc. 97**.

1   That is, elector Georg Wilhelm of Brandenburg-Prussia who was chairing the meeting.
2   That is, Wallenstein.

such low regard, any proposals from him must be treated as dangerous, and he might give the same poison later to both electors. If he separates them [the electors], he has all the more opportunity to then fall on the necks of both electors or the other evangelical imperial Estates ...

Source: The opinion of Chancellor Götze recorded in the minutes of the Privy Council meeting 7 February 1634 that discussed Wallenstein's peace proposals that had been forwarded to Brandenburg by the Saxon commander, General Arnim; printed in Georg Irmer (ed.), *Die Verhandlungen Schwedens und seiner Verbündeten mit Wallenstein und dem Kaiser von 1631 bis 1634*, 3 vols (Stuttgart, 1888–91), vol. III, p. 222.

---

100. The decision to remove Wallenstein: Prince Gundacker von Liechtenstein's memorandum, 11 January 1634

(1) There are two reasons for Your Imperial Majesty's current evil situation: one is spiritual deriving from the oppression of the poor and the inadequate administration of justice (which is a universal complaint) that penetrates heaven and brings down divine punishment.

(2) The other is political, being firstly the generalissimo's insubordination [and] second that the army depends on him and not Your Imperial Majesty. The insubordination is manifest in that, contrary to Your Majesty's order, he unnecessarily occupied [winter] quarters in your Hereditary Lands rather than outside them, and that he did not pursue Weimar[1] despite Your Majesty's urgent and repeated orders. It is clear that the army does not depend on Your Majesty because it does not do what you want and Baron de Suys does not obey Your Majesty's regulations.[2]

(3) The evil has grown so great that the Hereditary Lands are being entirely exhausted, the honourable House of Austria is being consumed, and Your Majesty is losing respect and authority amongst friends and foes, while the Generalissimo gains these, because they see that he, not Your Majesty, commands the army, and he attracts the soldiers' love, while their hatred is directed against Your Majesty.

Many dangers arise from this evil. Your Majesty will lose the means to continue the war and the enemy will find no better way to triumph without a shot and to force you to accept harsh peace terms. Electoral Bavaria will lose

---

[1] Bernhard of Weimar who captured the imperial city of Regensburg on 14 November 1633 and threatened Bavaria.

[2] The emperor had ordered Colonel Ernst Roland Baron Suys (died in1645) to march his detachment to reinforce the Bavarians on the river Inn. Wallenstein countermanded this as soon as he heard of it, and told Suys to remain in billets in Upper Austria. Suys followed Wallenstein's instructions. Suys changed his allegiances in time and was promoted to major general after Wallenstein's murder.

heart and defect, and Electoral Cologne and Mainz will follow and join France and will make either France or one of them king of the Romans alongside Your Majesty. Your Majesty will either lose both religion and lands, or be obliged to accept heresy in the peace. That the Generalissimo has the fate of your honourable house in his hands constitutes mutiny. If France or another of Your Majesty's enemies allies with him – and France, as they say, wants to ruin the House of Austria – they might suggest he could obtain the high honours he craves by using the power the command of the army gives him. They will help him and his associates to divide the lands of the House of Austria between them, and form an eternal alliance amongst themselves that they will strengthen by giving pieces of land to Saxony, Brandenburg, Sweden, Venice and Rákoczy.[3] He can easily keep the soldiers on his side if he allows them to rob the peasants (which neither Your Majesty nor the peasants will be able to prevent). He has made himself mighty and can help others to rise too if they remain at his side. If, God forbid, there was a death, the army would be bound closer still to him and the situation would become even more dangerous.

(4) This raises the question as to whether this can be expected from the Generalissimo? The answer is that while one should presume the best of everyone, in politics one should expect the worst that is probable and set about preventing it.

(5) I wouldn't put the above past France or Your Majesty's enemies or the Generalissimo when one considers, first the great opportunity he currently possesses and, second, he is naturally insatiable and ambitious (which is clear since he, a mere private cavalier, is not satisfied with three duchies[4] and other high privileges, that exceed those of anyone else in Austria, Spain or Germany). It has gone beyond the vice of greed and ambition that leads people to numerous enormities (as church and secular histories tell us), pitting brother against brother, son against father, not to mention servant against master. Third, it is to be feared that neither his conscience, which is the same as his actions, nor his love of Your Majesty will prevent this, since he strongly suspects Your Majesty will remove him from command. Fourth, it is clear he has lost all respect towards Your Majesty, in that he stirs Baron Suys against Your Majesty and chooses billets himself and moves troops into the [Hereditary] lands as he pleases.

It is also suspicious that, firstly, the enemy avoided his palace in Prague and the area where he has his principality.[5] Secondly, he did not want the Spanish troops, who are not under his command, to enter the Empire.[6] Third,

---

3 Györgi I Rákoczi (1593–1648), prince of Transylvania from 1630.

4 Friedland, Sagan and the Silesian duchy of Großglogau that he had received in lieu of Mecklenburg and that was lost to Sweden in 1631.

5 This refers to the Saxon invasion of Bohemia in 1632.

6 Wallenstein objected to the arrival of the Spanish army under the Duke of Feria which crossed the Alps into southern Germany in September 1633.

he could have defeated the enemy twice in Silesia but, as the soldiers report, did not do so.[7] Fourth, it is said he set free a prominent Frenchman with a gift of 1,000 ducats without demanding a ransom, and invited Jaras to see him.[8]

Your Majesty will no doubt know many further particulars. I only wished to recount these to show Your Majesty the basis for my opinion.

(6) All this places Your Majesty's person and the sovereignty of your house, the welfare of your lands and religion itself in grave danger, likewise exposing many innocents to oppression. Your Majesty's conscience dictates that it should be remedied.

The remedy is to remove the *causus mali* [cause of this evil]. There are two ways to do this. (6a) One is spiritual, in that Your Majesty preserves your right intention towards God, trusts in God's grace and omnipotence (as God never abandons those who trust him in their hour of greatest need), instructs the clergy to promote piety in town and country and improves the administration of justice (which is the most important public task pleasing to God after religion itself). (6b) The other remedy is secular and has two elements. The first is to end the Generalissimo's insubordination. This cannot be achieved through benevolence, since he is not used to subordination as his disobedience to your orders indicates.

It would not help Your Majesty if he immediately showed subordination now whilst retaining his current authority, as there would always be the risk he would become insubordinate again when he chose. This would pose an even greater danger to Your Majesty, since it would be clear that he could not be tamed by obedience. For this reason, as I see it, it would be futile and dangerous to try and assert authority by benevolent means. The other way is to bring the army under Your Majesty's control. This can be achieved by reducing his authority over it (particularly by asserting Your Majesty's control over appointments to senior command and to regimental command, the income from contributions and confiscations, as well as billeting). He would take such offence at this that he would continue to pose a danger to Your Majesty as long as he commanded the army. Thus, there is no other way than to remove him from command. (Even if the officers and colonels are devoted to Your Majesty, if he retains command he can soon put the army into such a state that it will either be ruined by the enemy or forced to surrender.) I believe it is impossible to achieve this removal through kind means, firstly because he loves command over the army above all else and will never relinquish it even if required to. Second, it will be dangerous to try, since he will resist as soon as he perceives any such attempt and this will be to the greatest disadvantage to Your Majesty.

---

[7]   A reference to the two truces with the Saxons in summer 1633.

[8]   Jaras possibly refers to a suspected French agent. The prominent 'Frenchman' is possibly Heinrich Jakob MacDougall (1589–1634), a Scot raised in Mecklenburg who became a Swedish officer and was captured by Wallenstein at the second battle of Steinau in October 1633. Many accounts present him as French. He escaped captivity, but died soon after.

(7) I conclude that he can best be removed without loss of his life by securing the loyalty of the other generals first, so that if he resists, he cannot do
Your Majesty harm, and so that he does not suspect that the court is acting
against him. There are, in my opinion, no objections to such action, since
he has already demonstrated his guilt through his insubordination and lack
of respect, and placed Your Majesty, your house, lands and religion in such
danger and damage through caprice and his hatred of Bavaria. (It is better
that he suffers as the guilty party, rather than the aforementioned innocent
one suffers and remains threatened.) It can do Your Majesty no harm, since
you lose nothing as he has achieved nothing with his command. (I neither
wish to diminish his merits nor exaggerate his demerits, but to present
them in comparison for Your Majesty to consider.) The Generalissimo has
raised an army in a new manner for Your Majesty's service. However, this
could have been done another way without his extortion and burdens that
contravened the imperial constitution and the privileges of the electors and
princes, greatly offending them and making Your Majesty and house hated
throughout the Empire. It is noted that he captured much land, but Your
Majesty received none of it[9] and it was merely plundered by the soldiers. He
won the battle of Dessau Bridge [1626]. Mansfeld and Weimar[10] then
advanced 80 [German] miles into Your Majesty's lands. He pursued, but did
not fight Bethlen, despite outnumbering him, thereby increasing the Turks'
opinion of Bethlen whilst diminishing the Turks' and Hungarians' view of
German soldiers, and using up the army, billeting it in the Hereditary Lands
and allowing it to waste away.[11] He raised a second army for Your Majesty's
service [in 1632], but only by ruining the [Hereditary] lands. It is said that
he did not attack the Swedes outside Nuremberg because they were stronger
than him.[12] The battle [Lützen] in which the king of Sweden fell, ended
well, but the lands were again eaten up with billets. It is said that last
summer [1633] he did not defeat the enemy, though he could have. He
defeated Count Thurn and part of the enemy army,[13] but did not relieve
Regensburg. He selected billets according to his caprice rather than need
outside the Empire in the Hereditary Lands, contrary to Your Majesty's
order.

---

[9] A reference to Wallenstein's conquest of mainland Denmark which was returned at the
Peace of Lübeck in 1629 [see **Doc. 45**].

[10] Johann Ernst von Sachsen-Weimar (1594–1626) commanded a Danish detachment
cooperating with Mansfeld.

[11] Bethlen broke his truce with the emperor, but only skirmished with imperial outposts
because he distrusted Mansfeld and Weimar, who had no money to pay his troops. Both
the imperial army and its opponents were ravaged by plague that killed both Mansfeld
and Weimar at the end of 1626.

[12] A reference to the prolonged stand-off outside Nuremberg which ended in the costly
Swedish assault on Wallenstein's entrenched camp at Alte Veste that the imperialists
repulsed.

[13] At Steinau, 11 October 1633. See note 8 above.

(8) Once he has been removed, Your Majesty can have him tried to see whether he deserves reward or punishment and act accordingly.

(9) However, if it were found that Your Majesty could not remove him safely without depriving him of his life, I would advise, since actions should be guided by justice and human blood is not ox's blood, that two or three of your privy councillors, conscientious and learned in law, should convene in secret and study thoroughly what the Generalissimo has done against Your Majesty, what indications there are of his intentions, what particulars have occurred, what danger threatens Your Majesty's person, honourable house, lands and religion. They should advise whether Your Majesty can deprive him of his life without offending justice if his removal cannot be achieved otherwise. Nothing can be done if they find against this, as no one should act in this world against God. However, if justice permits this, Your Majesty's person, house, lands, religion and so many tyrannised innocents will be freed from danger and oppression. It would be an injustice if Your Majesty were to deprive him of his life against the law, but if this were lawful, it would be unjust not to take the extreme measures necessary to conserve the state and which are not contrary to God.[14]

(10) Before Your Majesty removes the Generalissimo, it is necessary to decide a replacement. I believe His Royal Highness [Ferdinand III] would be best to assert authority over the generals. The soldiers would be delighted to have such a prominent commander who will protect the [Hereditary] lands and strike terror amongst the enemy, not to mention the universal acclaim that will greet His Royal Majesty. It will also be necessary to discuss the methods of war finance, since these are useless.

(11) A full solution to these problems and to stabilise Your Majesty's house requires that peace be made as best as possible. It is necessary because Your Majesty's situation deteriorates and, if the enemy simply retain their existing means, Your Majesty will not be able to maintain the army in the coming winter without ruining and destroying part of the [Hereditary] lands. Only mutiny and arson can be expected. As You cannot make the peace you would like, it would be better to make the peace you can. Though this may entail harsh terms, no peace is more prejudicial or ignominious (if there be no alternative to save the state) than loss of status, since if this is retained it is easier to repair an ignominious peace than recover status. Your Majesty accepted harsh terms from Bethlen,[15] a very weak enemy, in order to save your land from robbery and fire, and there is all the more need to do so now against more numerous and powerful enemies who are not as exhausted as Your Majesty, and to accept harsh peace terms to save your lands and entire

---

14 The final decision on Wallenstein's fate was taken by Ferdinand II and his closest advisors shortly afterwards. See **Doc. 165**, para. 15.

15 The Peace of Pressburg, December 1626, that ceded part of Upper Hungary to Bethlen.

honourable house. Loss of status is the greatest evil and ridicule such a high potentate can suffer.

Source: Oskar Frhr v. Mitis, 'Gundacker von Liechtensteins Anteil an der kaiserlichen Zentralverwaltung (1606–1654)', *Beiträge zur neueren Geschichte Österreichs*, (1909), pp. 103–10.

_____

101. The First Pilsner Reverse, 12 January 1634

Declaration of obligation of the officers to their commander, Pilsen, 12 January 1634:

Authenticated and empowered through this: we the undersigned generals, colonels and other regiments commanders have received news that His Highness, the noble-born Prince and Lord, Albrecht Duke of Mecklenburg, Friedland, Sagan and Grossglogau, etc., has decided not only to stop the most necessary, indispensable maintenance of the army, but to quit the service and retire entirely on account of various highly injurious *Disgusti* [slanders], as well as dangerous machinations against him. However, we believe that this intended resignation of His Princely Grace will not only be the cause of the certain destruction of His Imperial Majesty's service, the *bonum publicum* [common good] and the imperial armies, but in particular we will all be ruined and lose the only hope of gracious recognition and recompense for our loyal service that rests in the word of the same prince and in which we have placed our hope, lives and property, if we are robbed of our gracious princely patron and his constant care. In particular and disregarding numerous other previous examples, if we reflect on the contents of the imperial instructions produced by Lord von Questenberg,[1] these produced consternation. Especially to prevent the complete ruin of ourselves and the entire army and its soldiers that will follow the resignation of His Princely Grace etc. ..., Field Marshal von Ilow[2] etc. and his four adjutants, colonels Mohr von Waldt,[3] Bredow,[4] Losy[5] and Henderson,[6] have remonstrated and pleaded to be left with His Grace's protection and fatherly care, until His Princely Grace graciously resolved to delay his resignation, that was intended through such important motives, for as long as was required to see what means can be

_____

[1] Gerhard Freiherr von Questenberg (1580–1646), Vice President of the Imperial War Council. See also **Doc. 60.**

[2] Christian Freiherr von Ilow (1585–1634), who was murdered along with Wallenstein in February 1634.

[3] Franz Wilhelm Mohr von Waldt (died 1643), Knight of the Teutonic Order. Later lost his regiment as punishment for having signed the document.

[4] Hans Rudolf von Bredow (c.1595–1640), escaped punishment.

[5] Petrus von Losy.

[6] John Henderson, a Scot who had defected from the Swedes in 1633. Escaped punishment.

found to maintain the army. In return, we all hereby certify in lieu of a bodily oath to remain true and loyal to His Princely Grace for this time and not abandon him in any way, but to promote all that is necessary to preserve the army and His Princely grace to our utmost ability and the last drops of our blood. In the event of one or other opposing this or trying to leave, we will pursue him as a faithless breaker of oaths who must pay with his property, body and life. All this is to be honourably observed and to confirm it we have signed and sealed this [document] personally. Done at Headquarters in Pilsen, on the twelfth of January in the year 1634.

Source: Hermann Hallwich, *Wallenstein's Ende. Ungedrückte Briefe und Acten* (Vienna, 1879), vol. II, pp. 186–7.

102. Appeal for charity: Wallenstein's widow to Ferdinand II, 1634

Most Serene Emperor etc.

Most gracious lord, as much as the crimes against Your Imperial Majesty and your arch dynasty committed by my husband through divine fate concern me, so it pains me no less that his principality and property have been appropriated and assigned to the royal treasury. However, I was assured by my marriage contract and donations *inter uiuos* [between partners] of my dowager's seat of the Lordship of Neuschloss and the house in Prague, as well as two other lordships of Weisswasser and Hirssperg, that all lie within the Principality of Friedland. I live in hope, since I never did anything against Your Imperial Majesty and your arch dynasty, and am innocent that I will not be punished and will receive what is mine.

Therefore, I humbly request that Your Imperial Majesty will order the commissioners entrusted with confiscating the above-mentioned properties, that they not only immediately return them, but also desist from spoiling and devastating them, so that I may have something of my indispensable maintenance, can house and accommodate myself, [and] that I will not forget Your Imperial Majesty and your arch dynasty in my humble prayers to God and render myself to Your Imperial grace.

Your Imperial Majesty's most humble servant

Isabella Duchess of Mecklenburg

Source: Karl Oberleitner, 'Beiträge zur Geschichte des Dreissigjährigen Krieges mit besondere Berücksichtigung des Österreichischen Finanz- und Kriegswesens', *Archiv für österreichische Geschichte*, 19 (1858), pp. 43–4.

13

The Peace of Prague, 1635

Wallenstein's death removed a principal obstacle to Saxony's desire to change sides by allowing it to negotiate with the emperor through more reliable channels. The Swedes were aware of what was happening, but were unwilling to challenge Saxony openly for fear of discouraging their other, equally lukewarm, German allies. The crushing imperial victory at Nördlingen on 6 September 1634 finally made it safe for Saxony to defect. One half of the Swedish army retreated precipitously to the Rhine, while the other half withdrew northwards to defend Pomerania.

Ferdinand had learnt his lesson and abandoned much of his earlier inflexibility over the Edict of Restitution. Saxony secured significant advantages in the Peace of Prague agreed on 30 May 1635 [**Doc. 103**]. This was intended as a general settlement of the Empire's problems. Other imperial Estates were invited to join it and back a common effort to expel the Swedes. To this end, all other alliances were annulled and separate armies were to be merged with the imperial forces. Bavaria accepted this, even though it entailed the dissolution of the League, because the Peace confirmed its possession of the Palatine lands and titles. Brandenburg and most other imperial Estates also abandoned Sweden and joined the emperor. Despite the concessions over the Edict, the settlement represented a major triumph for Ferdinand by confirming the re-Catholicisation and property confiscation undertaken in his hereditary lands since 1620. It was to defend these gains that the emperor kept fighting for another thirteen years.

Prague dealt Sweden a serious blow. Germans comprised the majority of its soldiers, without whom it had no hope of extracting any benefit from its costly intervention in the Empire. Ferdinand commissioned Saxony to persuade Sweden to accept Prague and leave the Empire. The recent political and military successes made the emperor fatally overconfident, while Bavaria and the other Catholics were in no mood to be generous to Sweden having suffered its depredations for five years. All expected Saxony and the Protestant Germans to pay Sweden to disband its army and leave without any territorial gains. Saxony appealed to the German officers' patriotism in an effort to persuade them to accept its offer. Many officers were willing, especially once they discovered that Oxenstierna had deliberately misrepresented the terms of the Peace to them. They seized the chancellor when he arrived in the camp of Sweden's army in north Germany. The result was the Powder Barrel Convention, whereby Oxenstierna secured the army's loyalty by promising to include the officers' pay demands in any peace terms [**Doc. 104**].

While personal greed and ambition clearly drove many of Sweden's German officers, some were genuinely alarmed at Saxony's failure to secure better terms at Prague. The most significant omission was the exclusion of several important territories from the imperial amnesty granted to most of Sweden's German supporters. Those excluded from the amnesty were still free to accept the Peace, but only on harsher terms dictated by the emperor. Hessen-Kassel was the most significant of the excluded territories, because it was the only one with a large army and had captured many towns in Westphalia after 1631. Its prince initially remained neutral, refusing to back Sweden actively, but equally not withdrawing his troops from the Catholic lands they had occupied. Negotiations to include Hessen-Kassel in the Peace dragged on into 1640 when it finally declared for Sweden [**Doc. 105**].

103. The Peace of Prague, 30 May 1635

1 All are hereby told and informed that the Roman Emperor, king of Hungary and Bohemia, Royal majesty, our gracious lord, as supreme head, together with his electoral highness of Saxony etc., as a leading pillar of the Holy Roman Empire have faithfully discussed how and by what means a Christian, general, honourable, just and secure peace can be re-established for the Holy Roman Empire and, after such long wars and resulting misery, poverty, and destruction, the bloodshed can be finally stopped and the beloved fatherland of the most noble German Nation can be saved from ruin.

2 Because they were unable to hold a general assembly of the Empire or any other conference safely, particularly in view of the foreign nations and armies on the Empire's soil, they sent their mutual representatives initially to Leitmeritz and then to Pirna, and finally to Prague, to pursue this beneficial public end and have agreed and concluded the following general peace in the common interest and for the good and honour of the Empire, the German Nation and its respective kingdoms, electorates, lands and peoples.

3 Concerning all the mediate diocese, monasteries and other ecclesiastical properties and their appurtenances that were already secularised before the agreement at Passau by the electors and imperial estates who are members of the Augsburg Confession, they shall all remain according to the clear letter and direction of the established, highly esteemed, Religious Peace.

4 However, concerning the immediate diocese and ecclesiastical lands and properties that were secularised before the agreement at Passau,[1] as well as those ecclesiastical lands and properties that have fallen into the hands of members of the Augsburg Confession after the conclusion of the Passau agreement, whether they be mediate or immediate, we have finally agreed that those electors and imperial estates who held these lands on 12 November 1627, new style, shall have complete and free control of the same for a period

---

[1]   The Treaty of Passau 1552. See **Doc. 1**, article 19.

of forty years from the date of this concluded agreement. And any authority that has been deprived of such lands since 12 November 1627 shall have them returned, yet without any right to claim costs or damages.

[Arts 4–9 cover further detailed provision of the arrangements in art. 3, including guaranteeing that Lutherans who held ecclesiastical territories on 12 November 1627 could retain these for forty years, including exercise of all associated political rights. They were, however, to tolerate Catholic worship in these lands at the state it had been exercised in 1627.]

10 To prevent posterity being troubled again by unrest or complications after the end of the oft-mentioned forty-year period, and so that good will and harmony are preserved, a meeting of peace-loving Estates, or their plenipotentiaries, ambassadors and representatives, of both religions in equal number, are to convene prior to the end of the agreed forty years and to use every effort, care and energy to find a definitive, mutually acceptable solution to the matter of the ecclesiastical property. This assembly is to start at the latest within the next ten years from the date of this peace, to ensure that this agreement does not take too long nor is postponed till the last minute, and to conclude as far as is humanly possible.

[Art. 11: if no agreement can be reached, the status quo of 1627 was to remain in force.]

12 His Imperial Majesty reserves for himself and his heirs in the Empire, as supreme head, the proper authority and jurisdiction in the case of non-agreement or further disputes to settle the disputes between the parties through the Reichshofrat (but in consultation with councillors from some electors and Estates of the Empire, in equal numbers from both, the Catholic Religion and the Augsburg Confession, who will be accepted for this purpose and swear by a special oath to do their duty, in the name of their masters according to the Religious Peace and the Imperial Constitution without respect to the status of their person and the religion of their party), as well as through the Reichskammergericht in each case following sufficient prior hearing and according to due process, discussing every case separately, as well as maintaining the Religious and profane Peace on account of the high imperial office, according to the terms of the Imperial Recess and Imperial Electoral Agreement.[2]

[Art. 13: reinforced the terms of art. 4 by stating that the Catholics were not to be deprived of any further archbishoprics, monasteries and ecclesiastical properties and permitted them to seek redress through the imperial courts should this occur. Art. 14: does the same for Protestants, without expressly mentioning recourse to justice.]

---

[2] The Imperial Electoral Agreement (*Wahlkapitulation*) was the document each new emperor had agreed with the electors since 1519 confirming (and often extending) their privileges and other aspects of the imperial constitution.

15 Concerning the Archbishopric of Magdeburg and in order to secure dear peace, it has been agreed that his princely grace the Duke August of Saxony, Jülich, Cleves and Berg, the much loved son of His Electoral Highness of Saxony,[3] can keep and enjoy the same for the rest of his life and not be disturbed or hindered in this.

[Arts 16–19 detailed the terms regarding Magdeburg. Art. 20 confirmed the validity of the Peace of Lübeck.[4] Art. 21 recognised Leopold Wilhelm, son of Emperor Ferdinand, as ruler of Halberstadt, and that the status quo of 1627 was to apply to the confessional status in the Archbishopric of Bremen. Art. 22 conceded free exercise of religion according to the Religious Peace of Augsburg to the imperial knights.]

23 Those agreements between His Imperial Majesty and the imperial cities that have been made during this war are to remain in force, but all others are to remain according to the Religious Peace.

[Art. 24: permitted the restitution of Donauwörth once the elector of Bavaria had been repaid his expenses.[5]]

25 Concerning His Roman Imperial Majesty's hereditary kingdom of Bohemia and other Austrian hereditary lands, His Electoral Highness has diligently urged His Imperial Majesty that the free exercise of the Augsburg Confession should remain unhindered as it was in every place in 1612, and has also urged from a variety of motives and does not want to deviate from this. However, despite the frequent requests, His Imperial Majesty was not to be moved, but on the contrary had numerous concerns against this, not least that the Augsburg Confession adherents' own rule is that the introduction of religion is dependent on princely territorial sovereignty and [the emperor] has no desire to withdraw this and it would be too much if the rights granted each Estate in the Empire were denied to His Imperial Majesty Himself. Because of this, His Imperial Majesty could not agree to what His Electoral Highness wanted. Because His Imperial Majesty insisted upon this, things have been left as they were and His Imperial Majesty has made a separate resolution concerning Silesia. A separate treaty has been concluded with His Electoral Highness regarding Lusatia.[6]

26 His Electoral Highness had also requested and desired that there was greater parity of religion in the Reichskammergericht and that after the

---

3 August of Sachsen-Weissenfels (1614–80), younger son of Elector Johann Georg. His possession of Magdeburg was confirmed in the Peace of Westphalia, but only for his own lifetime: see **Doc. 171**, art. XI, para. 6.

4 See **Doc. 45**.

5 See **Doc. 3**. This issue was quietly dropped later and Bavaria retained Donauwörth as part of its territory.

6 This treaty permitted Saxony to keep both Upper and Lower Lusatia in lieu of the expenses it had incurred assisting in the suppression of the Bohemian revolt. See also **Doc. 23**.

current Catholic Cameral Judge [had completed his term] one of the Augsburg Confession would follow, and after him, a Catholic again and so on *per vices*, four presidents, including two Catholics and two of the Augsburg Confession would be appointed and that the number of assistant judges from the Augsburg Confession would be the same as those of the Catholics. [It has been agreed] that this article will be put to debate at the earliest meeting of the Imperial Estates of both religions. In the meantime things are to remain according to the previous common Reichskammergericht Ordinance without alteration and dear justice be administered without delay. In addition, the previous Ordinance will apply to the maintenance and payment of the Cameral Court.

[Art. 27 dealt with the visitations and revision of the court verdicts.]

28 Concerning the Reichshofrat, His Imperial Majesty's representatives have again explained that the draft Reichshofrat Ordinance prepared according to the Electoral Agreement will be presented to the next Imperial Diet and advice sought from the electors, and the same be implemented without delay so that the Imperial Estates are not faced with commissions, nor *Mandata sine clausula indifferenter* [general mandates], and are not judged except according to their rights and through due process. [The question of appointing Lutheran judges was postponed for further negotiation.]

[Art. 29 regulated the status of procurators and agents of the Lutheran Estates at the court. Art. 30 stipulated that cases pending at the Reichskammergericht could not be transferred by the emperor to the Reichshofrat, and that the Reichskammergericht could not issue 'imperial law' without the knowledge of the Imperial Estates.]

31 In the case of the Palatine matter that has been the source of unrest and complaint for years, His Electoral Highness has urged that this, including the matter of the electoral title, as well as the territories, be settled once and for all. However, it is known throughout the world that the outlawed Palatine Elector Frederick is a chief cause and instigator of all the evil that occurred in His Imperial Majesty's hereditary kingdom of Bohemia and subsequently in the Roman Empire, and has caused His Imperial Majesty and his most esteemed family more than many millions of debts and other great damages that also affect parts of his hereditary lands because of the associated war costs. Accordingly, he was not moved from his resolve, no matter how hard and assiduously His Electoral Highness pressed the matter. Everything is to remain as arranged by His Imperial Majesty for His Electoral Highness of Bavaria and the Wilhelmine line[7] regarding the said electoral title and lands, as well as other property of Palatine servants. However, Elector Frederick the Fifth's Lady Widow[8] will be left her widow's pension, as far as she has properly liquidated

---

[7] The descendants of Wilhelm V of Bavaria (1548–1626), father of Elector Maximilian I.
[8] Elisabeth Stuart (1596–1662), daughter of James I of England.

these, and her outlawed children will receive a princely allowance from Imperial grace rather than obligation, once they have humbly submitted themselves to His Imperial Majesty.

[Art. 32 ordered the Duke of Brunswick to pay 400,000 talers to Tilly's heirs over eight years.[9]]

33 Concerning the dukes of Mecklenburg, His Imperial Majesty has decided, in the interests of general peace and his high-born goodwill, as well as following the insistent intercession of His Electoral Highness of Saxony, to accept the two dukes back into imperial homage and grace, and leave them peacefully with their entire lands and people (in return for which they gratefully accept the present peace and will respect it, as well as their separate memorandum they have delivered).

34 Regarding the Restitution, the adherents of the Augsburg Confession will immediately evacuate and restore to His Imperial Majesty, his arch-dynasty, as well as the electors and Estates assisting him, including military personnel and their advisors, servants, territorial estates, and subjects, as well as members of religious orders and in general all and every member of spiritual and secular society, without exception, particularly the Duke of Lorraine and his followers, all their electorates, principalities, counties and lordships, lands and people, castles, passes, fortresses, grounds, and all rents, dues, usage, income and all places that have been taken from His Imperial Majesty and his allied Estates since the disorder following the arrival of King Gustavus Adolphus of Sweden on imperial soil in 1630, or are claimed by them, whether they possessed them in 1630 or not. However, this is to be done without compensation, war damages and other expenses, or demolishing [fortification] or inflicting other additional damages, such as taking away artillery or other property, other than the pieces and ammunition they brought with them. And the subjects are to be counted at the place where they owe their obedience.

35 Concerning the foreign potentates and nations, in particular the crowns of France, Sweden and others, who are neither Imperial Estates, nor members of the Empire, nor are currently recognised as such, nor were once formerly, and who do not accept this peace, nor will abide by it, His Electoral Highness of Saxony, together with other adherents of the Augsburg Confession, electors and Estates, if they wish to enjoy this peace, must assist His Roman Imperial Majesty and the Catholics with their entire strength without any delay to restore and recover peace by the power of this treaty, as well as the general Public Peace and Imperial ordinances and discuss the ways and means to implement the peace agreement.

---

9   This was a fine imposed on Brunswick in 1627 for having backed Danish intervention. The money was then assigned to Tilly in lieu of his expenses, but had not been paid by 1635. The claim was annulled by the Peace of Osnabrück, art. XIII, para. 11 [**Doc. 171**].

36 However, it is to be understood that the above-mentioned restitution terms are not intended for the immediate future, and do not include those spiritual and secular properties that were still in Catholic hands in 1630, but according to various terms of this peace, are to remain in the possession of the adherents of the Augsburg Confession.

[Art. 37 restored the Protestant lands occupied by the emperor and Catholics since 1630 according to the same terms as art. 34. Art. 38 covered restitution of the places occupied by the emperor's forces in Lower Saxony since 1625, including Wolfenbüttel.[10] Art. 39 required Saxony to restore places taken in Silesia and Bohemia to the emperor, pull out its troops and surrender fortresses. Art. 40 states that, in return, the emperor will restore places taken from Saxony.]

41 His Electoral Highness wishes to assist the new Imperial Army, so that the Catholics in the Empire can recover their possessions as soon as possible, whether the other adherents of the Augsburg Confession do likewise or not.

42 In return, His Imperial Majesty and the Catholics will also place their entire strength to assist, save and rescue those adherents of the Augsburg Confession who accept and abide by this peace.

43 In addition it is expressly agreed that, if His Electoral Highness of Brandenburg accepts this peace in all its entirety (from which he is not excluded, nor exempt from the amnesty terms), he can expect to be enfeoffed with the Pomeranian lands, and otherwise will certainly be protected by His Imperial Majesty.

44 Not only because of the Pomeranian lands, but in general it is agreed to *Conjunctis viribus* [use combined forces] to liberate the Upper and Lower Saxon Kreise from foreigners, especially the Swedes and the other troops lying there who do not abide by this peace, and remove them from imperial soil, and if they do not go willingly, to drive them out with combined force, free the places they have occupied and return them without delay to their former rulers according to the terms of this peace.

[Art. 45 specified the same for other parts of the Empire and the Hereditary Lands. Art. 46 dealt with the details, namely the restitution of the fortresses belonging to the Guelph dukes of Brunswick. Art. 47 defined restitution in general. Art. 48 covered it in the Rhenish and south German Kreise. Art. 49 governed the maintenance of imperial garrisons that had not yet withdrawn from these areas. Art. 50 specified the restoration of the duke of Lorraine. Art.

---

10 The town of Wolfenbüttel was the capital of the duchy of Brunswick which had (rather unwillingly) backed Danish intervention in 1625. It had been captured by imperial forces in 1627. The imperialists remained in Wolfenbüttel, because the duke's relation, the duke of Lüneburg, refused to restore the bishopric of Hildesheim to Cologne. The imperial garrison only withdrew in 1643 once Lüneburg had been defeated and accepted the Peace of Prague. See also art. 46 below.

51 specified that the fortress of Philippsburg was excluded from restitution because the emperor had decided to keep it. Art. 52 stipulated that no one was to derive claims to anything based on how the war had been conducted since 1630. Art. 53 arranged the exchange of prisoners.]

54 There is a complete amnesty between, on the one side, His Roman Imperial Majesty and allied Catholic electors and Estates, and on the other His Electoral Highness and all other adherents of the Augsburg Confession who were previously at war, provided they fully accept this Peace and its implementation with ten days of notification of its publication without delay. This covers all that has passed between them during the war since the arrival of the King of Sweden on imperial soil in 1630 and annuls all disagreement, displeasure and opposition, regardless of how it occurred, so that neither side shall think further ill of the other, nor threat or use action or the law against the other. In particular, His Imperial Majesty, His House and all Catholic electors, princes and Estates will not claim war costs or damages from the adherents of the Augsburg Confession, who do likewise with His Imperial Majesty, His House, and all Catholic Estates, neither now, nor in the future, but on the contrary these are annulled and removed by this Peace Treaty and by the emperor's absolute authority.

[Art. 55 specified that the amnesty stretched to the lowest soldier on both sides. Art. 56 removed any penalties for those failing to respond to Reichshofrat summons after 1630.]

57 However, His Imperial Majesty expressly excludes the Bohemian and Palatine affair from this amnesty. Because their suppression caused His Imperial Majesty and His House heavy burdens and forced them to leave behind and abandon several hereditary lands, His Imperial Majesty reserves the right to recover the war costs from those instigators, assistants and promoters [of the rebellion] with whom His Imperial Majesty has not yet made an agreement or reconciliation.

58 In addition, His Imperial Majesty excludes some people and property from the amnesty detailed in a special written communiqué sent to His Electoral Highness of Saxony, who has requested leniency, in the interests of peace and quiet, that the exclusions from the amnesty should not be extended beyond the terms of this Peace Treaty and in the special written communiqué.

59 Because His Imperial Majesty has most graciously insisted on such individual exemptions, His Electoral Highness felt obliged not to object further so as not to delay the salutary peace for the Empire an hour longer. Thus, these exceptions specified in a supplementary agreement on today's date are to have the same force and validity as this Peace, as if they were included word for word.

60 However, His Imperial Majesty has most graciously declared that, following the publication of the specified exceptions, if one or other

excluded individuals immediately present themselves and request mercy, He will, depending on the circumstances, not bar them the way to the imperial throne.

61 Those Estates who have already made individual agreements with His Imperial Majesty are to retain these, but are not to demand more from this Peace than what has been promised them already in their individual agreements.

62 The above mentioned amnesty, and in general the entire Peace Treaty, shall apply to those Estates, together with their councillors, subjects, territorial estates and subjects, that have remained neutral during the past hostilities, provided they accept this Peace Treaty and really help to implement it.

63 This Peace Treaty shall apply to those potentates and powers that have been allies of one or the other party during the past hostilities. However, they must return to its former owners everything they have taken during the current war since 1630 and the present, in particular since the peace treaty made with the king of France at Regensburg in 1630.[11] In which case, everything that has happened between these allies and this or that side shall be forgotten for ever more.

64 His Roman Imperial Majesty has most graciously agreed to publish and notify this Peace Treaty to each and every elector and Estate of the Empire, as well as the free knights, and coastal towns, and through imperial patents and attached letters and orders, to stress the high necessity, as well as duty, love and loyalty to the fatherland, as well as the solemn duty and oath binding them to His Roman Imperial Majesty and the Holy Empire, to exhort them to publish the current Peace Treaty in their territory and to accept and observe all its points, and then to actually withdraw his soldiers from his neighbours' lands, without thereby doing anyone any harm, and to combine these troops with His Imperial Majesty's army, and to maintain no more [soldiers] than are necessary to garrison their fortified places. In addition, upon acceptance of this Peace Treaty, they are to report how many troops can join the imperial army, and what condition they are currently in. However, if this is not possible within ten days of publication and notification of this Peace, because of the danger on the roads or the distance, they are to report clearly to His Royal Highness the King of Hungary and Bohemia etc., or to Their Electoral Highnesses of Mainz, Cologne, Bavaria and Saxony, or to the nearest imperial commander, instead of to His Imperial Highness.

65 This Peace is concluded with the intention that the worthy German Nation can be restored to its former integrity, tranquillity, liberty and security, and that His Imperial Majesty and His high dynasty, as well as all electors and Estates of the Empire who accept it, without distinction between the Catholic religion and Augsburg Confession, excepting those excluded, can recover and

---

[11]   See **Doc. 59**.

hold what is theirs. There will be no peace or celebration till this has been done.

66 To ensure the actual and happy implementation of all of this, His Imperial Majesty, as supreme head of the Empire, must remain armed. His Electoral Highness of Saxony and all other electors and Estates must send their soldiers to join him (except those mentioned above to be left to garrison their fortified places), and must assist His Imperial Majesty to implement and execute this Peace Treaty. Therefore, all armies are to be combined into a single main army to be called His Roman Imperial Majesty's and the Holy Roman Empire's Army. His Imperial Majesty will leave a considerable corps from this army to the command of the senior general of His Electoral Highness of Saxony, while all other troops will be under the immediate command of His Imperial Majesty's dear son, the King of Hungary and Bohemia as commander-in-chief, in whom His Imperial Majesty has already vested authority over all current and future forces. This Imperial Army and its various corps is to be used to implement this Peace Treaty against all who oppose this Peace, or those who refuse to restore what they should according to it, or who cause further unrest to His Imperial Majesty and the Empire. To this end a special memorandum has been prepared today detailing all the necessary measures.

67 All military personnel including the generals, lieutenant generals, field marshals and generally from the highest to the lowest shall swear loyalty, affection and obedience to His Roman Imperial Majesty and the Holy Empire, and to do their duty to His Roman Imperial Majesty as the sole supreme head and the Holy Roman Empire, in particular to implement this Peace Treaty and to follow what His Roman Imperial Majesty and the Holy Roman Empire have determined for the duty of soldiers in the Imperial Ordinances. Since the King of Hungary and Bohemia and the electors of the Empire, including His Electoral Highness of Saxony, exercise a general's rank in the name of His Roman Imperial Majesty and the Holy Empire, they do not need to swear a personal oath, and it is acceptable that their commands are valid without a solemn oath, because their royal and electoral dignity and honour, loyalty and honesty take the place of an oath. All other officers and men must actually swear the oath.

68 His Imperial Majesty desires that the instructions and articles of war, together with the Holy Imperial Recesses and Ordinances remain in force and are respected so that the already very exhausted fatherland is spared all insolence, that good military discipline is restored and that military operations can speedily secure the peace that is widely and highly desired. Moreover, that billeting can be organised equally without discrimination of religion or status, except that the residences and fortresses of the electors and Estates are exempt, as well as the imperial cities (which however, must provide billeting in the countryside, or other compensation).

69 Since it is impossible to summon an imperial diet, Kreis assemblies or an imperial deputation at present, yet means are required to maintain the troops

and (God willing) achieve immediate peace; So it is clear that no elector or Estate of the Empire, nor the free imperial knights or coastal cities, will object that acceptance of this Peace Treaty entails agreement to pay one hundred and twenty Roman Months in six equal instalments, namely 1 September and 1 December of this year, and 1 March, 1 June, 1 September and 1 December of the next year 1636 in the deposit cities according to imperial regulations and custom in good imperial currency, an imperial taler counting no more than one and a half florins or ninety kreuzer for which the Imperial Paymaster will issue receipts, so that *Disciplina Militaris* [military discipline] can be restored and to prevent those excesses and disorder that arise in the military from the lack of regular pay.

70 No Estate is liable to pay contributions as well, or to billet soldiers, or feed soldiers free of charge. On the contrary, the Emperor's and Empire's Commissariat are to arrange an equitable supply ordinance following this Treaty, and to deduct what the Estates or their subjects provide in provisions or forage from their contributions or to arrange for the Imperial Paymaster to refund them.

71 Since the common Estates will find it very difficult to bear the entire costs of the Imperial Army from now on, and because some Estates have suffered disproportionately from the war and have had their damages gradually deducted from their war contributions, nor is it the intention that the Estates should be required to pay more than the war contributions they owe to the Empire, but on the contrary out of the desire to avoid all unnecessary expense and to reduce the numbers of soldiers, the Imperial and Holy Roman Empire's Army and its corps will not be larger than necessary, and the soldiers will be entirely discharged once the Empire is completely pacified.

72 In addition, His Imperial Majesty wants, with the advice and desire of the electors, to summon an imperial diet as soon as possible to discuss all other matters to do with the *Militia* [military] properly with the assembled Estates.

73 In the meantime, neither the entire Empire of the German Nation, nor a single Estate of it, will be obliged to pay anything of the arrears or any other payment that they have not all agreed to. On the contrary, those who either reject this Peace Treaty or do not comply fully with it, and through their resistance to the fatherland are responsible for this costly army, can expect to be called upon to pay compensation according to the Imperial Ordinances.

74 Once the long-desired pacification of our dear fatherland of the German Nation (that is constantly and loyally sought) and been achieved, each and every military occupation, recruiting and mustering, war tax and other grievance against the laws of the Empire, with which the Empire has recently been burdened, is in future to cease entirely, and is never to be enforced again.

75 In like manner there shall never be another particular military constitution set up within the Holy Roman Empire, be it from the head or members,

that contradicts the Emperor's coronation oath, the laws of the Empire and of the Kreise.

76 In no matters, including those agreed in this Treaty or not, and above all those concerning the Palatinate affair, shall any armed foreign power be tolerated to come onto imperial soil, that contravenes the grant, order and permission of the emperor, and if this should occur then all effort shall be directed against it.

77 Furthermore, with the establishment and publication of this peace, all unions, leagues, federations and suchlike agreements, as well as all oaths and duties sworn on the same, are totally null and void, and only the imperial and Kreis laws shall be kept, although this shall in no way imply any dissolution of the electors' union.[12]

78 Equally exempt [from dissolution] are the hereditary inheritance pacts of His Roman Imperial Majesty and his high arch dynasty, as well as those of other electors, princes and Estates.

79 The ancient hereditary brotherly alliance between the three electoral and princely houses of Saxony, Brandenburg and Hessen, that has been confirmed by the Roman emperors, also remains unaffected.

80 His Roman Imperial Majesty wants to remain on good unanimity and trustworthy terms with those foreign Christian potentates and powers that do not hinder the peace, honour and dignity of the Holy Empire and to permit mutually reciprocal travel and unhindered free *Commercia* [trade] according to his imperial coronation oath and imperial law.

81 His Imperial Majesty also desires to treat all electors and Estates of the Holy Roman Empire justly according to the fundamental laws, Golden Bull[13] and other praiseworthy imperial constitutions, and to govern in accordance with this Treaty, and with gentleness and goodwill, and to display imperial friendship, homage, grace and goodwill, and remain in accordance with equity and justice, which is the foundation of the Empire and its happiness, and always maintain and defend the entire Roman Empire and its long-standing liberty, freedom and sovereignty, as well as the Religious and Profane Peace.

82 The electors, princes and Estates of the Empire shall all show all due humble respect, honour, obedience, love and loyalty towards His Imperial Majesty again and behave in all matters like true and loyal electors, princes and Estates.

---

[12] The electors' union was a pact between the electors made in 1338 and confirmed by the emperor in 1558. It was the practical expression of the electors' right to meet on their own initiative, whereas the imperial diet could only convene if invited by the emperor.

[13] The imperial law from 1356 regulating imperial elections and constituting a kind of Magna Carta for the Empire.

83 In addition, good old German trust shall be re-established between the Catholics and the adherents of the Augsburg Confession and be truly propagated, and all misunderstanding and disagreement willingly, diligently and expediently avoided in the interest of the common good.

84 Both the Catholics, the adherents of the Augsburg Confession, the electors and Estates shall confer truthfully with each other to implement peace and justice and show all due respect, obedience and assistance to His Imperial Majesty as their overlord.

85 Since the Holy Roman Empire cannot exist without the wise Public Peace, this should always be observed by head and members [i.e. emperor and Estates], all the more during these cruel times with the numerous disorders and crimes committed almost without fear, and all those who break it are to be punished without regard to their person to the full penalty, as a deterrent to the others.

86 One or other Estates have recruited soldiers contrary to Imperial Law and the Executive Ordinance and this Peace Treaty and have not wanted to disband them, despite being properly notified by His Imperial Majesty and by the Convening Princes of the nearby Kreise.[14] They shall be proceeded against with imperial seriousness according to the terms of the Empire's fundamental laws and other salutary constitutions, as well as this pacification, and thereby the Holy Empire's laws and ordinances shall always be enforced and observed.

87 Those matters that are not dealt with specifically in this Peace Treaty and its attached agreements are to be dealt with according to the Holy Roman Empire's fundamental laws, including the high and valuable Religious and Profane Peace, as well as other salutary imperial constitutions and ordinances, and if these do not cover them, then according to customary imperial law.

[Art. 88 declared everything that contradicted the Peace to be null and void and asserted the Peace's permanent validity. Art. 89 bound the emperor and his descendants to observe it, while art. 90 did likewise for the elector of Saxony. Art. 91 asserted the Treaty as imperial law and made it binding on the two imperial supreme courts.]

92 His Electoral Highness shall swiftly forward to all adherents of the Augsburg Confession the guarantee from the Catholic electors and Estates, or most of them, concerning the high archbishoprics and bishoprics, as well as the cathedral chapter benefices. Moreover, no Estate from either Religion is permitted an excuse or delay, but should observe full parity and behave truthfully, like Germans, and upright in all matters and can be assured of what is agreed here by His Imperial Majesty and His Electoral Highness of Saxony.

---

14 One or two princes in each Kreis were recognised as Convenors who were empowered to summon the other territories of that region to attend its assembly.

93 Finally, His Imperial Majesty and His Electoral Highness of Saxony have considered that such high matters cannot be decided for the entire Empire without a general imperial diet, or at least an Imperial Deputation. His Imperial Majesty and His Electoral Highness would very much have liked to observe this (if there had not been the current great difficulties and no exceptional rescue measures had been required). It is stressed that the method used during this unavoidable emergency will not have prejudicial consequences for the Holy Roman Empire or its members at any time, nor can be used as a precedent by anyone.

94 Presented in three original copies on parchment and signed personally by His Roman Imperial Majesty and His Electoral Highness of Saxony for themselves and on behalf of their descendants, and authenticated with their imperial and Electoral seals, and one copy given to His Imperial Majesty, the second to His Electoral Highness of Mainz and the third to His Electoral Highness of Saxony. Done at Prague on the thirtieth of May in the year of Christ our saviour sixteen hundred and thirty-five.

Source: *Neue und vollständige Sammlung der Reichs-Abschiede*, 4 vols (Frankfurt, 1747), vol. III, pp. 534–48.

---

104. The Powder Barrel Convention, 1635

Preliminary declaration of the officers to the Chancellor, camp at Neu Gattersleben, 30 July 1635 [OS]:

The Royal and Imperial Swedish Councillor, Chancellor and Plenipotentiary Legate in the German lands and with the army, as well as Director of the Evangelical League [of Heilbronn], the right honourable lord Axel Oxenstierna, Baron of Kymitho, Lord of Fihölmen and Tydoen etc. addressed all the major generals, colonels and lieutenant colonels of this honourable evangelical army on 25 July and explained the generally dire situation following the Peace of Prague that has divided the evangelical Estates and caused such widespread collapse that there is now no human help (beyond God) left than our honourable army. His Excellency saw that the army was in such a condition, thank god, that it enjoys respect amongst friends and foes. If our army was also to go, the entire cause would be lost. The soldiery would not only not be content, but each and every cavalier serving in this army could expect all kinds of unpleasantness, even threat to body, life, honour and property, not to mention that only insults and ridicule would reward the right honourable Swedish crown, His Excellency's beloved fatherland and above all the blood of its most glorious late king.

The only way, other than God, to prevent this and to try and obtain a good, reputable peace, and to provide some satisfaction to the soldiery as well as the right honourable Swedish crown, was for His Excellency to be empowered by his beloved fatherland and for the soldiery to unite and to stand firmly and resolutely together until we die or God Almighty grants a desirable and honourable peace, either through negotiation or by force of arms. His Excellency then left the major generals, colonels and lieutenant colonels to confer. They sent some to declare that the senior officers wished none other than to declare their immediate affection for His Excellency. They were unanimous in agreeing to remain firmly united until a satisfactory treaty [was agreed upon]. However, opinions differed as to what to do if the treaty could not be agreed and it was necessary to fight the elector of Saxony, because the officers were from different nations, with various interests and considerations. The matter was so important that they humbly requested His Excellency to grant a few days more time to reach a common decision they would present to him in writing. His Excellency replied there were no real differences of opinion, but that they should agree immediately to remain united till death and not to separate unless both the soldiery and the Swedish crown obtained satisfaction. He promised them he would not negotiate or agree anything without the knowledge and consent of the senior officers. To this end two to three cavalry colonels and a similar number from the infantry were to join the negotiations as a committee to represent the interests of the soldiery and ensure nothing prejudicial was agreed. After this offer from His Excellency the Chancellor, the colonels shook hands agreeing to send their definitive decision within three or four days. To this end the undersigned colonels and lieutenant colonels met again and discussed this with the captains (since this also concerns them) and agreed unanimously on their honour that the colonels and lieutenant colonels should select four or six individuals and empower them to represent them in the negotiations so that no peace or war shall be agreed without their knowledge or consent. They wish to remain firmly united until God almighty grants the desired peace treaty with the elector of Saxony.

However, they expressly reserve the condition that, should the negotiations not bring peace, each officer shall be free to resign the service honourably if he wishes. This is to be done as far as possible without harming his regiment or company. Some notice is to be given so as not to weaken the service of the royal Swedish crown.

This honourable discharge is not to affect any officer's legitimate claims to [pay] arrears which it is to be hoped can be settled in cash.

Those officers and soldiers who will see this through to the end, should it lead to fighting with the elector of Saxony and should this cause them suffering or (God Almighty forbid) should they be driven by force from Germany, wish to be assured that their loyal service thus far will be rewarded and their pay settled, or [advised as] to whom they should turn for this.

The above has been pledged by the undersigned colonels and lieutenant colonels with His Excellency the Chancellor by handshake. Affirmed by all the undersigned. Camp at Neu Gattersleben, 30 July 1630.

Source: O.S. Rydberg and Carl Hallendorf (eds), *Sveriges Tractater med främmande magter jemte andra dit hörande handlingar*, 5 vols (Stockholm, 1902–9), vol. V, part 2, pp. 330–3.

105. Heinrich Schlick urges Peter Melander to change sides, 31 October 1637[1]

Most noble and gracious etc.

My particular, dear sir will no doubt remember well that we have been in trusted correspondence that should continue despite these objectionable times. I am writing now, because of the death of his princely grace, Landgrave Wilhelm of Hessen [-Kassel], who was a bad child who helped inflict no little damage and ruin on our fatherland, the Holy Roman Empire. I would like to remind you of our long friendship and to encourage you to reflect on the evil our dear fatherland has suffered and the great dangers that remain and how foreigners laugh at us and heartily rejoice at the devastation we are inflicting upon ourselves (to their best utility and advantage). I would like to seek you to turn to the proper pillar that is our Roman emperor and to oppose the destruction of our dear fatherland. You will be received with honour and a good position, and will see that it is I who wishes only your advantage from true German affection. I can only hope that you will discuss this with Field Marshal Count Götz or Artillery General Count von Wahl[2] (and through them send me your decision). I remain as always

Your willing servant

Heinrich Schlick Count of Passau
Prague 31 October 1637

Source: Horst Conrad and Gunnar Teske (eds), *Sterbezeiten. Der Dreißigjährige Krieg im Herzogtum Westfalen* (Münster, 2000), p. 190.

---

1   Heinrich Schlick (1580–1650) served the Moravian Estates 1619–20 and fought at White Mountain (see **Doc. 25**, note 10), but joined the Habsburgs in February 1621 and became president of the Imperial War Council. Peter Melander (1589–1648) was a Calvinist peasant from Nassau who rose through Dutch, Venetian and Swiss service to command the Hessian army 1633–40. After prolonged negotiations, of which this letter was part, Melander changed sides, was elevated as Count Holzapfel and eventually became imperial commander in 1647.

2   Johann von Götz (1599–1645), a Lüneburg Lutheran who served the Bohemian Estates and then Mansfeld, before joining the imperial army in 1622; Joachim Christian Baron (later Imperial Count) von Wahl (1590–1644), a minor Weimar noble who converted from Lutheranism to Catholicism before 1618 and became Bavarian commander 1639–42.

14

War and politics, 1635–40

Despite securing the army's loyalty in the Powder Barrel Convention **[see Doc. 104]**, there seemed little prospect in 1635 of Sweden defeating the emperor. Swedish forces had been halved by the loss of the south German army under Bernhard of Weimar who retreated to the Rhine after Nördlingen and later took his men into French service (for an English translation of this arrangement, see G. Symcox (ed.), *War, Diplomacy and Imperialism, 1618–1763* (London, 1974), pp. 117–25). Many in Sweden's regency council initially urged Oxenstierna to make peace, but all were reluctant to leave Germany without at least some compensation **[Doc. 106]**.

The outbreak of a separate Franco-Spanish war in April 1635 provided some encouragement. Though this distracted France and reduced the likelihood of immediate French military assistance, it nonetheless increased Richelieu's interest in retaining Sweden as an ally. Still unable to reach a firm agreement with Bavaria, Richelieu needed Sweden to keep Austria busy and prevent it from assisting Spain **[Docs 109–10]**.

With Sweden unwilling to leave Germany empty-handed, Saxony was obliged to begin military operations. These were hopelessly mismanaged **[Doc. 111]**, encouraging Sweden to reject further peace proposals **[Doc. 107]**. Oxenstierna welcomed French financial support, but hesitated to forge a closer alliance for fear of losing the freedom to make a separate peace with the emperor should a suitable opportunity appear. The defection of Bernhard of Weimar and the south German army heightened his suspicions of French intentions in the Empire **[Doc. 108]**. The combination of modest French assistance, renewed Swedish resolve and lacklustre Saxon military performance dashed initial hopes that the Peace of Prague would end the war. Maximilian of Bavaria became increasingly pessimistic towards 1637, but remained committed to his alliance with the emperor who had guaranteed his possession of the Palatine lands and titles **[Doc. 112]**.

SWEDISH POLICY

106. Minutes of the Council of the Realm, September–October 1635

(1)

17 September 1635. Discussion as to what is to be written to the Chancellor [Axel Oxenstierna was still in Germany], and whether it would not be advisable for him frankly to pull out of Germany by degrees, and devote his efforts

to doing it without loss of security and reputation, and without forfeiting German goodwill: if he can secure something over and above, so much the better. The view was that if the Chancellor should win a victory, we may no doubt hope for reasonable peace-terms; if he loses a battle, he will be forced to retire northwards to a place of safety. In the meantime that he keep in close touch with the French, so that he may shape his conduct according to how things develop. He should make every effort to hang on to the most important places, as far as he can.

Decided that the Chancellor is to abide by Her Majesty's former instructions. If he can obtain any territory [at a possible peace], that would be best; if not, to take satisfaction in money; and if he cannot get that, to try every means consistent with reputation and safety to extricate himself from the German business.

(2)

9 October. Discussion whether the news that the Elector of Saxony and the German Princes have separated themselves from us shall be publicly laid before the Estates. The view was that a gloss must be put upon it, and the information be conveyed in softened terms … Since the Elector of Saxony wants to drive us out of Germany by force, it is plain that we must prepare to defend ourselves, in particular by providing garrisons and ample supplies for the coastlands, since our main armies are steadily falling back nearer and nearer to the coast.

Herr Per Banér[1] urged that we could not simply get out of Germany, as once the King of Denmark did: he could see nothing for it but that we must fight.

Count Per Brahe[2] said that we could not accept compensation in money, and preserve our honour. If the crown of Sweden could obtain satisfaction in land, that would be the best solution. … In any case our armies could hardly be paid off for less than 4 or 5 millions. It would seem best, therefore, if we cannot reach any respectable agreement with the Emperor, that we go on fighting. If we win a victory, we must exploit it; if we are beaten, then that disposes of the soldiers' arrears, and we can defend the strong places on the coast with the survivors.

(3)

10 October. *The Court Chancellor* [Johan Adler Salvius] gave the Regents his views about the possibility of negotiation with the Elector of Saxony, to the effect that since the Elector is hardly likely to be willing to let us arrange a general peace, he will try to prevent our negotiating directly with the Emperor, with whom he (and he alone) has made his dishonourable agreement … The Court-Chancellor was of opinion that … it was quite possible to negotiate with the Elector, just as other Princes and Republics had done, and by doing so get

---

[1]   Per Banér (1588–1644), councillor of state and brother of Sweden's commanding general, Johan Banér. See **Doc. 117**, note 2.

[2]   Count Per Brahe (1602–80) was an important Swedish noble who served with Gustavus before taking up a seat in the council of state in 1632. He negotiated the renewal of the 1629 truce with Poland in September 1635, thus ensuring Sweden did not have to fight a war on two fronts.

what we wanted; for the longer the German business lasts, the worse for us. If it does come to a breach [with Saxony], our own German troops will desert us. If our army consisted of French, Scots and Swedes, we could no doubt put up a fight; but as it is, our army is entirely composed of Germans. Conscription at home is at the moment out of the question. The Chancellor [Oxenstierna], in his anxiety to escape humiliation, is firmly determined to die over there in Germany; but this will hardly do the country much good: we shall be forced to make peace just the same. The burden of defence will be intolerable in the long run; and in any case peace will have to be made sooner or later.

(4)
23 October. It was considered wisest and best to start a negotiation with the Emperor, and extricate ourselves from the German war: if it cannot be done on honourable terms, then let us content ourselves with whatever terms we can get; for the resources of the country are not adequate to the maintenance of great armies.

...

The Court-Chancellor said also, that we wage war in Germany as auxiliaries, and not as principals. If the principals have now done a deal with the enemy, who can say that we are behaving dishonourably, if we cut ourselves off from the whole business?

Source: Michael Roberts (ed.), *Sweden as a Great Power 1611–1697. Government: Society: Foreign Policy* (London, 1968), pp. 149–51.

_____

107. Resolution of the Regency rejecting the Peace, 1 August 1636

Whereas the Chancellor upon his return has reported on the position in Germany at the time of his departure, and particularly on the negotiations for peace with the Emperor and the Elector of Saxony, which have been proceeding for almost a year, through the intermediary of Duke Adolf Friedrich of Mecklenburg[1] ...; the Regency and the Council have found these draft-terms reasonable, useful and honourable to the Queen and country ...

... We have given all these things our careful attention, and having entreated God, have now by His aid reached the following conclusions:

First, that we ought to pitch the terms of the sixth article (concerning restitution of the oppressed Protestant Electors, Prince and Estates) as high as is practicable; for (i) it is our Christian duty to take up their cause, and so try to preserve God's congregation in those places; (ii) it is conformable to the attitude and actions of our late King, who shed his blood for that cause; (iii) the safety of this country depends upon the liberties of the Estates in Germany

_____

[1] Duke Adolf Friedrich of Mecklenburg (1588–1658, r.1592) was one of the two dukes deposed in 1628 for having backed Denmark. He was restored in the Peace of Prague and undertook in November 1635 to assist Saxon negotiations with Sweden.

not being transformed into a servitude, under the absolute domination of the House of Austria, and especially in keeping that House away from the Baltic; (iv) it is a question of honour, which in politics can never be ignored; (v) it gives us the goodwill and affection of all our neighbours, and of many Estates and soldiers in the Holy Roman Empire; (vi) and lastly, it seems unwise to give up this point before we are sure of the two others (the Crown's indemnity and the contentment of the soldiery), since if the first point were let go, either our adversary would seize the opportunity to evade the other two, or else if the negotiation broke down on them, all concerned would be alienated from us, and their jealousy of us would be even greater than before. For these and other reasons we have decided that this point must be stuck to as firmly as possible, and that we should aim at keeping the discussion of it going, while we press on in the meantime with ... the negotiation of the two other points. But since (1) the state of the country does not permit us to continue the war, unless it be unavoidably necessary; (2) the advantages of the war now fall to our neighbours, while the damage falls upon us; (3) the Evangelical Electors, Princes and Estates have not stood by us either constantly or sincerely: most of them have left the League [of Heilbronn],[2] and (which is worse) attached themselves to the enemy; the most important of the rest are carrying on separate negotiations with him, and if there are still a few who are not, that is only because they have no hope of obtaining terms; (4) consequently we can expect no assistance from any state, but (5) have much more reason to fear that not only the German princes, but also foreign potentates may be induced to make common cause with our enemies ... For these and other reasons, the Regency and Council do not consider it either reasonable or advisable that we should in the last resort persist with the war for the sake of others; but as soon as the two points of the Crown's indemnity and the contentment of the soldiery shall have been settled, then, when all reasonable means to aid the German [i.e. imperial] Estates have been tried without success, we should drop the contentious article about the extent of the [emperor's] amnesty and the restitution of the [imperial] Estates, and should leave it to the Estates themselves to deal with. Thereafter we should give them all possible assistance, not with the sword and under the hazards of war, but by intercession and other amicable means, and without prejudice to our own attempts to find an acceptable means of withdrawing from the war.

...

Concerning the Crown's indemnity, we must insist that the treaty provide a considerable sum of money – up to 6 million *riksdaler* or more, if we are to abandon all lands and towns, though if need be we might accept 3 million *rdr*, together with the payment of the Crown's debts incurred here and there in Germany. But if the Crown were freed from all claims of the soldiery, as well as from its own outstanding debts in Germany, we might press for a sizeable cash payment, and thereby (since the situation of the German [i.e. imperial]

---

[2]   See **Doc. 96.**

Estates is not such at present that they can find the money) keep possession of some of the harbours under the guise of security: the total sum might be abated by at the most a million *rdr*, and the main security should be in western Pomerania, Rügen, Kolberg and Wismar, and we should so arrange it that the garrisons be maintained without cost to the crown. Some concessions, as has been said, may well be made on this point of indemnity, and it is reasonable rather to give way than at this critical time to deprive the country of its gains, and commit it to a perpetual war, to the advantage of others and the hurt and danger of ourselves. But above all things we must try to obtain the contentment of the soldiery, and relieve Her Majesty and the crown of that burden, which should not and must not be placed upon her, since she receives no benefit from them, but rather hurt and extortion. Nevertheless since it would not be advisable nor honourable to the country to leave the soldiery entirely unsatisfied, the burden must be taken from our shoulders and transferred by agreement to those of the German Estates; and on this we must strictly insist.

As regards the ratification of the alliance with France, there is certainly something to be said for it, if in the end we are forced to go on fighting: but since it would bind our hands too tightly, and we should thereby be compelled to keep in the war even though an opportunity might arise to get out of it, it seems most advisable to defer the ratification as long as we can, on one pretext or another, till we see what happens to the Duke of Mecklenburg's negotiation. If it goes well, we had best cut loose from the war. If it sticks, we must ratify the alliance, and commend our cause to God.

Source: Michael Roberts (ed.), *Sweden as a Great Power 1611–1697. Government: Society: Foreign Policy* (London, 1968), pp. 151–4, from *Axel Oxenstiernas skrifter och brevvexling*, vol. I, part i, pp. 574–9.

108. Oxenstierna on the French alliance, 1640

The Chancellor: I say, as I have always said, that there are many arguments to dissuade me from the French alliance. I have had experience of their tricks in former years. They commit hostile acts against us, under a mask of friendship. When we remonstrate with them about [taking] Breisach, and how they debauched the Army of [Bernard of] Weimar, they make long speeches, and trot out excuses, and shrug their shoulders. Our late King often tore his hair at the impertinences he had to put up with from them. But what could he do? Necessity is a great argument, and for a handful of gold one must often sacrifice reputation.

Source: Michael Roberts (ed.), *Sweden as a Great Power 1611–1697. Government: Society: Foreign Policy* (London, 1968), p. 154, from *Svenska riksradets protokoll*, vol. VIII, p. 329.

FRENCH INTERVENTION

109. Richelieu's reflections on French policy after 1630

[At the Diet of Regensburg, 1630[1]] the discontent felt toward the Emperor and the Spaniards by the Duke of Bavaria, who until then had been inseparably attached to the House of Austria, and the fear felt by all the Electors, both Catholic and Protestant, that they would be deprived of their estates, as many other princes had already been by the Emperor's [Edict of Restitution], made them secretly seek your support. You negotiated with them so adroitly and with so much success that they prevented, in the presence of the Emperor himself, the election of the King of the Romans, even though the Diet of Regensburg had been convoked for this sole reason.[2]

Then, to please Bavaria, to satisfy the Electors and various other princes, and to fortify all of them in their resolution to make the Catholic League independent, not of the Emperor, but of Spain, which was usurping its leadership, your ambassadors ... helped these princes to depose Wallenstein from the command of the armies of the Empire (which helped not a little to slow down the affairs of his master) ...

A little later the King of Sweden embarked on his enterprise to prevent the oppression of the princes of the Empire in Germany, and this plan was no sooner known to you than Your Majesty, to prevent any prejudice to the Catholic religion, concluded a treaty with him which obliged him not to disturb its exercise in any of the areas of his conquests.[3]

I know well that your enemies, who hope to justify their actions by criticizing yours, have overlooked nothing in their effort to make this agreement seem odious. But their plan has had no effect other than to reveal their malice. The innocence of Your Majesty is absolutely clear, because his ambassador did not enter into any treaty with this conqueror until he had been in Germany for six months. This easily proves that the treaties made with this prince were the remedy for the wrong and not its cause.

The treaties concluded not only with this great King, but also with many other princes of Germany, were justified anyway because they were absolutely necessary for the safety of the Duke of Mantua, who had been unjustly attacked, and for the security of all Italy, over which the Spaniards had no less right than they did over the lands of this poor prince, since they considered their convenience sufficient legitimacy ...

If it is an action of singular wisdom to have kept all the forces of the enemies of your State occupied for ten years by the armies of your allies, using your treasury and not your weapons, then, when your allies could no longer survive on their own, it was an act of both courage and wisdom to enter into

---

[1] Like many outsiders, the French referred to all important gatherings in the Empire as a 'diet'. The meeting in 1630 was actually an electoral congress, not a full imperial diet.

[2] See **Docs 59–60**. For the Edict of Restitution, see **Doc. 62**.

[3] A reference to the Treaty of Bärwalde. See **Doc. 77**.

open war. This shows that, in managing the security of the kingdom, you have acted like those stewards who, having been careful to save money, know when to spend it to prevent a greater loss ...

You attacked in various places at the same time ... in order to keep your enemies occupied on all sides so that they could be invincible in none.

The war in Germany was virtually unavoidable, since this part of Europe had been the theatre where it had opened long before.

Although the war in Flanders did not achieve the success one might have expected, it was impossible not to regard it as advantageous in its aims.

The war in the Grisons was necessary so as to encourage the Italian princes to take up arms by removing their fear of the Germans ...

The war in Italy was no less important, as much because this was the best way to get the Duke of Savoy on our side, as because the Milanese, the heart of the States possessed by Spain, was the territory he had to attack.

As for the rest, if one considers that Your Majesty had allies on all sides who had to join forces with you, it is common sense that the Spaniards, attacked in various places by such a union, would succumb under the force of your power ...

During the course of this war ... nothing went wrong for you without seeming to have happened only for your glory ...

Various things are worthy of note about this war.

The first is that Your Majesty did not enter the war until it was unavoidable, and did not leave it until he had to. This observation sheds great glory on Your Majesty, because when at peace France was often urged by its allies to take up arms, though reluctant to do so. And during the war his enemies often proposed a separate peace, but he would never consider it because France could not be separated from the interests of its allies.

Those who know that Your Majesty was abandoned by several princes allied to France, and that nonetheless he did not wish to abandon anyone; that moreover some of those who remained loyal let him down in several important matters, yet still received from Your Majesty the treatment they were promised; those people, I say, understand that if the good fortune of Your Majesty is apparent in the success of his endeavors, his virtue is no less great than his good fortune. I know well that if France had broken its word, its reputation would have suffered badly, and the least loss of this kind means that a great prince has nothing further to lose. But it was no small matter to have lived up to one's obligations on various occasions when the natural desire for vengeance and peace after a war gave way to an opposite course of action.

You needed wisdom no less than force, an effort of will no less than one of arms, to persevere almost alone in those very designs which you had hoped would succeed by the union of many ...

The second observation on this subject worthy of great note is that Your Majesty did not, so as to protect himself from the peril of war, expose Christianity to Ottoman arms, which were often offered to us.

He was not unaware that he could have accepted such assistance with justification. Yet this knowledge was not strong enough to make him take a step which endangered religion, however advantageous it might have been for securing peace.

The example of some of his predecessors, and various princes of the House of Austria, who especially try to appear as religious before God as he is in fact in his private beliefs, was too weak to carry him into what history teaches us has been practiced by others a number of times ...

If I add that his many preoccupations did not prevent him from properly fortifying, at the same time, all his frontiers, which previously had been open on all sides to his enemies, then their present state can only be cause for astonishment. It will be an innovation no less important to posterity that, having gained security for ever, this kingdom will in the future gather as many of the fruits of Your Majesty's labours and efforts as he has received in the past.

Those to whom history will reveal the crosses Your Majesty encountered in all his great designs: through the envy his successes, and the fear his power, aroused among various princes, including occasionally some of his allies; through the disloyalty of his evil subjects; through a brother badly advised; through a mother always possessed of evil intentions;[4] ... they will realize that such obstacles have in no small way increased your glory, and they will re-realize also that great courage cannot be diverted by the difficulties it encounters.

If they consider further the natural frivolity of this nation, the impatience of its soldiers who are little accustomed to hard work, and finally the weakness of the instruments which by necessity you had to use on these occasions – among which I hold the first place – they will have to admit that nothing made up for the failings of your implements except the excellence of Your Majesty, who was the artisan.

Finally, if they realize that after overcoming all these obstacles you succeeded in concluding a peace, in which ... you returned territory that you yourself had conquered, they cannot fail to realize that your generosity equals your power, and in your conduct wisdom and the blessing of God march side by side ...

Source: Amand Jean du Plessis, Cardinal and duc de Richelieu, *Testament Politique*, ed. Louis André (Paris, 1947), as translated in Theodore K. Rabb (ed.), *The Thirty Years War* (Chicago, 1964), pp. 77–9.

---

4   Louis XIII had a difficult relationship with his mother, Marie de Medici (1573–1642), and brother Gaston d'Orleans (1608–60). Marie eventually fled into exile in June 1631 having failed to oust Richelieu and to control her son. Gaston also fled, but was briefly reconciled in 1636, before fleeing again in 1641 after another failed plot.

110. French declaration of war against Spain, 19 May 1635

To be read out by the French herald, Jehan Gratiollet de Daubas

I am summoned here on the part of the king my master, my one sovereign lord, to inform you as follows: Since you have failed to release the archbishop of Trier, elector of the Holy Roman Empire,[1] who had placed himself under his protection, when he was unable to receive it from the emperor or any other prince; and since contrary to the dignity of the Empire and the law of nations you are holding as prisoner a sovereign prince with whom you are not at war; now therefore His Majesty declares that his is resolved to avenge this offence by force of arms, for it is of concern to all the princes of Christendom.

Source: D.P. O'Connell, *Richelieu* (London, 1968), p. 311.

IMPERIAL FAILURE

111. Lacklustre Saxon military performance[1]

On 3 July in the year 1635 [OS] His Electoral Highness [of Saxony] after made peace with His Roman Imperial Majesty, left his court at Dresden as Imperial Commissioner and Plenipotentiary with the intention of forcing those who did not accept the peace willingly to see reason …

On the 19th [July 1635] Lt General Arnim[2] held a banquet at Schreiner's house on the market place [in Leipzig] and invited His Electoral Grace himself and his court and all officers. Everything went magnificently. His Highness was very jolly at this banquet and paid the said Lt General many extraordinary compliments, thinking he would persuade him to resume command, but in vain. Many have criticised Arnim for resigning his command, which they found unreasonable, but those in the know say he did the right thing, though those who told me of the foolish talk in Linz, that will be recounted later, have also conceded he did right. I asked the Saxon officers to think of ways and means to persuade Arnim to resume command of the army, and

---

[1] Philipp Christoph von Sötern (1567–1652), bishop of Speyer from 1610 and elector of Trier from 1624, had accepted French protection on 9 April 1632 and signed a treaty of neutrality with Sweden shortly after. He was seized by Spanish troops on 26 March 1635 and later handed over to the emperor.

[1] The following is an extract from the diary of Colonel Christian Vitzthum von Eckstädt (1586–1652) serving in the Saxon army. Vitzthum came from a family of Lutheran Saxon nobles. Two of his relations were Saxon generals. Older works incorrectly identify the author as Augustin, another of Christian's relations, who was an imperial colonel.

[2] Hans Georg von Arnim [see **Doc. 66**]. His position became untenable once Saxony returned to the imperial side after the Peace of Prague, and he resigned.

offered 1,000tlr, and if the others had done the same, we would have got some 30,000tlr together to offer to the General. But they didn't want to, saying they had learned their art as well as Arnim. I think one has seen what they have learned, given that the emperor and the elector nearly lost their lands and peoples ...

On the 27th they started negotiating with Baudissin[3] to offer him Lt General Arnim's place. Never in my life have I seen anything as loathsome as these quite damaging negotiations. I urged my cousin and brother to oppose them, since I would bet my life that we would lose half the infantry within two months, as happened within six weeks, as will be recounted. But no one wanted to believe me ...

On the 6th [August 1635] my brother was sent again to negotiate with the Weimar regiments. That evening His Highness summoned Major General Lohausen and Schwallenberg to dinner, but not Brandenstein.[4] His Highness told Lohausen, among other things, ... get out of the Empire, I will cover your back, so that the Imperials don't do anything, but if you don't go willingly, you will be forced. It was well said, but to poor effect. In short, we conducted the negotiations badly, without subtlety or discretion, using few kind words, but instead harsh and tough threats as if the entire world was ours already. I had advised to bribe Schwallenberg, and to grease his palm with a councillor's post, and to employ Brandenstein and so not to treat him so harshly and poorly, and to attract the Swedish officers to us with money.

On the 7th the Swedish representatives returned to Halle in displeasure ...

[On 24 August 1635 the elector finally set out from Leipzig with 21,500 infantry and 13,600 cavalry] And His Electoral Highness in person with his court made their first night camp at Zorbitz. The army, however, camped in the field at Scheidiz, with the general staff in Scheidiz.

Earlier at the rendezvous [outside Leipzig], my cousins, brother and many colonels came to me and complained at Baudissin's little understanding. He didn't know how to direct a march, and if he continued like this, we would lose and be defeated, as happened shortly afterwards. However, I think they were more to blame than Baudissin, since they refused to follow my advice to oppose him, and chose to serve under him instead.

[Later Vitzthum gave the elector the following advice in January 1636:]

---

3   Wolfgang Heinrich Christoph von Baudissin (1597–1646) had served Venice, Denmark and Sweden, but resigned in March 1633 after disagreements with the Swedish regency government.

4   These were officers in the army under Duke Wilhelm of Weimar (1598–1662) that retreated separately from the main Swedish forces to Erfurt. Wilhelm Calchum von Lohausen (1584–1640) was a key figure in the Powder Barrel mutiny [see **Doc. 104**] who eventually quit Swedish service in April 1636 [see also **Doc. 139**]. Christoph Carl von Brandenstein (1593–1637) had transferred from Saxon to Swedish service early in 1633 and acted as treasurer of the Heilbronn League. Elector Johann Georg of Saxony hated him for having accepted the small principality of Querfurt as a Swedish donation that contravened Saxon jurisdiction. He was later arrested and died in prison in Dresden.

And I think it certain that if Your Highness does not remedy the following five points, you will have a miserable war.

1 First, all officers should remain at their posts and not wait in the suite [of the elector, but] be cashiered or punished [if they do], because Dietrich Taube, the major general of the right wing, never goes to his regiments, but hangs around the elector's neck.

2 The commissariat should act a little more diligently and provide provisions at the proper time, putting things in order won't do any harm.

3 Not to say anything about the war to your pages, servants and courtiers, because they spread it amongst the troops, as has happened a few times already.

4 Discharge those who don't have a place in the army, regardless of their estate.

5 And fifthly, get better intelligence and pay for it.

Everything will end badly if these things aren't remedied quickly.

And though some think that the elector has done a fine thing by putting the troops into winter quarters by the water, one will soon see. And the imperial generals will try to see what they can get out of it ...

The army has now spent 32 weeks in the field and doesn't know when it will enter quarters. The enemy has quite ruined the quarters, and there has been no mention of pay for some months, while the lieutenants and ensigns must drink water and suffer want. This must be remedied or the army will be ruined ... [Vitzthum complains his suggestions were laughed at.]

The elector personally spent much effort with the artillery and was present at its limbering up and marching, but appointed a lazy officer as his general of artillery, who sat in his coach and paraded in front of the pieces with his women, and didn't care whether they arrived, or got stuck ...

In the meantime everything goes slowly and sleepily ...

Source: Vitzthum's diary published by F. Budczies (ed.), 'Der Feldzug der sächsischen Armee durch die Mark Brandenburg im Jahre 1635 und 1636', *Märkische Forschungen*, 16 (1881), pp. 303–86.

112. Maximilian of Bavaria reflects on the course of the war, *c.*1637

It is well-known that God Almighty blessed the arms of His Imperial Majesty and the honourable Catholic League with many imposing victories after the recapture of the city of Prague and the kingdom of Bohemia and its incorporated lands.[1] The non-Catholics and their supporters and adherents were

---

[1] In 1620.

thereby weakened and so humbled that Emperor Ferdinand II, God rest his soul, judged the year 1629 appropriate to promote the acceptance of Catholicism. With the advice and knowledge of the Catholic electors he issued the imperial Edict of Restitution to recover the archbishoprics, bishoprics and ecclesiastical land alienated since the Passau Treaty and seized by the non-Catholic electors and Estates contrary to law. The Edict was published throughout the Empire and its implementation so organised that, with God's help and support, all abbeys, monasteries and foundations in the Swabian Kreis and Württemberg were recovered from the non-Catholics who had taken them after the Passau Treaty. Catholic worship was restored to various imperial cities, especially Augsburg, Memmingen, Lindau and Kaufbeuren, and Catholic councils resumed proper power and direction. Above all, Catholic authority was stablised in the bishoprics of Osnabrück, Minden and Verden, which had already been recovered by force of arms, through the appointment of Catholic bishops, while the bishopric of Halberstadt, bishopric and town of Hildesheim and the city and archbishopric of Magdeburg were captured and restored, and even in the archbishopric of Bremen matters were advanced so far that Archduke Leopold Wilhelm[2] succeeded there as well as in Magdeburg and Halberstadt. The Catholics thus acquired so many impressive and numerous ecclesiastical lands that there was a lack of qualified people to occupy all these archbishoprics, bishoprics, abbeys, monasteries and other ecclesiastical foundations, or to teach and maintain the several million souls won for the Catholic faith.

Meanwhile, the costly maintenance of such a strong army running into the twelfth consecutive year had so stressed and exhausted His Imperial Majesty and the electors, princes and Estates of the Catholic League that many true-hearted people now felt it better and safer to consider more appropriate means for peace, respite, recovery, stabilisation of conquests and to secure the many and impressive archbishoprics, bishoprics and lands that had been recovered, rather than continue the war, for which the means were already noticeably lacking and which would expose what had been recovered, as well as existing Catholic possessions, to the uncertainties of military events. Moreover, the non-Catholic electors, princes and Estates gathered at the congress of Regensburg in 1630 not only favoured peace, but were prepared to accept the loss of the restored ecclesiastical lands and let the Catholics keep what they already possessed, and allow the Catholics to claim the remaining territories alienated after the Passau treaty.

However, soon after the congress began in Regensburg it became clear that the clergy ignored the important and urgent motives for peace and even the

---

2   Leopold Wilhelm (1614–62), Ferdinand II's younger son, was elected bishop of Passau (1626), Strasbourg (1626), Halberstadt (1627), and archbishop of Magdeburg (1631–8) and Bremen (1635–45). He commanded the imperial army in 1639–43 and 1645–6 and Spain's Army of Flanders in 1647–56, but continued his career in the imperial church becoming bishop of Olmütz (1638) and Breslau (1656), as well as Teutonic grand master (1639).

clear absence of means to continue the war, and instead from inappropriate zeal opposed the most reputable and necessary peace that was within grasp, and unashamedly and openly threatened censure and excommunication, even making difficulties for His Imperial Majesty and the Catholic electors. [The clergy claimed] that continuing military success was certain, enabling a full recovery of the few remaining poor ecclesiastical lands in Pomerania and other distant places. In the end, the opportunity for concluding the desirable and reputable peace was lost and it was resolved to continue the war despite the lack of the necessary means and assistance of Catholic potentates, thereby exchanging certainty for uncertainty, much for less, and exposing many millions of souls to danger and the most regrettable ruination that has followed since then.

The non-Catholic electors, princes and Estates, along with foreign kings and potentates, both Catholic and of the Augsburg Confession, noticed that the Catholics were not content with the impressive and acceptable peace terms they had been offered, but wished to continue the war to the bitter end and – so they assumed – the complete extirpation of non-Catholics. This drove them to desperation and they staged a general convention at Leipzig immediately after the Regensburg congress, opening correspondence and signing treaties with foreign potentates, notably the king of Sweden, mobilising their maximum strength, making all sorts of strong military preparations, promoting the most destructive alliance between the French and Swedish crowns,[3] and bringing not only the Swedish and later the French armies into the Empire, but also thereby causing a most lamentable bloodletting, even bringing the Roman Empire to a miserable, wretched and ruined state and plunging the Catholic electors, princes and Estates and their lands and peoples into extreme need and ruin, as is unfortunately so clear to see and more to cry over than describe. Not only have the above-mentioned impressive archbishoprics, bishoprics and ecclesiastical lands and the many millions of souls that were happily recovered now been lost again, but the [Catholics'] own lands have largely been ruined and are at risk of being lost altogether.

Matters have reached a crisis. The Catholic electors, princes and Estates, together with their lands and peoples, have been largely exhausted and have lost the means to continue the war. The imperialists and Austrians have shoved the burden from their lands onto others. Even the Pope has excused himself from helping the Catholics in the Empire who are fiercely attacked and oppressed by foreign Catholic and non-Catholic potentates and have been reduced to such a condition that they and the Catholic faith are threatened with complete destruction. It is thus appropriate and timely to consider who is to blame for this, so as to promote a peace as good as the current situation permits (because the much better one was rejected before), and whether it is better and appropriate before God and posterity to take this last means (since no one, not even those who oppose this current peace, has proposed

---

3   The Treaty of Bärwalde, 23 January 1631 (see **Doc. 77**).

an alternative) to preserve what remains of the archbishoprics, bishoprics and ecclesiastical lands together with Catholicism in Germany and the many millions of souls, or to continue the war that, as all Catholic imperial Estates know from experience, threatens the total ruin of the aforementioned arch-bishoprics, bishoprics and Catholic lands, along with the Catholic religion and so many millions of souls.

Source: Dieter Albrecht, *Die auswärtige Politik Maximilians von Bayern 1618–1635* (Göttingen, 1962), pp. 379–81.

15

Military organisation and the war economy

Much of the writing on the war conveys the impression it was waged by debauched mercenaries with no loyalty other than to the highest bidder. Mercenaries already had a poor reputation in the sixteenth century when they were shunned socially by the pious who condemned their trade in killing. In fact, mercenaries were simply those who enlisted for a bounty and received pay. Most were subjects of their paymaster, to whom they were already bound by feudal jurisdiction, dynastic and confessional loyalty. Some were drafted under the limited forms of conscription which existed in Denmark, Sweden and most German territories. These systems invariably stated the principle of universal service to defend hearth and home, but then elaborated numerous exemptions based on social and marital status, occupation, age and fitness. The Scandinavian systems placed men directly in the regular army, which also contained units of mercenaries, i.e. professionals. The conscripts were at least nominally reserved for national defence and the Danish constitution contained provisions restricting their use outside the country.

German conscription was more obviously restricted as a militia, recruiting men who remained civilians except when embodied by mobilisation. Such militias dated from at least the late fifteenth century and were legitimated by feudal obligations and customary requirements for the able-bodied male population to assist in combating natural disasters like floods, repelling invaders and pursuing criminals.

The development of effective gunpowder weaponry since the 1450s made such militias increasingly obsolete. The new guns went by a bewildering variety of names which gradually simplified to muskets, for the long-barrelled infantry weapons, and shorter pistols, which could be held and fired in one hand and so used whilst on horseback. The new handguns had greater penetrating power than other missile weapons (like crossbows), but they were still fairly ineffective if used individually, since their optimal range was only around 100 metres and the chance of hitting a selected target under battlefield conditions was slight. Their true potential was exploited by deploying large numbers of musketeers together, relying on the speed and volume of fire, not individual accuracy. The process of loading and firing was simpler and faster than often thought, but musketeers were still vulnerable to attack by fast-moving cavalry. They were protected by grouping them with other infantry armed with pikes – steel-tipped poles around five metres long which could be used in defence or attack by pointing them in the enemy's face. Pikes too were ineffective individually, but potent when used en masse. Effective use of these weapons required personal courage, training, collective discipline and subordination to a clear hierarchy of command; four factors noticeably absent from most early modern militias.

These deficiencies were addressed by the counts of Nassau from the 1570s. The counts' small territories in the Rhineland were close to the civil wars in France and the Netherlands. To improve security, the counts reorganised their militia which, like that of most of the other imperial Estates, had existed largely only on paper. The new militia were armed, trained and commanded like professional soldiers, but would only be embodied in emergencies. They were never intended to replace expensive mercenaries for major operations, but only to provide local defence and supplement regulars if necessary. The reforms were copied throughout the Empire so that most territories had a new model militia by 1610. What caught the imagination of rulers was not only the promised improved effectiveness, but also the underlying philosophy that military drill would transform indolent, recalcitrant peasants into thrifty, obedient and pious subjects [Doc. 113].

Though often labelled 'militia' in secondary accounts, the troops of the Bohemian rebels were in fact professionals serving under officers appointed by the Estates of the kingdom's five provinces [see Doc. 25]. Attempts to mobilise an additional, genuine militia failed in 1618–19. Militia formed a significant proportion of the Palatine army and that of Frederick V's supporter, Margrave Georg Friedrich of Baden-Durlach (1573–1638, r.1577–1622). They were also used by other territories, notably Bavaria and Württemberg, but always with mixed success. The problems are revealed in a series of reports during the Bavarian mobilisation against the Swedish invasion of 1632 [Doc. 114]. As these show, militia could fight well if defending their own homes.

Frequently, peasants resorted to self-help, ambushing small detachments and murdering stragglers or soldiers left injured on a battlefield. Such guerrilla activity was frowned upon by the authorities for whom war was intended as an orderly application of force to achieve specific goals. Popular resistance was hard to control and was often directed against a ruler's own, ill-disciplined troops. It could prove successful, but generally met with merciless, bloody reprisals from soldiers [see Docs 135–6].

The war witnessed the rapid growth in army size. The Habsburgs started with fewer than 2,000 regular troops, plus their militia guarding the Hungarian frontier. Relentless recruiting and the arrival of foreign and allied contingents soon pushed the average combined total of all combatant forces in the Empire to 80–100,000 men between late 1618 and 1626. Such numbers had not been seen in the Empire for over 70 years. Moreover, unlike earlier conflicts which ended after a few campaigns, this one saw three decades of nearly continuous fighting. The relentless growth of Wallenstein's new imperial army raised the total under arms to 160,000 men by 1629, including the much smaller League and Danish forces. A peak of 250,000 was reached by mid-1632 following Sweden's intervention and the rapid spread of the war to all parts of the Empire. Widespread devastation, depopulation and imminent state bankruptcy made it impossible to sustain such numbers and the slow but steady decline is clear from an assessment by the Habsburg War Council in 1637 [**Doc. 115**]. Nonetheless, overall army size remained above that of the opening phase and represented a terrible burden [**see Doc. 173**].

The purpose of such numbers was to force the enemy to make an acceptable peace by achieving a decisive victory. Military experts disagreed in their approach to this, with some advocating the capture of strategic towns or valuable territory, while others argued it was necessary to defeat the enemy army in battle [**Doc. 116**]. Battles involved up to 76,000 men (as at Breitenfeld in 1631) facing each other at close quarters. Opinions differed as to the best form of deployment, with that of Gustavus Adolphus attracting considerable attention after the unexpected scale of his victory at Breitenfeld [**Doc. 117**]. Actions rarely lasted more than a few hours, but were frequently bloody, with a fifth of more killed or maimed.

Losses were heaviest amongst the infantry of the defeated side, since they usually found it hardest to escape. However, cavalry could also suffer, especially if hit by artillery fire or routed by their opponents, as in the case of the imperialists and Saxons at the Second Battle of Breitenfeld on 2 November 1642 [**Doc. 118**]. The large numbers of troopers left dismounted after that battle indicate the high level of animal casualties that were another grisly characteristic. The strength return also shows the growing difficulty of keeping regiments up to strength and supplied with the appropriate number of senior officers: few of the imperial and Saxon regiments listed have a full complement of company commanders, while none has the required number of at least 100 troopers per company.

The Second Battle of Breitenfeld was one of several important battles in the later stages of the war lost through the poor cohesion and discipline of the impe-rial army. An initial success was ruined when several cavalry regiments on the left wing turned and fled without receiving a Swedish counter-attack. Some sense of the commanders' disappointment and resentment comes through the official published account of the subsequent punishments inflicted on the offending regi-ments [**Doc. 119**]. Repeated efforts were made to reform the army, but they were constantly undermined by a chronic lack of funds [**Doc. 120**].

No army was paid punctually or in full. All participants raised more men than they could afford, relying on assistance from allies and whatever they could extort from the local population to make good the shortfall. Extortion took many forms, but is generally labelled 'contributions'. At their worst, contributions were extracted by threatening to devastate crops or burn houses [**see Doc. 146**]. Such extortion was practised in hostile territory by raiding parties or by armies which lacked a secure base and were constantly on the move. Mansfeld's is a good example of the latter, and was notorious for its plundering [**Doc. 121**]. Most commanders preferred more reliable, regular payments made through established systems of taxation [**Doc. 122**]. Cash payments were but one of numerous impo-sitions. Armies consumed huge quantities of food, drink, fodder, boots, clothing and other materials demanded in kind. They also expected the local population to dig entrenchments, build or demolish fortifications and transport all manner of things [**Doc. 123**].

Military demands brooked no delay. Soldiers could not grow food or make what they needed, and any disruption in supply threatened an army's existence. Pre-war taxes were levied with only an imperfect knowledge of actual resources and often a poor regard of people's ability to pay. War made this much worse and many communities swiftly became over-burdened to the point that it threatened their survival [**Doc. 124**]. Outright refusal was dangerous in the face of military violence. Most communities preferred to bargain, offering bribes to commanders to moderate their demands [**Doc. 125**]. Such graft was endemic and hardly unusual at a time when public officials were expected to find most of their income by charging fees for their services. However, bribes and gifts were no guarantee that officers would not make further demands or fail to curb their soldiers' bad behaviour [**Doc. 126**].

Contributions supplemented regular taxes which were also increased, but the conflict disrupted social and economic relations and diminished returns. The Habsburg monarchy received about 5.4 million florins in annual taxation and income from the dynasty's personal property in 1618. Even assuming the figures in their treasury's calculations for 1618–40 are correct [**Doc. 127**], actual revenue declined slightly to under 5.3 million a year, despite money from subsidies, forced loans, property confiscation and other extortion. Costs far exceeded income. Estimates prepared in November 1638 for two-thirds of the imperial and allied army put the total pay and provision bill at 7.4 million – and this was just for eight months and made no allowance for other items like artillery and transport [**Doc. 128**]. The Peace of Prague authorised the emperor to demand taxes from all imperial Estates using the Empire's administrative structure of ten Kreise [**see Docs 103 and 128**]. These never produced the expected return, not least because many territories were occupied by, or allied to, the Swedes.

Subsidies from foreign allies have attracted disproportionate interest amongst later historians. Subsidies brought in far less than contributions or regular taxation and were often tied to policies the donor wished to impose on the recipient [**Docs 129–30**]. Their chief value was that the arrival of modest amounts of cash served as collateral for far more substantial loans that the recipient had raised from bankers or his own subjects.

Bavaria was the best administered territory in the Empire, and, at least on paper, balanced its books during the war [**Doc. 131**]. Such official figures should be treated with caution, but they are nonetheless indicative of the relative significance of different sources of income and items of expenditure.

Military administration rested on several tiers of officials. Bailiffs, mayors and other local officials were responsible for collecting taxes, contributions and other direct payments, as well as arranging billets and transport [**see Docs 122–3, 146**]. Central coordination was provided by the war councils and treasuries which existed in all European kingdoms and most German territories [**see Docs 115, 128**]. These bodies were mainly concerned with strategy and planning, while most actual administration was devolved to the regimental colonels and company captains who were expected to recruit, equip, command and often pay their units from their own pockets. A few made fortunes, but many were engaged in long, fruitless efforts to persuade their nominal paymaster to honour promises to reimburse their expenses [**Doc. 132**].

MILITIA

113. Territorial defence ordinance of Count Johann of Nassau-Siegen, 1596

Because it has been suggested that it is better to use subjects for defence than strangers and foreigners, the reasons will be summarised briefly:

I want to demonstrate how subjects can be persuaded to serve willingly on horse and foot, and what manner one must train and instruct them, so that they are of more effect and use in an emergency than soldiers, indeed more than untrained soldiers.

Therefore, a lord or an authority has to explain to all his subjects, young and old, how burdensome and dangerous wars can be, and how they will persist for some good time more, probably because of our sins. And show them in detail how disorderly forces that are sitting on the doorstep have destroyed and burnt prominent, distinguished electorates and principalities, land and people, without provocation, and have even flayed women and children in front of their eyes and martyred them with cruel, unheard of and unbelievable tyranny and lamentably murdered them and that to offer justice there is no other means humanly possible, beyond God, than to resist. It is clear from *iuris divini* and *naturalis* [divine and natural law], as well as numerous examples, that those who resist have fared much better and suffered less than those who did nothing and trusted too well, thinking that they had offended no one, that no one would trespass against them, or that they were in no danger, because the others were of their religion and faction, but in practice were spared as little as the others. Never mind that we Evangelicals are so hated by other religions that they think they do God a service when they kill us, whom they call heretics, and eradicate us totally, and so it is necessary in such times to keep your eyes open and treat such matters seriously, to avoid such lament and dire straits.

For God gives the sword to every Christian ruler, not only to execute evildoers, but also to protect and shelter subjects from illegal force.

Therefore, if rulers are to preserve their conscience before God, they must think of ways and means to put such into practice with the least burden and damage to themselves and their subjects, and in case a ruler acts irresponsibly he will not only incur God's wrath but the inextinguishable disgrace, curse and ridicule of posterity and his neighbours, because he let his land and people suffer and be ruined. For God the lord provides every ruler with enough ways and means to protect and shelter the subjects entrusted to him, if one only reflects with reason and proper consideration.

To achieve such an end, one has either to accept foreign soldiers and keep them ready permanently in expensive employment, or better the subjects must do this themselves, since it concerns them the most, and select at times a contingent from the lads and hearty men who are best qualified for and can cope with such a task.

It says: when one keeps a sword sheathed, the opponent will see that one is ready and will think ten times before he undertakes anything, in particular because he knows what advantages one has from the mountains, passes and rivers.

Further, those [people] who give no cause for such destruction, that they then suffer, not from the main force [of soldiers], but from the baggage and riff-raff and rogues who, contrary to the knowledge and will of their masters, engage in such business, [and] when they encounter no resistance they don't go away, but follow the rest, *quia occasio facit furem* [as the fancy takes them], in order to get something, because they lack *conscientia* [conscience], religion, understanding or innocence. Indeed, sadly, experience has often proved sufficiently that neither sorrow nor belief has any presence amongst them.

By contrast, when they encounter blows instead of booty, and so can gain little fame, where they have started such action on their own initiative, they think twice before starting such a dangerous business. Each of such folk clearly understands that he has the hare in his chest and in particular because he lacks direction or order for such activity or business.

Source: Eugen von Frauenholz (ed.), *Das Heerwesen in der Zeit des Dreissigjährigen Krieges*, 2 vols (Munich, 1938–9), vol. II, pp. 47–8.

---

114. The failure of the Bavarian militia: reports to Elector Maximilian, January–December 1632

(i) Elector Maximilian to Tilly, 5 or 6 January 1632:

... We are already responding to your advice and are in the process of ordering across the land that the militia should be put into such a state of readiness and condition that it can be used immediately when needed. To this end, we order you to arrange training at home, so that the militia can be made ready faster and a few days earlier. A number of single peasant sons can be drafted and de facto taken from our lands of Bavaria so that the infantry regiments that have lost heavily can be brought nearly back up to strength, because it is difficult to get enough regulars. We have started to implement this in this tax district and want to see what can be done by the end of the month, of which we shall report to you in due course.

(ii) Report of the local government of Amberg to the Elector of Bavaria, 14 February 1632:

Around 2,000 single Bavarian subjects have arrived here already, and many more are coming. However, they have to be distributed in 29 billets, until the marauders have gone away, and a good drill instructor is needed for each billet, because otherwise the fine strong people will have guns in their hands and not know how to use them, and will on no account advance ... Therefore, we respectfully request Your Electoral Highness to despatch some good drill instructors ...

(iii) Report of Councillor and Tax Official Sickenhauser to the Elector, from Amberg, 22 April 1632:

I respectfully report, however, that although 3,380 men were summoned, we have got scarcely 300, because the others have nearly all run away, to get to Nuremberg, and, as can be seen from the enclosed report of the overseer in Haimburg, the single men in his district have failed to report after two summons, and on the contrary declared they will leave the country rather than be drafted. Other districts report the same and we have enough to do just to prevent a general rising ...

(iv) Report of Lieutenant Colonel Hans Jacob von Fendten to Colonel Hannibal von Herliberg, 6 May 1632:

... Therefore, I left 40 horse and 100 musketeers in Freising and 40 horse and musketeers in Mosburg. However, because the militia cavalry are useless for patrolling, I had the lieutenant from Fugger with 40 horse, whom I left at Mosburg ... The country people have nearly all fled from nothing, back to their houses, and if I didn't have regular troops with me, I would have been forced to retreat, [and] just had to string up one of the fellows, or otherwise it's no good. The rural militia cavalry that I left at Freising didn't want to stay there, but wanted to remain with their company, [they] are a very ill-disciplined lot. God help us that we don't have to fight ...

(v) Report of the governor and commander of Kronach, 31 July 1632:

... between 7 and 8 o'clock in the evening on Monday 17 of last month May, the above-mentioned [Swedish] Colonel Hastuer with three companies of regular infantry, six companies of horse and 1,500 Saxon militia[1] attacked the Hasslacher Gate in the suburbs here with great fury ..., but through God's particular great grace the citizens resisted so strongly for 17 hours throughout the night until midday between 12 and 1 o'clock the next day, with constant skirmishing and fighting, that they [the enemy] had to retreat, their militia fled completely, together with some of the regulars, and according to the prisoners, left over 300 dead ... Having stayed here two days less than four weeks, they retreated in the night of 11 June ... According to the enemy's own reports they lost over 800 in addition to the wounded in this siege, while the burghers and militia only lost around 40 dead, as well as a young artillery officer. When we were filling in their batteries and trenches we discovered that they had treated our prisoners in such an un-Christian and abominable manner, that is scarcely heard of from the Turks, in that they had flayed five of them alive and other unheard of torture, that we cannot write of honourably ...

---

[1]   These were not from electoral Saxony, but the small duchy of Sachsen-Coburg whose prince joined Sweden late in 1632. Kronach and Forchheim were small fortified towns in the bishopric of Bamberg that resisted all Swedish attempts to take them during the war.

(vi) Mandate replacing militia service with a tax, 10 December 1632:

Maximilian, Elector etc.

Highly learned, dear subjects. Experience has proved that conscription of subjects is of no use whatsoever, and that any expenditure on them is nearly futile and a waste. To remedy this and to promote better the defence of our dear fatherland during these on-going dangerous enemy actions, we have carefully considered, wished, resolved and ordered herewith that you immediately demand three imperial talers from each conscripted subject in the district entrusted to you, with which money we shall without delay, in view of the time and the need, recruit and raise able-bodied troops, in return for which the conscripts shall be free from personal service. If some of the conscripts are too poor to pay three imperial talers to you, others should be selected who could have been drafted and made to pay in their place, and this liability for three imperial talers applies not only to those who have already been drafted, but also to those who have died in the ranks, or otherwise left the service, and whose places in the muster rolls must be filled with others, from whom such money can be demanded, including those of the nobility in your district. They are to be notified immediately by the power of this [decree] and sent a copy of our order. When all such money has been collected, it is to be sent to the captaincy to which the conscripts belonged and thence directed to the proper place. You are hereby instructed to implement this impartially on pain of our inevitable punishment and displeasure.

Dated Munich, 10 December 1632.

Source: Eugen von Frauenholz (ed.), *Das Heerwesen in der Zeit des Dreissigjährigen Krieges*, 2 vols (Munich, 1938–9), vol. II, pp. 247–8.

REGULAR WARFARE

115. Army size: Count Schlick's estimates of the rival forces in 1637[1]

First, the most accurate calculations of the imperial army, including the electoral Bavarian and Saxon contingents, give together 73,000 men, excluding the recruits who have been ordered, totalling another 10,000, to give 83,000 altogether.

The enemy are estimated at the most as 36,000 Swedes and 74,000 French.

At least 18,000 infantry and 12,000 cavalry must remain in Germany to fight the Swedes, excluding those who will be needed against Landgrave Wilhelm of Hessen [-Kassel] to which end another 4,000 will probably need

---

[1] Count Heinrich Schlick, president of the Imperial War Council. See **Doc. 25**, note 10 and **Doc. 105**, note 1.

to join Landgrave Georg and Geleen,[2] thus giving a total of 40,000 men remaining in Germany.

These 18,000 [infantry] men can be split into two parts, and 9,000 of them together with 3,000 cavalry, sent across the Elbe, the other 9,000 [infantry] retained this side [of the river] with the remaining 9,000 cavalry ready to attack the enemy should he cross the Elbe.

The above calculations leave 45,000 men with Piccolomini's troops[3] and the aforementioned recruits against the French. From these another 4 or 5,000 must remain on the Rhine and Saar, and a similar number in the Westphalian garrisons and on the Weser.

Source: Schlick's memorandum, edited by Eugen von Frauenholz as 'Zur Geschichte des Dreißigjährigen Krieges', *Zeitschrift für Bayerische Landesgeschichte*, 13 (1941/42), pp. 254–5.

___

116. Strategy: Henri de Rohan, Le Parfait Capitaine, 1647

Of battles and field engagements. To give battle is the most prestigious and important thing about war. Winning one or two captures or overturns entire kingdoms. All wars have been waged with battles since antiquity, because these are the quickest way to victory. Today, one fights more as a fox, than a lion, and sees war more as sieges than battles. There are still various peoples who fight most of their wars through battles, notably the Turks and the Persians. One also saw many battles in Germany amongst the Christians a few years ago … And a well-disciplined army that fought no battles enjoyed a great advantage over those that had fought like that. Therefore, although it is now no longer so common to risk battle, one must not neglect the study of such …

Source: Henri, duc de Rohan, *Le parfait capitaine* (Cologne, 1642, German translation), ch. 7.

___

117. Tactics: The Swedish deployment at Breitenfeld, 1631

The King of Sweden deployed his men in two lines, each of a body mainly of infantry, flanked by two detachments of cavalry. The first line had, on the right

---

2   Georg II (1605–61), the Lutheran landgrave of Hessen-Darmstadt from 1626 who backed the emperor throughout the war; Gottfried Huyn von Geleen (c.1590–1657), commander of the autonomous Westphalian army 1634–44. The discrepancy in Schlick's figures is probably explained by the Westphalians who numbered around 6,000 at this point.

3   Octavio Piccolomini (1599–1656) commanded a corps of about 12,000 imperial troops sent in 1636 to reinforce the Spanish in the Netherlands against the French (but not the Dutch!). He remained there until 1639. See also **Doc. 119.**

as the most distinguished flank, the Swedish and Finnish infantry[1] regiments, namely the East Goth, Schmaländer, West Goth and two regiments of Finns. Behind these stood the Rheingraf's Regiment in reserve. In the other line on the right stood the Livonians, Courlanders and the two regiments of colonels Damnitz and Sperreuter. The king was personally present on this wing, but because, as commander-in-chief, he could not stay in one place in the order of battle, but had to be everywhere as needed, General Johan Banér[2] was ordered to remain there to watch this wing. In the first line on the left there were two companies of Field Marshal Gustav Horn's regiment, as well as those of Kulmbach and Baudissin, while in the second [there were] the Hall and Courville [regiments]. This entire wing, which, considering that the electoral Saxons stood further to the left, was the middle and therefore the main place of battle, had been entrusted to the above mentioned field marshal deliberately by the king.

Between the cavalry regiments, particularly in the first line, the king had placed a good number of detached musketeers, partly from General Johan Banér's Regiment that was entirely musketeers, and partly from the strongest regiments. The weak infantry regiments were amalgamated in the centre to make stronger brigades and the first line consisted of four infantry brigades. The first was composed entirely of Swedes, under Ako Oxenstierna, colonel of the Dalekarl Regiment. The second was the Yellow or King's Life Guard Regiment, under Colonel Maximilian Teuffel. The third, was partly Swedish, partly German, under Colonel Erich Hand. The fourth, was the Old Blue Regiment, under Colonel Winckel. The King's Life Guard Cavalry Regiment, under Colonel Uslar, and three strong troops of foot under colonels Ramsay, Hamilton and Monro were held in reserve behind this first line. In the second line there were three brigades under Count Thurn, colonels Hepburn and Vitzthum.[3] Cochitzky and Colonel Schaffmann stood behind the main body with their cavalry. The great cannon were moved in front of the centre, [and] each brigade had its own regimental pieces for its own defence, each pulled

---

1   *sic.* In fact, these were cavalry.

2   Johan Banér (1596–1641) came from a distinguished Swedish family on the losing side in that country's brief civil war in 1600. He joined the army in 1617 and rose rapidly to become one of Gustavus's most trusted generals. Oxenstierna gave him command of Sweden's army in northern Germany after Nördlingen. He had a violent temper, but was a superb strategist and played a major part in recovering Sweden's position in the Empire before his death through illness. See also **Doc. 106**, note 1.

3   Johann Vitzthum von Eckstädt (*c.*1590–1648) was a cousin of Christian, author of **Doc. 111**. Unlike the rest of the family, he remained loyal to Sweden after 1635, but was a poor general and almost lost Banér the battle of Wittstock in 1636. Johann Jakob Count Thurn (1602–*c.*1643) was a son of Matthias Thurn, the instigator of the Defenestration [**Doc. 11**]. Sir James Ramsay (1589–1639) and Sir James Hepburn (1598–1636) (a Catholic!) were among the many Scots in the Swedish army. Robert Monro (1590–1680), another Scot, commanded the regiment originally raised for Danish service by Donald MacKay [**Doc. 131**] and wrote its famous regimental history. Johann Georg aus dem Winckel (died in 1639) was one of several prominent German officers who defected to the emperor after the Peace of Prague [see **Docs 103, 105**].

by one horse, or moved by two or three men if necessary, that could be turned and fired very quickly.

Source: Boguslav von Chemnitz, *Königlich Schwedischer in Teutschland geführter Krieg*, 2 vols (Stettin 1648, Stockholm, 1653), I part 3, p. 32.

118. Casualties: strength returns for the Imperial Cavalry after the Second Battle of Breitenfeld, November 1642

Regiment	Coys	Officers[1]	Fit	Dismounted	Detached	Lost[2]	Wounded
Brigade Borneval							
KR Borneval	8	6	123	85	34	42	37
ARK Wartowsky	6	3	72	15	15	32	–
KR Spiegel	6	3	126	119	24	23	–
CR Callenberg[3]	10	10	242	188	36	206	–
KR Capaun	8	8	121	91	86	122	–
ARK Münster	6	6	63	145	71	74	–
? Gerstorff[4]	10	10	200	95	90	63	12
? Rambsdorff	8	6	77	30	21	47	14
CR Hanau[3]	10	9	237	189	85	43	49
KR Lüttich[5]	10	8	168	85	31	146	13
KR Burgsdorf[5]	6	5	87	92	37	72	16
	88	74	1,526	1,134	530	872	121
Brigade Puchheim							
KR Gonzaga	12	5	233	163	142	72	40
KR Puchheim	10	4	138	70	138	89	–
KR Nicola	10	7	145	275	42	31	36
DR Gall	8	4	106	97	98	287	–
DR Craft	3	2	55	8	85	32	6
KR Wintz	6	4	123	53	116	60	9
CR Jung-Schleinitz[3]	10	8	137	103	69	114	41
KR Alt-Heister	11	5	130	81	37	64	–
KR Jung-Heister	6	4	80	292	12	21	–
KR Pompei	6	6	112	23	23	–	16
unnamed	6	6	70	41	164	52	6
ARK Madlo[6]	6	6	81	–	206	42	–
	104	61	1,568	1,279	1,209	972	134

---

[1] Captains and above.
[2] Killed, missing or captured in the battle.
[3] Saxon regiments attached to the imperial army.
[4] Probably a Saxon unit.
[5] Brandenburg regiments attached to the imperial army to discharge the electorate's obligations to the Empire (as permitted in its truce with Sweden).
[6] See **Doc. 119**.

Regiment	Coys	Officers	Fit	Dismounted	Detached	Lost	Wounded
Brigade Bruay							
KR Leib Piccolomini	12	8	197	208	49	159	38
KR Bruay	7	3	225	124	47	111	–
KR Mislik	8	6	138	149	47	92	8
KR Des Fours	8	7	147	100	40	120	10
KR Sperreuter	8	2	66	48	26	42	15
KR Jung	6	6	78	47	13	24	6
KR Montecuccoli	9	5	177	29	26	74	–
KR Neu Piccolomini	10	5	330	138	47	104	–
	68	43	1,158	843	294	726	99

Key

ARK	arquebusier regiment
Coys	companies
CR	cavalry regiment (i.e. *Reiter*)
DR	dragoon regiment
KR	cuirassier regiment

NB The above list omits a fourth brigade that fought on the imperial right wing behind Brigade (the other two were on the left), as well as the Croat regiments.

Source: Haus-, Hof-, und Staatsarchiv Vienna, Kriegsakten 110 (neu), fol. 295–304.

119. Discipline: punishment of imperial deserters after the Second Battle of Breitenfeld, 1642

Proceedings, verdict and execution of the Imperial Cavalry Regiment Madlo, that wilfully broke at the battle at Breitenfeld, near Leipzig, in the year 1642, and thereby robbed the imperial army of its victory.

The imperial army relieved the besieged city of Leipzig at the beginning of November. The Swedes pulled back to a village called Breitenfeld, while the Imperials camped not far from them at night so that both sides were positioned for battle. Both moved at the break of day the following morning and closed in proper battle order and engaged each other for two hours when, after various changes of fortune, the Imperials left the field. This is sufficiently well-known to the world, not to need further discussion here.

The primary cause of this misfortune was recognised that, against all expectations, the Imperial side had to see that its regiments suddenly turned their backs on the enemy, squadrons and indeed entire units at a time with their colours flying, and prematurely and carelessly abandoned the army that was still locked in battle. The enemy was thereby all the more encouraged, while our side was assaulted by great force and finally forced to flee the field with great loss.

Neither martial law nor any dispassionate man of the world can condone or excuse such an unlikely flight, and all those who are at least interested will accept that those who did so must be punished with full rigour by God and the regulations. Therefore, our gracious lord and generalissimo, His Archducal Highness,[1] has graciously resolved to punish this terrible crime that was committed in the open field with the utmost rigour and in public.

Since it is recognised that this shameful flight gripped one regiment more than the others, since it fled first, it has been decided to conduct the execution of the delinquents in front of the cavalry.

Therefore, they left Prague with Field Marshal Piccolomini[2] on 25 November and went by the direct route to the town of Rokezan, around which the cavalry were then quartered. They arrived there on 26th and started an investigation that revealed not only through denunciations of many high and lowly persons who had been on the field, but also from the accounts of the deserters, that the regiment of Colonel Hanß George von Madlo[3] shamefully left the field first, and neither honour nor the admonishments and shouts of other honourable officers could stop it.

Though others also fled, this [regiment] was observed to be the first and principal shameful culprit. Accordingly, it should be the first to receive the due rigour that has been resolved upon. To make this example more imposing and terrifying for the entire army, six nearby regiments that behaved well in the battle (the Alt- and Neu-Piccolomini, Puchheim, Nicolai, Lüttich and Ramsdorff), as well as the accused Madlo [regiment], were ordered that day to assemble early the next morning, the 27th, in good order at Rokezan camp and await further instructions.

As soon as these regiments, which expected nothing other than an execution, were assembled at the appointed time, His Archducal Highness appeared in person in the field along with the field marshal and had the regiments directed into the town by Don Hannibal, Marquis of Gonzaga,[4] the commanding general of the cavalry, and led to the marketplace and neighbouring squares and streets, after which the Madlo regiment was moved through the others to form up on the marketplace before the generalissimo's lodgings.

Once this had been done, His Highness the generalissimo finally left Field Marshal Piccolomini and went into Rokezan between the regiments. And once he had seen that the orders had been carried out, he had the imperial

---

[1] Archduke Leopold Wilhelm, the imperial commander-in-chief (see **Doc. 112**, note 2).

[2] See **Doc. 115**, note 3.

[3] Madlo had taken command of the regiment of mounted arquebusiers in 1641, which had been raised in Silesia two years before. He was also executed and the unit disbanded.

[4] Hannibal Franceso Maria Gonzaga (1602–68), a relation of Ferdinand II's second wife Eleonore (1598–1655), was one of the many Italian aristocrats in the senior ranks of the imperial army. His career was not impaired by the fact he had signed the First Pilsner Reverse (**Doc. 101**).

army's senior Auditor General, Heinrich Graaß, read out what had been resolved regarding the Madlo regiment in the presence of the generals and many cavaliers from the country and the army, and then order the Provost General present to carry out the execution.

This grave resolution provoked not a little fear and considerable terror amongst the accused, as well as frightening the men of the other regiments, to which the presence and authority of the generals and prominent country lords made this act appear all the more admirable. The large number of otherwise tough and fearless soldiers then fell silent and remained so for a little while, whereupon the General Auditor began to address them with the following proclamation:

All well knew of the unsuccessful and unhoped-for outcome for the imperial arms in the action on the 2nd of this month in the vicinity of Leipzig, in the district of Meissen, against the enemies of His Imperial Majesty and the Holy Empire, and that this was mainly because the present Madlo Regiment and others of its sort had failed to do their duty, but had precipitated the defeat by breaking their oath, and shamefully fleeing the field, abandoning the imperial army, the generalissimo, the field marshal and other generals, and the post assigned to them, and carelessly leaving the battlefield like deserters, scoundrels and villains, taking their standards with them in their flight, and thereby angered so many brave soldiers who never flee, and so being the principal cause of the defeat that robbed their master and generalissimo of a particular triumph, and all the more shamefully robbing His Roman Imperial Majesty, their most gracious commander and paymaster, of his victory.

[The regiment was informed it would be punished.]

Once this had been announced, the field marshal ordered the punishment to begin, first by ordering those ensigns who had fled with their standards to step forward from the mounted ranks and be disarmed by placing their swords on the ground and surrendering to the Provost General. This was repeated with the sergeants, and lieutenants who laid their guns before the Provost General's feet and placed themselves in his power.

Lastly, the lieutenant colonel and major, who had remained mounted under guard, were reminded again of their particular mistakes by the Auditor General. Once this was done, the six companies of the regiment were ordered individually to dismount, leave their horses and muster together as a group in the middle of the square. Their horses were distributed amongst the [other] regiments and their arms were laid on the ground.

Once this had been done and the horses led from the square, the weapons and standards laid on the ground and everyone had assumed their position, the aforementioned Auditor General read out the account of the shameful behaviour on that day on the battlefield. The Provost General's secretary then rode forward and read out the following punishments:

[The defeat was again blamed on the regiment's 'shameful' unauthorised flight. The colonel, lieutenant colonel and major were to be held in custody until their sentence had been decided. The entire regiment was to be decimated, i.e. every tenth man to be executed, with the victims selected by all men throwing dice. Captains and lieutenants who were selected would be beheaded, but the ensigns would be hung like the NCOs and men, because their flight from the field with the regimental standards was considered especially dishonourable.]

Once this had been promulgated, the executioner broke the ensigns' swords, and the standards were ripped to shreds with a fury by the onlooking soldiers. However, the evening was now drawing on and there was no longer time to complete the rest of the punishment, so the NCOs and men of the Madlo Regiment were led away into the custody of the Provost General. Once they were securely held, those tenth men who had been selected by dice throw were drawn out to prepare themselves for execution and were provided with clergymen.

The following morning all the captains, lieutenants, ensigns, NCOs and men were led by the Provost General out of the town along the Pilsen road to the place of execution where the other regiments had drawn up the day before, except those who could prove they had remained behind in the battle. The Provost General then ordered the executioner to commence the approved punishments, starting with the troopers and the sergeant who had substituted for an ensign and fled the battle with a standard. All were bound to trees with rope and hanged until dead.

His Archducal Highness the generalissimo had meanwhile granted the appeal from two captains to be freed from the executioner's hands and to die honourably. They were shot in the customary military manner by the dragoons guarding them, each despatched with a single shot. The others, comprising another captain, a lieutenant, two ensigns and a sergeant, were pardoned by His Highness the generalissimo on account of their manly deeds in previous campaigns and the numerous petitions from senior generals and other officers on their behalf. The captain-lieutenant was held back for special reasons. Thus, none were touched by the executioner and instead they were led back to the town and were reminded just outside by the Auditor General of the difference between death in their lord's service at the enemy's hand and that through the rigour of justice. They received their pardon with humble thanks and were allowed back into the town. Thus, the Madlo Regiment received its well-deserved punishment.

Source: Johann Christian Lünig (ed.), *Corpus iuris militaris*, 2 vols (Leipzig, 1723), vol. II, pp. 211–17.

---

120. Mandate on the reform of the Imperial Army, 19 October 1647

We Ferdinand the Third by the grace of God elected Roman Emperor, perpetual enlarger of the Empire etc. offer our imperial grace and all the best to each and every spiritual and secular authority, subjects and loyal followers, as well as all our high and low commanders and military personnel on foot and horse, regardless of nationality, dignity, estate or form, and graciously inform you hereby that:

We have striven until now to restore military discipline that has declined and even entirely collapsed amongst the soldiery by repeatedly issuing patents in the Holy Roman Empire, as well as in our hereditary kingdoms and lands, to ensure that it is observed again. However, against all hope nothing has come of this than that all serious and beneficial orders, publicised patents, safeguards, letters of protection, passes, strictures and prohibitions have all not only been ignored, but insolence has grown from one time to the next, till even our imperial diplomas and orders are not obeyed. We have seen that the desire of the territories to participate in military operations declines when they are given no protection, but instead are ruined by such plundering and robbery, and have graciously considered a means to stop the insubordination of the soldiery and the marauding bands and to give the land proper protection against them, and retain them in good affection and to encourage the army and military operations.

Therefore, all previous patents, publications, safeguards, letters of protection and the like open orders are hereby repeated. We hereby order all and everyone, our supreme field marshal in particular, and in their absence their deputies and other commanders in all territories, not to allow any officer or soldier of the armies, regiments, troops or garrisons under their command to travel on private business in the Holy Roman Empire or our hereditary kingdoms and lands without good cause, as has often happened before. If they must travel, they are to be given sufficient new passes and to be strictly told they are not to use these passes as a pretext for insolence, but are to behave modestly, quietly and peacefully at all times, and not burden the land with arbitrary billeting, contributions, plundering, theft of cattle, horses or property, or other excesses, but if they are travelling on authentic passes for necessary purposes in our service, they must report to the authorities, the district commissariat, or their subordinates for billets at night, and peacefully accept a modest, necessary accommodation. In order to put a stop at last to this evil, we hereby entrust our loyal Estates and all subjects of the Holy Roman Empire, as well as of our hereditary kingdoms and lands, with the power and authority to watch for such marauding and robbing bands and to alert each village and warn and use their own means to arrest such delinquents and highwaymen, especially if there are officers amongst them, and if they encounter armed resistance to proceed as if against common robbers and use force against force. Furthermore, following an arrest they are to provide information together with an estimate of the damage to us as well as our supreme field marshal, or whoever has command in the territory at the time, so that the delinquents can be caught and, according to circumstances, made a terrible example of, either in the headquarters in their regiment or in the territory itself, by being punished with death.

And it is most important that the officers watch the non-commissioned officers, so that the soldiers do not run without authorisation and in disorder.

Therefore, our supreme field marshal and commandants in every territory are to ensure that the delinquents and deserters are not only punished according to their crimes, but the senior officers are to be compelled to refund the damage, so that they all seek to avoid damage and keep the non-commissioned officers and common soldiery in the best order and discipline and thereby fulfil our gracious and serious order, will and opinion. Given in our royal palace in Prague on the nineteenth day of the month of October in sixteen hundred and forty-seven, the eleventh year of our reign as emperor, the twenty-second as king of Hungary, and twentieth as king of Bohemia.

Ferdinand

Source: Johann Christian Lünig (ed.), *Corpus iuris militaris*, 2 vols (Leipzig, 1723), vol. I, pp. 80–1.

CONTRIBUTIONS

121. 'The Mansfeld Sauna, together with a Jolly Conversation', 1622

[A composite broadsheet from 1622. The picture shows six figures representing the social groups in the rhymed text. Each is in his underwear, and distinguishable only by his hat. They are sitting in two rows on benches and all are sweating coins which are being collected by Mansfeld, also in his underwear, but still wearing his plumed hat and field marshal's sash.]

Bath Attendant Mansfeld:
I had a free facility
To which I invite many notables
They can be my friends or not
I don't care
They can be old, young, poor or rich
Clergy, laity, all the same to me
I just have to run the show
And fleece one and all.

Protesting Prince:
We princes, counts, potentates
Follow the Bath Attendant's advice
Hold out our hands to him
And are now bathing together with our lands and peoples.

Imperial City:
We are also heavily involved
But obtain little enjoyment
Have him now as our lord
He's fleecing us too.

Clergy:
We didn't pay attention to what was happening
With our hands in front of our eyes
Now we're in the same heat
And must sweat many 1,000 florins.

Knights and Noblemen:
We burghers and nobles
Have striven for greater booty
Piled burdens upon our subjects
Now we're dripping and sweating too.

Artisan:
Woe, woe, wonder upon wonder
How sour sweat pours from us
I think we must do penance
With bitter soapy water.

Peasant:
No one bathes as hot as us
Many have lost much from sweating blood
There's no end to our misery
Inflicted by this Bath Attendant
But I believe those who ordered him
Can get rid of him too
If only we of this world
Loved God and our neighbours more than money
He will deliver this Bath Attendant into our power
Think he will have to make amends
When God, one day, will let the bath out.
In 1622

Source: John Roger Paas (ed.), *The German Political Broadsheet 1600–1700*, 8 vols (Wiesbaden, 1994), vol. IV, p. 74.

---

122. Instructions for levying contributions in the Duchy of Westphalia, 20 March 1636

The Westphalian Estates and poor subjects have unfortunately been almost entirely exhausted and ruined by the heavy billeting and damaging passage of troops for some time. Until now the soldiery have also extorted a weekly tax for their own maintenance from the poor inhabitants. This burden and inconvenience is now hereby remedied through a new distribution of the tax across the entire country for the general staff and the Westphalian Regiment of nine companies that are billeted here. Henceforth, every taxpayer in each and every town, district or jurisdiction shall pay one and a half gold florins per month for every gold florin of their tax assessment or, in other words, a one and a half tax levy every month. This contribution shall be delivered to whichever garrison to which the community has been assigned according to a list already specially prepared for this purpose. Six Kopfstücke[1] shall be paid to the soldiery for every florin of tax assessment, with the remaining one and half Kopfstücke being delivered immediately to the treasury to pay for other needs. Subjects can pay in coin, meat, corn or forage to the garrison. This contribution takes effect today, 20 March, and is to be made correctly eight days prior to the end of each month to the treasury. All officials, treasury and contribution receivers are to observe this strictly. Done, Arnsberg 20 March 1636.

Source: Horst Conrad and Gunnar Teske (eds), *Sterbezeiten. Der Dreißigjährige Krieg im Herzogtum Westfalen* (Münster, 2000), pp. 280–1.

123. Instructions for peasant labour and transport to assist the Imperial Army, 30 July 1644

The generals have recently renewed the daily transport duty at Stadtberge[1] of 40 people and extended it for six weeks because of pressing need. Accordingly, the communities named below that have recently provided weekly duty at Stadtberge are now to do this every one and half weeks – every period reckoned at nine days after the deduction of Sundays and holidays – or face military execution.[2]

The first period of nine days starts on 8 August 1644 for the town of Brilon. The fourth period of nine days starts on 12 September for the jurisdictions of Olpe, Drolshagen, Wenden, Stockum, Allendorf, Hagen, Sunderen, Langenscheidt, Friggenoll, the town of Balve, Balve district, Affeln, Hüsten, Menden town and district, Nehm, [to provide] daily 40 workers and two wagons.

Arnsberg, 30 July 1644.

Source: Horst Conrad and Gunnar Teske (eds), *Sterbezeiten. Der Dreißigjährige Krieg im Herzogtum Westfalen* (Münster, 2000), pp. 292–3.

---

1   Coins worth two-ninths of an imperial taler.

1   The fortress of Stadtberge (also called Obermarsberg) was an important strong point for the imperial and electoral Cologne troops in the duchy of Westphalia until its destruction in 1646. The duty was to help strengthen its defences.

2   That is, punishment enforced by soldiers, usually a fine.

124. Response to demands: the inhabitants of Balve District threaten emigration, June 1644

Inhabitants of Balve District
Appeal to Elector Ferdinand of Cologne
[Undated, but mid-June, 1644.]

Most worthy and serene elector and gracious lord.

We, Your Electoral Highness's poor and ruined subjects and inhabitants of Balve District, are driven by unavoidable great need to complain most humbly and miserably about the onerous contributions assigned to this district of Balve by Your Electoral Highness's Westphalian Estates. We have always willingly and obediently paid everything we could in the hope that we would then be free of such heavy contributions.

However, they have continued till now and it has become completely impossible to meet our monthly quota, because we have been completely exhausted and ruined by paying the contributions (not to mention the devastating passage of friends and foes and the heavy burden of war). More than half the farms in this district of Balve are now wasteland and so it has become impossible to continue paying obediently without us all soon being forced to emigrate as beggars.

God willing, Your Electoral Highness will receive our humble petition and will be moved by our piteous state to paternal and princely compassion and will graciously order a reduction of our quota by at least a third if not a half on account of half the farms lying waste. Otherwise, it is to be feared that this district will soon be entirely devastated and will have to follow those of our neighbours who have already emigrated to the county of Mark.

We earnestly pray for this daily to God.

All Your Electoral Highness's humble and obedient subjects of Balve District.

Source: Horst Conrad and Gunnar Teske (eds), *Sterbezeiten. Der Dreißigjährige Krieg im Herzogtum Westfalen* (Münster, 2000), pp. 299–300.

---

125. Negotiating contributions: the Swedes in Olmütz, June 1642

Once Colonel Miniati marched out at the appointed time with the Neu Krackow regiment, Major General Wittenberg and Colonel Dörffling[1] arrived around noon on 15 June, and immediately showed the Council a commission

---

[1] Miniati commanded the imperial garrison which had just surrendered Olmütz in return for free passage to the Swedes. Arvid Wittenberg (1606–57), a Finn, was instrumental in ensuring the loyalty of Sweden's army in Germany when Johan Banér died in 1641. He was made commander of the Swedish forces in Movaria and Silesia in 1646 [see **Doc. 176**].

in the name of His Excellency, the Swedish Field Marshal,[2] and demanded that the city pay 150,000 imperial talers ransom at once. This was impossible, so we bargained for a day and a night, at last reducing it to 30,000 by secretly promising 4,000 imperial talers to the commissioners, to be let off the rest. The Field Marshal marched away with the money and the rest of the troops on the 16th, while three regiments were let in as garrison, to wit the Horn and Hammerstein cavalry and the infantry regiment under Colonel Königam who was also made commandant.

Colonel Königam was ordered to march away on St John the Baptist's Day, and Colonel Georg Paikul replaced him, soon demanding 100 imperial taler a week on top of the agreed sum, which the town councillors were to pay from their own pockets.

Horn's cavalry regiment marched out, heading for Silesia on 1 July, having plundered many of the leading burghers' houses. Lieutenant colonel Wancke then arrived with the Guard Dragoon Regiment. Soldiers and especially their officers stole noteworthy precious items and whatever they could find from the leading burghers' houses.

Source: The diary of the Friedrich Flade, the Olmütz town clerk, published in B. Dudik (ed.), 'Tagebuch des feindlichen Einfalls der Schweden in das Markgrafenthum Mähren während ihres Aufenthaltes in der Stadt Olmütz 1642–1650', *Archiv für österreichische Geschichte*, 65 (1884), p. 318.

126. Cost of a garrison: the Swedes in Olmütz, 1642–3

List of all and every current expenditure from 12 June 1642 to 20 June 1643, as well as a memorandum handed into His Excellency, as follows [in imperial talers]:

For the ransom	30,000
The extraordinary	4,000
Extra payments on the fortifications	1,350
To the commandant and other officers from the councillors' own pockets	12,172
For shoes and stockings for the infantry and dragoons of the garrison	1,538
More given to them on 30 July 1642	5,910
More given to them in the winter for clothing	1,605
For 33 barrels of wine delivered to the magazine at the cost of 100 rthlr each	3,300
Another 40 barrels confiscated and taken away	4,000
Construction costs for the city fortifications	594

---

[2] Lennart Torstensson (1603–51), commander of the Swedish army in Germany after Johan Banér's death until 1645. See also **Doc. 166.**

Hops, 384 measures purchased	512
Brewing costs	640
Over 26 banks of salt, each half reckoned at 20 hundred weight ...	3,466
Costs of the remaining citizens for lost houses and yards and on exile ...	41,437
Total	110,694

[Then follow detailed calculations of provisions provided in kind.]

NB There were initially 475 houses available to billet the garrison here, and now there are no more than about 170, the remaining 300 are either completely ruined or abandoned because of serious damage. There are 965 infantry and cavalrymen in the 170 houses according to the reports handed down by the senior officers and NCOs.

Of the sergeants, NCOs, corporals, cavalry, artillerymen, drummers, medics, there are over 200 who must be accommodated by the poor citizens.

Source: The diary of Friedrich Flade, the Olmütz town clerk, published in B. Dudik (ed.), 'Tagebuch des feindlichen Einfalls der Schweden in das Markgrafenthum Mähren während ihres Aufenthaltes in der Stadt Olmütz 1642–1650', *Archiv für österreichische Geschichte*, 65 (1884), pp. 400–5.

IMPERIAL WAR FINANCE

127. Revenue raised for military purposes, 1618–40

Source	Amount (florins)	%
Lower Austrian Estates	3,800,000	3.2
Upper Austrian Estates	700,000	0.6
Inner Austrian Estates	900,000	0.7
Bohemian Estates	22,731,725*	19.6
Prague City 1632–4	1,100,290	0.9
Prague Jews 1632–5	1,099,000	0.9
Moravian Estates	2,569,583	2.2
Silesian Estates	7,727,860	6.6
Bohemian crown lands	800,710	0.6
Alsace (in 1621)	23,583	0.02
Austrian districts and individuals	30,000,000	25.8
	(71,452,751)	(61.5)
Papal subsidies	944,613	0.8
Spanish subsidies	1,718,145	1.4
	(2,662,758)	(2.2)

Source	Amount (florins)	%
Provisions, money claimed from Saxony etc.	30,000,000	25.8
Bavarian costs set against Upper Austria	13,000,000	11.2
Overall total	c.117,000,000	(100.0)

* Includes confiscation from rebels.

Source: Compiled from Karl Oberleitner, 'Beiträge zur Geschichte des Dreissigjährigen Krieges mit besondere Berücksichtigung des Österreichischen Finanz- und Kriegswesens', *Archiv für österreichische Geschichte*, 19 (1858), pp. 45–8.

128. Cost estimates for November 1638

(i) To bring the main imperial army and the attached electoral Saxon and Brandenburg troops back to 26,000 men[1] as follows:

	[monthly costs in florins]
General staff[2]	26,000
Infantry	193,554
Cavalry	166,920
[Total]	386,474
Total for eight months	3,091,792

To be funded by 150 Roman Months[3] from the Upper and Lower Saxon Kreise.

(ii) Imperial army on the Upper Rhine with a projected strength of 10,000 imperialists and 9,000 Bavarians:

	[monthly cost in florins]
3 imperial infantry regiments	62,154
3 Bavarian infantry regiments	61,104
3,000 imperial cavalry	63,368
1,000 Croats	18,000
3,000 Bavarian cavalry	62,520
General staff	14,100
[Total]	279,846 [actually 281,246]
Total for eight months	2,238,768

---

[1] Organised into 12 infantry regiments of various sizes totalling 18,000 men, and 12 cavalry regiments totalling 8,000.

[2] Comprising 29 generals and administrators.

[3] A unit of account calculated on each imperial Estate's basic quota of imperial taxation. See also **Doc. 4**, note 6.

To be funded by 150 Roman Months from the Bavarian, Franconian and Electoral Rhine Kreise.

(iii) Garrisons at 257,504 fl a month, for eight months   2,060,032

(iv) Total value of a levy of 150 Roman Months by Kreise
Upper Saxony (excluding Austrian territory and Pomerania)	1,391,400
Lower Saxony	1,704,000
Westphalia (less 50,400 from Osnabrück and Verden)	120,600 [*sic*]
Franconia	1,155,000
Electoral Rhine	1,075,500
Bavaria	1,020,000
Swabia	2,082,000
Upper Rhine	1,320,900[4]
[Total]	[9,869,400]

Expected income after deducting quotas of areas under enemy occupation:
The two Saxon Kreise	3,095,400
Westphalia, Franconia and Electoral Rhine[5]	2,522,100
Bavaria, Swabia, Upper Rhine	2,349,500
[Total]	7,967,000

Source: Haus-, Hof-, und Staatsarchiv Vienna, Kriegsakten Fasz. 94 (neu), fols 255–61.

---

129. Spanish subsidies to the Emperor, 1618–48 (in florins)

Year	Direct to treasury	Indirect
1618	300,000	10,000
1619	200,000	360,000
1620	530,000	201,000
1621	–	–
1622	–	–
1623	–	–
1624	–	–
1625	–	–
1626	650,000	–
1627	160,000	–
1628	670,000	930,000

---

[4] Only 909,000fl were expected at the most from the Upper Rhine.

[5] These were assigned to support the army under Piccolomini that defended the Lower Rhine. The cost estimate omits any calculation of its strength.

Year	Direct to treasury	Indirect
1629	–	80,000
1630	520,000	–
1631	100,000	970,000
1632	400,000	–
1633	600,000	–
1634	150,000	–
1635	430,000	559,000
1636	681,000	467,000*
1637	100,000	266,000**
1638	310,000	–
1639	585,000	50,000***
1640	426,000	–
1641	12,000	415,000***
1642	60,000+	330,000***
1643–8	–	–
Total	6,884,000	4,638,000

* 85,000 in lieu of troops, plus 382,000 to recruit troops in the Empire.
** for recruiting in the Empire.
*** for imperial troops transferred into Spanish service.
+ as a loan.

NB Spain also paid 505,000fl in subsidies to the Liga 1620–37, including 280,000fl direct to Bavaria 1634–7, as well as 50,000fl a month to Wallenstein, May 1632 to October 1633 (900,000fl in total), with another 100,000fl in November–December 1633.

Source: Compiled from Hildegard Ernst, *Madrid und Wien 1632–1637. Politik und Finanzen in den Beziehungen zwischen Philipp IV. und Ferdinand II.* (Münster, 1991), pp. 79, 277, 279.

130. Papal subsidies to the Emperor, 1618–48 (in florins)

Year	Direct to Treasury	Indirect	
1618	40,000 ⎫		
1619	120,000 ⎬	380,000	
1620	220,000 ⎭		
1621	230,000	130,000 ⎫	
1622	240,000	360,000 ⎬	(paid in devalued coin)
1623	160,000	210,000 ⎭	
1624–30	–	–	
1631	30,000	–	
1632	120,000	–	

Year	Direct to Treasury	Indirect
1633	240,000	–
1634	180,000	–
1635–48	–	–
Total	1,580,000	700,000

NB The papacy paid 1,529,000fl to the Liga over the same period.
(Popes: 1605–21 Paul V; 1621–3 Gregory XV; 1623–44 Urban VIII; 1644–55 Innocent X.)

Source: Compiled from Dieter Albrecht, 'Zur Finanzierung der Dreißigjährigen Krieges: Die Subsidien der Kurie für Kaiser und Liga 1618–1635', *Zeitschrift für Bayerische Landesgeschichte*, 19 (1956), pp. 534–67; and Karl Oberleitner, 'Beiträge zur Geschichte des Dreissigjährigen Krieges mit besondere Berücksichtigung des Österreichischen Finanz- und Kriegswesens', *Archiv für österreichische Geschichte*, 19 (1858), p. 47.

131. Bavarian military expenditure and revenue, 1618–48

(1) Expenditure (in florins)

Item	1619–34	%	1635–49	%	Total
General staff	1,091,786	2.34	31,019	0.24	1,122,805
Administrative staff	853,422	1.83	189,765	1.48	1,043,187
Tilly's staff	147,682	0.31	–	–	147,682
Soldiers					
a) Cavalry	8,658,525	18.57	3,753,826	29.38	12,412,351
b) Infantry	15,090,009	32.37	1,829,954	14.32	16,919,963
c) Free companies	4,188,120	8.98	854,720	6.69	5,042,840
d) Remounts	307,218	0.65	2,192,255	17.15	2,499,473
Field hopsital	139,852	0.30	138,826	1.08	278,678
Artillery	3,436,200	7.73	543,569	4.25	3,979,769
Commissariat	4,132,343	8.88	1,909,694	14.95	6,042,037
Elector's field staff	185,111	0.39	–	–	185,111
Militia (horse and foot)	691,612	1.50	–	–	691,612
Various other troops	80,698	0.17	322,788	2.52	403,486
Ingolstadt garrison	58,492	0.12	128,656	1.00	187,148
Travel and envoys' expenses	1,324,572	2.86	783,113	6.12	2,107,685
Gifts, honours, compensation	124,220	0.26	67,566	0.60	191,786
Loss through coinage devaluation	6,004,305	12.90	–	–	6,004,305
Field treasury losses to the enemy	97,197	0.20	29,715	0.23	126,912
Total	46,611,364	100	12,775,466	100	59,386,830

(2) Income (in florins)

Item	1619–34	%	1635–49	%	Total
Liga contributions					
a) Rhenish directory	3,386,509	7.21	–	–	3,386,509
b) Bavarian members (excl. Bav.)	3,831,684	8.16	38,400	0.32	3,870,084
c) Swabian supporters	229,262	0.50	3,000	0.02	232,262
d) Swabian counts and lords*	13,624	0.02	140,233	1.20	153,857
Catholic Imperial Estates	27,402	0.05	10,500	0.08	37,902
Subsidies	1,890,975	4.02	111,500	0.93	2,002,475
Bavarian Kreis (excl. Bavaria)	507,466	1.10	2,219,424	18.69	2,726,890
Bavaria	31,779,253	67.70	8,897,766	74.92	40,677,019
Imperial subsidies	–	–	–	–	–
Borrowing	101,277	0.21	–	–	101,277
Contributions	1,247,481	2.65	437,149	3.70	1,684,630
Commissariat income	1,318,157	2.80	17,388	0.14	1,335,545
Profit from coinage inflation	2,620,352	5.58	–	–	2,620,352
Total	46,953,442	100	11,875,357	100	58,828,799

* voluntary contributions.

Source: Cordula Kapser, *Die bayerische Kriegsorganisation in der zweiten Hälfte des Dreißigjährigen Krieges 1635–1648/49* (Münster, 1997), pp. 282, 285.

MILITARY ENTREPRENEURSHIP

132. Papers of Colonel Donald MacKay, July 1628–April 1632[1]

(i) Petition of Colonel Donald MacKay to King Christian IV of Denmark, July 1628

The soldiers wounded and maimed, and the remainder fighting persistently against the enemy, run to me and beg that I recompense them in some way for their own suffering and bloodshed, for the death of their comrades, the mutilation of their limbs; or that I permit them to return to their own country, to their homes and friends.

[The regiment transferred to Swedish service in October 1629 and was largely destroyed at Neu Brandenburg, March 1631.]

---

[1] Sir Donald MacKay (1591–1651) succeeded to the clan headship in 1614 and was made first Baron Reay by James I. He was authorised by Charles I to raise 3,000 men to assist Mansfeld's expedition, for which the king promised £4,000, but since Mansfeld had died the regiment directly entered Danish service. He was the most active of all the Scottish recruiters, raising another 10,000 men for Sweden between 1629 and the mid-1630s. He joined the Royalists during the British Civil Wars in 1644, but was captured later that year and retired to Denmark after he had been released.

(ii) King Gustavus Adolphus to MacKay, 14 May 1631

We have also given orders to our Commissary Larsson that he should pay to you 9,600 imperial taler for the enlisting of your regiment; and we request of you that if we should be a little tardy in paying, you should, nevertheless, prosecute the levy by your own means and be persuaded that the money advanced by you in this business will be immediately repaid by us.

[MacKay recruited the unit back to strength, but in the meantime became involved in a law suit at home by accusing another Scottish noble of treason.]

(iii) MacKay to Lord Carlisle, April 1632

Right Honourable. May it please your honour that a real friend is best known in adversity ... Good my lord, so is my present estate that I am brought to so low an ebb of means and monies that I know not what way to subsist until the day of my trial, neither know I what way to furnish myself with any kind of equipage fit for my birth or quality, except his Majesty [Charles I] be so graciously pleased as to cause to be given me part of the monies which is due unto me. I caused a petition to be presented to his Majesty but had no answer thereof, so that I most humbly request your Lordship to present this my other petition to his Majesty and to return to me an answer ... His Majesty oweth me as yet two thousand five hundred pounds. I desire now but the odd five hundred pounds to do my present business, which is his Majesty's own service more than mine; and I am willing not to press the other two thousand pounds till God make an end of this trial, although his Majesty did owe me more. Yet without offence I may say His Majesty is obliged in honour not to suffer me to come to ruin or disgrace at this time, seeing it is for his royal safety that I have brought myself into this necessity. As your Lordship has ever been my surest patron and truest friend, I expect this favour once more amongst the rest of your Lordship's manifold courtesies shown to me ...

[Charles I failed to pay his debts and MacKay was forced to come to terms with his creditors.]

Source: Printed in Ian Grimble, 'The Royal Payment of MacKay's Regiment', *Scottish Gaelic Studies*, 6 (1961), pp. 23–38.

16

Experience

Most civilians encountered soldiers as unwelcome intruders who disturbed the peace of their community. Often, the troops were only passing through, stopping just long enough to rest and consume anything worth taking. Others stayed longer as expensive garrisons in strategic towns [see **Docs 125–6**]. Civic officials found themselves overruled by commandants who did as they pleased. The community's normal routine was completely suspended if the other side approached and the garrison prepared for a siege [**Doc. 133**]. The consequences of prolonged but ultimately unsuccessful resistance were all too graphically demonstrated by Magdeburg's fate [**see Docs 79–90**].

Individual encounters were often antagonistic. Peasants and townsfolk feared and resented soldiers, and took brutal revenge when they could. More mundane motives like robbery were also often behind attacks on soldiers. Soldiers were recruited from the same rural and urban worlds which they understood and often longed to return to. However, they regarded resistance as unwarranted attacks on their personal and collective honour [**Docs 134–6**]. The abject failure of armies to protect civilian lives and property fuelled a widespread critique of soldiers as useless parasites [**Doc. 137**]. Yet, the military world still fascinated many, especially those who had not yet experienced its horrors [**Doc. 138**].

Contemporary diaries are full of dread as their writers recorded mounting anxiety at the news of the war and reports of approaching soldiers. This is pronounced in nuns' accounts. As all-female communities in convents outside or on the edge of towns, nuns felt acutely exposed. One of the most revealing of several surviving nuns' diaries is that kept by Maria Anna Junius who had been placed in the Heiligengrab Convent outside Bamberg for safety by her father who fell victim to a vile sequence of witchcraft trials which only ended in 1630 [**Doc. 139**]. Junius reveals her mixed feelings at her encounters with the Swedes who often turned out to be very different from what she had expected. Her diary also recounts the system of 'safe guards' (*Salvaguardia*), or sentries posted to protect communities, generally at their expense. Like the Swedish officers who stopped Junius's convent from being plundered, some of those in other armies strove for good relations with civilians and recognised that their men were often at fault [**Doc. 140**].

Soldiers experienced lives of sharp contrasts: periods of rest and plenty mixed with gnawing hunger and gruelling marches. This is clear from the diary of an anonymous soldier, thought to be Peter Hagendorf from a family of skilled artisans near Magdeburg [**Doc. 141; see also Docs 88, 134**]. This remarkable document was only discovered in 1993 and covers the period 1624–49, during which its writer served Bavaria and, briefly, Sweden, with what appears to have been equal diligence. Hagendorf is frank about his desire for plunder [see Doc. 88], but equally about his concern for his family and the deaths of some of his children.

Soldiers' wives and children were part of a wider military community which included other non-combatants like hucksters and prostitutes [see Doc. 141]. Many teenagers attached themselves to the army as 'boys', or servants who carried weapons, looked after the horses and helped scavenge and plunder. Plundering was often well-organised and systematic [Doc. 142; see also Doc. 152]. Plunder was essential to supplement irregular pay and meagre rations, but many commentators including officers recognised its debilitating effect on discipline, military efficiency and public order [Doc. 143]. The profits from plunder and the financial stake held by officers in their units led many to accuse soldiers of deliberately prolonging the war [Doc. 144].

Though contemporaries and many later writers present it as ravaging a previously flourishing land, it is clear that many of the Empire's inhabitants already lived in abject poverty before 1618. Nonetheless, the war made matters much worse, dislocating trade and production, as well as destroying valuable tools and buildings. Attempts to cover the initial shortfall in war finance, by coinage debasement and speculation, fuelled a period of hyperinflation known as the 'Kipper and Wipper' period 1621–2 [Doc. 145].

The episodic character of the war experience is captured in the diary of Hans Dobel, an inhabitant of the village of Virnesberg in Franconia [Doc. 146]. There is little sense here of the constitutional or theological issues influencing decisions for war or peace. The various contending parties do not appear as Catholic or Protestant, but usually simply by the name of their commanding officer, along with the nature of their demands on local resources and the level of violence they used to get what they wanted. Events are recorded without comment, in contrast to diaries kept by nuns or pastors who frequently refer to the theological purpose of suffering and the importance of maintaining faith in adversity [see Docs 139, 150].

Relentless demands and repeated destruction drove survivors to leave their homes. Many sources record abandoned farms and even whole villages with too few people, tools and animals left to revive the economy [Doc. 147]. However, there were considerable variations across time and space, making it difficult to draw general conclusions about the overall impact. Travellers encountered some areas of total devastation, while others appeared largely untouched. A good example is the official diary kept by the secretary of Thomas Howard, Earl of Arundel and Surrey (1585–1646) who travelled up the Rhine in 1636 at the head of one of several of the expensive, but fruitless, embassies sent by James I and his son Charles I to petition the emperor to reinstate the elector Palatine [Doc. 148]. Arundel travelled through areas which had recently experienced some of the worst fighting and at the height of the plague epidemic which ravaged the Empire after 1631.

Diaries like those of Junius, Dobel and Arundel's secretary have the immediacy of eyewitness accounts. However, they often include hearsay and material copied from contemporary newspapers or even cut and pasted into their notebooks.

Many incidents reported third hand appear strikingly similar in different texts, as do certain metaphors and phrases. References to cannibalism are a good example, as this was a stock motif for horror exceeding all bounds [**Doc. 149**].

The social status of the writer also needs to be considered. Their peacetime wealth and experience affected how they judged the war's impact. Prominent citizens and officials often had a harder time than their poorer neighbours, because they were deliberately targeted by soldiers, either for plunder or to ensure the wider community's compliance with demands [**see Doc. 146**]. However, the rich were better placed to survive periods of scarcity, and often had wider contacts in other communities who could offer shelter or assistance [**Doc. 150**].

It is important, given the horror stories, to remember that most peoples' lives were full of other experiences. Even Hans Dobel's wife was able to attend a wedding amidst skirmishing between parties of Swedes and imperialists [**see Doc. 146**]. While few lives were completely untouched by the war, personal misfortune clearly could have other causes [**Doc. 151**].

Eyewitness accounts, such as the examples presented here, have been published since the eighteenth century, but they have only recently attracted serious interest from historians. Literary and artistic depictions proved much more accessible and have profoundly shaped how later generations remembered the conflict. The most prominent example is the novel *The Adventurous Simplicissimus* by Johann Jacob Christoffel von Grimmelshausen (1622–76) which first appeared in 1668, but was clearly based on the author's own wartime experience. The book has been variously interpreted as an anti-militarist polemic, criticism of religion and the established order, an exhortation to greater piety, or purely escapist entertainment designed to make its author rich. Like other seventeenth-century works, it appeared as several consecutive parts and combined a mix of narrative, commentary, classical allusions, middle-brow philosophising, bawdy jokes and travelogue, making it hard to form a simple overall judgement [**Doc. 152**].

Visual evidence is also often hard to decipher. Numerous prints were produced during the war, often for a mass market which grew exponentially after 1618 with the thirst for news. Some pieces were issued as polemics or propaganda [**see Docs 20, 26, 46**], but many seem deliberately ambiguous [**see Docs 89–90**]. Some show horror still within stylistic conventions, such as Rudolf Meyer's (1605–38) peasant supplicating before a fashionably dressed officer. Others have a rawer quality, like those by Hans Ulrich Franck (1603–75). However, Franck equally depicted soldiers plundering civilians and peasants taking their brutal revenge [**Doc 153**]. These images were part of a wider market for 'genre scenes', with illustrations of soldiers in camp or brawling being another variation on pictures of drunken peasants and other social groups. Some illustrations were primarily practical, like the famous set by Jacob de Gheyn (1565–1629) accompanying a published version of the Nassau counts' drill manual [**see Doc. 113**]. They show soldiers as their commanders wished them to appear: orderly, disciplined subordinates performing their required tasks [**Doc. 154**]. Individual artists produced works of more than one type, making it hard to see whether they used art for personal statements. Jacques Callot (1592–1635) is a good example, noted for his two cycles of engravings entitled the 'Greater' and the 'Lesser Miseries of War'. Callot worked for Duke Charles IV of Lorraine (1604–75, r.1622), a prince who backed the emperor from 1631 and whose troops were frequently guilty of the crimes depicted in the engravings [Docs 155–6]. Another of Callot's cycles includes images which can be interpreted as a warning of the consequences of military life, but which also possibly evoke sympathy for soldiers' fate. Works professing to offer direct commentary are often some of the most ambiguous.

CIVILIAN ENCOUNTERS WITH SOLDIERS

133. Preparations for a siege: Olmütz, July 1642

On the 11th the commandant ordered the honourable council to ensure that the citizens provided themselves with six months provisions, while the remaining artisans, healthy, non-resident burghers, peasants and beggars who could not feed themselves for this time, were to leave the city, with the threat that if this did not happen and supplies ran short later, not only the poor but the rich would be driven from the city. Further all secret correspondence was to stop, and if there was the slightest trouble, the entire city would be set on fire and our necks would be the first to be broken.

Further after midday on the 10th and early on the 11th the hospitals, monasteries and clergy were inspected, and the suspected men and guns searched for.

On the 15th some troops of the imperial cavalry appeared as an advance guard, with His Excellency Count Piccolomini said to be among them, followed by the entire army on the next day and the 17th.

Source: The diary of Friedrich Flade, the Olmütz town clerk, published in B. Dudik (ed.), 'Tagebuch des feindlichen Einfalls der Schweden in das Markgrafenthum Mähren während ihres Aufenthaltes in der Stadt Olmütz 1642–1650', *Archiv für österreichische Geschichte*, 65 (1884), p. 322.

134. Peasant resistance: the mugging of Peter Hagendorf, June 1642

Here I had a bit to drink in the evening and fell behind my regiment in the morning, because of a hangover. Three peasants hiding in a hedge beat me up thoroughly and took my coat, satchel, everything. By divine intervention they suddenly ran off, as if being chased, even though no one was behind them. Thus beaten up, without coat or bag, I rejoined my regiment and was laughed at.

Source: Peter Hagendorf's diary entry for his experience at Dierdorf, north-west of Limburg on the Lahn, June 1642: in J. Peters (ed.), *Ein Söldnerleben aus dem Dreißigjährigen Krieg* (Berlin, 1993), p. 103.

135. Swedish account of Bavarian resistance, 1631

Although the land was in a pretty bad way, we could easily have got a lot more from it if the people had not brought a great misfortune down upon their necks. Wherever they were strong and encountered small numbers of Royal Swedish cavalry and soldiers, some of whom had been sent to protect them as *Salvaguardien*, they set upon them terribly and most cruelly executed them, cut off their hands and feet, poked out their eyes, cut off noses and ears, and (pardon the liberty) private parts, and otherwise martyred them inhumanly. These evil deeds and murders provoked such bitterness on the Royal Swedish side towards the Bavarian peasants, that they returned and took their revenge most grimly with fire and sword. Thereby, not a few were cut down and several hundred villages burnt to the ground ...

Source: Boguslav von Chemnitz, *Königlich Schwedischer in Teutschland geführter Krieg*, 2 vols (Stettin, 1648; Stockholm, 1653), vol. I, book 4, p. 18.

136. Swedish account of Brandenburg resistance, 1642

Torstensson took quarters in part of the Altmark ... The country folk and peasants proved very unwilling and disobedient, and only accepted a few of the *Salvaguardien* that were offered them. Most of them held these in contempt and said they wanted to insure and protect themselves. They used the Drömling and other marshes to protect themselves and did the Swedes a lot of damage, but also suffered damage and losses themselves. They did not remain on the defensive, but sortied out of pure sin and mischief and insulted those who were only travelling to and from the army, even though no one had done them any harm ...

Source: Boguslav von Chemnitz, *Königlich Schwedischer in Teutschland geführter Krieg*, 2 vols (Stettin, 1648; Stockholm, 1653), vol. IV, book 2, p. 6.

137. Civilian view of the utility of soldiers

Tuesday 5th September [1634]. The Forchheim soldiers were again driven back by the Swedes and saved themselves by coming to Bamberg where they caused further fright in the city. The burghers did not want to give them any quarters and told them: 'You soldiers won't be able to resist here, still less protect us and the city against the enemy. Your use is merely to bring misfortune to us poor burghers.' So they got no lodgings and all had to spend the night in the square.

Source: Sister Maria Anna Junius, 'Bamberg im Schweden-Kriege', *Bericht des Historischen Vereins zu Bamberg*, 53 (1891), p. 209.

138. A child's first sight of soldiers at a check point

Friedrich Friese recalls the journey to Magdeburg in October 1628 when his father moved from their home in Leipzig to take up an appointment with the city council:

It was already quite cold. Then we had to pass through the Dessau entrenchment that was held by the Imperials. It counted for a major work at that time. We required three days for this trip and arrived very late in the evening on 22 October in front of the Zollschanze [custom's house fort] by Magdeburg. One of the two horsemen with us rode out in front and arranged for us to be allowed through. However, we did not reach the Zollschanze before 12 o'clock, because the road was so bad. We had to wait and freeze a few hours, until the key was fetched from the mayor, Dr Martin Braun, who was well-disposed towards my father. All drawbridges, gates and locks were opened; that took nearly two hours. It is impossible to describe what this business was for mother and us children. We saw musketeers with burning matches at that point that we had never seen before. Father took me as the eldest son with him together with the tutor. We walked next to the coach and saw how each drawbridge was lowered, the gates opened and closed once the coach had passed. We had to wait a good half hour on the Elbe bridge. I can't say what crying arose from my little siblings. Although I was suffering from terrible frost, I followed my father all the time like a calf and stuck to him like a chain. We heard the rushing of the water through the stone arches on the Elbe bridge, and saw the fires on the boats. The smell of the matches struck us as very strange. Mother nearly died. But my father's sister, Barbara Friese, came with us and accompanied him. She normally lived in Eisleben and had suffered much hardship. She often consoled my mother that she should be patient. Finally we arrived in the city and in the house assigned to us by the honourable council.

Source: Karl Lohmann (ed.), *Die Zerstörung Magdeburgs von Otto von Guericke und andere Denkwürdigkeiten aus dem Dreißigjährigen Kriege* (Berlin, 1913), pp. 186–7.

---

139. From fear to friendship: Sister Junius encounters the Swedes, 1632–4

Wednesday the 11th [February 1632] as I was in the church at my early morning prayers at 5 a.m. there was such a barking that I thought all the dogs in the city were baying. I wondered what this meant for a while, until a lad ran passed our wall and cried: 'Thank God I'm out of the city.' I was gripped by mortal fear and wondered what he could mean.

Soon all the bells were ringing in the city and we all ran from the church heartily frightened to ask where the fire was. They told us the city was not on fire, but that the enemy were already at the Kaulberger Gate. We did not know what to do from anxiety and fear, but ran around like lost sheep until we finally sent someone into the city to ask how things were. We were told the enemy was there, but we still had enough time to escape. However, others said it was not the enemy, but merely peasants who were fleeing from the enemy with their wives and children, and this news calmed us a little.

Then at noon our priest arrived and told us the enemy were really already on the Kaulberg Hill. The burghers drove them off the hill. The enemy refused to give up, but demanded only accommodation in the city, or that they be given merely beer and bread. No one sent us any troops, so the mayors decided not to resist any longer. They brought the keys to the enemy and negotiated terms. The enemy promised not to harm the town or its inhabitants. Just as the terms were being agreed, a detachment of our rural militia arrived and objected to the surrender. The mayor told them they were only making matters worse and should desist, but his pleas were ignored and they soon opened a fierce fire on the enemy and drove them out of the city again. At last the bridge was raised so that the enemy could not re-enter the city. This appeared to anger them greatly as they returned with their entire force, broke in again and ordered no one to be spared, but all to be cut down except for [those in] the convents. This finally panicked the burghers who began fleeing the city in droves, men, women and children, 50 or 60 a time, to spend the night hiding in woods and villages.

As we were sitting at table that night, a sister came to us from our confessor who was still living with us. She told us that Father Vincent and Father Balthasar had hurried across the courtyard and told the confessor he should escape, because everyone was being murdered. He immediately ran away with them without saying a word. Just as we were stricken with great fear and concern, a Jesuit arrived and said: 'Dear Sisters, the enemy is certainly here, but stay in your convent and no harm will befall you … but I must escape.' Then the shooting started around 6 p.m. and lasted until 1 a.m. Some burghers apparently barricaded themselves in the city hall and opened fire on the enemy so fiercely that none of them could risk going onto the streets without being swiftly shot down. We heard all this and, when we looked into the city, we saw nothing but fire that lit up our convent. The entire Kaulberg district burnt down. We were told the enemy were angry that the agreement had been broken and that they would spare no one. Oh what fright and mortal fear gripped us then. Oh what terrible thoughts filled our minds as we did not know whether to run or stay. We might be killed at any minute … but we placed ourselves entirely at the aid and mercy of our beloved Jesus and firmly resolved to remain in our convent.

[The Swedes secured control of Bamberg. The nuns sent their gardener to the city in the morning to fetch a safe guard (*Salvaguarda*) for their convent.] As he arrived, he found that Colonel Wildenstein was still asleep in his billets in the Goose Inn in the Marketplace. Our gardener would have to wait a long time, so he begged the cook for the love of God that she wake the colonel, because the virgin nuns were dying from fear. He said this to the colonel who immediately … sent his nobleman friend with five musketeers to stand guard

for us. Oh God, what fear and mortal anxiety gripped us, because we thought
the gardener had been killed and we would be next at any minute ... Then a
sister arrived and said: 'Don't worry dear sisters, the gardener is coming with
soldiers ... to stand guard.' On hearing this we were a little comforted as we
waited. Then we went to the window where the soldiers saw us in floods of
tears. They told us we should not cry, for no harm would befall us. The nobleman also greeted us warmly and said his gracious cousin [Colonel
Wildenstein] sent his best wishes to all the nuns and had ordered him and the
musketeers to guard us. We should not be frightened at all, because we would
not be harmed. We thanked him profusely and immediately sent them food
and drink, because we were so happy we could stay in our convent. Oh who
was ever happier than us? It was as if we had risen from the dead. If we had
not obtained protection so soon, we would have been trice plundered before
noon, because our guards had such a pushing and shoving by our gate. This
left us frightened for the rest of the day and night ...

Wednesday 18th. A captain and his wife arrived at noon and asked to see
inside the convent. The sisters went to the window and told him it was not
our custom to let laity into our convent ... He replied angrily he would open
the door himself if we did not let him in. We had to let him in, but as we
showed him around, we heard a great commotion in the courtyard. We were
told a lot of soldiers from the Solms Regiment were there and wanted to force
away our guards and break into the convent. We were stricken with fear and
thought we had been tricked and were going to be plundered. Our nobleman
was not in the courtyard, but we immediately sent a musketeer into the city
to fetch him and told the captain with us that we had done so. He immediately went to the soldiers and quietened them. Our nobleman arrived meanwhile and swiftly drove them all out ...

[Later that month.] Colonels often visited us, but always left their servants
outside if they entered. We sisters stayed in our cells and spun or got on with
our chores. They greeted us warmly and went from one to another of us, offering us their hand. They conversed with us for a while. They behaved so
politely and friendly, correct and properly towards us, that we were
constantly amazed ... We were fortunate that we could remain in our convent
without any harm and we thanked them heartily for this. However, our hearts
were always heavy with fear and anxiety ...

[The Swedes were temporarily driven out of Bamberg by an imperial
counter-attack, but returned for a second occupation.]

Tuesday 15th [March 1633]. The [Swedish] commissary together with
several officers and Duke Bernhard's court preacher visited us. They went to
the St Clare's sisters and had dinner with them ...

Thursday 17th, St Gertrude's Day. The doorbell rang loudly at 4 p.m. and
we were told to open up, because the prince [Duke Bernhard of Weimar] was
coming. But we were not to be afraid. We went to the gate and waited as he
entered. He went up to each sister and shook her by the hand from the most
senior to the most junior. Then he went into our garden and looked all round
our church. He spoke to the sisters and asked who was the founder of our

order. A sister told him it was St Catherina of Siena, who had done a lot of good for Christendom by promoting peace and harmony. [1] He replied with a sigh that God desired another of us should arise and make peace now. Then he asked us all to sing as he liked to hear singing. He stood in the chancel and watched while we sang … Once this was over, he went round the cells and promised us his goodwill, and rode swiftly away …

The 27th [March 1633]. Early on Holy Easter Day the younger Lohausen rode to Halstadt and had the bridge dismantled. He arrived here alone around 9 a.m. and was followed by Colonel Rost and four individuals who visited us and the convent at noon. News came around 1 p.m. that the prince [Bernhard] and General Lohausen[2] had departed together with all the troops, leaving only the mob [of camp followers]. Our visitors stood up immediately and took their leave. However, we said we were frightened that the mob would attack us. Colonel Rost ordered those of the soldiers he had detached to guard us to remain another day and to stay alert. He would send for them once the mob had also left. This was a great relief. The younger Lohausen then returned and said: 'I have seen my father and he is staying here,' and so he had returned quickly to the dear little convent, because we were frightened and concerned. As evening drew on, it was said that the dragoons were already plundering the street. We begged the younger Lohausen to spend the night in our courtyard, but he replied we should not be frightened and ordered our guard to keep a sharp look out that night. He wanted to leave and inspect the sentries. When he reached the street he quickly quietened the dragoons: one was strung up and the others fled.

Monday 28th. Colonel Lohausen left at 5 a.m. with the army and his father Georg Wilhelm von Lohausen who had done us and the entire city so much good. The elder Lohausen had already marched a [German] mile out of Bamberg the day before, but returned because he feared the mob would sack the city … [The Swedes then temporarily returned to Bamberg again.]

[Last entry dated 12 September 1634 as the Swedes evacuated Bamberg following the defeat of their main army at Nördlingen six days before.] It is not easy for me to think of all this, still less to write about it. When one thinks of the danger we have been in, as can be read in this little book, one will soon see how chivalrously we, as weak women, have survived these times. It is still more wonderful to recount how the enemy themselves expressed their astonishment that we, as women, remained alone in this isolated house throughout this dangerous time. When one reflects, the only explanation is that God Almighty had preserved us because we, as unworthy guardians of his holy

---

1   St Catherine (1347–80) negotiated peace between Pope Gregory XI and Florence and helped end the Babylonian Captivity by persuading the pope to return to Rome from Avignon in 1376.

2   Junius calls him Georg Wilhelm, but he is generally known as Wilhelm Calchum von Lohausen (1584–1640). He was a cultured and educated man from Berg in Westphalia, who served Denmark, the city of Bremen, Mecklenburg and then Sweden until he left after the Peace of Prague. See also **Doc. 111**, note 3.

grave, remained constant throughout this dreadful time when our little convent was often threatened by force. We earnestly desired and still desire to remain here, preferring to die in this holy place than to live outside. We only desire that Jesus preserves us in our little convent and preserves our virginal honour, as has been until this day, God be praised. People said many bad things about us, but I can testify before God that not a single sister of our convent lost the slightest of her virginity. Though the Swedes visited us daily, they always behaved correctly and honourably towards us. Though they had appeared terrible towards us, as soon as they saw us and talked to us, they became patient and tender little lambs.

Source: Sister Maria Anna Junius, 'Bamberg im Schweden-Kriege', *Bericht des Historischen Vereins zu Bamberg*, 52 (1890), pp. 53, 123, 125–6, 130–1; (1891), pp. 221–2.

140. Colonel Lintelo reflects on military–civil relations, 30 March 1623

Colonel Lintelo[1] to the town of Rüthen, 30 March 1623

Since I have garrisoned your town and others in the Archbishopric of Cologne, I have never ceased to hope that I have done my utmost to guard against the soldiers who threaten to ruin the entire archbishopric and its subjects. In all truth, no one can say otherwise. I must concede, I understand the great hostility and aversion often shown towards me. I have now received new orders not to return to you in [the Duchy of] Westphalia, but to take up new quarters elsewhere. Accordingly, I would like to take my leave from the learned electoral councillors in Arnsberg,[2] as well as the councillors in Rüthen, and to thank them for all the courtesy and friendship they have shown me.

I would also like to request that the councillors will arrange for my baggage to be maintained until it can be collected – which will occur shortly.

Source: Horst Conrad and Gunnar Teske (eds), *Sterbeweiten. Der Dreißigjährige Krieg im Herzogtum Westfalen* (Münster, 2000), pp. 311–12.

---

[1] Tilmann Dietrich von Lintelo (died in 1635) was from Westphalia and became a colonel in the Bavarian army in March 1616. He commanded a Catholic League cavalry regiment after 1618. Though there were numerous complaints about the bad behaviour of his troops, he seems to have kept good order whilst garrisoning Rüthen between November 1622 and March 1623.

[2] The administrative capital of the Duchy of Westphalia which belonged to the Electorate of Cologne.

SOLDIERS' DAILY LIVES

141. Peter Hagendorf's diary

To Aldorf, in the Margraviate of Baden. Here we lay in quarters, guzzling and boozing. It was wonderful [1627].

On Good Friday we had bread and meat enough, but on Holy Easter Sunday we couldn't get even a mouthful of bread [1628].

From Stralsund we all went by the river, that is called the Schwine, in two boats into the region of Kaschubia, a very wild land, but with splendid cattle breeding of all sorts. We didn't want to eat beef any more; we had to have goose, duck or chicken. Where we spent the night, the landlord had to give each of us one and a half taler, but because we were content with him, we left him his cattle in peace. And so we marched about with 2,000 men, with fresh quarters each day for seven weeks. We stayed put at Neustettin for two days. Here the officers equipped themselves well with cows, horses, sheep, because there was enough of everything [1629].

Bread was really scarce in our camp this time, 2 lb bread cost 45 Kreuzer, but 1 lb of meat cost [only] 2 Kreuzer ... here the bread and meat were hung on the highest nail again because of the number of soldiers [September–October 1635].

At this time there was such a famine in the army that no horse in the stables was safe from the soldiers. They would stab a horse in the chest with a knife and then creep away leaving it to bleed to death. Then they would eat it. This didn't last long, however. Only five days ... Set out again on 24 February [1636] to Andernach on the Rhine and to the lordship of Breisig, a town, lying on the Rhine, that belongs to the Archbishopric of Cologne. We were supposed to get billets here for our regiment, but here was neither cat nor dog in this place. So we returned to Andernach, [and on to] Münstermaifeld, to Kaisersesch, to Wittlich and to Schweich on the Mosel. Here we stayed till 30 March. The we set out and marched to Hillesheim in Cologne territory, to Malmedy across the Eifel, a desolate place. Then on to Lissra [?] and Spa, to Liege, a very large town and beautiful land.

We besieged this town on 10 April in the year 1636 with five regiments of foot and two of horse. Johann von Werth commanded them all. Here we stayed by the Maas [river Meuse] and had a boat bridge.

A very beautiful country. All the hills are fertile, with the most beautiful gardens full of all kinds of fruit. There is a lot of animal husbandry in this area and fine corn cultivation. But there is not a lot of wood, instead the people all burn coal which they dig out of the ground. [Then Hagendorf's unit moved on to the town of Charlemont in Spanish Brabant.] Here I was detached with 12 men from the regiment to fetch fish for our regiment. Because we came across sheep in the forest, we rounded them up. We brought them onto the plain, [where] they began to cry and bleat. All the [other] sheep came running out of the forest, so that 2,000 sheep came together, so that I began to become anxious and afraid. Still, we got into camp. Then the whole camp had enough sheep. I took two for myself and slaughtered them [December 1635–June 1636].

We went to Stühlingen again, to Blumberg, to Fürstenberg, a beautiful palace. To Geisingen on the Danube, to Pfullendorf. Stayed put for 14 days; celebrated Christmas with water from the Danube and didn't have a bite of bread [December 1638].

[In operations in Hessen, August 1640.] Here we started to entrench. I supplied myself with forage at the outset. My wife and I threshed a whole sack of barley and rye. This proved very useful later, because Banér, who commanded the Swedish army, came up to us on 31 August and visited us with a strong convoy. But when he saw that we too were strongly entrenched and he couldn't get passed, he took position on a hill and blocked the way. We stayed this way until 30 September in the year 1640.

Meanwhile, our situation deteriorated badly. One pound of bread cost a crown, a measure of salt 3 Gulden, a measure of wine 3 Taler, a pound of tobacco 6 Taler, a pair of shoes 3 Gulden. Our best dish at this time was peas [and] beans. I had enough bread for myself and my wife. Even sold some, because we made ourselves a mill from two grindstones and dug an oven in the ground and baked bread.

When we wanted to go foraging, we had to take 5,000 or 6,000 horses with us. Then everyone who could run, women and children, left the camp. [They] brought in apples, pears, beans, peas, and such became their meals. But the soldiers had enough money [August–September 1640].

Source: J. Peters (ed.), *Ein Söldnerleben aus dem Dreißigjährigen Krieg* (Berlin, 1993), pp. 42–4, 65–74, 87, 94–5.

142. The 'Garte': the time without pay

How does the soldier prepare himself for the Garte? First of all, he takes two, three or four boys, so that he can demand more from the peasants, because as he talks to the peasant, his boys go into the barns after the hens, ducks, geese and whatever they can catch. What doesn't want to be taken is carried off, and so the boys are taught well from an early age how to steal and hunt like a marauder. A fine trade, a fine guild … Our marauders load up, however, since that's what they call stealing. And so that the peasants don't notice, and pick up their trade, the marauders use many other words, so they say everything in good German, but with the wrong words, and this is called *Rothwelsch* [cant]. For example, a goose is called a straw brush, and catching is called interrogation, so that to interrogate a straw brush is to catch a goose, and also sorts of other expressions. The ropes they use to catch chickens are called regiments. You see how prettily they honour their units: their robber's tools are called regiments as if a regiment did nothing more [than rob and steal]. This is how these brothers honour military discipline.

Source: Johann Jacob von Wallhausen, *Kriegskunst zu Fuß* (Oppenheim, 1615), p. 20.

143. The good old days

So let's just compare the present war with those of the past that were conducted during the reigns of the emperors Maximilian II and Rudolph II, and you can easily see the considerable difference between the warriors of the past and the soldiers of today. To be brief, you must accept that current military ways are but a shadow of those of the past ... Wasn't there a fine universal order in the Roman Empire? If there had to be a war between it and its hereditary and open enemies, it had to be done with the advice and agreement of the electors and Estates. Then each Kreis was assigned and paid its share of the burden, like a general tax, to support the war effort. No one knew anything about *Extraordinari Contributionibus, Exactionibus*, and similar extortions. Honourable, brave colonels and captains were appointed, who enjoyed a good name and high standing amongst the cavalry and foot soldiers, and these quickly collected brave men together at the muster sites and led them against the enemy. It was rare that a regiment was kept together for more than a year, unless it guarded the frontier; we were discharged before the winter, so that the poor country folk weren't burdened with winter quarters. Today, you hear nothing but billeting, mustering, contributions and other exorbitant matters. The colonels are either foreigners or skivers, swindlers, stone masons, smiths and the like, who, once they have collected enough money and property, pack their bags and leave the others to look out for themselves, especially when the campaign starts.

Source: Pamphlet entitled *Gespräch Hauptmann Schnepfs mit Veit Schrammen und Lentze Kumhold* (1631), quoted in Eugen von Frauenholz (ed.), *Das Heerwesen in der Zeit des Dreißigjährigen Krieges*, 2 vols (Munich, 1938–9), vol. I, p. 6, note 3.

---

144. A soldier's comment on being told the Emperor had made Peace

Can he make peace without even asking me? ... Does he not owe all his victories to me? Have I not shot down the Swedish king? ... Have I not conquered Saxony? Have I not earned my reputation in Denmark? How would the battle on White Mountain have ended without me? What glory have I not earned in the battle with the Grand Turk? Fie upon you! Get out of my sight; for I get mortally vexed when I fly into a real rage: overpowered by hot and boiling wrath and savage ire I am capable of seizing the spire of St Stephen's Cathedral in Vienna and bending it down so hard that the whole world will turn upside down like a skittle ball.

Source: *Horribilicribrifx*, a comedy drama written by the Silesian poet Andreas Gryphius (1616–64) around 1648–50 but not published until 1663.

DESTRUCTION

145. 'Kipper and Wipper' hyperinflation: Pastor Bötzinger's memoirs

In 1620 I went from Coburg to Jena where I received a student grant of 60fl
for two years from the local church treasury for my studies. However, the
'Kipper time' started that year and one could scarcely do anything with that
money. The 30fl were in good coin and 5fl would have been enough for
another two years after my studies. God bless the Church and those who
become pastors. But in Jena in 1621 a one pound loaf of home-baked bread
cost 1 Groschen, or even 15 pence, a measure[1] of beer 1gr., a measure of Jena
wine 4gr., a pair of shoes 3 or even 5fl, a pair of boots 10fl.

Source: Pastor Martin Bötzinger, 'Vitae curriculo', *Beyträge zur Erläuterung der
Hochfürstl. Sachsen-Hildburghäusischen Kirchen-, Schul- und Landes-Historie*, 1
(1750), p. 349.

----

146. The impact of military operations: Hans Dobel's diary for 1631

[The Swedes approached Franconia in October 1631.] Anno 1631. On 16 and
6 October [i.e. OS and NS] the bailiff [Burkhard Seyfried] left here and drove
to Öttingen, together with his wife and little daughter, the Silesian woman
and the secretary's maid. On 20 and 10 October our noble master the Lord
Commander[1] also went to Öttingen, together with the secretary and his
servants.

On a Thursday [23 October] the Swedish cavalry first appeared and plundered.

Register of everything that happened in the year 1632.
On 1 January Carpenter Hans and two horsemen came into the castle and
stayed there till 5 January. Six musketeers arrived from [the imperial City of]
Windsheim and stayed there until 12 January, then they returned to
Windsheim. And they took ten table hooks with them and went on to
Höchstatt/Aisch. Lieutenant Colonel Johann Lord of Zerotin was killed there
and several soldiers wounded. And the town was taken over 14 days later and
another lieutenant colonel was shot, then they went to Forchheim. There
Count von Solmitz was shot through the arm, so they retreated because of the
high water.

On 25 January the cavalry from Lichtenau [a fortress belonging to
Nuremberg] rode passed towards Unteraltenbernheim and around Buch

----

[1]   Equivalent to 0.92 litres.

[1]   Johann Theobald Hundbiss von Waldrams, Commander [i.e. governor] of the property
       of the Teutonic Order at Virnsberg in Franconia.

harnessed around 25 horses and took the peasants from Ickelheim with them. The peasants had to be ransomed with 100 taler.

On 17 February the horsemen from Lichtenau plundered our village [of Virnsberg] and harnessed several horses and rode away. On Wednesday, 29 February in the old calendar, the Imperial troops attacked Bamberg and drove out the Swedes. In the night of 8 March my noble master was at Lichtenau. On 6 March soldiers came to Ickelheim. On the 9th they wrote to Unteraltenbernheim that they should be sent a back of meat and a barrel of wine and 50 loaves each day and [that] Fröschendorf and Buech and Hechelbach had to pay 10 imperial talers each day to Lieutenant Colonel Johann Winckler.[2] Tuesday 13 March the Swedes arrived at Windsheim. On the 14th 15 horsemen went to Flachslanden [a village south of Virnsberg] and took 24 horses and shot a peasant from Ottenhofen.

Thursday 15 March, nine horsemen took two horses from Kontz the joiner and made schoolteacher Wolf ride with them as far as Undernbibert [southeast of Virnsberg]. They were given 20 taler, afterwards they went to Unteraltenbernheim where they were given 25 taler and they took seven lambs.

Monday 19 March, the Swedish king left Windsheim and marched to Nuremberg.

On the 18th of this month, the cavalry plundered Boxau [near Virnsberg] and drove away six head of cattle.

Tuesday 20 March, the Weimar Regiment camped here and at Sondernohe [east of Virnsberg] and at Unteraltenbernheim for two nights and Lieutenant Colonel Mayer and his company occupied Virnsberg castle.

Tuesday 27 March, the lieutenant colonel from Windsheim was here and took three wagons of hay.

Thursday the 29th of this month, sent four cartloads of hay from the Kammathhof[3] to Windsheim and this day Bernhard [of Weimar] left.

Friday the 30th of this month, the judge returned to the castle and did the accounts.

Tuesday 3 April, they drove four oxen and three cows from Windsheim to Virnsberg. Sunday 8 April, they fished the Kammathhof and took the fish to Windsheim on two wagons. And three wagons were loaded with hay at the Kammathhof and two wagons were loaded at the castle and one with feed, and all taken to Windsheim. The mayor and another man, called Becken Hans, from Ickelheim were with them.

Tuesday 17 April, it was the gamekeeper's wedding at Oberdachstetten; his name is Leinhard Ungelein from Öttingen in Swabia. My wife was at the wedding. Horsemen came into the village that day.

Tuesday 17 April, a letter arrived in Virnsberg from Windsheim. The subjects were told to give money: 1 imperial taler from each full farmer, half

---

2   This was a detachment of Bernhard von Weimar's army.
3   A farm attached to the Teutonic Order Commandery of Virnsberg.

a taler from those with a large farm, 8 kreuzer from those with a small one, and 9 kreuzer from a cottager. To be paid within two days. The judge collected [the money] and recorded it.

Thursday 19 April, I, Hans Dobel, went to Sulzfeld and carried a barrel full of wine with Hans Suhr of Sundernau.

Saturday 5 May, Michel Bittheuser [the district overseer] returned to Virnsberg and drove in nine cows and a calf.

Tuesday, 8 May, Bittheuser summoned the village headmen and told them they had to give him money. One imperial taler from a full peasant, half a taler from a large farm, a quarter taler from a small one. And so this was done on Friday, the 11th of this month. And they are supposed to send the bailiff's corn as well.

On the 11th of this month a cartload of hay was sent to Windsheim.

Saturday 12 May, von Rigland was in the castle with the mayor of Ickelheim, a corporal and six soldiers from Windsheim. They had lunch and afterwards the mayor and those from Windsheim went to Dietenhofen [northeast of Ansbach] and took the castle.

Wednesday 30 May, they took the tin from the well, roughly three hundred weight. They took the stonemason's cloth [?] and, when only half came out, he said it was all gone. The gardener was standing there and said to the district overseer [Bittheuser], no, they shouldn't stop because there were over a hundred pieces in there.

Saturday 9 June, the Swedish horsemen took the horses of the ploughmen on the Order's field.

Tuesday, the 26th of this month, around four wagons arrived at Virnsberg from the Swedish camp and requested billets, but were refused. So they went to Wippenauhof [south of Virnsberg]. Stayed there two days, afterwards they went to Nuremberg into the camp.

Sunday, 1 July in the old calender, the Imperials took Schwabach [near Nuremberg] an hour before nightfall and afterwards advanced towards Nuremberg and moved their base. They plundered Ansbach and Neustadt [on the Aisch] and Erlbach [northeast of Virnsberg] and Leutershausen [near Ansbach] and Brückenfels [south of Virnsberg] and Rügland [southeast of Virnsberg] and Schillingsfürst and all the places and villages and castles. Neustadt on the Aisch and Erlbach were set on fire. Saturday 7 July, the district overseer [Bittheuser] and the preacher [Johann Nikolaus Pomeranus] went to Windsheim in the morning. Imperial horsemen arrived at Virnsberg castle at 2 o'clock in the afternoon and were given bread and corn each day for 14 days. Monday the 9th of this month the gatekeeper was shot in the thigh and died six days later and was buried at Sundernau.

Sunday 22 July, Bernhardt Breytygam, together with the Bosler's boy and Schmidt of Kemmathen's son went into the Imperial camp.

Friday 27 July, Bernhardt Breytygam was captured by the old bailiff Eberlein of Underbibert and peasant lads at Fladengreuth [east of Virnsberg] and delivered to Windsheim.

Thursday 9 August, around 300 Swedish horsemen were at Boxau and fed their horses on the lower meadow. They took the bailiff's cows and slaughtered some pigs. And they took a pair of boots and two shirts from me.

Friday 10 August, around a hundred Imperials came through Sundernau to Unterzeichen and met the Swedes and laid some low.

Wednesday 15 August, Bittheuser and six horsemen returned from Windsheim.

Monday 20 August, the horsemen left the castle and took 19 horses and two wagons from the Imperials. The gamekeeper and the castle miller [Hans Kuhn] rode with them.

Tuesday 21 August, Bernhardt Breitygam, born in Mehrstadt, who was an official at Virnsberg, was beheaded in Windsheim, while Hans Schreiner from Sundernau was strangled, because they are said to have wanted to betray the town.[4]

Thursday 23 August, they fought each other for the first time in front of Nuremberg. Von Weimrich was captured.[5]

Sunday 26 August, the Swedish horsemen sortied from the castle again and took 21 horses from the Imperials. The gamekeeper, the miller and Jergen's son-in-law rode with them.

Monday 27 August, Bittheuser and his horsemen fled from the castle to Windsheim.

Thursday 30 August, 17 Swedish horsemen were in the castle and looked for the old judge.

Friday the 31st of this month, they arrived at Leonrodt [near Dietenhofen] and afterwards celebrated in Windsheim. Gettlein was among them.

Friday 31 August, a large body of imperial horses were at Sundernau and Boxau, threshed corn at Sundernau mill and took a cart and three measures of corn from my sister, [also] a measure of corn from me.

Saturday 1 September, the old judge was released from Windsheim and a horseman was shot dead beside the school.

Friday 7 September, the Imperial cavalry took farmer Michel Eckhardt and his son and boys with them. He had wanted to skewer a horseman with a pitchfork.

Saturday 8 September, I buried my godfather, a farmer called Hans Resch, at Ickelheim.

[The diary breaks off at this point: possibly its author was a victim of the war.]

Source: Quoted in Gerhard Rechter, 'Der Obere Zehngrund im Zeitalter des Dreißigjährigen Krieges', *Jahrbuch für fränkische Landesforschung*, 38 (1978), pp. 110–13.

---

4   The Swedes suspected them of being imperial spies.
5   A reference to the battle of Alte Veste in September 1632.

147. Damage and reconstruction

[Report of Johann Daut, steward for Colonel Dietrich von Sperreuther, on the condition of the knight's fief of Trautskirchen in Franconia, 1641:]

The following desolate farms and properties are currently at Trautskirchen castle:

1. The bath house, the barn has fallen down.
2. Nicolaus Schöller's property, a burnt patch.
3. Stephan Herbt's property, the barn has fallen down and the house is very dilapidated.
4. Barthel Neuber's, two burnt patches, on which a barn still stands.
5. Contzens Köhler's property there, the house is very dilapidated.
6. Hans Winterlein's property, in which the house is very dilapidated.
7. The smithy, where the barn has fallen down.
8. Michael Rössner, burnt down, where a small barn still stands.

Einersdorf, a property where the house has fallen down.
Stökkach, a farm, where the buildings are much in need of repair.
Dagenbach, three farms and a property, that can be made habitable at little expense.
Oberheßbach, a farm in which the rooms could be repaired at little cost.
Gräfenbuch, a farm and two properties in which some rooms have partly collapsed already, while others are very dilapidated.
The total of these desolate farms and properties is 20 hearths.

… to reoccupy these only capable people will do and, if they are available, they need more than dear peace and good health. Quite a good supply of money and draught animals and necessary farm equipment. Then they need support through the six months of planting, whatever that might be, and the hard work. One will also need fertiliser, since such ruined fields will initially produce little and can be scarcely cultivated within two years. For this it is essential that the above-mentioned properties are exempt from tax, contributions and services for at least six years, and in particular are exempt from dues for three years, so that meanwhile all possible savings can be made. If, however, the perpetual transit, billeting and similar burdens of war continue, everything will be pointless and the poor country man cannot make progress.

Source: Printed in Gerhard Rechter, 'Der Obere Zehngrund im Zeitalter des Dreißigjährigen Krieges', *Jahrbuch für fränkische Landesforschung*, 38 (1978), p. 119.

---

148. Foreign observation: the Earl of Arundel's trip along the Main, 1636

We left Mainz the next day, May 3 [1636], leaving the Rhine one and a half miles above the city on our right hand and entering a shallow river called the

Main … then to the stately city of Frankfurt, near the left side of the Main. Here we landed and stayed.

From Cologne to Frankfurt all the towns, villages and castles are battered, pillaged and burnt and every one of our halts we remained on board [the boat], every man taking his turn on guard duty. Here we stayed for four days until our carriages were prepared for us to continue our journey … [After sight-seeing in Frankfurt:] On Sunday, May 7, leaving the Main on our left hand, we set off with our wagons, through the city and over two bridges which are always guarded by soldiers. And because of the dangers to travellers we took with us a convoy of musketeers and passed by Offenbach and Seligenstadt, between our route and the Main, and through a great forest where we considered ourselves to be in considerable danger for we could hear the rapid discharge of the great guns at Hanau, less than three miles away, which the Swedes formerly captured and which was, at this time, besieged by the Emperor's forces.[1]

Emerging from the forest, we travelled for two miles by the side of a great mountain whose lower slopes were covered with vines until we arrived at a humble little village where we halted and cooked our food, departing thence, after dinner, over level country until we reached the Main and were ferried over into the town of Klingenberg. Passing through this town, we climbed for two miles over rocky ground to the top of a very high hill. Then, after passing through a wood, we came to a wretched little village called Neukirchen, which we found quite uninhabited yet with one house on fire. Here, since it was now late, we were obliged to stay all night, for the nearest town was four miles away; but we spent that night walking up and down with carbines in our hands, and listening fearfully to the sound of shots in the woods around us. We did, however, make use of some of the burning fragments of the house that was on fire for we used them to roast the meat that was prepared for His Excellency's supper.

Early next morning, His Excellency went to inspect the church and found it had been plundered and that the pictures and the altar had been desecrated. In the churchyard we saw a dead body, scraped out of the grave, while outside the churchyard we found another dead body. Moreover, we entered many houses but found that all were empty. We hurried from this unhappy place and learnt later that the villagers had fled on account of the plague and had set that particular house on fire in order to prevent travellers from catching the infection.

Source: Francis C. Springell (ed.), *Connoisseur and Diplomat: The Earl of Arundel's Embassy to Germany in 1636 as Recounted in William Crowne's Diary* (London, 1963), pp. 59–60.

---

[1] Hanau had been captured in 1631 and was held after 1634 by Sir James Ramsey (1589–1639), a colonel in Bernhard of Weimar's army. Ramsey and his garrison defected with Bernhard to the French in 1635. He was wounded when the fortress was finally captured by the Imperialists on 23 February 1638. See also **Doc. 117**.

149. Accounts of cannibalism at the Siege of Breisach, 1638

Two accounts of cannibalism amongst the Protestant prisoners held by the imperial garrison besieged in Breisach, autumn 1638.

(i)

A soldier died in prison on 12 December. When the Provost wanted to have him buried, the other prisoners fell violently on the corpse and ripped it apart with their teeth and ate it raw.

Eight burgher's children are known to have gone missing in the Fischerhalten alone by 10 December and were presumed eaten, because no one knew where they had gone, excluding the foreigners' and beggars' children, of whom no one knew anything. Also ten corpses were found in a square one morning, excluding the others found in the dung heaps and in the alleys.

Source: *Kurzes summarisches Verzeichnis etlicher denkwürdiger und zum Teil sonst in Historien nicht viel erhörter Sachen, so sich in der Belagerung von Breisach ... von einem hohen und virnehmen Offizier zum Gedächtnis aufzuschrieben* (1638).

(ii)

A soldier died in prison on 12 December. When the Provost wanted to have him buried, the other prisoners fell violently on the corpse and ripped it apart with their teeth and ate it raw. Soldiers had to be chased away on several [other] occasions to stop them catching children to slaughter so that the burghers did not let their children out of the house ...

Eight children are known to have gone missing in the Fischerhalten alone by 10 December and were presumed eaten, excluding those of the refugees. A large number of dead soldiers and other people are found early each morning piled up in the alleys and dung heaps.

Source: *Brysachsche Hungersnot und umstandliche Verzeichnis aller denkwüdigen Sachen, so sich während der achtzehnwöchentlichen Belagerung* (Bern, 1639).

Both from Fritz Julius, 'Angebliche Menschenfresserei im Dreißigjährigen Krieg', *Mitteilungen des Historischen Vereins der Pfalz*, 45 (1927), p. 71.

---

150. Poverty is relative: Pastor Ludolph complains about food, 1642[1]

Anno 1642: Everything continued as badly as the previous year, only that the sorrows pressed more heavily still. In such times one had to hold baptisms and festivals without meat soup, without boiled or braised meat. We had to learn to eat green cabbage, pea soup without dripping! Well over a year has passed during which I, a pastor, have not been able – in a whole year – to have

---

1   Lorenz Ludolph (b.1608), pastor of Reichensachsen and Langenhain, two villages in Hessen.

a dish on my table. Anyone who has not themselves seen and endured such a state of affairs will not believe what I set down here for remembrance. There continues to be a shortage of cattle, no pigs, not a goose to be found in the village, and even the road is overgrown with grass, and even corn, oats and barley. One can buy the best and largest field for two loads of wood or the like, often for just one. Those who were once the most distinguished and richest in Reichensachsen, are now the poorest. They have carried loads of wood or some corn across the fields for payment or for themselves; barefoot or just in stockings, and without shoes, for they had none, just to earn their bread. I don't want to name them, as it is not their disgrace. It is better that they should not reject Christ's cross or God's wondrous rule and salvation, but instead accept this and praise God thankfully that they have grown poor in Christ's example and remember David that God thereby honoured, Psalm 66. Reichensachsen and Langenhain should not forget the content of this Psalm! I must stop describing this state of affairs, not only because it is impossible to describe it, but because I did not intend to write a chronicle of Reichensachsen, but to compile a record of baptisms and marriages.

[Entry in 1652:] I have had to give up maintaining the death registers altogether in such miserable times. I have had a great deal to do and am glad that I have managed to keep the baptismal and marriage registers, which are more important. My successor can now keep the death register better under his own times.

Source: Walter Kürschner (ed.), 'Aus dem Kirchenbuch von Reichensachsen (und Langenhain) von 1639–1653', *Archiv für hessische Geschichte und Altertumskunde*, new series 9 (1913), pp. 53–4.

---

151. A misspent youth: student Stephan Behaim is upbraided by his guardians, 28 December 1630

Guardians to Stephan Carl Behaim (1612–38)

Our friendly greeting and obliging will, dear foster son. We received your letter of 18 December on the 25th, and we understand well enough from it your defence [of the use] of the money you have received and your late accounting of it. But because your letter is so completely contradictory and bewildering, we have great difficulty believing it, so let us again remind you to send us a detailed statement of all the money you have received during your entire stay in Altenburg, and [this time] indicate to us in an orderly manner, item by item, on a full or half sheet of paper, not on so many little tattered scraps, just how you have spent it. Then we can properly inform ourselves. Also, since you indicate that you are still in need of a suit of clothes, Herr Sternenbecker will be written to and instructed to accommodate you as economically as possible, if you do need it.

As for your wish to go to a university, indeed, to Wittenberg, we guardians, pursuant to our duty, have together and in consultation with your mother, carefully and fully considered it. We simply cannot in conscience find it advisable at the present time to grant your wish, considering that everything is now so corrupt and perverted in the universities. Unfortunately, one now learns more evil than good there (even when one arrives with good intentions and is resolute). One could cite many and varied examples of such corruption of youth [in the universities]. In consideration of this one fact alone, we have unanimously decided that it is in your best interest to be placed instead with an eminent doctor of law and advocate at the imperial [cameral] court in Speyer.[1] There you will have the desired opportunity, by constant practice, not only to learn fine, elegant handwriting and how to write orthographically and compose properly, but also with effort to acquaint yourself with imperial law and judicial procedure. Such knowledge will be useful to you in the future and give you an advantage over others not so experienced, should God want you to have a position in government. You need not in the least be ashamed of such [training]. Others of your rank, at great effort, have also spent time there. For example, your cousin who is now a forestry official. Herr Georg Seyfried Kohler, and others. Indeed, a Harssdörffer, Haller, and a Schedel are now there.[2] One may hope that for you also [such training] will not defame your honour, but redound to your benefit. However, for the present, you must keep these plans to yourself and diligently serve [Herr von Bünau] and be loyal to your peers [in Altenburg], showing everyone there respect and avoiding bad company. If you conduct yourself according to God's commandments, there is no doubt that He will give you fortune and success in all that you undertake, so that his divine honour and what is best both for you and for the common good may be served. All of which we wish you from the bottom of our hearts together with the start of a happy new year. May the divine omnipotence bless us all. Nuremberg, 28 December, 1630.

Your willing and loyal guardians,
Lucas Friedrich Behaim
Hans Heinrich Weiss
Conrad Baier

Source: Steven Ozment (ed.), *Three Behaim boys: Growing up in Early Modern Germany* (New Haven, 1990), pp. 217–18.

LITERARY EVIDENCE

152. Grimmelshausen's *Simplicissimus* [extracts]

Book 1 Chapter 3: The sympathetic suffering of a loyal bag-pipe.

---

[1] That is, the Reichskammergericht.
[2] Like the Behaims, these were all prominent families in the imperial city of Nuremberg.

[The character Simplicissimus is a boy shepherd in the Spessart region of northern Germany.]

So I began to make such ado with my bagpipe and such noise that 'twas enough to poison all the toads in the garden, and so I thought myself safe enough from the wolf that was ever in my mind ... So far and no further could I get with my song; for in a moment I was surrounded, sheep and all, by a troop of cuirassiers that had lost their way in the thick wood and were brought back to the right path by my music and my calls to my flock. 'Aha,' I said to myself, 'these be the right rouges! These be the four legged knaves and thieves my dad told me of!' For at first I took horse and man (as did the Americans when they saw the Spanish cavalry) to be but one beast, and could not but think that these were the wolves; and so would sound the retreat for these horrible centaurs and send them flying. But scarcely had I blown up my bellows to that end, when one of them catches me by the shoulder and swings me roughly upon a spare farm horse they had stolen with other booty ... So away my horse went with me at a good trot ... for my dad's farm.

Strange and fantastic notions now filled my brain; for I thought, because I sat upon such a beast as I had never seen before, that I too would be changed into an iron man. And because such a change didn't come, I thought these strange creatures were simply there to help me drive my sheep home; especially as none was devouring the sheep, but all, with one accord, made for my dad's farm. So I looked anxiously when my dad and my mammy should come out and bid us welcome, but they did not. For they and our Ursula, my dad's only and dearest daughter, had done a bunk through the back door and did not want to welcome our guests.

Book 1 Chapter 4: How Simplicissimus's palace was stormed, plundered and ruined, and in what sorry fashion the soldiers kept house there.

Although it was not my intention to take the peace-loving reader with these merry troopers to my dad's house and farm, seeing that matters will go ill there, yet the course of my story demands that I should leave to kind posterity an account of what manner of cruelties were sometimes practised in our German war. And, moreover, testify by my own example that such evils were necessarily sent to us for our own good by the kindness of Almighty God. For, dear reader, who would ever have taught me that there was a God in Heaven if these soldiers had not destroyed my dad's house, and by such a deed driven me out among folk who gave me all fitting instruction thereupon? Only a little while before, I neither knew nor could fancy to myself that there were any people on earth save only my dad, my mother and me, and the rest of our household, nor did I know of any human habitation but that where I daily went out and in. But soon afterwards I understood the ways of men's coming into this world, and how they must leave it again. I was only in shape a man and in name a Christian; for the rest I was but a beast. Yet the almighty looked upon my innocence with a forgiving eye, and wanted me to come to the knowledge of Himself and of myself. And although He had a thousand ways for this purpose, yet He undoubtedly wanted to use as an example to others that one only by which my dad and my mother should be punished for their heathenish upbringing of me.

The first thing these troopers did was to stable their horses in the nice black rooms of the house. Then each fell to his appointed task: which was more or less death and destruction. For though some began to slaughter and to boil and to roast so that it looked as if there would be a merry banquet afterwards, others stormed through the house ransacking upstairs and down; not even the privy closet was safe, as if the golden fleece of Colchis was hidden there. Still others stowed together great parcels of cloth and clothing and all manner of household stuff, as if they were going to hold a jumble sale somewhere. All that they had no mind to take with them they cut to pieces. Some thrust their swords through the hay and straw as if they had not enough sheep and swine to slaughter; and some shook the feathers out of the beds and in their place stuffed bacon and other dried meat and provisions as if such were better and softer to sleep on. Others broke the stove and the windows as if forecasting a never-ending summer. Houseware of copper and pewter they beat flat, and packed such vessels, all bent and spoiled, in with the rest. Bedsteads, tables, chairs and benches they burned, though there were many cords of dry wood in the yard. Jars and crocks, pots and casseroles, must all go to pieces, either because they would eat none but roast meat, or because their purpose was to make just one meal with us.

Our maid was handled so roughly in the barn that she was unable to walk away, I am ashamed to say. They stretched out our hired man on the ground, thrust a wooded wedge into his mouth to keep it open, and poured a milk churn full of stinking manure drippings down his throat; they call it the Swedish cocktail. He didn't find it tasty and made a very wry face. This way they forced him to take a raiding party to some other place where they captured men and beasts and brought them back to our farm, in which company were my dad, my mother and our Ursula.

Then they got started: first they took the flints out of their pistols and jammed the peasants' thumbs in their place and so to torture the poor peasants as if they wanted to burn witches. Though he confessed to nothing, they put one of the prisoners into the bake oven and lighted a fire under him. As for another, they put a rope around his neck and twisted it so tight with a piece of wood that the blood gushed from his mouth, nose and ears. In short, each had his own device to torture the peasants, and each peasant his special torture. But it seemed to me that my dad was the luckiest, for he confessed with a laugh what others were forced to say in pain and miserable lamentation. Such an honour no doubt fell to him as head of the household. For they put him close to a fire and bound him so fast that he could neither stir hand nor foot, and smeared the soles of his feet with wet salt, and made our old goat lick it off, and tickle him that he nearly burst his sides laughing. And this seemed to me such a merry thing, for I had never seem him laugh so much, that I had to laugh too to keep him company, or perhaps to hide my ignorance. In the midst of such glee he had to tell them everything they demanded, and indeed revealed the whereabouts of hidden treasure much richer in gold, pearls and jewellery than might have been expected on a farm.

Of the women, girls and maids they took, I can't say much, for the soldiers didn't let me watch their doings. Yet, this I do remember, that I heard some of them scream piteously from various dark corners of the house, and I guess that my mother and our Ursel [Ursula] fared no better than the rest. Amid all this horror, I was busy turning the roasting spit, and in the afternoon gave the horses drink, and so got to see our hired girl in the barn. She looked wondrously messed up so that I didn't recognise her at first. She said to me in a sickly voice: 'Boy, get out of this place, or the troopers will take you with them. Try to get away; you can see that they are up to no good!' And she could say no more.

Source: Hans Jacob Christoffel von Grimmelshausen, *Der abenteuerliche Simplicissimus Teutsch* (Nuremberg, 1668).

VISUAL EVIDENCE

153. *Peasants' Revenge*: engraving by Hans Ulrich Franck (1643)

154. *The Enrollment of Troops,* no. 2 in the Greater Miseries of War series by Jacques Callot

155. *The Hanging,* no.11 in the Greater Miseries of War series by Jacques Callot

156. *The Old Soldier,* no. 14 in Beggar series by Jacques Callot

17

Peace making, 1641–8

The initial optimism generated by the Peace of Prague [see Doc. 103] had long evaporated by the time Ferdinand III succeeded his father in February 1637. The new emperor was more pragmatic, but equally determined to preserve the gains his father had secured in 1635. He summoned the imperial diet in 1640 for the first meeting since 1613. Though the assembled imperial Estates agreed continued support for the war against Sweden and France, many were clearly growing disillusioned. After the negotiations through the Saxon elector collapsed in 1636, peace talks were shifted to Hamburg, a financial centre which all sides found expedient to regard as neutral. The deteriorating military and political situation obliged Ferdinand III to accept the Hamburg Peace Preliminaries in December 1641 [Doc. 157]. These settled the form, but not the content of the peace, by arranging for a general congress to meet in the two Westphalian towns of Münster and Osnabrück.

Fighting continued because all parties hoped further victories would enable them to open the talks in a stronger position. The emperor also wanted to reserve representation of the Empire for himself to deny the imperial Estates a chance to erode Habsburg gains. Envoys began arriving at the congress venues during 1643, but serious negotiations only began two years later. Defeats such as the Second Battle of Breitenfeld [see Docs 118–19] exposed the emperor's inability to protect the princes who had joined him in the Peace of Prague. Brandenburg led the way in a steady drift towards neutrality after 1641. Neutrality was illegal under the imperial constitution, as well as reviled morally for allowing evil to go unpunished. Princes excused themselves by saying Sweden gave them no choice. The terms agreed by Brandenburg are fairly typical of these arrangements [Doc. 158].

To stem this trend, Ferdinand finally invited all imperial Estates to the congress in August 1645 [Doc. 159]. This proved an astute move, countering much of the earlier criticism and ensuring that negotiations were conducted through the established status groups of electors, princes and imperial cities regardless of confession or alliances. This made it much harder for France and Sweden to manipulate political or religious issues to divide the imperial Estates, most of whom still looked to the emperor for guidance.

A string of imperial and Bavarian defeats during 1645 prevented Ferdinand III from aiding Saxony which was partly overrun by the Swedes. Elector Johann Georg reluctantly followed Brandenburg's example and agreed an armistice at Kötzschenbroda on 6 September. Further pressure obliged him to extend this as the truce of Eilenburg in March 1646 to last until peace could be concluded at the Westphalian congress. Alongside Bavaria, Saxony had been the emperor's most steadfast ally in the Empire since 1635. Ferdinand III accepted that peace could now only be obtained by offering serious concessions. Alone in his room in Linz castle, he personally wrote secret instructions to his most trusted envoy, Count Maximilian von Trauttmannsdorff (1584–1650) [**Doc. 160**]. Trauttmannsdorff was authorised to give ground in a carefully staged sequence until the enemy made peace. The order of priorities and Ferdinand's accompanying comments reveal how he interpreted the war and why he continued fighting. If somewhat self-congratulatory, Trauttmannsdorff's final report on his negotiations demonstrates his skill in keeping the actual concessions to a minimum, as well as listing the real gains the Habsburgs made during the war [**Doc. 161**].

Sweden's objectives were spelt out in the resolution of its governing Council of the Realm in May 1643 [**Doc. 162**]. The timing of this resolution is significant, since it determined Swedish policy before the young Queen Christina was declared of age and assumed a more active role in government in 1644. It included the decision to open a new war with Denmark which had remained neutral since 1629. Victory by August 1645 removed any chance of Denmark chairing the Westphalian congress and thus of it influencing the outcome to Sweden's disadvantage. The document also reveals the necessity of concealing the extent of Sweden's territorial demands in the Empire so as not to alienate Protestant opinion and undermine claims to be fighting for 'German Liberty'. Subsequent events divided the councillors and diplomats. Johan Oxenstierna (1612–57), the chancellor's son and head of Sweden's delegation at Westphalia, led the hardliners who wanted to extract the maximum 'security' and 'satisfaction' from the Empire. Oxenstierna's assistant, Johan Adler Salvius (1590–1652), urged a more pragmatic, flexible approach to end the conflict quickly. As her correspondence indicates, Christina clearly preferred Salvius's line, but was unable to change the basic course of Swedish policy [**Docs 163–4**].

The French delegation was also divided between those who wanted peace quickly and others demanding greater concessions. France and Sweden had agreed in 1641 to continue fighting until both achieved their objectives in the Empire. Their envoys outwardly presented a united front at the congress, but internal memoranda indicate how far the aims of the two allies diverged. France still hoped an understanding with Bavaria would provide a more effective means of countering perceived Habsburg threats than continued alliance with Sweden [**Doc. 165**].

France appeared to achieve its goal when further defeats forced Maximilian of Bavaria to sign the Truce of Ulm in March 1647 [**Doc. 166**]. Unlike those agreed by Brandenburg and Saxony, Maximilian did not have to pay contributions to his enemies in return for them respecting his neutrality. He did have to surrender key towns in south-west Germany which improved France's grip on the Upper Rhine. The Truce left Ferdinand III isolated, and he took immediate steps to recover Maximilian's trust by, for example, trying to improve the efficiency of the battered imperial army [**see Doc. 120**]. More directly, he renewed his guarantee for Maximilian's possession of the Palatine electoral title and the Upper (eastern) Palatinate, and Trauttmannsdorff ensured international recognition for this in the Westphalian peace [**see Doc. 167**]. The Truce also increased tension between

Ferdinand's enemies, because France did as Sweden had feared and switched its army from Germany to strengthen the forces fighting Spain. Maximilian rejoined the war on 7 September 1647, obliging France to recall its troops to Germany and renew active support of Sweden. The final campaign saw further imperial and Bavarian defeats, but no clear victory of their enemies.

IMPERIAL POLICY

157. The Hamburg Peace Preliminaries, 25 December 1641

His Holy Roman Imperial Majesty's and the Imperial Aulic Councillor Konrad von Lützow, armed with plenipotentiary powers to negotiate in the Lower Saxon Kreis and in the talks on the peace preliminaries, wishes to announce to all to whom it may concern, that after many years of negotiations over the basis to start general peace talks, and after the most diverse difficulties arose from the preliminaries, finally, thanks to divine assistance and the intervention of the authority of the serene king of Denmark as mediator, the following preliminaries have been agreed:

The general discussions are to take place in Osnabrück and Münster in Westphalia from which, after the exchange of the letters of safe conduct ... the garrisons of the belligerents are to be withdrawn immediately. Both sides are to swear that the two cities are to remain neutral for the duration of the congress.

The councils are permitted to retain their own militias and citizen volunteers to protect their cities during this time. They are to promise through a declaration to be loyal to the congress and to protect it, to regard the property, persons and entourage of the negotiators as inviolable and to protect them. And if something is demanded of them in the common good of the treaty, they are to provide it willingly, but not carry out orders from one party only, but on the contrary those agreed by both negotiating teams.

Both congresses should be regarded as one, and accordingly not only should the road between them be safe for all who need to travel from one to the other, but all intervening places as deemed advantageous in mutual agreement between the two sides, are to enjoy security too.

The import or export of all documents, food and all things that are required by such an important congress is free and not to be disrupted by anyone for whatever reason, but on the contrary promoted by every possible means. ...

Letters of safe conduct for both congresses are to be exchanged by all participants within two months of this convention.

[There follows a list of all those who must provide letters of safe conduct.]

The date for both congresses at Osnabrück and Münster to open formally has been fixed as 25 March of the coming year. May it please God that this ends happily and favourably for Christianity! ...

Source: B. Roeck (ed.), *Deutsche Geschichte in Quellen und Darstellung, Vol. IV Gegenreformation und Dreißigjähriger Krieg 1555–1648* (Stuttgart, 1996), pp. 366–7.

158. Truce between Sweden and Brandenburg, 15 June 1644

Let it be hereby known to all that Queen Christina [full title] and the honourable Swedish crown has garrisoned the two towns of Frankfurt and Crossen on the Oder for a number of years for military reasons, and has built an entrenchment by the river above Züllichow.[1] Elector Friedrich Wilhelm of Brandenburg [full title] has expressed a particular desire to recover these from Her Majesty and the Swedish crown to avoid any damage to his electoral lands should, contrary to hope, they be attacked, and additionally to allow his widowed mother[2] to enjoy her proper dowager seat in the duchy of Crossen. The elector knew of no better way to achieve this and to free himself from danger than to turn to Her Majesty, the Swedish crown and its councillor and field marshal, Lennart Torstenson [full title],[3] and request the evacuation of both towns and the entrenchment. These thoughts and proposals were conveyed by various means to His Excellency the field marshal. He believed these places were well provisioned and in no danger of being captured, as they could easily be reinforced in time if necessary, and so voiced serious reservations against surrendering the advantage they gave Her Majesty and the crown. Nonetheless, His Excellency's desire to grant the elector's request and alleviate his concerns, as well as securing his widowed mother's dowager seat, and to provide the necessary means to sustain the university of Frankfurt [an der Oder], outweighed other considerations, and he resolved to return the two towns of Frankfurt and Crossen, and the entrenchment, to the elector under certain conditions. Her Majesty's privy councillor, the right honourable Johan Nicodemi Lilienströhm, and His Electoral Highness's privy councillor and lord lieutenant of the county of Ruppin, the right honourable Gerhard Romilian von Kalcheim, called Leuchtmarn, were empowered to arrange this at Schwedt and agree the terms of this evacuation, subject to their rulers' ratification.

1 His Electoral Highness of Brandenburg promises to do his utmost to ensure that Crossen, Frankfurt and the entrenchment do not fall into hostile hands once they have been restored to him by Her Majesty and the Swedish crown. He assures this is binding upon his successors and the entire electoral family.

2 The royal Swedish army or detachments from it retain the freedom to cross through Frankfurt and Crossen, like any other electoral town, at any time. His

---

1 Brandenburg had agreed a two-year ceasefire on 24 July 1641, leaving Sweden in possession of Gardelegen, Driesen, Landsberg, Crossen and Frankfurt on the Oder, thereby securing access between Pomerania and Silesia. In addition, Brandenburg agreed regular contributions to maintain the Swedish garrisons. The agreement was converted into an armistice on 9 May 1643 to last until the end of the war, in return for Sweden returning control of the countryside to Brandenburg administration.

2 Elisabeth Charlotte of Pfalz-Simmern (1597–1660).

3 The Swedish commander. See also **Docs 125 and 162.**

Electoral Highness will expressly instruct his commandant of the entrenchment to allow all Swedish troops, regiments and couriers, or indeed the entire
army, to pass without hindrance.

3 There is to be free and unhindered access through the aforementioned
places at all times for Swedish post and correspondence.

4 The sustenance agreed temporarily by His Electoral Highness in the
armistice [of 1643] for the Crossen and Frankfurt garrisons (calculated at half
a taler for each measure of grain, to total 43,000 talers) is to be reduced to
28,000 talers. The Swedish garrisons that are withdrawn, regardless of their
destination, are to receive 2,333 and 1/3 talers punctually each month, paid
to the Swedish receiver at Landsberg or to whoever is designated by Sweden
for that purpose.

5 His Electoral Highness fervently assures his officials will deliver the agreed
amount punctually before the end of each month without fail. His Electoral
Highness agrees that Sweden may send troops to those communities in
Brandenburg which fail to meet their obligations should, contrary to expectation, any shortfall or delay of more than eight days occur.

6 His Electoral Highness is to be relieved of half of any arrears of any contributions found owing from the two towns after the accounts have been
completed following the evacuation. The remaining half is to be paid in two
instalments to Her Majesty, the first within fourteen days of the evacuations,
and the other fourteen days later, punctually, without fail to appointed
Swedish agents. Troops will be sent to collect the arrears should payment not
be made punctually.

7 All material, ammunition, supplies, troops and reinforcements that may be
sent to Silesia or elsewhere along the Oder through Stettin, Driesen and
Landsberg shall be free to pass Küstrin,[4] Frankfurt and Crossen without
paying tolls, as agreed in the armistice, using barges and boatmen paid
according to the customary rates.

8 The withdrawal of both garrisons is to proceed orderly and none of the
departing troops are to be insulted or harmed.

9 The bridge at Crossen is to be completely destroyed before the garrison's
departure and is not to be rebuilt during the current war without Her
Majesty's permission.

10 The redoubt at Spütlaw is also to be demolished before the troops' departure with the assistance of the electoral subjects. His Electoral Highness is not
to construct any fortifications here or elsewhere during the present war without Her Majesty's permission.

---

[4]   A key fortress on the Oder that remained garrisoned by Brandenburg throughout the
      war.

11 His Electoral Highness's subjects are to provide the necessary ships and transport free of charge to evacuate ammunition, supplies, material and the like belonging to Her Majesty and the Swedish crown. Everything belonging to His Electoral Highness and the towns is to be left behind.

12 All ships, transport oxen and horses used in the evacuation are to be returned afterwards. Should this not occur the equivalent cost is to be deducted from the contributions.

13 This agreement does not affect the treaty of armistice in any way.

The above is to be observed firmly by both parties, and not infringed or altered in any way. Affirmed by the signatures of Her Majesty's and His Electoral Highness's councillors and sent for immediate ratification to His Excellency the field marshal on behalf of Her Majesty and the Swedish crown, and to His Electoral Highness. Done at Greifenhagen, 15 June 1644.

Source: O.S. Rydberg and Carl Hallendorf (eds), *Sveriges Tractater med främmande magter jemte andra dit hörande handlingar*, 5 vols (Stockholm, 1902–9), vol. V, part 2, pp. 576–81.

---

159. Emperor Ferdinand III's invitation to the Imperial Estates to the Westphalian Congress, 29 August 1645

Circular Letter to the various Imperial Estates to send representatives and deputies to the coming Peace Conference, or to empower others there on their behalf.
Dated St Pölten, 29 August 1645. Ferdinand.

You will be aware what was recently discussed and agreed between us and the electors and Estates of the Empire, and the councillors, ambassadors and envoys at the imperial diet at Regensburg and incorporated into the Imperial Recess, that we and the Holy Roman electors found it good and advisable, either in general or individually, to be represented at the coming peace negotiations, as is also permitted and allowed to all other imperial princes by the authority of that Imperial Recess, that they may also send representatives to communicate with our imperial commissioners of the Holy Empire and our principal negotiators. We have followed this agreed Imperial Decision at all times and all and every elector and Estates of the Empire can send their representatives to the said peace talks to join and assist our imperial envoys with advice and thereby exercise their free *Jus suffragii* [rights of suffrage] freely confessed and unhindered by us, as we have already graciously given the Franconian and Swabian Kreise, as well as some princes, to understand through a special reply that we reaffirm here. Our imperial envoys have already proposed proper peace terms at Münster and Osnabrück to the plenipotentiaries of both crowns, France and Sweden, who have also revealed their propositions on 11 June, the Day of the Holy Trinity, at both places, Münster and Osnabrück, and now we have given these propositions mature discussion and consideration and thereby found that they are of notable concern to the electors and Estates of the Empire. We, however, do not want to detract from their current and customary rights and justice in the slightest, and are resolved once and for all and have instructed our envoys accordingly, that they should discuss with the electors' and Estates' representatives, councillors and ambassadors and then respond to the plenipotentiaries of both crowns. Therefore, we have wanted to explain matters to you, and wish, with your gracious request, that you, if you have not already done so, either send your envoy to the said negotiations with sufficient instructions and powers, or entrust another of the Imperial Estates with such powers, and instruct them to appear at the peace negotiations and on their arrival there to assemble and continue with the others in the three imperial curia as is customary in the Holy Roman Empire, as well as to assist our imperial envoys with true word and deed, because we do not want to delay promoting the said peace negotiations and, with God's help, bring them to the desired conclusion as far as the foreign crowns will be content with honourable, proper and Christian means. So to your knowledge etc., given at the town of [St] Pölten, 29 August 1645.

Source: B. Roeck (ed.), *Deutsche Geschichte in Quellen und Darstellung, vol. IV Gegenreformation und Dreißjähriger Krieg 1555–1648* (Stuttgart, 1996), pp. 371–4.

---

160. Ferdinand III's secret instructions to Count Trauttmannsdorff, 16 October 1645

I have considered the long duration of the present war, the ruin thereby inflicted on the Holy Roman Empire and on my hereditary kingdoms and lands in particular, the ever increasing enemy forces and strength against my own ever declining forces and strength and that of my allies, the almost exhausted means, the general sighs for peace and its necessity because of all this. I have also considered the good qualities, long experience in *negotiis* [negotiations] and the constant enthusiastic engagement for my and the common good displayed by Count Trauttmannsdorff, my Senior Court Chamberlain. I am resolved ... to appoint the said Count Trauttmannsdorff to the peace negotiations in Münster and Osnabrück (as my plenipotentiary) and to give him the following secret instructions, which he is to follow and to make peace (*in extremo casu* [as a last resort] and when nothing else can be done).

[1] First, he is (in addition to assisting and promoting the negotiations with the foreign crowns so that no time is lost) to work zealously to ensure that the Estates of the Empire unite as members with myself as head and father, that the disrupted *harmonia imperii* [harmony of the empire] is restored, that the good old trust is reestablished, [and] the proper combination of all Estates is consolidated again so that the foreign enemy crowns are brought to a proper

peace, or that by forcing them back we can resist them more readily. This settlement or unification of the Estates principally involves *duobus capitibus nempe in puncto amnystiae et in puncto gravaminum* [the disputed points of the amnesty and the complaints].

[2] Concerning the *punctum amnystiae* matters are to remain as stated already in the reply to the foreign crowns *in hoc puncto* [on this point]. However, since it is likely that the Estates will not be satisfied with this, this [the amnesty] can be extended in the Empire to 1627 and finaly *in extremo casu* (if the peace or the unification of the Estates cannot be otherwise obtained) granted to the year 1618 (but then only *in imperio* [in the empire]), *exceptis omnimode et per expressum meis regnis et provinciis hereditariis atque negotio Palatino* [but always expressly excluding my kingdoms and hereditary provinces and the Palatine affair] (of which more will be said later). In *meis provinciis* the following *limitationes* [limitations] may be granted (if it is not possible otherwise), that all those who (*vigore amnistiae usque ad annum 30um vel 27um* [by the power of the amnesty of 1630 or 1627]) are to be given back their property in my hereditary lands, are to be tolerated to enjoy and possess the same, or at least (as is the case with other members of the estates in my lands) not hurried away with short emigration deadlines and to keep an eye on the relaxation of the like and not to punish them so strictly.

[3] The difficulties about the complaints relate to the ecclesiastical reservation, the possession of ecclesiastical property and the parity *in camera et consilio aulico* [of appointments in the Reichskammergericht and Reichshofrat]. Trauttmannsdorff is *in genere* [in general] to strive to ensure that these points are settled by the Estates themselves, if possible permanently, or at least settled for a certain time so that the agreement only requires my assent or *confirmatio* [confirmation].

[4] *Ad specialia* [in particular] no concessions are to be made regarding the ecclesiastical reservation, which on the contrary is to remain in *favorem catholicorum* [the Catholics' favour]. The ecclesiastical property should remain *in statu quo* [as at present] or, if the amnesty in the Empire is extended to the year 1618, then to that date, *cum assecuratione reciproca nihil in posterum immutandi* [with mutual assurance, that nothing will be changed in the future].

[5] Concerning parity of religion, things can remain as they are, but three or four Lutherans can be granted in the *consilio aulico*. However, if this point alone holds up peace or unification of the Estates, then religious parity can also be granted, *statutis tamen prius certis normis et regulis, secundum quas in negotiis religionis procedi debeat et non aliter* [after certain norms and rules have been fixed to regulate religious matters and not before].

[The next section discusses the results of the negotiations to this point and instructs Trauttmannsdorff to support Hessen-Darmstadt's claims in the Marburg succession dispute since these have 'justice' on their side.]

[7] Concerning the *negotium Palatiniorum* that were *origo huius belli* [the cause of this war], they must be considered at its end and settled in this treaty. This does not entail, as the other side claims *in plenaria restitutione Palatini, tam quoad dignitatem quam provincias* [the full restitution of the Count Palatine, including both his electoral title and his lands]. Concerning the *dignitet* [dignity, i.e. the electoral title] this must be settled on the basis of the *alternatio* [held alternately with Bavaria] *et nisi ad extremum* [and even in the last resort] this point must not be relinquished, but if finally there is no other way and the electors and Estates consent and regard it as proper, then it can be granted *in octavum electorem* [as an eighth electoral title], but on the condition *ut et nonus ex nostra domo fiat* [that a ninth is created from our lands]. Finally, however, this can also be relinquished if there is no other way.

[8] Concerning the lands, matters are to remain for the Lower Palatinate as agreed already. Regarding the Upper [Palatinate], negotiations are to be directed towards leaving part of the Palatine lands in Bavarian hands, that Bavaria be paid some millions, that the Empire, England and *amici et fautires Palatini* [friends and supports of the Palatinate] contribute something towards this and I do the same (but my contributions should not exceed 3 million payable across six or eight years) and meanwhile Bavaria shall retain a part of the Upper Palatinate *secundum proportionem quotae* [in proportion to the size of the quota] as security for this payment. If it should come *ad restitutionem* [to the restitution] of the lands, the status quo regarding the Catholic religion must be preserved. This completes the matters concerning the Estates of the Empire.

[9] The second part [of the instructions] concerns the foreign crowns. Here the Count must first ensure that all *morae* [obstacles] are removed and the treaty not delayed any longer. Secondly, he must try to reach an agreement with one of the two crowns (which will clearly not want to negotiate, let alone agree, separately). Should he spot an opportunity, however, to negotiate and agree with one or the other crowns, he should press the one with whom he can reach an agreement most easily on proper, easy and secure *conditionibus* [terms]. And since Sweden has given grounds for some separate negotiations, he should negotiate or, failing that, seek grounds for this himself in order to secure agreement with this crown as soon as possible. The *puncto satisfactionis propriae* [issue of settling their claims] concerns the two crowns the most (because the business with the Estates is more a pretext and has already been covered above).

[10] As far as Sweden is concerned, the starting point is the Schönebeck negotiations.[1] Because we had already *in secreto* [secretly] offered them half of Pomerania before this point, it is likely that they will not budge from this

---

[1]   A reference to the negotiations between Sweden and Saxony at Schönebeck on the Elbe in October–November 1635 where, among other things, it was proposed that the German Baltic coast be demilitarised. Sweden rejected the offer as insufficient 'satisfaction' for its involvement in the war.

and, moreover, not be satisfied with it, all of Pomerania may eventually be offered to them, including the bishoprics, [and] if there is no choice, what adjoins the archbishopric of Bremen, as well as Stralsund, Wismar and Rostock, *ad certos annos vel in perpetuum* [for a limited time, or in perpetuity], but on the condition *in feudum praesenti reginae et ipsius lineae masculinae vel tandem etiam foemininae et ultimo etiam ipsis coronae tamen in feudum tantum* [as a fief of the present queen and her male descendants, or also in the female line, and as a last resort of the crown itself, but then only as a fief]. It should be understood that all this is only to be conceded *gradatim* [gradually] one after the other *et non nisi in ultimo necessitatis gradu* [and only as a matter of the last resort].

[11] It is likely that those that [also] want these lands will object, so Electoral Brandenburg can be offered my jurisdiction over the Duchy of Crossen[2] together with a sum of money and so put off as long as possible. If it is not satisfied with this, it can be given Halberstadt as well, together with some districts from Magdeburg, meanwhile the holder of the archbishopric of Magdeburg, as well as Bremen and Mecklenburg, can be given financial compensation. The money must be provided by the Imperial Estates, instead of those that would have been given to Sweden according to the Schönebeck agreement.

[12] Thirdly, to turn to the French and what concerns their satisfaction, the Count is solemnly instructed to stick as long as possible to what was contained in my letter to Electoral Bavaria of 3 April of this year, [but if necessary] finally to grant them Alsace along the Rhine if they return the fortress of Breisach. If this cannot be obtained, also to attach Breisach, and, if peace sticks solely on the Breisgau, finally to drop this as well, but only *non nisi in desperatissmo casu* [in the most desperate circumstances], especially as it is to be hoped that France will not ask for it, or at least will not insist on it, because up till now it has only claimed Alsace up to the Rhine. This point has to be settled with the archduke's representatives.[3] If they will not agree to it, then *in extremo casu* [as a final resort, Trauttmannsdorff] must act before they do.

[13] However, since the Innsbruck line will certainly not surrender this without compensation, a certain sum of money should be agreed with them *pro satisfactione* [as recompense] and part of Carinthia pawned to them, or if necessary nothing. It is better to achieve a peace, even if it excludes another

---

2 Crossen had been pawned to Brandenburg in 1482 and later as a crown fief held from Bohemia, but the Habsburgs claimed Brandenburg remained obliged to pay the duchy's share of Bohemian taxes.

3 This line, known as the Innsbruck or Tirol branch of the Habsburgs, had been created in 1626 when Ferdinand II gave the Tirol, Alsace and the Breisgau to his younger brother, Leopold (1586–1632). The archduke at this point was Leopold's son, Ferdinand Karl (1628–62), who was succeeded in turn by his younger brother Sigismund Franz (1630–65). Their possessions reverted to the main branch in 1665.

line of my house, than to continue the war (the *eventus* [outcome] of which
is *dubius* [doubtful]) [and] the county of Görz [Gorizia] can be sold to the
Venetians. Count Trauttmannsdorff is to exert himself to ensure that, as far as
possible, the Innsbruck line has no claims against me, but rather *amore pacis*
[for the love of peace] bites into this bitter apple.

[The next section covers compensation to the Tirol line of the Habsburg
family if it had to give up Alsace and Breisach.]

[14] It is likely that France will want to claim *sessionem et votum* [a seat and a
vote] in the Empire. Such claims are to be rejected entirely and opposed with
all strength. If, however, they will not budge, this issue is to be postponed
until *ad ultimum* [last] and once all other matters are agreed, and only this
remains, and the electors and Estates of the Empire consent to it, then the
Count is to submit his opinion in a memorandum and await my decision.

[15] Fourthly, most of this will concern the Spaniards. It is known that all our
enemies' *dissegni, intentiones* [plans, intentions], effort and work is directed to
separate the Germans from the Spanish *et secundum illud, divide et vinces* [and
according to the principle divide and conquer], defeat one or the other or
both successively. Therefore, Count von Trauttmannsdorff will above all
ensure that it will not come to such a separation, and will rather let all go to
rack and ruin than this to happen. To avoid this danger, one must ensure that
Spain is included in the peace. Therefore, the Count will remain in good faith
and correspondence with the Spanish plenipotentiaries, stressing to them the
danger, the impossibility of continuing the war, the necessity of peace and a
swift conclusion. Should they reject this, however, or claim they have no
instructions, he should indicate to them that I cannot leave this business, but
will request that the King of Spain, my dearest cousin, brother-in-law and
brother,[4] *cum praefixo certo termino* [with a previously agreed deadline] will
agree to the peace, or, if he does not, he should not hold it against me that I
can no longer assist him. And therefore *in extremo casu* the French can be
given Roussillon and a place in the Netherlands (that one can agree on) so
that they make peace and renounce all *foederibus* [alliances] (that they have
with Portugal, Braganza and Catalonia) and no longer provide aid *sub quovis
praetextu* [under any pretext]. And a deadline of six months is to be set ...

[The next section covers arrangements for an armistice, discharge of the
soldiers and possible financial compensation for the emperor and security for
the peace.]

And this is what I give to von Trauttmannsdorff *loco instructionis* [as
instructions], that he realises that he is to proceed *gradatim* in everything,
and not concede this or that too hastily, but according to circumstances

---

4   Philip IV (1605–65, r.1621). The term 'brother' is used here to denote family solidarity,
     rather than direct relationship. However, Philip was Ferdinand III's brother-in-law, since
     his sister Maria Anna (1608–46) was the emperor's first wife.

and the *ultimos gradus* only *ad ultimum et extremum necessitatis gradum* [final stages only as the last resort in dire straits] and when all hope is gone. I place my gracious trust in his prudence, skill, experience and loyalty, that he will observe the correct tempo and will not act too soon or too late. He and his family remain in my grace and I remain his gracious emperor. Done at my castle in Linz 16 October 1645.

Ferdinand [signed]

Source: Fritz Dickmann, Kriemhild Goronzy, Emil Schieche, Hans Wagner and Ernst Manfred Wermter (eds), *Acta Pacis Westphalicae, series I: Instruktionen, vol. I: Frankreich – Schweden – Kaiser* (Münster, 1962), pp. 440–52.

161. Trauttmannsdorff's final report on his negotiations, 2 February 1649

Most gracious emperor and lord etc.
Now that the German peace is concluded through God's grace, I must report briefly about my negotiations in Münster and Osnabrück and how the terms correspond to Your Imperial Majesty's secret instructions written in your own hand (the original of which is enclosed here).

1 First, Your Imperial Majesty ordered me in the aforementioned instruction of 16 October 1645 above all to achieve peace amongst the imperial Estates and between them and Your Imperial Majesty. Although Bavaria strongly opposed this in 1646 and urged treating first with France in order to obtain better terms from Sweden and the Estates later, events proved that the resolution of the Estates' complaints and the amnesty would form the core of these negotiations, and without agreement on these points no peace could be made with the foreign crowns. Matters thus conformed to Your Imperial Majesty's instructions on this point.

2 Your Imperial Majesty graciously permitted settlement of the amnesty in the Empire by granting restoration of the situation as far back as that of 1618. The settlement is in fact based on the situation six years later in 1624, thus preserving Catholicism in the Upper Palatinate and throughout the imperial Hereditary Lands apart from three small [Protestant] churches to be maintained in Silesia, and Your Imperial Majesty only has to tolerate non-Catholicism in Austria amongst the counts, lords and nobles. In addition, all the confiscations enacted prior to the French and Swedish wars are confirmed.

3 The instructions permitted dealing with the complaints as far as granting religious parity in the Reichshofrat. The result is better and limited to only a few adherents of the Augsburg Confession to be included in the Reichshofrat. In addition, throughout my negotiations, and regardless of what was agreed

in my absence at Osnabrück in May 1647, nothing more was conceded concerning the [imperial] city of Augsburg than restoring its political and religious state to that of 1624. Above all, more of the archbishoprics and bishoprics that were to be granted to the Protestants or to Sweden as satisfaction or compensation were saved for Catholicism than specified in the instructions, as well as thwarting the demand (already conceded by some Catholic electors and princes) for [Protestant worship in]Your Imperial Majesty's lands.

4 The Hessian matter was settled by the participants without the involvement of Your Imperial Majesty's servants and without cost to Your Imperial Majesty.

5 The Palatine matter was settled, so that instead of the three million florins allowed in the instructions Your Imperial Majesty only has to pay 400,000 tlr or 600,000 fl in four years, 20,000 tlr or 30,000 fl to Frederick of the Palatinate's widow, and 10,000 tlr or 15,000 fl to each of the two Palatine princesses should they marry, in all 660,000 fl. In just this point I have saved Your Imperial Majesty 2,340,000 fl.

6 Concerning Sweden's satisfaction, Your Imperial Majesty permitted cession of part of the archbishopric of Bremen, together with all Pomerania and [the port of] Rostock, as well as 1,200,000 tlr specified in imperial orders to your envoys at Osnabrück. On this point Sweden has settled for only half Pomerania, Rostock[1] and only half the 1,200,000 tlr, of which Your Imperial Majesty only has to pay 200,000 tlr, thereby saving one million.

7 Concerning the compensation for Brandenburg, Your Imperial Majesty granted the remainder of the duchy of Crossen[2] some cash and lastly authorised by letter to me to surrender the duchies of Gross-Glogau and Sagan. This matter has been settled without costing Your Imperial Majesty a penny or a hand's breadth of land, and even the duchy of Jägerndorf has been fully preserved.[3]

8 France's satisfaction was settled according to Your Imperial Majesty's instructions with the Breisgau, the four Forest Towns and the bailiwick of the Ortenau. The Innsbruck line[4] was compensated with part of the duchy of Carinthia and three million francs. If the Empire, contrary to hope, fails to grant the Upper Austrian [imperial] line recompense, Your Imperial Majesty is

---

1   In fact, the Mecklenburg port of Wismar, not Rostock, was ceded to Sweden.

2   See **Doc. 160**, note 2.

3   The duchy of Jägerndorf was an autonomous part of the duchy of Silesia that belonged to a junior branch of the Hohenzollerns since 1523. It had been confiscated by Ferdinand II after its ruler, Margrave Johann Georg (1577–1624), had backed the Bohemian Revolt. Brandenburg asserted the claims of Johann Georg's son, Margrave Ernst (1617–42), for its return.

4   The Tirolean branch of the Habsburgs. See **Doc. 160**, para. 13, and **Doc. 168**, articles 73 and 78.

obliged to pay no more than 200,000 tlr of the capital and 10,000 tlr annual interest.

9 Spain was included in the negotiations as long as I was at Münster and there was no separation [of Austria and Spain].

10 Your Imperial Majesty neither granted nor concluded either a particular or a general armistice.

11 The satisfaction of the Swedish military was concluded by Sweden and the imperial Estates long after my departure.

12 Military demobilisation and the restitution of territory [according to the 1624 normative year] is yet to be agreed, so that I cannot be blamed for its outcome.[5]

13 I do not wish to conceal anything from this most loyal account of my dutiful service to Your Imperial Majesty in these peace negotiations. To the best of my knowledge, no one else knew of the powers entrusted me by the imperial instructions and personal letters, but I have dedicated (without vain fame) my loyal silence and industry. Without the concessions I have made, it would not have been possible to make the peace, because the great hopes France had to conquer Naples, Milan and thereby all Italy encouraged Swedish hopes to win more in Germany.

14 This peace finally ended the obligations to Bavaria regarding Upper Austria, but I had already recovered the full use and possession of this province for Your Imperial Majesty's late father at Munich[6] in 1628. Accounts show that Your Imperial Majesty has enjoyed around 20 million florins revenue from Upper Austria between then and this peace, much to Bavaria's regret. Its recovery in the peace was thought to be difficult, because the enemy crowns and imperial Estates would have preferred to have restored the Upper Palatinate to the Heidelberg line,[7] and compensated Bavaria with Upper Austria instead.

15 Your Imperial Majesty is graciously aware of my role in dampening the Friedland fire. Both crown and sceptre were imperiled at that point, and I was one of the few advising the emperor when the final decision was taken.[8]

---

5   These matters were decided at the Nuremberg Execution Congress, see **Docs. 170** and **171**.

6   Trauttmannsdorff negotiated the Treaty of Munich 22 February 1628 that recovered Upper Austria from Bavaria as part of the deal over Ferdinand II's recognition of Bavaria's possession of the Palatine electoral title.

7   That is, Frederick V's son Karl Ludwig (1618–80) who was restored as elector Palatine ruling the Lower Palatinate.

8   Along with Prince Eggenberg and Bishop Anton Wolfradt of Vienna, Trauttmannsdorff was the only person involved in Ferdinand II's final decision in January 1634 to sanction Wallenstein's murder [see also **Doc. 100**].

16 I was the only person Your Imperial Majesty consulted in [your] heroic decision to remain in January 1641 (when Banér appeared in force outside Regensburg), which brought Your Imperial Majesty great renown throughout the Empire and the world.[9]

17 I give my humble thanks that my dutiful service has been richly rewarded with property and honours from Your Imperial Majesty's father and yourself and humbly acknowledge what Your Imperial Majesty and the imperial Estates have freely granted with respect to the present peace.

18 Such merits (without claiming vain fame) allege no value, nor does the grace shown me require any consequence. I pledge myself entirely and most obediently to Your Imperial Majesty, your most honourable family and your descendants, and hope Your Imperial Majesty will remember my many children and their future descendants who may humbly seek promotion (as for me, it is likely God will grant my own final end). I hereby submit myself to your imperial grace. Vienna, Candlemas Day, Anno 1649.

Source: Fritz Dickmann, Kriemhild Goronzy, Emil Schieche, Hans Wagner and Ernst Manfred Wermter (eds), *Acta Pacis Westphalicae, series I: Instruktionen, vol. I: Frankreich – Schweden – Kaiser* (Münster, 1962), pp. 453–7.

SWEDISH POLICY

162. Resolution of the Council of the Realm on War with Denmark and Conditions for Peace in Germany, May 1643

First. It is obvious, from the King of Denmark's public conduct and secret intrigues, that he is contemplating war against us. This appears from a variety of his recent actions; and particularly the provocation he has given us by his occupation of Pinneberg and the diocese of Bremen,[1] ... by his unreasonable treatment of Swedish denizens and subjects (and particularly merchants) at the Sound, and by his assisting the departure of Her Majesty's mother, the Queen Dowager, from this realm.[2] And even though we were to suffer these things (and others like them) in patience, and postpone a reckoning to a more

---

[9] Ferdinand III stayed at the imperial diet when Banér briefly bombarded Regensburg.

[1] This statement ignores the fact that Sweden had no legal jurisdiction in the Empire. The emperor had allowed one of Christian IV's sons to become administrator of the archbishopric of Bremen after the death of the previous administrator in 1634. It was precisely this sort of imperial–Danish cooperation that alarmed Sweden.

[2] A reference to Gustavus's grief-stricken widow, Maria Eleonora of Brandenburg (1599–1645), who fell out with both her daughter, Christina, and Chancellor Oxenstierna after her husband's death. She escaped disguised as a commoner to Denmark where she was given temporary asylum by a reluctant Christian IV.

convenient time, there are now added to them such practices and enterprises as can neither be passed over nor postponed without the irremediable injury and certain destruction of the realm, since they openly proclaim that the determination to make war against us is already taken, and all they are working for now is to prepare a proper opportunity: as may be seen from their intrigues in Poland and Russia, and also from the way they treat us at the Sound, which is insufferable, and contrary to their agreements. For they now lay an excise on all imports of foreign liquor, and they arrest, unload and confiscate practically all Swedish ships and cargoes, under one pretext or another, so that scarcely anybody now may venture to avail himself of his right to sail the seas and trade freely; ... and lastly their intentions are reflected in the innovations which they have introduced [in the tolls] at Ruden, in the recent Danish demonstration (undertaken without any imminent danger), when the King of Denmark put to sea with his entire fleet, and mobilized all his forces on land – either with a view to attacking us at home or abroad, or to intervene as a third party (as they say) and force us to accept such a settlement of the [German] war as may suit himself, and thereafter turn his arms against us. These are matters of such importance that they must be considered in good time; and we must take counsel together how such misfortunes may (with God's help) be averted, and whether we have cause enough to justify a war? And if so, whether we ought to take the initiative against the enemy, or await his attack?

2. Next, assuming that we have full and satisfactory grounds for waging a just war, what steps we can take to avoid it, so that the country does not become involved in hostilities at an untimely moment; or, if we do become involved in them, how the war is to be conducted?

3. Since the peace-negotiations [at Westphalia] have been generally agreed upon, and the day fixed upon which the congress is to meet, it is necessary to discuss what indemnity is to be proposed, and what insisted on; in which connection we must make up our minds whether it will be advisable to demand and insist upon Pomerania, or whether it would not be better to consider some other satisfaction, so that our diplomats and soldiers may shape their conduct accordingly.

All these matters having been fully canvassed in the course of the last few days, and argument heard for and against, in the light of such reports as have come to hand and such information as could be elicited, we have at length decided and resolved as follows:

I

First. That it is the King of Denmark's intention to hurt, hinder, belittle and bring into contempt Her Majesty and the crown of Sweden, wherever and whenever he can; to incite one enemy after another against us; to distract our forces as much as possible; and to stir up trouble in the country as he shall find opportunity. Against these things we must take counter-measures in good time, suffering some of them in patience, and avoiding a conflict (as hitherto) as long as it is a question only of plans and intentions, rather than of overt acts. But now that projects are turning into realities, it is no longer possible to sit still in cover, or try to gain time: we must either oppose a timely resistance, and look to the country's interests, or expect to be overwhelmed by a sudden attack ... And therefore the lords of the Council find that the grounds and reasons for war with Denmark are sound, strong and satisfactory; and that we may begin hostilities with a good conscience, as being a righteous war; ... so that if the King of Denmark continues taking toll, confiscating, interrupting navigation in the Sound, and other such proceedings, and is not to be moved from that course of action, then our best course would be to begin the war (as well now as later!) and rather throw its burdens upon him, than sit waiting to be attacked by him at home.

II

Next, it seems necessary and prudent to make an attempt to smooth out the disputes with Denmark by trying the means which are provided by treaty, and have been usual in the past ... It would not be a bad thing, either, to seek an opportunity to revive our old friendship with the Tsar by sending an embassy to him, and thus as far as possible forestall any Danish plots and take the edge off any controversies that may arise. It is particularly necessary to get in touch with Field Marshal Lindorm [i.e. Lennart] Torstensson,[3] and put him in the picture about the whole situation, and our policy in regard to it; and to order him to give the highest priority to keeping his army in such a state that he may be able to move to the coast in the autumn, either through the Mark of Brandenburg or on the other side of the Elbe through Lüneburg territory, as he may find most convenient, so that when the Danish forces withdraw he may be able to follow them and take up his winter quarters in Holstein and Jutland ... In the meantime, while all this is being quietly and secretly arranged, it might be as well to give advance notice to some of the leading Estates, confidentially inform them of the position, and get their approval, by way of additional security in case things should turn out ill: this has been usual in the past, and was always done by His late Majesty in important matters which involved serious consequences. And since we concluded an alliance with the States-General of the Netherlands three years ago for no other purpose than to safeguard trade and navigation in the Baltic and North Seas, and in the Sound, they too should be written to, their assistance should be sought, and they should be stimulated to make the alliance effective by cooperating with us. Private merchants and shippers in Holland should also be induced to help us, either with money, or by such other evidences of goodwill as may be most convenient ...

---

3   Torstensson had commanded Sweden's army in Germany since 1641 and was campaigning in Moravia and Silesia when the Council made this resolution. His health had been broken during his captivity in an imperial prison 1632–3 and he resigned command after defeating Denmark in 1645. See also **Docs. 125** and **158**.

III

Concerning the indemnity for the crown of Sweden, ... and the terms which we must formulate and insist on in the peace negotiations, it seems very clear that this was the real reason why the King of Denmark put himself forward as mediator; his idea being that he could put obstacles in the way of our gaining anything that would be convenient or useful to us, and also obtain some advantages for himself. It is also the case that this question of indemnity has deterred many from seeking our friendship, and particularly the Elector of Brandenburg, who is afraid that we may seek our satisfaction in Pomerania. And this is not less a matter of concern to the King of Denmark – indeed, it is the thing which he finds hardest to swallow; it made him arm this year; it provoked the lively correspondence between Denmark and Poland. Since Pomerania is such a thorn in the flesh both to our neighbours and to many others, and arouses such jealousy against us, we have hitherto claimed indemnity in general terms, and neither specified nor pressed for Pomerania. But if the thing be soberly considered, there is certainly no solution more convenient, more practicable and more honourable for the Holy Roman Empire than to allow the Swedish crown to keep Pomerania as satisfaction for war expenses, to recognize the crown as holding an imperial fief, in the same way as the King of Denmark holds Holstein, and to allow the crown a vote in the Upper Saxon Kreis, at the imperial diet and at all other meetings of the Estates. We should be permitted to retain the Pomeranian ports in order to secure the Baltic coast against the House of Austria, and other ill-disposed powers; with full freedom to raise mercenaries, and to refuse this privilege to our neighbours. It would give us the possibility of always being able to keep an eye on our neighbours at close range, and in time of war we should be in a position to take them in the rear. There are many such reasons; and they apply equally to Wismar. But when we consider all the opposition which the proposal will arouse, and the counter-mines which Poland and Denmark are preparing, and will prepare; the great difficulty of bringing the Emperor to assent to it; and the antagonistic reaction it will produce in the Elector of Brandenburg (now, after the extinction of the ducal house of Pomerania, the guaranteed successor) – there is no doubt that while we may certainly propose Pomerania as our indemnity we shall not get it unless we are prepared to go on fighting for it; and it is easy to envisage what difficulties that might land us in, especially if the peace negotiations were to break down on that point only. All this is to say nothing of the fact that even in peace-time Pomerania can be held only if it is given strong garrisons; for the towns and Estates of Pomerania dislike Swedish rule, and malevolent neighbours will always have designs on it, especially at times when the Swedish crown may happen to be in difficulties, either at home or with some neighbour. So that if one looks squarely at the problem, it is clear that satisfaction in Pomerania is not obtainable by negotiation, but is bound to provoke all sorts of cabals and conspiracies against us in one place or another; and therefore it would be wisest not to incur the odium of it, especially since there are few powers who look with any favour on the demand for satisfaction, even when framed in general terms, and still fewer, when it is particularized. If we pitch on some other territory, the same objections will apply, and someone else will have to pay the price, wherever we choose; to say nothing of the fact that no other territory lies so conveniently for Sweden. It seems therefore that the most practicable line is not directly to declare our views on Pomerania, but to press as strongly as possible for the payment of the army's arrears, either in money or in land, without specifying where; and if they choose to pay in money, to ask then that Pomerania and Wismar be handed over as security, and that the terms of payment, and the instalments, be carefully laid down; and if these terms are not complied with, that the securities fall to the crown in perpetual possession ... This, it seems, might be proposed with some show of reason, and without arousing the jealousy of any interested party; and in such a case it might be possible to reach agreement in advance with the Elector of Brandenburg (as the party principally concerned) and by playing on his hope of acquiring Pomerania induce him to cooperate in the peace negotiations, and in the contentment of the soldiery, or at the very least keep him in play so that he did not actually enter into an alliance with Denmark and Poland against us ...

The amount of money which might reasonably be asked, and should be asked, for our expenses, might first be fixed at 2 million rdr for every year of the war, which makes 26 millions, since the war is now in its 13th year; but this might be gradually cut down to a million a year, or 13 millions in all. And if the contentment of the soldiery be deducted from that, this seems not unreasonable. If we estimate the soldier's arrears at from 1 to 5 millions, and the [imperial] Estates undertook to pay it, the crown would receive (over and above the demands of the army) some 8 or at the absolute minimum 6 millions, and besides that would hold in pawn either the whole of Pomerania, or Western Pomerania, Wismar and certain dependent territories.

These are to be declared to be the minimum terms upon which Her Majesty will be satisfied, and it is to be presumed that nobody can reasonably object to them if the crown can be induced to part with the territorial advantages now in its hands. [Better terms should, however, be obtained if at all possible.] These are the ultimate and final proposals for indemnity; and the members of the Council do not support them as good in themselves, but because seeing the great dangers which threaten the country if the war goes on, as well as others which seem probable, they think such terms preferable to a continuance of hostilities ...

Source: Michael Roberts (ed.), *Sweden as a Great Power 1611–1697. Government: Society: Foreign Policy* (London, 1968), pp. 155–60; from *Axel Oxenstiernas skrifter och brevvexling*, vol. I, part i, pp. 580–7.

163. Negotiations in Westphalia: Queen Christina to Johan Oxenstierna and Johan Adler Salvius, 10 April 1647 [OS]

Gentlemen,

I add these few words in my own hand to my official letter, in order to discover to you my alarm lest the peace negotiations, which until this moment have borne so favourable an aspect, should be blocked; and this for reasons of which I am totally ignorant. And that you may be in no uncertainty as to my wishes, [this is to inform you that] you may certainly take it for granted that I desire above all things a safe and honourable peace. And since the question of our indemnity has already been disposed of, and the only matters still to be arranged are the contentment of the soldiery and the grievances of the [E]states of the Empire, it is my will that you keep the negotiations going on an amicable footing, until Erskine has arrived and acquainted you with the nature of his commission; after which you will without delay bring the negotiation to a satisfactory conclusion: for the [imperial] [E]states, and in the matter of our indemnity and the contentment of the soldiery, you will obtain the best terms that are to be had without risk of a rupture; and you will refrain from protracting the negotiations, as you have done in the past. And if you fail in this, you may look to it how you will answer for it to God, to the Estates of the Realm, and to me. If it is a matter of concern to you to escape my severest displeasure, if you have no ambition to answer for your conduct in my presence, and be forced to stand before me with a countenance alternating between white and red, you will take care not to allow yourselves to be deflected from your object by the imaginings of ambitious men. For you may be perfectly assured that neither personal eminence, nor aristocratic backing, will deter me from manifesting to the whole world the displeasure with which I view unreasonable proceedings. For I am very sure that if it went ill with the treaty I should find myself, by your fault, involved in a labyrinth from which neither you, nor those whose intrigues were responsible, would be very likely to extricate me. You will do well, then, to have a care what you do. I have no doubt that you will; and I write this simply for your information, having such full reliance upon your discretion that I confidently expect (with God's help) a successful outcome to these long-drawn negotiations. And if in these matters you continue to give evidence of your fidelity, you may rest assured that upon your return you will find me always your well-affectioned
Christina.

Source: Michael Roberts (ed.), *Sweden as a Great Power 1611–1697. Government: Society: Foreign Policy* (London, 1968), pp. 160–1; from Arckenholtz, *Mémoires concernant Christine, Reine de Suède*, vol i, pp. 110–11.

164. Christina to Salvius, 10 April 1647 [OS]

Your various letters have given me a clear idea of the present state of the peace negotiations; and I see very plainly how hard you have been working to put an end to the long and bloody war which for so many years has afflicted the whole of Europe. But I also deduce from all this that there are those who are doing their best to spin out the discussions, if not indeed to wreck the treaty altogether. I shall not fail to reward your zeal and fidelity. As to the other party, I intend to act in such a way that the whole world will know that the fault does not lie with me; and I shall let them see that not even the R.C. [Rikscantzler: i.e. Axel Oxenstierna] can move the world with his little finger ... The letter which accompanies this [**Doc. 163**] is directed to both of you, and you are to deliver it to G[reve, i.e. count] J[ohan] O[xenstierna]: although I say harsh things about you in it, they are not meant to apply to you, but to him only. Contrive that d'Avaux[1] is made aware of the contents, so that they may know where the fault lies: I should not like them to get wrong ideas about me. I am sending Erskine to you to let you know more at large about the contentment of the soldiery: I have done as much as I could about this, and do not doubt that you will continue to do everything possible to help on the negotiation: you may be entirely assured that I will support you on this question, and when at last God sends you home with a peace, I will reward your services by appointing you to the Council of the Realm, which as you know is the highest honour to which any Swede may aspire; and if there were any higher degree of honour, I would not hesitate to confer it on you. But it will not be done, I fancy, without arousing a good deal of ill-feeling ... For the rest, I trust you to press on with the negotiations with the same admirable fidelity which you have always shown upon all occasions. Try above all to keep the French in a good opinion of me, so that the dislike of that nation shown by a certain party [Johan Oxenstierna] does not rebound to my hurt. I hope my actions will make it clear what my real sentiments are.

I recommend to you the interests of Count Magnus[2] as though they were my own. If you could give me a hint or a suggestion as to how I could confer Benfeld[3] upon him, or some other considerable territory, I should be only too pleased. I would much like to give him Benfeld, but I hesitate to do so until I know your opinion. Keep this to yourself at all costs, until I can find out whether it can be done ... But speak to M. d'Avaux about it. I flatter myself that he is too courteous to make any difficulty about doing so considerable a

---

[1]   One of the main French diplomats at the peace congress. See **Doc. 165**, note 1.

[2]   Count Magnus de la Gardie (1623–86) was Christina's favourite courtier and Swedish ambassador to France. He headed the regency for Charles X during 1660–72 and was chancellor until dismissed in 1676.

[3]   Benfeld was a small fortified town in southern Alsace which the Swedes had captured in 1632. The local Swedish commander handed over all other Alsatian towns to the French during the crisis following the defeat at Nördlingen. Benfeld's significance grew as it became obvious that France wanted to annex Alsace.

service to one of his most affectionate friends and servants; or rather, I think he would not take it amiss if I were to say to him that by working for a friend of mine (and thereby making him a friend *of his*) he would give me one of the most signal marks of affection that I ever solicited of him. I beg you, then, to assure M. d'Avaux of the esteem I have for his person; tell him that the private services he has rendered me are so considerable that I should be mortally disappointed if I were deprived of the hope of repaying at least a part of what he has done for me.

With this I close. God keep you. Take care that the roan doesn't kick over the traces! I am your always well-affectioned
Christine.
Do let me know what sort of a face G.J.O. makes when he reads my letter to you both.

Source: Michael Roberts (ed.), *Sweden as a Great Power 1611–1697. Government: Society: Foreign Policy* (London, 1968), pp. 161–3; from Arckenholtz, *Mémoires concernant Christine, Reine de Suède*, vol. i, pp. 112–15.

FRENCH POLICY

165. Abel Servien's memorandum, 3 February 1646[1]

I have just been told by Count Wittgenstein that the Brandenburg elector has finally decided to recognise the king's title of majesty in his letters. His Eminence[2] is very glad that, during his ministry, a new honour has been bestowed upon his majesty, despite his very young age. Indeed, no such recognition was ever given to his predecessors by the electors of Saxony, Brandenburg or the Palatinate. It is to His Eminence's glory to have achieved this, especially as I have become aware that less advantageous discussions had taken place with the Brandenburg envoy.

We think highly of the Duke of Bavaria's actions towards the king; so highly in fact that we would recommend that we should not attack or ruin him as we have done in previous years. It is certain that if he has neither army nor credit in these negotiations, the king's affairs will suffer for it. We also

----

[1] Abel Servien (1593–1659) was an experienced French diplomat who had helped secure the Peace of Cherasco ending the Mantuan War (1628–31) and was chief negotiator at the Westphalian Congress alongside Claude de Mesmes, Count d'Avaux (1595–1650). He championed a pragmatic foreign policy intended to maximise French territorial gains, in contrast to d'Avaux who favoured solidarity with the Catholic powers. Servien's memorandum was sent to Hughes de Lionne (1611–71), secretary to Cardinal Jules Mazarin (1602–61), who was the leading statesman during the minority of Louis XIV (1638–1715) after 1643.

[2] A reference to Mazarin. Withholding recognition was one of the few bargaining options open to minor powers like Brandenburg.

recognise that the Swedes disagree with him over the transfer of Alsace to France. You will see this yourself from the pamphlet in Latin I am enclosing here which has been distributed here by the Spanish in which he [Bavaria] fares no better than ourselves.

I therefore believe we could propose a ceasefire in the Empire to last two to three months, in case an important military incident changes the current trend of events which favours peace for France. If Bavaria is defeated, we will lose a great deal. If the Imperialists are defeated, the Swedes will become insufferable. If the Swedish army is ruined, it will be even worse: the emperor will harden his terms and Bavaria will no longer be as favourable towards us. Moreover, how would the king's army survive after crossing the Rhine? It would certainly be doomed if sent back there without first securing a base and line of retreat. All things considered, I am sure that a ceasefire at the start of the campaign would be useful. Perhaps we could secure some freedom of action this side of the Rhine and attempt to recapture the places still held there by the Spanish.

[Servien argues that if the Swedes opposed a ceasefire, France could still let Bavaria know informally that the French army would not cross the Rhine provided the Bavarians did not fight the Swedish and Hessen-Kassel forces. The French could concentrate on taking fortresses like Frankenthal, Ehrenbreitstein and Benfeld (all west of the Rhine) whilst pointing to the lack of bases east of the river as an excuse to the Swedes for not crossing.]

These are my own thoughts and I would rather His Eminence than myself considered them to identify the problems they may contain. His Eminence will be able to do this much better than me. It seems to me that our distrust of Bavaria's behaviour prevents us from arranging such a truce before. Today, however, it inclines so towards France that, in this particular negotiation at least, we have nothing to fear.

I forgot to mention that we asked Count Courval[3] to befriend the elector of Mainz since we are nearing the conclusion of our affairs and need all the friends we can get. I know that not everything depends on them, but it is good to have powerful allies in the Empire to promote our interests. As regards a separate treaty,[4] we know that the Catholic princes and the Calvinists will never agree to it, but the Swedes and the Protestants would favour it.

During the past few days we have had a little disagreement with the imperial Estates gathered in this town [Münster] concerning the difficulties they encountered in sending us a deputation, similar to those the ones in Osnabrück sometimes send to the Swedish plenipotentiaries.[5] We were upset

---

3   Charles Christophe de Mazencourt (1608–50), viscount de Courval, commandant of Mainz city after its capture by France in October 1644.
4   The fear that Sweden would sign a separate peace with the emperor.
5   The envoys of the Catholic imperial Estates met in Münster, where the French delegation was based, while those of the Protestants gathered in Osnabrück where the Swedes were. The Catholics followed the imperial lead in maintaining the Empire should negotiate as a whole, and not separately.

at first, as we cannot have them do less for us than for the Swedes. On the other hand, we had to be gracious to the envoys of this assembly, since it is in our interest to retain their friendship. Their excuse for refusing to meet us was that the emperor's plenipotentiaries do not summon the Estates' envoys to see them, but instead go to the assembly themselves when they have business to conclude with the Estates. They claimed the envoys sent to the Swedes were not part of the assembly of Osnabrück, but individuals who, as friends of the Swedish plenipotentiaries, will have discussed current affairs with them and reported back to the assembly. They added that the assembly at Osnabrück is not as regimented or solemn as the assembly in Münster where proceedings are more dignified. In the end, the disagreement was resolved to the satisfaction of both parties. We have just been told that the envoys will be joined by the Brandenburg envoy in addition to those of Mainz and Bavaria who led the deputation. They will meet us on the first day to ask for clarification on some points of our formal reply [to the imperial proposals], especially the question of [territorial] satisfaction. We believe that they will not forget to add more arguments to compel us to withdraw some of our demands.

(If France were to follow the example of the Dutch in their negotiations with Spain and firmly refuse to give any ground, Spain would be obliged to submit itself to us, just as they did to the Dutch.[6])

Source: Elke Jarnut and Rita Bohlen (eds), *Acta Pacis Westphalicae, series I: Korrespondenzen, section B, vol. 3, part 1: Die französische Korrespondenzen 1645–6* (Münster, 1999), pp. 357–60.

BAVARIAN POLICY

166. The Truce of Ulm, 14 March 1647

1. The two crowns of Sweden and France, together with their allies and adherents in Germany[1] have solemnly agreed with His Electoral Highness of Bavaria, and his brother, His Electoral Highness of Cologne, together with their coadjutors,[2] to suspend hostilities from this day until a general peace in the empire. Sweden, France and their allies will take no hostile act in word or deed against their Electoral Highness of Bavaria and Cologne who are free to use all the Bavarian, Upper and Lower Palatine lands and subjects (except those of the bishopric of Eichstätt) to support their own troops. Likewise,

---

6   The Spanish had just offered a truce to the Dutch on 28 January 1646, which was converted into peace on 8 January 1647 and eventually ratified and formally enacted on 15 March 1648 at Münster.

1   That is, Hessen-Kassel.

2   That is, the successors designate in Ferdinand of Cologne's ecclesiastical territories.

their Electoral Highnesses of Bavaria and Cologne agree to reciprocate and in addition His Electoral Highness of Bavaria agrees to withdraw his imperial army corps from the forces of His Roman Imperial Majesty and will not burden any land outside his own with transit or billets.

[A formulaic statement followed that the treaty was not intended to harm the emperor or Empire. Article 2 permitted both Sweden and the emperor, if he so demanded, to transit through all Bavarian territory except the core duchies.]

3 It is further agreed that Sweden is allowed to occupy the two [imperial] cities of Memmingen and Überlingen to enhance its own security until the general peace. Sweden has long insisted on this and the electoral Bavarian deputies have consented to evacuate the Bavarian garrisons after obtaining agreement from envoys of both cities. Sweden has also promised to remove its garrisons from the [Bavarian] towns of Rain, Donauwörth, Wembdingen and Mindelheim and their associated villages and possessions and to return these to His Electoral Highness of Bavaria for his better security. [Both sides agreed to return captured artillery.]

[Article 4 obliged Bavaria to return occupied fortresses and towns to Duke Eberhard III of Württemberg after ratification of the truce, except for Heidenheim which the French held. Article 5 neutralised and demilitarised the imperial city of Augsburg where the Protestant inhabitants were promised the 'free exercise of religion' and to be treated the same as Catholics for military tax purposes. Article 6 allowed discharged Bavarian soldiers to be recruited by France, Sweden and their allies, but not by their enemies, except Venice which had just been attacked by the Turks. Article 7 allowed military personnel to travel between billets provided they obtained special passes. Article 8 stipulated extradition of deserters and delinquents. Article 9 stated that marauding would not constitute breach of the truce, but also that marauders were to be punished. Article 10 allowed free trade throughout the lands covered by the truce, except for trade in arms and ammunition to enemies of France and Sweden. Article 11 proposed an exchange of prisoners. Article 12 obliged the elector of Cologne, once he ratified the truce, to provide France and Sweden with a list of all imperial troops and his own forces in his lands and to 'clear' the imperialists from his lands. Bavaria and Cologne were not to permit Hessen-Darmstadt to recruit in their territories nor to hinder the Allied Crowns and their allies from driving their enemies from the lands of His Electoral Highness of Cologne, should he not do this himself.]

13 Furthermore, it is agreed that this separate armistice shall not prejudice any general armistice agreed at Osnabrück and Münster on the basis of *uti possidetis* [current possessions], or indeed any general peace treaty that may be concluded …

Source: Jean Du Mont (ed.), *Corps universal diplomatique du droit des gens*, 8 vols (Amsterdam and Brussels, 1726–31), vol. 6, part 1, pp. 380–3.

18

The Peace of Westphalia

The Westphalian congress convened in 1643 in the form agreed in the Hamburg Peace Preliminaries of December 1641 [**see Doc. 157**]. France and Sweden presented a united front, but their delegations were quartered respectively in Münster and Osnabrück. This reflected the Habsburg interpretation of the issues as two separate wars; one against Sweden which began in 1630, the other with France after 1635. Sweden's championing of German Liberty meant that constitutional and religious matters were mainly discussed in Osnabrück along with Swedish demands for territorial 'satisfaction' and the financial 'contentment' of its army. The latter was essential to allow Sweden to make peace, since it did not have enough money to meet its obligations to its officers under the Powder Barrel Convention [**see Doc. 104**].

The separation of the delegations was also convenient for France which wanted to disassociate itself from any concessions within the Empire which would undermine German Catholicism. The imperial Estates' representatives convened separately, with the Protestants assembling in Osnabrück and the Catholics in Münster. Individual envoys dealt directly with the French, Swedish and imperial delegations, but all formal negotiations were conducted through the constitutional framework of the three status groups of electors, princes and imperial cities. This contributed to the length of the talks, since letters had to be exchanged between Münster and Osnabrück, but it preserved the Empire's established structure in the face of Swedish-backed plans from the radical Protestant minority to reorganise the imperial Estates along confessional lines. This had been the Palatine programme in the Protestant Union and had been adopted by Sweden in the League of Heilbronn [**see Docs 4, 69, 96**]. Its realisation would have entrenched religious division in the Empire by replacing traditional status distinctions with confessional ones. The defeat of this programme, which was opposed by France, enabled the peacemakers to defuse religious tensions. Special safeguards were included in the constitutional revisions, allowing Protestant and Catholic imperial Estates to vote separately in two confessional blocks in the imperial diet when religious issues proved controversial.

The congress was intended to settle the parallel Spanish–Dutch and Franco-Spanish wars. Negotiations to end both were conducted in Münster, but only Spain and the Dutch reached agreement in their Treaty of Münster, signed on 15 May 1648 (English translation available in C. Jenkinson (ed.), *A Collection of All the Treaties of Peace, Alliance, and Commerce between Great Britain and other Powers* 3 vols (London, 1785; reprint: New York, 1969), vol. I, pp. 10–44). Spain abandoned its efforts to subdue the Dutch and recognised their republic as an independent state. Unfortunately, peace with the Dutch enabled Spain to concentrate its dwindling resources for its other war with France. Meanwhile, the prospect of peace in the Empire encouraged the French government to believe it could now defeat Spain. French and Spanish representatives continued talking in Münster until the summer of 1649, but failed to reach agreement. Both powers fought for another decade before accepting the Peace of the Pyrenees on much the same terms they had before them in Münster.

Peace in the Empire came when Ferdinand III finally granted French demands and promised not to support Spain in the ongoing Franco-Spanish conflict. This concession was contained in the treaty signed in Münster on 24 October 1648 by France with representatives of the emperor and Empire. The original was in Latin and called *Instrumentum Pacis Monasteriense* (IPM). The *Instrumentum Pacis Osnabrugense* (IPO) was signed the same day in Osnabrück between Sweden and representatives of the emperor and Empire. Both treaties were considered part of the same settlement and many terms were identical [**Docs 167–8**]. The IPO settled the constitutional and religious issues in the Empire by adjusting the Peace of Prague, but confirmed the emperor's gains in his hereditary lands. It also satisfied most of Sweden's territorial demands and arranged compensation for those (mainly Protestant) princes who suffered from this. The compensation involved converting the north German ecclesiastical lands previously under elected Protestant administrators into fully secularised hereditary principalities. The IPM confirmed these arrangements and settled France's territorial demands in Alsace and the obligation that Austria would not assist Spain in its current war.

Thousands of copies were printed for distribution throughout Europe and were soon translated into the major languages. Each treaty runs to around 20,000 words. As there are a number of easily accessible older English translations of most terms of both treaties (see http://www.pax-westphalica.de), presentation here concentrates on summarising *all* terms and highlighting how far the IPM corresponded to the IPO.

167. The Peace of Osnabrück, 24 October 1648

[The passages in Roman type are direct translations from the original text, whereas those in italics are summaries of the relevant articles.]

[Divine invocation:]
In the name of the most holy and indivisible Trinity, amen.

[Preamble:]
Be it known to each and everyone it may concern in whatever way: that after the disputes and internal troubles which began many years ago in the Roman Empire and spread to such an extent that they drew in not only all Germany, but also several neighbouring kingdoms, especially Sweden and France, thereby causing a long and bitter war [lists the principal belligerents].

Consequently, the plenipotentiary envoys of both sides gathered at the appointed place and time [lists the principal envoys] and agreed in the presence of, and with the acceptance and consent of the electors, princes and Estates of the Holy Roman Empire to the honour of God and the salvation of Christendom, the following terms of peace and friendship.

Art. I [Universal peace] [= 1 IPM][1]

That there be a Christian, universal and perpetual peace, and a true and sincere friendship and amity between his sacred imperial majesty, the House of Austria, and all his allies and adherents, and the heirs and successors of each and everyone of them, chiefly the Catholic king [of Spain], and the electors, princes and Estates of the Empire, on the one side; and her sacred royal majesty, the kingdom of Sweden, her allies and adherents, and the heirs and successors of each of them, especially his most Christian majesty [of France] and the relevant electors, princes and Estates of the Empire, on the other side; and that this peace shall be observed and cultivated sincerely and seriously, so that each party promotes the other's benefit, honour and advantage, and that a true neighbourliness, sincere peace and genuine friendship grows afresh and flourishes between the Roman Empire and the kingdom of Sweden.

Art. II [Comprehensive amnesty] [= 2 IPM]

Both sides grant the other a perpetual oblivion and amnesty for all that, wherever and however, has been done to the other since the beginning of these troubles, so that neither for any of those things, nor upon any other account or pretext whatsoever, any act of hostility, enmity, vexation or hindrance shall be exercised, suffered or caused to be exercised, either to persons or their status, property or security, either by oneself or by others, in private or openly, directly or indirectly, under the form of law, or by violence, either within or in any place whatsoever without the Empire, notwithstanding all former compacts to the contrary. Instead, each and every injury, act of violence, hostility, damage and expense inflicted by either side, both before and during the war, by words, in writing or by deed, shall be entirely forgotten without regard to persons or things, so that whatever [recompense] may be demanded by the other, shall be entirely forgotten.

Art. III [General restitution on the basis of the amnesty]

Art. III para. 1 [= 5 IPM] *The imperial Estates (including the imperial knights) and their subjects were to be restored to their status of 1618*

Art. III para. 2 [+/– 6 IPM] *There were exceptions to this general reservation, to be specified in other clauses, but it was to guide all subsequent court verdicts in future disputes*

---

1   The notes correlate the terms of the Peace of Osnabrück (IPO) between the Empire, emperor and Sweden with those of the Peace of Münster (IPM) signed on the same day between the Empire, emperor and France. Key: +/– denotes approximately the same wording; = denotes identical or nearly identical wording.

Art. IV [Specific restitution terms]

Art. IV para. 1 [= 7 IPM] *Certain cases were to be handled differently, but those which were not expressly mentioned were not to be considered as unsettled*

Art. IV para. 2 [= 10 IPM] *The Palatinate was one such special case*

Art. IV para. 3 [= 11 IPM] *The Palatine electoral title (4th in order of precedence), along with the Upper Palatinate and the county of Cham, were to be retained by Maximilian of Bavaria and his successors*

Art. IV para. 4 [= 12 IPM] *Bavaria relinquished its claim that the emperor refund its war expenses (set at 13 million fl) or grant Upper Austria in lieu of this*

Art. IV para. 5 [= 13 IPM] *The Palatinate was compensated with a new electoral title, ranked eighth*

Art. IV para. 6 [= 14 IPM] *The Lower Palatinate was to be restored to its political and religious status of 1618*

Art. IV para. 7 [= 15 IPM] *The elector of Mainz was permitted to redeem the districts of the Forest Road [Bergstraße] that had been pawned to the Palatinate in 1463*

Art. IV para. 8 [= 16 IPM] *The elector of Trier, in his capacity as bishop of Speyer and Worms, was free to petition the courts to resolve a long-standing dispute over his right to ecclesiastical revenues from the Palatinate*

Art. IV para. 9 [= 17 IPM] *The Palatine branch of the Wittelsbachs would recover the fourth electoral title and the Upper Palatinate, should the Bavarian branch die out. If this occurred, the new eighth title would cease*

Art. IV para. 10 [= 18 IPM] *These terms did not affect the rights of the Neuburg branch of the Wittelsbachs, as previously agreed with the Palatine branch in agreements confirmed by former emperors*

Art. IV para. 11 [= 19 IPM] *The Palatinate could obtain any vacant part of the Jülich inheritance, provided it could prove its claim*

Art. IV para. 12 [= 20 IPM] *The emperor would pay 100,000 tlr annually for four years from 1649 to enable Elector Palatine Karl Ludwig to discharge his obligations to provide for his brothers*[2]

Art. IV para. 13 [= 21 IPM] *The Palatine family and their servants were not to be excluded from the general amnesty*

Art. IV para. 14 [= 22 IPM] *The elector Palatine and his brothers were to renounce claims to the Upper Palatinate as long as the Bavarian line continued, and were to be loyal to the emperor and Empire*

Art. IV para. 15 [= 23 IPM] *The emperor would make a one-off payment of 20,000 tlr to the elector Palatine's widowed mother plus 10,000 tlr to each of his sisters if they married*[3]

Art. IV para. 16 [= 24 IPM] *The Palatinate was not to infringe the rights of the counts of Leiningen and Dagsburg*

---

[2] Karl Ludwig (1618–80), eldest surviving son of Frederick V. At that point, he had four surviving brothers: Ruprecht (1619–80, better known as Prince Rupert of the Rhine), Moritz (1621–52), Eduard (1624–63) and Philipp (1627–50).

[3] Elizabeth Stuart (1596–1662), wife of Frederick V. The four surviving daughters were Elisabeth (1619–80), Louise Maria (1622–1709), Henriette Maria (1626–51) and Sophie (1630–1714). Only the latter two married.

Art. IV para. 17 [= 25 IPM] *nor infringe those of the Franconian, Swabian and Rhenish imperial knights*

Art. IV para. 18 [= 26 IPM] *Four of the emperor's supporters were allowed to retain the Palatine fiefs they had received during the war, but were to accept Palatine overlordship*

Art. IV para. 19 [= 27 IPM] *Freedom of worship was guaranteed for Lutherans in the Palatinate in the areas they occupied in 1624*

Art. IV para. 20 [+/– 28 IPM] *Ludwig Philipp Count Palatine of Simmern and Lautern was restored to the lands held by his family in 1618*

Art. IV para. 21 [+/– 28 IPM] *Duke Friedrich of Pfalz-Zweibrücken recovered his rights to the Rhine tolls at Vilzbach (in Mainz) and the monastery of Hornbach*

Art. IV para. 22 [+/– 28 IPM] *Leopold Count Palatine of Veldenz recovered his lands*

Art. IV para. 23 [= 29 IPM] *The bishop of Bamberg and Würzburg was to return the fortress of Wülzburg to the margrave of Ansbach, and both he and the margraves of Ansbach and Kulmbach were to settle their dispute over the town and district of Kitzingen within two years or be forced to accept a settlement*

Art. IV para. 24 [+/– 31 IPM] *Württemberg was restored to the political and religious status of 1618*

Art. IV para. 25 [+/– 32 IPM] *The counts of Mömpelgard[4] were to be restored, specifically to the enclaves of Clerval and Passavant in Alsace, and their status as members of the Empire was confirmed*

Art. IV para. 26 [= 33 IPM] *Personal amnesty for Margrave Friedrich of Baden-Durlach, his family and servants, with full restoration of their land and political rights*

Art. IV para. 27 [= 34 IPM] *Baden-Durlach's claims to the lordship of Herrengeroldseck were to be settled by the courts within two years*

Art. IV para. 28 [+/– 35 IPM] *Duke Ernst Bogislav of Croy and Aerschot was included in the amnesty and recovered the lordship of Finstingen*

Art. IV para. 29 [+/– 35 IPM] *The dispute between the [Catholic and Protestant] branches of Nassau-Siegen was to be settled by the courts*

Art. IV para. 30 [+/– 35 IPM] *Full restoration for the counts of Nassau-Saarbrücken*

Art. IV para. 31 [+/– 35 IPM] *The house of Hanau recovered the districts of Babenhausen, Rheinbischofsheim and Willstätt*

Art. IV para. 32 [+/– 35 IPM] *Count Johann Albrecht II von Solms-Braunfels recovered the town of Butzbach and its four adjacent villages*

Art. IV para. 33 [+/– 35 IPM] *Full restoration for the counts of Solms-Hohensolms*

Art. IV para. 34 [+/– 35 IPM] *Amnesty for the counts of Isenburg-Büdingen*

Art. IV para. 35 [+/– 35 IPM] *The Wild- und Rheingrafen [counts] recovered their rights in the districts of Dhronecken and Wildenburg, and the lordship of Mörchingen*

---

4   A junior branch of the family ruling Württemberg. Their county was at the south-western extremity of the Empire between Basel and Alsace.

Art. IV para. 36 [+/– 35 IPM] *Luise Juliane countess of Erbach, widow of Count Ernst of Sayn-Wittgenstein, recovered the district of Hachenburg and the village of Bendorf*

Art. IV para. 37 [+/– 35 IPM] *The castle and county of Flackenstein was to be restored to its [unnamed] rightful owner. The counts of Rasburg, called Löwenhaupt, recovered the district of Bretzenheim (a fief of Cologne) and the barony of Repoltzkirch in the Hunsruck*

Art. IV para. 38 [+/– 35 IPM] *The county of Waldeck recovered the rights it had enjoyed in 1624 in the lordship of Düdinghausen and four villages*

Art. IV para. 39 [+/– 35 IPM] *Count Joachim Ernst of Öttingen-Öttingen recovered his status of 1618*

Art. IV para. 40 [+/– 35 IPM] *The house of Hohenlohe recovered its possessions, especially Weikersheim and the former monastery of Scheffersheim*

Art. IV para. 41 [+/– 35 IPM] *Count Friedrich Ludwig of Löwenstein-Wertheim-Virneburg was restored to his status of 1618*

Art. IV para. 42 [+/– 35 IPM] *Count Ferdinand Karl of Löwenstein-Wertheim-Rochefort was restored to his status of 1618*

Art. IV para. 43 [+/– 35 IPM] *The house of Erbach recovered Schloß Breuberg*

Art. IV para. 44 [+/– 35 IPM] *The widow and heirs of Count Brandenstein recovered their property*

Art. IV para. 45 [+/– 35 IPM] *Paul Baron Khevenhüller and his half-brother Jakob Löffler, as well as the children and heirs of Marx Konrad Rehlinger, recovered their property*

Art. IV para. 46 [= 36 IPM] *All contracts, agreements, debts etc. that had been extorted during the war were declared null and void*

Art. IV paras. 47 and 48 [= 37 IPM] *Debtors were given a two-year suspension of interest payments in such cases as outlined in para. 46, but had to prove within that time the obligation resulted from extortion*

Art. IV para. 49 [= 38 IPM] *Problematic verdicts in wartime court cases involving secular matters were suspended pending a judicial review*

Art. IV para. 50 [= 39 IPM] *Vassals who had failed to pay homage during the war were not to lose their fiefs, but had to pay homage after the peace*

Art. IV para. 51 [= 40 IPM] *All officers, soldiers and their families were amnestied and restored to their personal and property status of 1618, except those who were vassals or subjects of the Austrian Habsburgs*

Art. IV para. 52 [= 41 IPM] *Habsburg vassals and subjects were free to return home and be amnestied, provided they accepted Habsburg laws*

Art. IV para. 53 [= 42 IPM] *Despite Swedish protests, it had been agreed that such Habsburg vassals and subjects would not recover the property confiscated before 1630*

Art. IV para. 54 [= 43 IPM] *but they would receive the property confiscated after 1630, though without compensation for any loss of use*

Art. IV para. 55 [= 44 IPM] *Adherents of the Augsburg Confession were to be treated the same as Catholics in civil court cases in the Habsburg lands*

Art. IV para. 56 [= 45 IPM] *The following were excluded from the general restitution: movable goods, personal possessions or things that had been consumed or destroyed, legally sold or given away* [i.e. restoration was to be in the physical condition of the property in 1648, not that of 1618]

Art. IV para. 57 [= 46 IPM] *The Jülich-Cleves inheritance dispute was to be settled as soon as possible, either through the imperial courts or amicable compromise to prevent it destabilising the peace*

Art. V [Religious settlement] [all +/– 47 IPM]

Art. V para. 1 *Confirmation of both the 1552 Treaty of Passau and the 1555 Peace of Augsburg. All disputed points were to be settled by this Peace of Osnabrück on the basis of* aequalitas exacta mutuaque *[parity] between the confessions*

Art. V para. 2 *The religious situation was restored to 1 January 1624 as the new normative date*

Art. V para. 3 *The confessional groups in the imperial cities of Augsburg, Dinkelsbühl, Biberach and Ravensburg were to have the religious rights and property they possessed on 1 January 1624, but civic government was henceforth to be shared equally*

Art. V paras 4–7 *Special provisions regulating how this was to be done for the Augsburg city council*

Art. V para. 8 *Oppression of another confessional group was expressly forbidden in Augsburg where the terms of the IPO were to be read aloud publicly every year*

Art. V para. 9 *Religious matters in Augsburg were not to be decided through majority decision*

Art. V para. 10 *Confirmed the 1555 Peace, civic ordinance of Charles V and regulations of 1584 and 1591 in Augsburg*

Art. V para. 11 *Established parity as the basis of civic government in Dinkelsbühl, Biberach and Ravensburg where, likewise, the peace terms were to be read aloud annually*

Art. V para. 12 *The dispute over Bavaria's possession of Donauwörth was postponed to the next imperial diet*

Art. V para. 13 *The 1624 normative year was not to affect anyone's rights under the amnesty clauses*

Art. V para. 14 *All ecclesiastical property to be restored to whoever possessed it on 1 January 1624, pending an eventual resolution of all religious differences*

Art. V para. 15 *Confirmation of the ecclesiastical reservation for both Protestants and Catholics. The Catholic ecclesiastical territories were to remain Catholic, regardless of whether their rulers converted. Likewise, former ecclesiastical territories ruled by Protestants would remain Protestant if their rulers converted*

Art. V para. 16 *The rules governing the election of clerics and rulers in the Catholic ecclesiastical and Protestant former ecclesiastical lands were to remain according to their own statutes, so far as these did not contravene the IPO or any other part of the imperial constitution*

Art. V para. 17 *The lands of the imperial church were not to be governed by hereditary rule, but instead through the election of suitable persons*

Art. V para. 18 *Confirmed the emperor's right of 'first prayer', i.e. to propose candidates in the imperial church, where this already existed*

Art. V para. 19 *The papacy had no right to collect dues from the ecclesiastical land now in Protestant hands and the Empire would not assist the pope to enforce such claims*

Art. V para. 20 *The pope could collect dues in those ecclesiastical lands now held jointly by Protestants and Catholics, if he already possessed such rights*

Art. V para. 21 *Preserved the emperor's right of investiture in the ecclesiastical lands ruled by Protestants, and confirmed that such lands had the rights of representation in imperial institutions*

Art. V para. 22 *Regulated the titles of the Protestant rulers of former ecclesiastical land and where they should sit in the Reichstag*

Art. V para. 23 *Fixed the possession of benefices amongst Protestants and Catholics as they were on 1 January 1624, and applied the same to the exercise of religion in ecclesiastical foundations*

Art. V para. 24 *Confirmed the validity of imperial law in the ecclesiastical lands ceded to Sweden and its allies, as far as this did not contradict arrangements in Articles X to XV*

Art. V para. 25 *Restored the Protestants' territorial church land to the status of 1 January 1624*

Art. V para. 26 *Applied the same for Catholics, and fixed possession and rights in mixed areas also as on 1 January 1624*

Art. V para. 27 *Property that had been pawned or occupied during the war was to be restored, but this should not affect the free exercise of religion for any inhabitants*

Art. V para. 28 *The imperial knights were to enjoy the same religious rights as other imperial Estates*

Art. V para. 29 *The same applied to the imperial cities where matters were expressly to be regulated according to the normative year of 1 January 1624 and the special clauses regarding the bi-confessional cities (paras 2–11)*

Art. V para. 30 *Confirmed the imperial Estates'* jus reformandi *[right of reformation, i.e. religious supervision of their subjects], as well as the subjects'* jus emigrandi *[right of emigration]. Rulers were not to proselytise or impose their religion on subjects of another imperial Estate*

Art. V para. 31 *Imposed limits on the powers confirmed in para. 30 by guaranteeing that dissenters with rights recognised on 1 January 1624 were free to exercise such rights*

Art. V para. 32 *Restored subjects' religious rights to the status of 1 January 1624*

Art. V para. 33 *Annulled all agreements between rulers and subjects that contravened the IPO*

Art. V para. 34 *Guaranteed toleration for subjects who converted to another faith between 1624 and 1648 and were now a dissenting minority within an imperial Estate provided they remained law-abiding. This toleration was expressed as private worship (within the home) or the right to attend services in a neighbouring territory, as well as the right to raise children in one's chosen faith*

Art. V para. 35 *No one was to be discriminated against on religious grounds, nor excluded from employment, business, inheritance, hospitals, alms houses, or other rights, and above all they were to be treated the same for burials*

Art. V para. 36 *Such dissenters who were asked to leave by their ruler, or who left voluntarily, were free to settle their affairs and keep or sell their property*

Art. V para. 37 *Such dissenters were to be given at least five years notice if they were to be expelled, as were those wishing to convert in the future. Dissenters wishing to emigrate were not to be hindered*

Art. V para. 38 *The Protestant princes of Brieg, Liegnitz and Münsterberg-Oels, as well as the city of Breslau (all in Silesia), retained their religious freedoms already granted by the emperor*[5]

Art. V para. 39 *Protestant nobles and their subjects in the Silesian principalities and in Lower Austria were permitted free exercise of religion as a special concession from the emperor*

Art. V para. 40 *Silesian Protestants were permitted to build churches in Schweidnitz, Jauer and Glogau [the so-called 'peace churches']*

Art. V para. 41 *Sweden and the Protestant imperial Estates reserved the right to urge the emperor in the future to grant wider freedoms to his Protestant subjects*

Art. V para. 42 *Feudal jurisdiction did not entail the right of reformation over vassals' lands*

Art. V para. 43 *In cases where the right of reformation was disputed, it was to remain in the possession of whoever had exercised it in 1624 pending a legal judgement. In the meantime, no one was to be coerced over religion. The normative year was to apply to the exercise of the right of religion in areas where rule was shared between more than one imperial Estate [i.e. condominia]*

Art. V para. 44 *No other jurisdictions could be construed as a basis for claiming a right of reformation*

Art. V para. 45 *The 1555 Peace of Augsburg was confirmed with regard to ecclesiastical revenue*

Art. V para. 46 *Such revenue rights were fixed according to the normative year of 1624*

Art. V para. 47 *Applied this to revenues attached to churches etc. that had been destroyed after 1624*

Art. V para. 48 *Suspended all Catholic spiritual jurisdiction over Protestant imperial Estates and their subjects, except where this had been acknowledged on 1 January 1624, or was related to revenues accepted on 1 January 1624*

Art. V para. 49 *Prohibited Catholic bishops from exercising spiritual jurisdiction over the Protestant subjects of bi-confessional imperial cities*

Art. V para. 50 *Forbade anyone to criticise the 1552 Peace of Passau, the 1555 Peace of Augsburg or the IPO on religious grounds. Any disputes should be settled amicably through imperial institutions*

Art. V para. 51 *Instituted religious parity for membership of the ordinary imperial Deputation, any deputations agreed by the imperial diet, and in imperial commissions*

Art. V para. 52 *Religious disputes were not to be resolved by majority vote, but by Protestants and Catholics meeting separately in two equal bodies [itio in partes] in the imperial diet to agree an amicable compromise*

---

5 This had been granted by Ferdinand II when Saxony returned Silesia to Habsburg control in 1622.

Art. V para. 53 *Postponed a decision on reforming the Reichskammergericht until the next imperial diet. However, to stabilise matters in the meantime, two of the four presidents were to be Protestants, and parity was to be enforced amongst the other judges whose number was increased to 50*

Art. V para. 54 *Instituted rules to prevent imperial Estates using religion to block appointments to the court. The emperor would also appoint Protestants to the Reichshofrat and ensure parity amongst its judges in cases touching religion*

Art. V para. 55 *The same procedural rules used by the Reichskammergericht were to apply to the Reichshofrat. Cases involving religion could be appealed to panels composed equally of Catholics and Protestants*

Art. V para. 56 *'Visitation' [i.e. review] of Reichshofrat cases was entrusted to the elector of Mainz, but the precise arrangements for this were to be determined at the next imperial diet. Cases where Reichshofrat panels were split equally by confession were to be referred to the imperial diet, but the court itself should settle those cases where panels were divided, but some Catholic judges sided with their Protestant colleagues and vice versa*

Art. V para. 57 *Provided a table allocating the appointment of the 24 Protestant Reichskammergericht judges amongst the Protestant imperial Estates*

Art. V para. 58 *The exclusion of the [few] Protestant imperial Estates of the Bavarian Kreis from this table was not to prejudice their rights*

Art. VI [Swiss 'independence'] [= 61 IPM]

Following the petition of the city of Basel at the peace congress, the entire Swiss Confederation was exempted from the jurisdiction of the imperial courts

Art. VII [Calvinists] [both +/– 47 IPM]

Art. VII para. 1 *Those of the Reformed religion [i.e. Calvinists] were granted equal status with Catholics and Lutherans in the imperial constitution. The same rules governing mutual autonomy between Catholics and Protestants were to apply between Lutherans and Calvinists, so that neither could claim jurisdiction over the other. Lutheran rulers were permitted to embrace Calvinism and vice versa; they could not impose this on their subjects, but could maintain their own religious establishment at court [the so-called Simultaneum]*

Art. VII para. 2 *Communities were free to follow voluntarily their ruler's change of faith between Lutheranism and Calvinism, and vice versa, at their own expense. Such rights were envisaged for the future, but were not to contradict those already possessed by the princes of Anhalt. The clause ended with the sentence:* Besides these aforementioned religions, no other shall be accepted or tolerated in the Holy Roman Empire.

Art. VIII [Imperial Estates]

Art. VIII para. 1 [= 62 IPM] *General confirmation of the existing rights of the imperial Estates*

Art. VIII para. 2 [= 63 IPM] *All imperial Estates to be represented in decisions concerning the Empire, including war and peace. In particular, all imperial Estates are free to ally amongst themselves, or with foreigners, for their preservation and* security. However, no such alliance shall be directed against the emperor, the Empire or its public peace, or contravene the oath binding each to the emperor and Empire

Art. VIII para. 3 [= 64 IPM] *Listed the* negotia remissa, *or constitutional matters postponed to the next imperial diet: proposed changes to the election of a king of the Romans, issue of a permanent 'electoral agreement', clarification of the imperial ban, revisions to membership of the Kreise, reform of imperial tax quotas, reduction of tax exemption, tax reduction, reform of the imperial police ordinance, reform of the imperial courts, changes to Reichskammergericht charges, and directorship of the three colleges at the imperial diet*

Art. VIII para. 4 [= 65 IPM] *Confirmed the voting rights of the imperial cities at the imperial diet, along with a general confirmation of the existing imperial constitution and constitutional practice*

Art. VIII para. 5 [= 66 IPM] *The emperor was to consult the two imperial courts for advice on how to deal with the problem of wartime debt and interest arrears. In the meantime, the courts were to judge cases and ensure no one was unduly burdened. This clause was not to apply to the duchy of Holstein [which had made other arrangements already]*

Art. IX [Economic clause]

Art. IX para. 1 [= 67 IPM] *Abolished all hindrances to trade and undue postage charges introduced during the war*

Art. IX para. 2 [= 68 IPM] *Imperial Estates could continue to levy those tolls that had been confirmed by the emperor with the electors' consent. Otherwise, free trade was proclaimed*

Art. X [Sweden's territorial satisfaction] [all omitted from IPM]

Art. X para. 1 *General statement that certain imperial territories had been ceded to Sweden in perpetuity, but remaining imperial fiefs, in return for Sweden withdrawing its troops elsewhere and agreeing peace*

Art. X para. 2 *Sweden obtained Western Pomerania, Rügen island and part of eastern Pomerania; the exact boundary of the latter to be fixed later but to include Stettin and other key towns*

Art. X para. 3 *Sweden was to enjoy all the former Duke of Pomerania's rights in these possessions, which were to be held as hereditary imperial fiefs*

Art. X para. 4 *Sweden and Brandenburg were to share Pomerania's rights in the bishopric of Kammin. Both the Swedish monarch and Brandenburg elector could call themselves 'Duke of Pomerania'*

Art. X para. 5 *Brandenburg renounced claims to Sweden's Pomeranian possessions and rights*

Art. X para. 6 *The Mecklenburg port of Wismar, fortress of Walfisch, the district of Poel (except the part belonging to the bishopric of Lübeck) and Neukloster were ceded to Sweden as imperial fiefs*

Art. X para. 7 *The archbishopric of Bremen, bishopric of Verden and district of Wildeshausen were ceded as secular imperial fiefs, including Bremen's jurisdiction over the Hamburg cathedral chapter, but without prejudice to the rights of*

the Duke of Holstein, and by ceding to Holstein-Gottorp 14 villages in the
districts of Reinbeck and Trittau that belonged to the Hamburg chapter

Art. X para. 8 *The city of Bremen was to be left with its present autonomy. Any
future disputes between it and Sweden or Holstein were to be settled amicably*

Art. X para. 9 *Sweden could exercise the rights of Pomerania, Bremen and Verden
as imperial Estates, with representation in the Reichstag*

Art. X para. 10 *Sweden also could exercise their rights in the Westphalian, Lower
and Upper Saxon Kreise. Directorship of the Lower Saxon Kreise was to alternate
between Bremen and Magdeburg as one director, with the other from the Guelph
dukes of Brunswick*

Art. X para. 11 *Sweden obtained exclusive use of Pomerania's vote in imperial
Deputations, but was to consult Brandenburg before exercising it*

Art. X para. 12 *Sweden obtained the* privilegium de non appellando *[exemption
from jurisdiction of the imperial courts] for its new possessions. However, it was
to establish a court of appeal to hear cases from them. If Sweden wished to pursue
a case in the imperial courts, it was free to choose between the
Reichskammergericht and the Reichshofrat*

Art. X para. 13 *Sweden was free to found a university in its territories, and free to
levy the existing tolls at its Pomeranian and Mecklenburg ports*

Art. X para. 14 *Inhabitants of the ceded lands were to obey Sweden; the emperor
promised to invest future Swedish monarchs with these fiefs and to protect
them*

Art. X para. 15 *Sweden was to seek investiture as required under imperial law*

Art. X para. 16 *Protestant religious rights were confirmed in Sweden's possessions,
including specifically Stralsund. Those towns that were also members of the
Hanseatic League retained their commercial privileges*

Art. XI [Brandenburg's compensation] [omitted from IPM]

Art. XI para. 1 *General statement that the bishopric of Halberstadt with its associated rights would be ceded as a secular imperial fief to Brandenburg in compensation for its renunciation of claims to western Pomerania and Rügen. Religion
was to remain as agreed during the war in a separate convention with Archduke
Leopold Wilhelm*[6] *guaranteeing the position of some Catholic canons in the
cathedral chapter*

Art. XI para. 2 *Extended this to include Halberstadt's share of the county of
Honstein (i.e. the districts of Lohra and Klettenberg)*

Art. XI para. 3 *Brandenburg had to accept Leopold Wilhelm's enfeoffment of the
count of Tattenbach with the county of Reinstein (also called Regenstein) that lay
under Halberstadt jurisdiction*

Art. XI para. 4 *In addition Brandenburg received the bishopric of Minden as a secular imperial fief, though some safeguards were confirmed for the autonomy of the
town of Minden*

---

6   Leopold Wilhelm (1614–62), younger brother of Ferdinand III, was imposed as bishop
    following the imperial victories in 1627.

Art. XI para. 5 *Brandenburg also received the bishopric of Kammin, and was entitled to incorporate this into its part of the duchy of Pomerania after the death of the present cathedral canons*

Art. XI para. 6 *Brandenburg would receive the archbishopric of Magdeburg as a secular imperial fief once its current Protestant administrator died*[7]

Art. XI para. 7 *The Magdeburg cathedral chapter, Estates and subjects were to swear they would accept Brandenburg rule once their current prince died*

Art. XI para. 8 *The emperor confirmed the civic privileges granted the city of Magdeburg by Emperor Otto I in 940 in a document subsequently lost, together with other privileges granted during the war*[8]

Art. XI para. 9 *Saxony could retain the four Magdeburg districts of Burg, Dahme, Jüterbog and Querfurt [acquired in the Peace of Prague], but had to shoulder their contributions to the Upper Saxon Kreis taxes. As compensation, Brandenburg was given the Magdeburg district of Egeln, and was permitted, once it secured possession of the archbishopric, to suppress a quarter of the cathedral canon benefices as their incumbents died out and divert their revenues to its own treasury*

Art. XI para. 10 *Regulated the payment of the present Magdeburg administrator's debts*

Art. XI para. 11 *Religion in the areas ceded to Brandenburg was to be handled according to IPO Art. V*

Art. XI para. 12 *Sweden renounced claims to eastern Pomerania, the port of Kolberg and the bishopric of Kammin*

Art. XI para. 13 *Sweden would evacuate its remaining garrisons from Brandenburg*

Art. XI para. 14 *Sweden would return church property lying outside its new German territories to the Knights of St John, as well as documents it had seized*

Art. XII [Mecklenburg's compensation] [omitted from IPM]

Art. XII para. 1 *General statement that the compensation was for the loss of Wismar to Sweden and consisted of the bishoprics of Schwerin and Ratzeburg that were to pass to Duke Adolf Friedrich of Mecklenburg-Schwerin and his male heirs with the option of incorporating them fully into the duchy once the existing canons died. Mecklenburg obtained the bishoprics' representation in the imperial diet and Lower Saxon Kreis. His relation, Duke Gustavus Adolphus of Mecklenburg-Güstrow, who had been administrator of Ratzeburg, was to receive two benefices in Magdeburg and Halberstadt as compensation*

---

[7] Duke August of Sachsen-Weissenfels (1614–80), younger son of Johann Georg of Saxony, had been elected archbishop by the Lutheran canons in 1628 in a desperate attempt to steer a middle course between Emperor Ferdinand II's attempted imposition of his own son, Leopold Wilhelm, and the reckless policies of the deposed former administrator Christian Wilhelm of Brandenburg (1587–1665) who had been placed under the imperial ban in 1625 for supporting Denmark. August's possession for his lifetime had been agreed with Saxony as Article 15 of the Peace of Prague [see **Doc. 103**].

[8] Like the town of Minden (see Art. X, para. 4), Magdeburg had petitioned unsuccessfully to be recognised as an imperial city.

Art. XII para. 2 *Confirmed Mecklenburg claims to two Protestant benefices in the bishopric of Strasbourg*

Art. XII para. 3 *The Schwerin line obtained the Knights of St John's property of Mirow, while that of Nemerow went to the Güstrow branch; both had to continue paying dues to the order and to Brandenburg as patron of the order*

Art. XII para. 4 *Confirmed Mecklenburg's tolls on the river Elbe and let it off the next 300,000 tlr of imperial taxes, except those intended to pay off the Swedish army*

Art. XIII [Brunswick's compensation] [omitted from IPM]

Art. XIII para. 1 *General statement that compensation was for renouncing the coadjutor positions in Magdeburg, Bremen, Halberstadt and Ratzeburg. Compensation came in the form of alternating control of the bishopric of Osnabrück*

Art. XIII para. 2 *Gustav Gustavsson renounced his claims in return for 80,000 tlr payable in four years by the present ruler of Osnabrück and, in the event of his death, his successor*[9]

Art. XIII para. 3 *Franz von Wartenberg was formally restored as bishop of Osnabrück*

Art. XIII para. 4 *Religion in the bishopric was to return to the status of 1 January 1624*

Art. XIII para. 5 *Duke Ernst August of Brunswick-Lüneburg was to become administrator after Wartenberg's death. The constitution of the cathedral chapter was to be altered to reflect this*

Art. XIII para. 6 *Regulated which of the Guelph dynasty ruling the Brunswick lands could rule Osnabrück in the event of Ernst August's death before he could become administrator, or if he left no children to enjoy his rights*

Art. XIII para. 7 *Confirmed this alternation between an elected Catholic bishop and a Brunswick duke was to continue without affecting the bishopric's religion or constitution*

Art. XIII para. 8 *The elector of Cologne was to exercise jurisdiction over the Catholic clergy during the periods of Guelph rule*

Art. XIII para. 9 *Guelph rights in Halberstadt and Hohnstein were annulled. In return, they were confirmed in possession of the monastery of Walkenried as an imperial fief*

Art. XIII para. 10 *The Guelphs had to return Gröningen monastery to Halberstadt, but retained their rights to the castle of Westerburg*

Art. XIII para. 11 *Annulled the claims of Tilly's nephew to payment from the Guelphs*[10]

---

[9]   Gustav Gustavsson (1616–53), illegitimate son of Gustavus Adolphus and a colonel in his army, had been given Osnabrück after its capture in 1633. The official bishop since 1627 was Franz Wilhelm von Wartenberg (1593–1661), from a junior line of the Bavarian Wittelsbachs. He led the Catholic zealots at the Westphalian congress.

[10] Werner von Tilly (1590–1655) had inherited his uncle's claim to a fine of 400,000 tlr imposed on Brunswick-Wolfenbüttel in 1627 for its support for Denmark. Ferdinand II had given Tilly claim to the money as a reward and in lieu of military expenses [see **Doc. 103**, Art. 32].

Art. XIII para. 12 *The Celle branch of the Guelphs was relieved of its obligation to pay 20,000 tlr annual interest to the bishopric of Ratzeburg. The original debt was also cancelled*

Art. XIII para. 13 *Duke August of Lüneburg was to renounce claims to a benefice in the bishopric of Strasbourg. In return, his two younger sons were to receive the next two vacant Protestant benefices*

Art. XIV [Former Magdeburg administrator] [all 30 IPM]

Art. XIV para. 14 *Christian Wilhelm, the deposed administrator of Magdeburg, was to receive the districts of Zinna and Loburg for his lifetime in lieu of the 12,000 tlr previously received from the archbishopric as his pension.[11] Since these areas were devastated, the current administrator [August of Weissenfels] was to pay 3,000 tlr immediately to Christian Wilhelm*

Art. XIV para. 15 *Christian Wilhelm's heirs were to enjoy possession of Zinna and Loburg for five years after his death, whereupon they were to revert to the arch-bishopric of Magdeburg*

Art. XV [Hessen-Kassel's satisfaction]

Art. XV para. 1 [= 48 IPM] *Hessen-Kassel was expressly included in the general amnesty, restitution and religious peace*

Art. XV para. 2 [= 49 IPM] *Hessen-Kassel could retain the former imperial abbey of Hersfeld (and the priory of Göllingen) in perpetuity as an imperial fief*

Art. XV para. 3 [= 50 IPM] *It also received use of the four districts of the county of Schaumburg previously under jurisdiction of the bishop of Minden*

Art. XV para. 4 [= 51 IPM] *Mainz, Cologne, Münster, Paderborn and Fulda were to pay 600,000 tlr to pay off the Hessian army in return for Hessian evacuation of their territory*

Art. XV para. 5 [= 52 IPM] *The Hessians could retain Neuss, Coesfeld and Neuhaus until the money was paid*

Art. XV para. 6 [= 53 IPM] *Regulated the garrisons of the three towns*

Art. XV paras 7–9 [= 54 and 55 IPM] *Neuss was to be evacuated once half the money had been paid; other detailed arrangements for payment and evacuation*

Art. XV paras 10–11 [= 56 IPM] *All other occupied areas were to be evacuated immediately after ratification of the IPO*

Art. XV para. 12 [= 57 IPM] *Those areas paying contributions to the Hessian army on 1 March 1648 were to continue doing so until the evacuation was complete*

Art. XV para. 13 [= 58 IPM] *Confirmed the agreement of 24 April 1648 between Kassel and Darmstadt settling their long dispute over Marburg*

Art. XV para. 14 [= 59 IPM] *Confirmed Kassel's treaty with Waldeck of 1635 and Darmstadt's recognition of this in 1648*

Art. XV para. 15 [= 60 IPM] *Confirmed primogeniture would govern the succession in both Kassel and Darmstadt*

---

[11] An arrangement made in the Peace of Prague. See note 7 above.

Art. XVI [Peace implementation, army satisfaction and withdrawal]

Art. XVI para. 1 [=98 IPM] *Hostilities to cease immediately after the peace had been signed*

Art. XVI para. 2 [=100 IPM] *The emperor was immediately to publish edicts throughout the Empire to implement the peace. Oversight of implementation was entrusted to the Kreis convenors*

Art. XVI paras 3–4 [=101 IPM] *The emperor and the affected parties [i.e. those making or receiving restitution etc.] were to name commissioners to implement the terms. Parity of confession to be observed in these appointments in cases involving parties of different confessions*

Art. XVI para. 5 [= 102 IPM] *All parties were to adhere immediately to the terms and not hinder implementation*

Art. XVI para. 6 [= 103 IPM] *Those delaying were threatened with military intervention*

Art. XVI para. 7 [= 104 IPM] *Generals to arrange release of all prisoners of war*

Art. XVI para. 8 [omitted from IPM] *The imperial Estates of the Electoral Rhenish, Upper Saxon, Franconian, Swabian, Upper Rhenish, Westphalian and Lower Saxon Kreise were to pay 5 million tlr 'satisfaction' to the Swedish army. Payments made according to the imperial tax quotas in three instalments, the first of 1.8 million followed by two of 1.2 million each*

Art. XVI para. 9 [omitted from IPM] *Provided general arrangements for payment, withdrawal and interim maintenance payments to Swedish garrisons*[12]

Art. XVI para. 10 [omitted from IPM] *No imperial Estate was to shirk its share or hinder others from paying*

Art. XVI para. 11 [omitted from IPM] *The Austrian and Bavarian Kreise were exempted from paying satisfaction to Sweden, as they were obliged respectively to pay off the imperial and Bavarian armies*

Art. XVI para. 12 [omitted from IPM] *The imperial Estates of the seven Kreise paying Sweden pledged to make good their obligations and to compel those falling behind to contribute their share*

Art. XVI para. 13 [= 105 IPM] *All garrisons from all parties were to be withdrawn without fail as soon as prisoners had been released, the treaty ratified and the satisfaction money paid*

Art. XVI para. 14 [= 106 and 107 IPM] *All parties were to withdraw simultaneously and were not to impose conditions to evacuate particular towns*

Art. XVI para. 15 [= 108 part 1 IPM] *All documents and material, such as artillery, that had been captured when the settlement was taken, and was currently still there, was to be returned*

Art. XVI para. 16 [= 108 part 2 IPM] *Local inhabitants were to assist and to provide transport, but officers were not to oblige them to travel beyond the boundaries of their territories during the evacuation*

---

[12]   These matters were resolved with greater precision by the Execution Congress at Nuremberg, see **Docs 170–1**.

Art. XVI para. 17 [= 109 part 1 IPM] *No new garrisons were to be placed in evacuated settlements*

Art. XVI para. 18 [= 109 part 2 IPM] *Evacuated towns and their inhabitants were to enjoy the full amnesty and political and religious rights of the peace treaty*

Art. XVI para. 19 [= 110 IPM] *Finally, all the troops and armies of the belligerent parties in the Empire are to be disbanded and discharged, and each imperial Estate is to maintain only as many [troops] in his own lands as are required for his security*

Art. XVI para. 20 [= 99 IPM] *The generals were to arrange a detailed schedule for the evacuation*[13]

Art. XVII [Legal status of the peace]

Art. XVII para. 1 [= 111 IPM] *Ratification to be completed within eight weeks*

Art. XVII para. 2 [= 112 IPM] To enhance the observance and security of all the terms, the present treaty is to be incorporated in the next imperial Recess and the next imperial election capitulation as a permanent fundamental imperial law like all other laws and fundamental constitutional documents of the Empire, and to be equally and perpetually binding upon all clergy and laity, whether they are imperial Estates or not, as well as imperial councillors and the councillors and servants of the cities, and further the judges and personnel of all courts.

Art. XVII para. 3 [= 113 IPM] No claims shall be advanced, received or heard, nor shall any judicial proceedings be initiated at any time or anywhere to assert rights, property, property claims or other procedures or the delegation of jurisdiction contrary to any article or clause of this treaty, whether they be on the basis of general or individual decisions of [church] councils, privileges, concessions, ordinances, judicial decisions, bans, instructions, decisions, pending claims, pronouncements from any time, judicial verdicts, imperial electoral capitulations and the statutes of holy orders or exemptions, protests already made or that shall be made,[14] objections, calls, assignment of ownership, agreements, oaths, renunciations, mortgages or other treaties, still less the decree of 1629 or the Prague Peace with its supplementary protocol or the concordats with the papacy or the Interim of 1548,[15] or any other secular or ecclesiastical decree, decision, dispensation, statement of release or the like of whatever name or title they might take.

---

[13] As note 12.

[14] A reference to the papal protests already presented orally during the peace congress and issued formally in a papal bull in August 1650 that was backdated to 26 November 1648 so as to pre-date the ratification of the treaty.

[15] That is, the 1629 Edict of Restitution [**Doc. 62**], the 1635 Prague Peace [**Doc. 103**] with the supplementary statement excluding Hessen-Kassel and others from its amnesty, papal concordats with the emperor and princes regarding ecclesiastical jurisdiction, and Emperor Charles V's 'Interim' or temporary settlement of the Empire's religious and political problems made prior to the 1555 Religious Peace [**Doc. 1**].

Art. XVII para. 4 [= 114 IPM] *Those criticising or contravening the peace in any way would be in breach of the Empire's public peace and would be dealt with accordingly*

Art. XVII para. 5 [= 115 IPM] *All parties were obliged to uphold the peace regardless of confession*

Art. XVII para. 6 [= 116 part 1 IPM] Should, however, such a dispute not be resolved through these means within three years, then all signatories are obliged to assist the injured party in word and deed following notification from the injured party that resolution through amicable compromise or judicial means was not possible, and to take arms to suppress the injustice, but without infringing anyone's jurisdiction or laws and ordinances that apply to every prince or Estate.

Art. XVII para. 7 [= 116 part 2 IPM] *No imperial Estates were to use force to settle disputes arising from the treaty; those doing so would be in breach of the public peace*

Art. XVII para. 8 [= 117 IPM] *The Kreise were to be revived to assist in upholding the public peace*

Art. XVII para. 9 [= 118 IPM] *Any troops that needed to pass through another territory had to observe the public peace and imperial law*

Art. XVII para. 10 [= 119 IPM] *Listed the parties on the emperor's side upon whom the treaty was binding. These included Spain*

Art. XVII para. 11 [= 119 IPM] *Did the same for Sweden and its allies, including France*

Art. XVII para. 12 [= 120 IPM] *Listed the signatories, including those of the imperial Estates*

Source: Karl Zeumer (ed.), *Quellensammlung zur Geschichte der Deutschen Reichsverfassung in Mittelalter und Neuzeit* (Tübingen, 1913), pp. 395–434.

168. The Peace of Münster, 24 October 1648

[The following lists the terms not included in the IPO. The passages in Roman type are direct translations from the original text, whereas those in italics are summaries of the relevant articles.]

[Exclusion of the Burgundian Kreis and Lorraine]
Art. 3
So that the mutual friendship between the emperor, His Most Christian Majesty [the king of France], the electors, princes and Estates of the Empire may be more firmly and sincerely preserved (without prejudice to the following guarantee clause),[1] no one shall assist the present or future enemies of the other with arms, money, soldiers, provisions, or receive, accommodate or

---

[1]   Art. 115 = IPO Art. XVII para. 5.

allow transit for any assistance or troops of another party against any of the signatories of this peace, for any legal reason, pretext, or on account of any dispute or war.

Though the Burgundian Kreis is and should remain part of the Empire and will be included in this peace once the hostilities between France and Spain are resolved, neither the emperor nor any imperial Estate shall interfere in the operations currently underway there.

If a dispute shall arise in the future between the [aforementioned] crowns, the promise between the entire Roman Empire and the king and kingdom of France not to assist each others' enemies will remain unaltered and in force.

Art. 4
The duchy of Lorraine (part of the Upper Rhenish Kreis) was also excluded until this could be resolved or included in a Franco-Spanish peace. The Empire was free to assist negotiations, but could not intervene militarily

[French territorial gains]
Art. 69 *The concessions had been agreed by both the emperor and the imperial Estates to secure peace*
Art. 70 *France was granted full sovereignty over the bishoprics of Metz, Toul and Verdun, which ceased to be part of the Empire, though remained under the spiritual jurisdiction of the elector of Trier*
Art. 71 *The bishopric of Verdun would be restored to Francis of Lorraine-Chaligny once he swore loyalty to France[2]*
Art. 72 *The emperor ceded imperial jurisdiction over Pinerolo[3]*
Art. 73 *The emperor ceded imperial and Habsburg jurisdiction over the town of Breisach, the bailiwick of Upper and Lower Alsace, the Sundgau and the imperial bailiwick of Hagenau*
Art. 74 *France renounced the imperial jurisdiction over these areas in favour of incorporating them directly into France*
Art. 75 *Catholicism was guaranteed in these areas, with any changes during the war to be reversed*
Art. 76 *France had the right to place a modest garrison in the fortress of Philippsburg (which belonged to the bishop of Speyer) and had free access to the Rhine to enable it to do so and to maintain its men there*

---

[2] The bishoprics of Metz, Toul and Verdun had been occupied by France since 1552, but maintained a precarious autonomy, especially through the role of members of the House of Lorraine as bishops. Duke Francis (1599–1661) became bishop of Verdun in 1623, but was deposed by France after its open breach with his relation, Charles IV (1604–75) the ruling duke of Lorraine.

[3] A town in the duchy of Savoy, and hence part of imperial Italy, i.e. the Italian territories still under the emperor's feudal jurisdiction. The French had captured Pinerolo in 1630 during the Mantuan War (1628–31). It commanded an important route over the Alps.

Art. 77 *The bishop and cathedral chapter of Speyer retained their rights in Philippsburg*

Art. 78 *The emperor, Empire and Archduke Ferdinand Karl[4] released all officials and subjects in the areas ceded under Art. 73. These were to swear loyalty to France. The emperor, Empire and archduke were to persuade Spain to renounce its claims to these lands[5]*

Art. 79 *No imperial law could contravene the cession of Alsace to France*

Art. 80 *The cession was to be recognised at the next Reichstag, and Alsace was to be removed from the imperial tax register*

Art. 81 *Demolition of the fortifications of those Alsatian towns not ceded to France: Benfeld, Rheinau, Saverne, Hohenbar, Neuenburg*

Art. 82 *The town of Saverne was declared neutral; French troops were permitted transit through it; no fortifications to be constructed along the eastern (imperial) bank of the Rhine between Basel and Philippsburg; no alteration to the course of the river Rhine*

Art. 83 *The archduke of Tirol remained responsible for a third of the debts of the former Austrian lands in Alsace that had been ceded to France*

Art. 84 *The size of the debts and their repayment schedule was to be determined jointly by France and Austria*

Art. 85 *France would evacuate all other Austrian and imperial areas it occupied and would not hinder trade on the Rhine*

Art. 86 *Private property of the inhabitants either side of the river was to be returned; all claims for war reparations were annulled*

Art. 87 *The bishops of Strasbourg and Basel, the imperial city of Strasbourg and all others with the status of imperial immediacy were to retain this status, though this was not to infringe French sovereignty[6]*

Art. 88 *France would pay the archduke of Tirol 3 million livres tournois within three years as compensation for the loss of Habsburg Alsatian land*

Art. 89 *France assumed responsibility for the other two-thirds of Habsburg Alsatian debts*

Art. 90 *France would return the Alsatian archive to the archduke*

Art. 91 *France could retain copies of any documents relevant to public administration of the territories*

---

[4] Ferdinand Karl (1628–62), then male head of the Tirolean branch of the Austrian Habsburgs. Ferdinand II had transferred Alsace to the Tirolean branch in 1625 [see **Docs. 160**, note 1 and **161**, para. 8].

[5] Claims that derived from the Oñate Treaty of 1617 (**Doc. 9**) which Ferdinand had himself broken by transferring Alsace to his Tirolean relations.

[6] This was a deliberately ambiguous clause, inserted by the imperial negotiators to prevent the total loss of Alsace for the Empire since the status of imperial immediacy implied subordination to no lord other than the emperor. Another example is Art. 73 which delineates the territorial concessions as various bailiwicks that in practice lacked clear boundaries. It was only the emperor's subsequent military decline relative to France that allowed Louis XIV to assert greater sovereignty in 1679–84. Nonetheless, many of the minor Alsatian imperial territories retained their autonomy until the French invasion of 1793.

[Mantuan dispute]

Art. 92 *The Franco-imperial treaty of Cherasco of June 1631 (ending the Mantuan war) was confirmed, though with the modification agreed between Savoy and France that ceded Pinerolo to the latter*

Art. 93 *No one was to act contrary to the treaty of Cherasco*

Art. 94 *France would pay the 494,000 fl Savoy owed Mantua as compensation for its annexation of Monferrato during the Mantuan War*

Art. 95 *The emperor enfeoffed Savoy with its share of Monferrato*

Art. 96 *Confirmed Savoy's sovereignty over its fiefs of Olmo, Céssole and Roccaverano; restored the first two and a quarter of the third to Count Scaglia*

Art. 97 *Restitution of various other minor fiefs*[7]

Source: J.J. Schmauss and H.C. von Senckenberg (eds), *Neue und vollständige Sammlung der Reichs-Abschiede*, 4 vols (Frankfurt, 1747), vol. III, pp. 604–20.

---

[7] Articles 96 and 97 settled problems arising from earlier attempts to resolve the Mantuan dispute by compensating other parties, and from the Savoyard civil war of 1637–42.

19

Peace implementation, celebration, commemoration

There were wide fears that the Westphalian settlement would not hold unless its terms were implemented swiftly. The Empire was still full of soldiers whose expensive presence retarded economic recovery and prolonged anxiety that peace would never come [**Doc. 169**]. France soon withdrew its small army which was needed for its continuing struggle against Spain. Bavaria and the emperor pulled their troops into their own lands to demonstrate goodwill and signal their intention to abide by the peace. The Bavarians were soon paid off with money from their immediate neighbours who were largely former members of the Catholic League. The imperial army was reduced and redeployed to Hungary to counter threats from the Ottoman Turks. Sweden refused to withdraw until its troops were paid off by the rest of the Empire. The generals met in Nuremberg to 'execute' (i.e. implement) the peace terms. A phased withdrawal was arranged in two 'execution recesses' in 1649 and 1650 [**Docs 170–1**]. A remarkable nine-tenths of the promised 5.2 million taler was paid to the Swedes by the June 1650 deadline, enabling a speedy withdrawal and demobilisation [**Doc. 172**]. Only 3 per cent of the money was still outstanding when the Swedes left their last German garrison in 1654.

Demobilised soldiers often found it hard to reintegrate into civil society. Many enlisted in the Spanish, French or Venetian armies: enlistment in the first two was officially illegal under the IPM, but recruitment for Venice was encouraged because, since 1645, that republic had been at war with the Ottomans who were considered a common enemy of all Christians. Thousands of soldiers joined other displaced persons living rough. The territorial authorities responded to popular anxiety with a series of mandates against marauders and other measures of public security [**Doc. 173**]. Actual violence soon subsided, but the horror of the war persisted in popular memory and was used by the authorities to justify tighter surveillance and social discipline linked to more absolute forms of princely government.

Article V of the IPO settled disputes over religious jurisdiction by ruling that the official faith of each territory was to remain as it had been on 1 January 1624. This included Calvinism which was now recognised within imperial law alongside Lutheranism and Catholicism. Dissenting minorities could retain any rights they had possessed in 1624. Rulers were expected to show patient toleration towards minorities without rights, but were equally free to expel them after due notice.

Efforts to impose conformity with official religion met with considerable passive resistance. Few rulers were willing to expel dissenters at a time when their economies and populations were still recovering from the war **[Doc. 174]**.

The successful withdrawal and demobilisation convinced people the peace would hold. A series of official celebrations were staged, soon becoming annual events of commemoration which continued in some areas into the nineteenth century. Celebration and commemoration drew on existing traditions of official giving of thanks through religious services for deliverance from dangers **[Doc. 175]**. Though the details varied, there was little to distinguish celebrations in Catholic areas **[e.g. Doc. 175]** from those staged by Protestants **[Doc. 176]**. All conveyed the official message endorsed by church and state that the war had been sent to the Empire as divine punishment for the population's sins. People were admonished to improve their behaviour and live thrifty and obedient lives to ensure such horrors would not be repeated.

DEMOBILISATION

169. Effective troop strengths in the Empire, October 1648

Anti-imperial forces

Army	Cavalry and dragoons	Infantry	Total
Swedish	23,480	40,218	63,698
French	4,500	4,500	9,000
Hessian	2,280	8,760	11,040
	30,260	53,478	83,738
Pro-imperial forces			
Imperial	20,300	22,000	42,300
Westphalian	3,200	9,300	12,500
Bavarian	9,435	11,128	20,538
Spanish	?	1,000	1,000+
	32,935	43,428	76,363

Source: P.H. Wilson, *Europe's Tragedy: A History of the Thirty Years War* (London, 2009), p. 770.

---

[1]   The above excludes Spanish forces in the Burgundian Kreis, those in imperial Italy, as well as Austrian Habsburg troops outside the Empire in Hungary. It also excludes the 6–7,000 Lorrainers (mainly in Luxembourg), as well as the neutral Brandenburg, Guelph and Saxon forces that probably totalled around 15,000. The figures for the Westphalian army relate to February 1649 by when some men had already been discharged. The total for October 1648 was probably around 15,000.

170. The First Execution Principal Recess, 21 September 1649

By the grace of God, we Carl Gustav,[1] Count Palatine on the Rhine, duke in Bavaria, Jülich, Cleves and Berg, Count of Veldenz, Spanheim, the Mark and Ravensberg, Lord of Ravenstein etc., Her Majesty's and the Crown of Sweden's Generalissimo over the armies and military personnel in Germany, hereby announce publicly: To execute the Peace agreed at Osnabrück and Münster on 14 October, old style, 24 October, new style, last year sixteen hundred and forty-eight, in accordance with Article XVI, we have met the high-born Prince and Lord Octavio Piccolomini de Aragona,[2] Knight of the Golden Fleece, His Roman Imperial as well as Royal Hungarian Majesty's Privy Councillor, Chamberlain, Captain of the Guard Halbardiers, Lieutenant General of His armies, Field Marshal and commissioned colonel etc., at a conference in the Holy Roman Imperial City of Nuremberg, through the authority of the Peace Treaty, as well as the plenipotentiary powers from His Roman Imperial and Her Royal Swedish Majesties, and have negotiated for a while with all the electors and Estates present here, as well as the envoys, councillors and ambassadors, and have concluded a preliminary agreement with all interested parties on 11 September, old style, 21 September, new style, which follows verbatim:

1 It is known that, through divine grace, a general peace was published in Germany after long negotiations at Osnabrück and Münster and ratified by all belligerents, that those points concerning its implementation were entrusted to His Roman Imperial and Her Royal Swedish Majesties' commanding generals, and that these met in person to this end in the Holy Roman Imperial City of Nuremberg, and after due deliberation, until the other points can be finally resolved, have concluded in the following points in a preliminary agreement in order to expedite an end to the heavy burden of billeting, in His Roman Imperial and Her Royal Swedish Majesties' names and with the consent, council and agreement of representatives present from the electors and Estates of the Holy Roman Empire, and will incorporate this verbatim in the final agreement once it is concluded.

[Arts 2–6 reaffirmed the implementation of the amnesty and the status of 1624 for religion in the Empire and declared all protests against these terms null and void.]

7 It is furthermore agreed that a start will be made on collecting the satisfaction money for the Royal Swedish military, as well as disbanding the troops and evacuating the places as agreed in the Peace Treaty, and that it will be

---

1   Carl Gustav Prince of Zweibrücken (1622–60) was Queen Christina's cousin. She named him Swedish commander in the Empire on 2 June 1648 as part of a long-term plan to groom him as her successor so she could avoid marrying. He became King Charles X after her abdication in 1654.

2   Octavio Piccolomini assumed command of the imperial army after Peter Melander Count Holzapfel was killed at the battle of Zusmarshausen on 17 May 1648 [see **Doc. 105**].

done in the following manner: His Princely Highness the Count Palatine and Generalissimo shall receive at his absolute disposal at each Kreis financial centre (in the case of the Upper Saxon Kreis there is an option between Brunswick or Magdeburg) payments within eight or ten days of the appointed deadline, with in total 1,800,000 imperial talers as first instalment, 600,000 imperial talers as second instalment, and 600,000 talers as third instalment, each time in cash with no deductions, or any [imperial] Estate falling into arrears.

[Arts 8–9 stipulated that the Swedes were to disband their troops in proportion to the payments they received. Art. 10 permitted them to retain some troops in the seven Kreise that were to pay the money, so they could compel those who fell behind to pay. Art. 11 specified lists of regiments to be disbanded and fortresses to be evacuated as the Swedes received their money. Art. 12 specified that the emperor was to receive 200,000 tlr in three equal instalments, in return for successively removing his troops from Bohemia, Moravia and Silesia. Arts 13–14 provided further detail of the towns to be mutually evacuated. Arts 15–20 discussed negotiations over the remaining 2 million tlr promised the Swedes and their concern not to withdraw without assurance of payment.]

21 To authenticate this, we, the appointed representatives, have signed this interim recess in our own hands, and both the Imperial plenipotentiary and ourselves have exchanged copies. Done in Nuremberg, 11 or 21 day of the month September, in the year of Christ 1649.

Source: J.J. Schmauss and H.C. von Senckenberg (eds), *Neue und vollständige Sammlung der Reichs-Abschiede*, 4 vols (Frankfurt, 1747), vol. III, pp. 625–40.

---

171. The Second Execution Principal Recess, 16 June 1650

[Art. 22 reaffirmed the First Recess, subject to changes noted in the Second. Arts 23–4 specified settlement within three months of numerous minor disputes over the implementation of 1624 as the religious status quo.]

25 Concerning the restitution of the Palatine Electorate as agreed in the Peace Treaty, we have mediated between the Electoral Bavarian and Electoral Palatine representatives, on the issue of that part of the Lower Palatine lands that the Elector of Bavaria has to restore. In return for Her Royal Swedish Majesty's evacuation of the places held by her forces in the Upper Palatinate, as well as the Elector Palatine ratifying the Peace and handing a declaration to His Electoral Highness of Mainz to the effect that he renounces the Upper Palatinate, His Electoral Highness of Bavaria will restore the castle and town of Heidelberg, together with the other places he holds in the Lower Palatinate. Furthermore, the declaration from His Electoral Highness of the Palatinate will confirm the renunciation of the Arch-Seneschal title and coat of arms, and all that pertain to them, in favour of His Electoral Highness of Bavaria,

until such a time as His Imperial Majesty confers a new arch office, title and coat of arms appropriate with electoral dignity. All this is expressly hereby confirmed and ratified by all sides.

[Arts 26–8, 30–4 specified arrangements for resolving the outstanding difficulties surrounding the implementation of 1624 as the religious norm.]

29 To expedite implementation His Roman Imperial Majesty will publish mandates throughout the Empire forbidding on pain of serious punishment all attacks, disputes and sermons against the Peace Treaty, as well as against imperial edicts, and their implementation in accordance with the aforementioned preliminary as well as principal recess, regardless what form these contraventions take, and all authorities are empowered to punish the delinquents in accordance with the *secundum Instrumentum Pacis* [second peace treaty].

[Arts 35–7, 39 authorised the use of force against those Estates that had fallen behind in their payment of the Swedish satisfaction money. Art. 38 ordered the seven Kreise to pay a total of 7,000 tlr a month to maintain the remaining Swedish troops until the arrears had been paid. Art. 40 reaffirmed that the Swedes would leave once the money had been paid. Art. 41 reaffirmed the arrangements specified in Art. 12 for the imperial evacuation of Moravia and Silesia that had fallen behind schedule.]

42 Hereafter the actual disbandment and withdrawal of the troops is to start in three stages each of fourteen days from the date of this agreement, so that the whole is completed in six weeks …

[Arts 43–5 listed towns to be mutually evacuated in the first of the three phases.]

46 Concerning the fortress of Frankenthal that should have been restored along with the other Lower Palatine lands and places to His Electoral Palatine Highness, but has not been done so, there is nonetheless good hope that it will be restored before the first evacuation deadline. In case this does not happen, we have agreed the following with His Electoral Palatine Highness:

47 His Imperial Majesty, together with the electors and Estates declare they will diligently seek the swift restoration of the fortress of Frankenthal to the Electoral Palatinate.[1]

[Arts 48–9 stated that in the meantime Heilbronn was to be entrusted to the elector, though it was to remain an imperial city. Arts 50–1 stated that to prevent the Frankenthal garrison causing trouble, the Upper Rhine Estates were authorised to continue paying contributions to it, while the emperor was to get his brother, Leopold Wilhelm, governor of the Spanish

---

[1]   The Spanish evacuated Frankenthal on 3 May 1652.

Netherlands, to ensure that the garrison did not disturb the peace. Art. 52 stated that the emperor promised that the Empire would pay 3,000 tlr a month to the Palatinate until Frankenthal was restored. Art. 53 specified arrangements to find the money. Arts 54–9 specified the towns to be evacuated in the second and third stages. Arts 60–1 specified arrangements for Pomerania and Osnabrück. Arts 62–4, 66–8 confirmed the arrangements to complete the evacuation and disbandment within six weeks. Art. 65 included Hessen-Kassel in the amnesty and gave it eight weeks to disband. Art. 69 listed the representatives who signed the recess on 16 June 1650.]

Source: *Neue und vollständige Sammlung der Reichs-Abschiede*, 4 vols (Frankfurt, 1747), vol. III, pp. 625–40.

---

172. The Swedes evacuate Olmütz, July 1650

On 4 July 1650 the welcome news arrived that His Excellency Count von Puchheim[1] would soon arrive for the evacuation of the City of Olmütz. The Council were ordered by the Lord Lieutenant of the province to collect meat, fish, chickens, game and all necessaries in return for cash payment.

At 9.30 on the 6th General Wittenberg[2] arrived, soon followed by General Lieutenant Field Marshal de Souches,[3] [and] around 7 o'clock General Field Marshal Count von Puchheim and the Lord Lieutenant Count von Rothal arrived together here.

On the 7th the general staff had the satisfaction payment, that is 70,000 tlr, counted, and the transport wagons collected from the countryside, after which there was an impressive fireworks display in the evening, the cannon were fired often and a toast made *pro Valedictione* [as a farewell].

On the 8th the full departure of the Swedes was continued, *pro qvo Soli Deo gloria* [glory to God].

Source: The diary of Friedrich Flade, the Olmütz town clerk, published in B. Dudik (ed.), 'Tagebuch des feindlichen Einfalls der Schweden in das Markgrafenthum Mähren während ihres Aufenthaltes in der Stadt Olmütz 1642–1650', *Archiv für österreichische Geschichte*, 65 (1884), p. 485.

---

1 Hans Christoph von Puchheim (1605–57), commander of the forces defending Austria, Moravia and Silesia since 1645.
2 Wittenberg had been involved in Olmütz's capture in 1642 [see **Doc. 125**].
3 Louis Raduit de Souches (1608–82), a Huguenot refugee who served Sweden, but defected to the emperor in 1642. He commanded the unsuccessful imperial attempt to retake Olmütz in 1644–5. He was named imperial commissioner to oversee the Swedish evacuation of Moravia in 1650.

173. Westphalian mandate against marauders, 17 June 1649

All sorts of marauding soldiers have appeared in the territory bent on theft and robbery, which is absolutely forbidden. Accordingly, all local authorities are strictly instructed to keep a sharp lookout and to arrest those found in *flagranti crimine* [committing crimes], or without a proper pass, whether in the countryside or the town. Such persons are to be sent immediately under guard to the electoral castle. Above all, the authorities are to report any deserters from the Lord Lieutenant's Regiment and to send them here or to Werl castle. There is a ten imperial taler reward for each one, but equally all are hereby warned they will be punished if such criminals are not arrested in their districts.

Approved and validated by the Lord Lieutenant's seal.

Arnsberg, 17 June 1649.

Source: Horst Conrad and Gunnar Teske (eds), *Sterbezeiten. Der Dreißigjährige Krieg im Herzogtum Westfalen* (Münster, 2000), pp. 433–4.

<hr>

IMPLEMENTING THE RELIGIOUS SETTLEMENT

174. Report of the Synod Visitation in the Bishopric of Paderborn, 27 May 1651

On 27 May 1651 the most worthy suffragan bishop of Paderborn[1] held a visitation in St Magnus Church in Marsberg Old Town …

The following non-Catholics appeared at Mayor Thelen's house after lunch:

The miller Johannes Hausmann, who remained stubborn. He was given until Michaelmas [29 September] to make a decision or accept that we were only acting in accordance with the peace terms.

Georg Barchmacher, also known as Leffler, promised to take instruction from a priest.

Michael Mölner, from Tundorf in Thuringia, wanted to keep his confession. The bishop gave him until Michaelmas to reconsider.

Gertrud Biggen, wife of church warden Johannes Hund, requested a little more time to think and promised to accompany her husband to communion.

Anna Scheven did not appear.

Source: Horst Conrad and Gunnar Teske (eds), *Sterbezeiten. Der Dreißigjährige Krieg im Herzogtum Westfalen* (Münster, 2000), pp. 383–4.

<hr>

[1]   Bernhard Frick (*c.*1600–55), suffragan bishop of Paderborn from 1644.

CELEBRATION AND COMMEMORATION

175. Institution of an Annual Day of Thanksgiving in the town of Arnsberg, 1646

For the eternal commemoration by the descendants of the town of Arnsberg.

No one should ever forget that the Swedish General Carl Gustav Wrangel[1] besieged the town of Höxter belonging to the abbey of Corvey on the Weser with a large force of cavalry and infantry in April 1646. Thanks to a vigorous attack and fearful bombardment, he captured the town within a few days, forcing the imperial garrison to surrender at his mercy. Once Höxter had been thoroughly plundered, all the towers and town walls were demolished.

Then the Swedish general advanced to the town of Paderborn with his entire force of cavalry and infantry on 11 May. A heavy bombardment forced it to surrender on 15 May and it was occupied by Hessian troops. The Swedish general of cavalry, Douglas,[2] meanwhile reconnoitred the electoral castle and town of Arnsberg with twelve cavalry regiments and two dragoon regiments. He nearly caught and destroyed the imperial Cavalry Regiment Holstein (that was partly here in Arnsberg with its colonel, Prince Holstein, and partly in the nearby towns of Grevenstein, Altendorf and Balve), but it escaped thanks to special divine intervention.

The town of Marsberg was likewise attacked by a large force and, within a few days, it was not only captured, but completely plundered, had its towers and walls destroyed and finally nearly entirely gutted by fire.

The Swedes robbed and plundered all the surrounding towns of Brilon, Rüden, Warstein, Hirschberg and Belecke, as well as their districts. Many people were brutally shot dead, kidnapped or likewise treated in an un-Christian manner. The entire territory and neighbouring lands were in complete terror, having lost virtually all hope of being saved by the imperialists who were far away and, in any case, outnumbered by the Swedes.

Then, between 6 and 7 a.m. on 16 May, a strong troop of cavalry appeared in the light wood on the Haar[3] and reconnoitred the castle and town. A party came down onto the fields outside the town and stole nearly 50 horses from the ploughs and manure wagons by the Monastery Gate Bridge. They returned to the main force that deployed in battle order, displaying 116 standards and flags. Rumbecke monastery was also fully plundered. However, Arnsberg escaped thanks to God's special grace, even though General Wrangel sent various trumpeters and drummers to summon the castle, as well as writing letters to the electoral officials to get the imperial garrison to leave.

---

1   Karl Gustav von Wrangel (1611–76), succeeded Torstensson as Swedish commander in Germany from late 1645 until June 1648.

2   Robert Douglas (1611–61).

3   A hill east of Arnsberg.

[The text continues with the claim that God and the town's patron St Norbert saved it when Hessen-Kassel troops tried to besiege it in July 1634.]

To honour and thank God for saving the town, the mayor, councillors and all the community have agreed to institute an annual procession from the parish churches through the town to the electoral castle every St Norbert's Day, 11 July, and have entered this into the civic record for the permanent remembrance of posterity. May Almighty God, through the intercession of our holy father and patron St Norbert, spare this town's inhabitants from all war, fire and misfortune.

So decided at Arnsberg town hall, 2 June 1646.

Source: Horst Conrad and Gunnar Teske (eds), *Sterbezeiten. Der Dreißigjährige Krieg im Herzogtum Westfalen* (Münster, 2000), pp. 228–31.

---

176. Description of the first annual peace celebration in Augsburg, August 1650

Wednesday the 3rd, the normal church service refrained from speaking *pro felici pacis executione* [of the execution of the peace], but by contrast both at the morning prayers at St Anna's [church] and in the evening after the children's service at St Anna's and St Ulrich's and at the Barfüssern a long paper was read with a fine announcement admonishing all to a proper thanksgiving to God for the long prayed for and now happily completed peace treaty, and it was announced that the thanksgiving festival for the peace organised by the Evangelical Council shall be celebrated on Monday the 8th (this is the same Monday that 21 years before in 1629 all the Evangelical ministers were abolished within two hours and the insufferable Reformation was introduced by the papists). It is arranged that next Sunday evening the midday service will be replaced by a service of preparation in all parishes, and on the following day of the festival a morning and evening service shall be held, and after the morning service at 6 a.m. the bells will be rung and all churches are to hold communion simultaneously ...

After the aforementioned Wednesday evening service another paper was also read, announcing that a special thanksgiving festival and service for the children shall be held from the following Monday for eight days for the eternal memory [of the peace], and after the service, instead of the catechism, the school children shall learn and recite special thanksgiving texts selected from the Old and New Testaments by an honourable minister, and that the older ones are to be clean and smartly dressed ... On Monday the 8th through God's special grace, as announced, the Evangelicals held a very fine festival of thanksgiving, peace and joy in all six parishes with music, singing, praying, thanking and preaching and communion, but the papists worked as if it was just another day, and even carried wood to the marketplace, because the gate was opened in the morning and remained so the whole day. And no one here can remember a finer festival. [Then follows a long description of how the churches were decorated with tapestries and flowers, including pictures of local dignitaries alongside Luther, Bernhard von Weimar, Gustavus Adolphus and Queen Christina. The children wore green leaves in their hair, while the civic soldiers fired salvos with their guns.]

Source: Printed in Bernd Roeck, 'Die Feier des Friedens', in Heinz Duchhardt (ed.), *Der Westfälische Friede* (Munich, 1998), pp. 653–9.

Guide to further reading

The literature on the Thirty Years War is immense, with well over 4,000 titles just on the concluding peace treaties. The following restricts itself to the most important recent works and those which English-speaking readers will find the most useful introductions to specific aspects.

There are a number of short surveys in English intended for university students, of which by far the best is R.G. Asch, *The Thirty Years War: The Holy Roman Empire and Europe, 1618–48* (Basingstoke, 1997). More substantial, comprehensive coverage can be found in P.H. Wilson, *Europe's Tragedy: A History of the Thirty Years War* (London, 2009). An alternative interpretation, presenting the war as a more general European conflict, is provided by G. Parker, *The Thirty Years War*, 2nd edn (London, 1997). A more extreme version of this perspective is the influential but unconvincing S. Steinberg, *The 'Thirty Years War' and the Conflict for European Hegemony 1600–1660* (London, 1966). Two works by the prolific Czech historian Josef Polisensky purport to be general studies, but in fact cover the war mainly from the Bohemians' perspective, nonetheless offering much insight and valuable detail: *The Thirty Years War* (London, 1971); *War and Peace in Europe 1618–1648* (Cambridge, 1978). The following older studies can still be read with profit: C.V. Wedgwood, *The Thirty Years War* (London, 1938); A. Gindely, *History of the Thirty Years War*, 2 vols (New York, 1892); H.G.R. Reade, *Sidelights on the Thirty Years War*, 3 vols (London, 1924). The latter does not cover all events, but offers considerable detail on the campaigns in the Rhineland 1621–3 and the Mantuan War 1627–31.

For those with German, the short survey by G. Schmidt, *Der Dreißigjährige Krieg*, 7th edn (Munich, 2006), offers a good introduction. There is a thought-provoking discussion of key issues by J. Burkhardt, *Der Dreißigjährige Krieg* (Frankfurt, 1992). The most recent German account is C. Kampmann, *Europa und das Reich im Dreißigjährigen Krieg* (Stuttgart, 2008), which presents the conflict as escalating into a general European war. The 450th anniversary of the 1648 peace was marked by several important conferences and exhibitions which led to numerous publications. The most extensive of these appeared in English as *1648: War and Peace in Europe*, 3 vols (Münster, 1998), edited by K. Bussmann and H. Schilling. In addition to providing an excellent compendium of the art produced during the war, this contains a useful volume of essays covering most topics in bite-size chunks.

The debate on the origins of the war is surveyed by P.H. Wilson, 'The Causes of the Thirty Years War 1618–48', *English Historical Review*, 123 (2008), pp. 554–86. Older work on the 1555 Religious Peace has been superseded by the thorough study of A. Gotthard, *Der Augsburger Religionsfrieden* (Münster, 2004) who remains sceptical towards the more positive assessment of the arrangements. There is little available in English that explains why the peace nonetheless proved remarkably durable, though the earlier stages are covered by P.S. Fichtner, *Emperor Maximilian II* (New Haven, 2001). The Empire's problems during the later sixteenth century also receive scant attention in English with most general works assuming general war was inevitably pre-programmed by the alleged failure of the 1555 arrangements. More material is available on the parallel difficulties in the Habsburg monarchy in a series of studies analysing the dynasty's programme to make Catholicism the basis for political loyalty: K.J. MacHardy, *War, Religion and Court Patronage in Habsburg Austria: The Social and Cultural Dimensions of Political Interaction, 1521–1622* (Basingstoke, 2003); J.F. Patrouch, *A Negotiated Settlement: The Counter-Reformation in Upper Austria under the Habsburgs* (Boston, 2000); R. Pörtner, *The Counter-Reformation in Central Europe: Styria 1580–1630* (Oxford, 2001). These detailed studies are not matched by works on high politics. Rudolf II's imperial policy remains under-researched, though his character and artistic patronage are well captured in R.J.W. Evans, *Rudolf II and His World*, 2nd edn (London, 1997).

The reasons why other European powers did not go to war over the Empire's problems earlier are explained by A.D. Anderson, *On the Verge of War: International Relations and the Jülich-Kleve Succession Crises (1609–1614)* (Boston, 1999). The international dimension of the Bohemian Revolt is explored by J. Polisensky, *Tragic Triangle: The Netherlands, Spain and Bohemia, 1617–1621* (Prague, 1991) and in a series of articles by Peter Brightwell, 'The Spanish Origins of the Thirty Years War', *European Studies Review*, 9 (1979), pp. 409–31; 'Spain and Bohemia: The Decision to Intervene, 1619', *European Studies Review*, 12 (1982), pp. 117–41; and 'Spain, Bohemia and Europe, 1619–21', *European Studies Review*, 12 (1982), pp. 371–99. The background to Transylvanian intervention is analysed by G. Murdock, *Calvinism on the Frontier 1600–1660* (Oxford, 2000). For the debate on religion as a factor causing and shaping the war, see P.H. Wilson, 'Dynasty, Constitution and Confession: The Role of Religion in the Thirty Years War', *International History Review*, 30 (2008), pp. 473–514.

The war is routinely presented as a decisive stage in the development of modern warfare by historians writing in English, but there has been little systematic analysis of the military aspects. There are a large number of older, detailed campaign and battle histories in German, many of which have been synthesised by William P. Guthrie in *Battles of the Thirty Years War from White Mountain to Nordlingen* [sic], *1618–1635* (Westport, 2002); and *The Later Thirty Years War from the Battle of Wittstock to the Treaty of Westphalia* (Westport, 2003). Those with French are directed to an important study of White Mountain by O. Chaline, *La bataille de la Montagne Blanche* (Paris, 1999). The best recent work offering new perspectives on organisation, strategy and tactics is D. Parrott, *Richelieu's Army: War, Government and Society in France, 1624–1642* (Cambridge, 2001).

Frederick V receives (perhaps too) favourable treatment by B.C. Pursell, *Frederick V of the Palatinate and the Coming of the Thirty Years War* (Aldershot, 2003) which, despite its title, in fact covers Palatine policy to 1632. The lack of foreign support is explained by M. Rüde, *England und Kurpfalz im werdenden Mächteeuropa (1608–1632)* (Stuttgart, 2007) with a good bibliography of more detailed works. Coverage of imperial policy is uneven and readers seeking works in English are directed to two works by the Jesuit historian Robert Bireley SJ, *Religion and Politics in the Age of the Counterreformation: Emperor Ferdinand II, William Lamormaini, SJ, and the Formation of Imperial Policy* (Chapel Hill, 1981); and *The Jesuits and the Thirty Years War* (Cambridge, 2003). Wallenstein has attracted considerable interest with a large number of biographies of varying quality. The best is J. Polisensky and J. Kollmann, *Wallenstein. Feldherr des Dreißigjährigen Krieges* (Cologne, 1997), but English-speaking readers are quite well served by G. Mann, *Wallenstein: His Life* (London, 1976) which offers a lot of detail on imperial policy and military operations during 1625–34. H.F. Schwarz, *The Imperial Privy Council in the Seventeenth Century* (Cambridge, MA, 1943) is an invaluable who's who of imperial advisors. Imperial policy during the latter part of the war and the peace negotiations is covered by L. Höbelt, *Ferdinand III (1608–1657). Friedenskaiser wider Willen* (Graz, 2008).

Bavarian involvement has been covered very well. Of several detailed studies, two are outstanding: D. Albrecht, *Maximilian I. von Bayern 1573–1651* (Munich, 1998) and M. Kaiser, *Politik und Kriegführung. Maximilian von Bayern, Tilly und die Katholische Liga im Dreißigjährigen Krieg* (Münster, 1999). None of this has yet appeared in English, but there is a superb study of Bavarian annexation policy by T. Johnson, *Magistrates, Madonnas and Miracles: The Counter Reformation in the Upper Palatinate* (Aldershot, 2009). This includes a summary of Bavarian policy in general. By contrast, there is still little on Saxon policy which is often misrepresented in general books as a complete failure. The most convincing explanation of what the Saxon elector was trying to do is offered in the unpublished thesis by D.M. Phelps, 'Reich, Religion and Dynasty: The Formation of Saxon Policy 1555–1619' (University of London, 2005). Readers with German can consult F. Müller, *Kursachsen und der Böhmische Aufstand 1618–1622* (Münster, 1997) which contains an extensive bibliography of specialist works.

The reasons behind Swedish intervention are explored by E. Ringmar, *Identity, Interest and Action: A Cultural Explanation of Sweden's Intervention in the Thirty Years War* (Cambridge, 1996) and P. Piirimäe, 'Just War in Theory and Practice: The Legitimation of Swedish Intervention in the Thirty Years War', *Historical Journal*, 45 (2002), pp. 499–523. Policy in Germany is covered in detail in the second volume of M. Roberts's biography of *Gustavus Adolphus*, 2 vols (London, 1953), and his 'Oxenstierna in Germany 1633–1636', *Scandia*, 48 (1982), pp. 61–105. There is nothing comparable in English for the later stages of Swedish involvement. The long negotiations with the emperor after 1635 are covered in German by J. Öhman, *Der Kampf um den Frieden. Schweden und der Kaiser im Dreißigjährigen Krieg* (Vienna, 2005). Denmark is well-represented by

P.D. Lockhart, *Denmark in the Thirty Years War, 1618–1648* (Selinsgrove, 1996), and the same author's *Denmark 1513–1660: The Rise and Decline of a Renaissance Monarchy* (Oxford, 2007), as well as S. Murdoch, *Britain, Denmark-Norway and the House of Stuart, 1603–1660* (East Linton, 2003).

The early stage of French involvement can be approached through the many biographies of Richelieu, of which the best remains D.P. O'Connell, *Richelieu* (London, 1968). Also of use is A.L. Moote, *Louis XIII the Just* (Berkeley, 1989). For the period after 1642 there is the excellent D. Croxton, *Peacemaking in Early Modern Europe: Cardinal Mazarin and the Congress of Westphalia, 1643–1648* (Selinsgrove, 1999) which also provides good coverage of the tensions between France and Sweden. Dutch policy is covered by the relevant sections of the encyclopaedic J.I. Israel, *The Dutch Republic* (Oxford, 1995). English-speaking readers are extremely well-served by works on Spain, of which the best include: A. Feros, *Kingship and Favouritism in the Spain of Philip III, 1598–1621* (Cambridge, 2000); J.H. Elliott, *The Count-Duke of Olivares* (New Haven, 1986); R.A. Stradling, *Philip IV and the Government of Spain, 1621–1665* (Cambridge, 1988); and the same author's *Spain's Struggle for Europe 1598–1668* (London, 1994). Further aspects, including the Mantuan War, are covered in a series of papers by David Parrott: 'The Mantuan Succession, 1627–31', *English Historical Review*, 117 (1997), pp. 20–65; 'A *prince souverain* and the French Crown: Charles de Nevers 1580–1637', in R.O. Oresko, G.C. Gibbs and H.M. Scott (eds), *Royal and Republican Sovereignty in Early Modern Europe* (Cambridge, 1997), pp. 149–87; 'The Causes of the Franco-Spanish War of 1635', in J. Black (ed.), *The Origins of War in Early Modern Europe* (Edinburgh, 1987), pp. 72–111.

Mercenaries from Britain have attracted considerable recent attention. The discussion is often illuminating, but at times rather magnifies their actual importance: S. Murdoch (ed.), *Scotland and the Thirty Years War, 1618–1648* (Leiden, 2001); D. Worthington, *Scots in Habsburg Service, 1618–1648* (Leiden, 2004). For matters of recruitment, organisation and the military economy, readers are still dependent on the first volume of Fritz Redlich's influential *The German Military Enterprizer and His Workforce*, 2 vols (Wiesbaden, 1964–5) which contains a mass of useful detail, but neglects political and cultural aspects. The wider problems of financing war are illustrated in the useful comparative study by J. Glete, *War and the State in Early Modern Europe: Spain, the Dutch Republic and Sweden as Fiscal–military States, 1500–1660* (London, 2002). Soldiers' appearance and weapons are well illustrated by E. Wagner, *European Weapons and Warfare 1618–1648* (London, 1979).

Civilian experience is explored in the recent literature on eyewitness accounts: G. Mortimer, *Eyewitness Accounts of the Thirty Years War 1618–48* (Basingstoke, 2002); C. Woodford, *Nuns as Historians in Early Modern Germany* (Oxford, 2002). The latter work is considerably more useful than its title suggests and includes detailed analysis of Junius's diary. The extensive recent German-language literature is summarised in English in three of the essays in J. Canning, H. Lehmann and J. Winter (eds), *Power, Violence and Mass Death in Pre-modern and Modern Times* (Aldershot, 2004), as well as the article by R.G.

Asch, 'Military Violence and Atrocities in the Thirty Years War Re-examined', *German History*, 18 (2000), pp. 291–309.

S.C. Ogilvie, 'Germany and the 17th Century Crisis', *Historical Journal*, 35 (1992), pp. 417–41 introduces the debates on the demographic and material impact of the war. More detail can be found in C.R. Friedrichs, *Urban Society in an Age of War: Nördlingen 1580–1720* (Princeton, 1979); T. Robisheaux, *Rural Society and the Search for Order in Early Modern Germany* (Cambridge, 1989); G.P. Sreenivasan, *The Peasants of Ottobeuren, 1487–1726* (Cambridge, 2004); J. Theibault, *German Villages in Crisis: Rural Life in Hesse-Kassel and the Thirty Years War, 1580–1720* (Atlantic Highlands, 1995).

There is an annotated guide to the literature on the Westphalian congress edited by D. Croxton and A. Tischler, *The Peace of Westphalia* (New York, 2001). There are a number of essays in English in the useful collection on peacemaking edited by Heinz Duchhardt, *Der Westfälische Friede* (Munich, 1998). There is wider assessment in D. Croxton, 'The Peace of Westphalia of 1648 and the Origins of Sovereignty', *International History Review*, 21 (1999), pp. 569–91.

The memory of the war and its influence on historical writing are explored by K. Cramer, *The Thirty Years War and German Memory in the Nineteenth Century* (Lincoln, Nebraska, 2007), and L.L. Ping, *Gustav Freytag and the Prussian Gospel* (Bern, 2006).

Readers seeking further contemporary documents in English can consult T. Helfferich (ed.), *The Thirty Years War: A Documentary History* (Indianapolis, 2009) and G. Benecke (ed.), *Germany in the Thirty Years War* (London, 1978). Material relating to James I's failed mediation has been published in S.R. Gardiner (ed.), *Letters and Other Documents Illustrating the Relations between England and Germany at the Commencement of the Thirty Years War* (London, 1865; reprint New York, 1968). Accounts by English soldiers include G. Davies (ed.), *Autobiography of Thomas Raymond* (London, 1917); W.S. Brockington (ed.), *Monro, His Expedition with the Worthy Scots Regiment Called Mac-Keys* (Westport, 1999); A.T.S. Goodrick (ed.), *The Relation of Sydham Poyntz 1624–1636* (London, 1908). E.A. Beller, 'Contemporary English Printed Sources for the Thirty Years War', *American Historical Review*, 32 (1927), pp. 276–82 offers a brief guide to other works, many of which can now be accessed through *Early English Books Online*. For a guide to other, still untranslated, eyewitness accounts, see B. von Krusenstjern (ed.), *Selbstzeugnisse der Zeit des Dreißigjährigen Krieges* (Berlin, 1997).

Index

Royalty and members of secular electoral families appear in order of their first names, while all other individuals are indexed by their family names (territory in the case of German rulers and nobility). Monarchs with similar first names are ranked in the contemporary order of their kingdoms.